Universitätsbibliothek Augsburg

Narrative Impact
Social and Cognitive Foundations

Narrative Impact
Social and Cognitive Foundations

Edited by

MELANIE C. GREEN
University of Pennsylvania

JEFFREY J. STRANGE
Public Insight

TIMOTHY C. BROCK
The Ohio State University

 LAWRENCE ERLBAUM ASSOCIATES, PUBLISHERS
2002 Mahwah, New Jersey   London

Copyright © 2002 by Lawrence Erlbaum Associates, Inc.

All rights reserved. No part of this book may be reproduced in any form, by photostat, microform, retrieval system, or any other means, without prior written permission of the publisher.

Lawrence Erlbaum Associates, Inc. Publishers
10 Industrial Avenue
Mahwah, NJ 07430

Copyright Permissions. For permission to quote: two lines from "Burnt Norton" (T. S. Eliot), we thank Harcourt Inc. (USA) and Faber & Faber (worldwide); one line from "Everyman" (anonymous), we thank copyright holders G. Cooper and G. Wortham; eight lines from "Elder Edda" (W. H. Auden), we thank Curtis Brown, LTD; four lines from "Ring of the Nibelung" (R. Wagner/S. Spencer) we thank Thames & Hudson; twenty-nine lines from William Shakespeare *The complete works* (1988), edited by Stanley Wells and Gary Taylor we thank Oxford University Press (Norton, 1997); five lines from *The first quarto of Hamlet*, (K. O. Irace), we thank Cambridge University Press. We acknowledge six lines from Keats' letters, in public domain.

Cover design by Kathryn Houghtaling Lacey

Cover painting: La Liseuse (Auguste Renoir).
Reprinted with permission.

Library of Congress Cataloging-in-Publication Data

Narrative Impact: Social and Cognitive Foundations, edited by Melanie C. Green, Jeffrey J. Strange, and Timothy C. Brock.
    p. cm.
Includes bibliographical references and indexes.
ISBN—0-8058-3124-X (cloth: alk. paper).
1. Public Narratives. 2. Impact of Fiction. I. Green, Melanie C.
   II. Strange, Jeffrey J. III. Brock, Timothy C.
PN3383.N35 N37   2002
808—dc21   2002069277

Books published by Lawrence Erlbaum Associates are printed on acid-free paper, and their bindings are chosen for strength and durability.

Printed in the United States of America
10 9 8 7 6 5 4 3 2

Contents

Foreword ... ix
Marcia K. Johnson

Preface ... xiii

1 Power Beyond Reckoning ... 1
An Introduction to Narrative Impact
Timothy C. Brock, Jeffrey J. Strange, and Melanie C. Green

Part I: The Experience of Stories

2 Mythic Structures in Narrative ... 17
The Domestication of Immortality
Victor Nell

3 Emotions and the Story Worlds of Fiction ... 39
Keith Oatley

4 "Get Up and Win!" ... 71
Participatory Responses to Narrative
James W. Polichak and Richard J. Gerrig

5 The Evolution of Interactive Media   97
   Toward "Being There" in Nonlinear Narrative Worlds
   Frank Biocca

Part II: Real-World Impact of Narratives

6 Controversial Narratives in the Schools   131
   Content, Values, and Conflicting Viewpoints
   Joan DelFattore

7 Entertainment Education and the Persuasive   157
   Impact of Narratives
   Michael D. Slater

8 Girls, Reading, and Narrative Gleaning   183
   Crafting Repertoires for Self-Fashioning Within Everyday Life
   Janice Radway

9 The Narrative Integration of Personal   205
   and Collective Identity in Social Movements
   Ronald N. Jacobs

Part III: Theoretical Perspectives

10 How Does the Mind Construct   229
   and Represent Stories?
   Arthur C. Graesser, Brent Olde, and Bianca Klettke

11 How Fictional Tales Wag Real-World Beliefs   263
   Models and Mechanisms of Narrative Influence
   Jeffrey J. Strange

12 The Pervasive Role of Stories in Knowledge   287
   and Action
   Roger C. Schank and Tamara R. Berman

13 In the Mind's Eye 315
Transportation-Imagery Model of Narrative Persuasion
Melanie C. Green and Timothy C. Brock

14 Insights and Research Implications 343
Epilogue to *Narrative Impact*
Timothy C. Brock, Melanie C. Green, and Jeffrey J. Strange

Author Index 355

Subject Index 365

Foreword

Marcia K. Johnson
Yale University

Narrative Impact: Social and Cognitive Foundations highlights the key role that stories play in shaping our memories, knowledge and beliefs. The editors, Melanie Green, Jeffrey Strange and Timothy Brock, have brought together an insightful group of investigators and their chapters collectively create a picture of an emerging and lively research domain with many questions of interest to various disciplines. At the heart of the endeavor is the idea that stories are a particularly compelling source of information and that public narratives (e.g., books, movies, news stories, TV programs) have the potential to have a profound and far-reaching influence on what we remember, know and believe. It is not hard to imagine a future where the influence of public narratives is even greater as the world increasingly is connected via television, movies, and the Internet. The focused and systematic study of the impact of narratives contributes to our understanding of cognition, emotion, and social processes in a number of ways.

This volume stimulates thinking about the cognitive and social mechanisms of learning and memory, and of persuasion and influence. Can we use available theoretical constructs (e.g., constructive and reconstructive processing, story schemas, situation models, causal chains, source monitoring, counterarguing, accessibility, social norms, social learning) to understand the impact of public narratives, or does this domain require new principles that might, in turn, broaden our conceptualization of cognitive and social processes in other domains? It causes us to think about how effective narratives are crafted, the relation between cognition and emotion, the techniques by which fictional accounts evoke emotions, individual differences in the tendency to be "transported" by stories, and about the relation between factual and narrative truth. It prompts reflection about the origins of self-identity. It challenges us to grapple with difficult and fundamental issues that require tradeoffs between values, such as freedom of expression and accountability. If the impact of narratives is potentially great, who should control the content and distribution of public narratives? Should we give more thought to self-censoring what we process?

We want our experiences to have an impact on us (create memories, knowledge, and beliefs). However, the fact that some experiences might have uninvited (or unwanted) impact creates a profound dilemma—how to segregate the wanted from the unwanted influences in any particular situation. Reality monitoring (or source monitoring, more generally) refers to the imperfect processes used to differentiate the multiple sources of the mental experiences we call memories, knowledge and beliefs. Investigating the impact of stories and public narratives on thought and behavior provides a useful way of investigating the joint operation of two aspects of reality monitoring—people's ability to accurately identify the sources of potential influence and their ability to evaluate and "correct" their memories, knowledge, and beliefs for specific sources of influence when they want to do so. It is tempting to think that we have control over the impact that narratives have on us (why else would we see some of the movies we do?), but how accurate is that belief? And if we do have some control, what is that nature of that control?

The application of findings and theoretical ideas from basic research is not always obvious to those who might be in the best situation to apply them. There have been some notable efforts to create such bridges, for example, in education, eyewitness testimony, jury decision-making, and reports of recovered memories of childhood sexual abuse. Through such efforts, teachers, police, lawyers, judges, and therapists can better see the relation between research findings and the way they present information to students or juries, conduct lineups, interview children, or explore adults' early childhood memories. Likewise, relevant empirical facts and theoretical ideas should be accessible to both the creators and consumers of public narratives. Such facts and theoretical ideas are most persuasive when demonstrated in ways that approximate real-world situations (e.g., showing that family planning discussions in soap operas affect viewers' attitudes or behavior)—that is, if they tell a good story. The chapters in *Narrative Impact* treat the influence of stories from applied as well as theoretical perspectives. They consider the influence of stories on education, health behavior, and political judgment, as well as the cognitive and social processes through which stories derive their force. The book will appeal not only to academicians, but also to creators, critics, and consumers of stories.

The study of narratives provides a clear bridge between examining cognition on an individual level and at the social–cultural level. Given what we know about the constructive and reconstructive nature of cognition, and our less than perfect reality monitoring processes, what is our obligation, and what strategies might we use, to protect ourselves and others from "false" information that might distort our memories, knowledge, and beliefs? What are the personal, social, and cultural consequences, if any, of experiencing the stories from newspapers, TV, movies, novels, video game worlds, the Internet, and the virtual reality experiences to come?

One line of argument is that, although there surely are influences from these narratives, we cannot predict the effect from the content of a narrative because individuals bring an infinite variety of unique combinations of experiences to any particular target event, and who knows what they will take from it? In short, if the influence cannot be predicted in any particular case, we can hardly be held accountable for producing or consuming any particular narrative. On the other hand, narratives (like any communication) derive much of their power not from the idiosyncrasies in our varied interpretations, but from the fact that there is some consensus in what people are likely to take from them. What creates shared narrative impact? Popular books, TV programs, movies, news sources, and so forth, provide a major source of the information consumed by people daily. To what extent do these sources create a shared cultural vision and what do we think about that vision? To what extent are public narratives sources of our expectations about people of different gender, ethnic, racial, and age groups, our understanding of typical behaviors in different professions, our trust or mistrust in public institutions, our beliefs about the origins of psychological problems, our expectations about what an abduction by aliens might be like, and so forth?

Whose narratives and visions of reality should prevail? News media, government, lawyers, scientists, religious groups, school boards, parents, producers of movies and TV programs? Is incidental influence of less or more concern than intended influence? Can the power of entertainment narratives to promote pro-social messages be harnessed in a way that does not elicit fears of brainwashing? Can the issue of quality control be addressed without eliciting fears of censorship? How do within and cross-institutional reality monitoring processes operate? How should they?

The collection of chapters in *Narrative Impact* instantiates an exciting, intellectually stimulating frontier of interdisciplinary research at the intersect among basic cognitive and social processes, sociology, political science, literary and film studies, and media studies. Furthermore, this domain of investigation raises important issues of professional practice and public policy. Different readers will come away intrigued by different aspects of this rich domain, but everyone will have a deeper appreciation of what is involved in the narrative experience, and of the potential influence of the stories in their past and their future.

—Marcia K. Johnson
Yale University
June 25, 2001

Preface

NARRATIVE IMPACT:
SOCIAL AND COGNITIVE FOUNDATIONS

This contributed volume draws on scholars in diverse branches of psychology and media research to explore the subjective experience of public narratives, the affordances of the narrative environment, and the roles played by narratives in both personal and collective spheres. The book brings together current theory and research on narratives, presented primarily from an empirical psychological and communications perspective, but with contributions from other areas as well such as literary theory, sociology, and censorship studies. Our goal was to obtain some diversity of perspectives, yet maintain sufficient common ground to generate a fruitful contribution to an inherently cross-disciplinary area of research.

Although the present book addresses persuasive impact, and although two of its three editors (Melanie Green & Timothy Brock) worked together at Ohio State University, the book should be distinguished from the previous Ohio State attitudes and persuasion series (e.g., Greenwald, Brock, & Ostrom, 1968, and successor volumes) as well as from the earlier Yale communication and persuasion series (e.g., Hovland, Mandell, Campbell, Brock, Luchins, Cohen, McGuire, Janis, Feierabend, & Anderson, 1957, and successor volumes).

Here is why.

The impact of public narratives has been so broad (including effects on beliefs and behavior, but extending beyond to emotion and personality), that the stakeholders in the process have been located across disciplines, across institutions, across governments, and, indeed, across epochs.

Therefore, we could not simply invite kindred scholars, from a single discipline (e.g., psychology), who had come to specialize in a relatively circumscribed domain within communication and persuasion, such as, for example, "order of presentation" (Hovland et al., 1957) or "attitude strength" (Petty & Krosnick, 1995).

Instead, the reach of the present volume and the roster of its contributors had to be broad enough to be commensurate with the scope of influence of public narratives. This scope includes the narrative mobilization of major social movements, the formation of self-concepts in young people, banning of texts in schools, the constraining impact of narratives on jurors in the court room, and the wide use of education entertainment (also called "edu-tainment") to cause social changes. The enormous scope includes, but is not limited to, the vast audiences for romances and for middlebrow literature.

With these very large arenas in mind, we looked at the psychology of individual recipients of public narratives and, finally, we showcased prevailing and new theoretical perspectives. In the case of individual respondents, we examined the role of emotion, of participation, of entrancement (transportation), and of safety-seeking amid mortality salience. In addition, we sought to project the future of public narrative impact in the interactive environments afforded by advancing cyberspace technologies. Our theoretical integrations include authoritative review chapters by experts in cognitive psychology, cognitive science, and social psychology.

ACKNOWLEDGMENTS

Our initial discussions were facilitated by stimulating encounters at national and international psychology conventions, where we began to share our cognate lines of empirical research on narrative impact (Strange & Leung,1999; Green & Brock, 2000). In addition, we were able to mount narrative persuasion symposia at some of these conventions; these panels in fact included some of our present contributors. At these presentations we were encouraged to proceed with an edited volume. Inevitably, one of the persons who encouraged us was Larry Erlbaum. We are indebted to him and to editors Bill Webber and Dr. Judi Amsel. Their commitment to the project has been vital to its completion.

Most of all we are grateful to our chapter contributors for their patience with several rounds of editing and for accommodating our editorial suggestions. In addition, we are indebted to our colleagues at Ohio State, at Lewis and Clark College, at the Annenberg School for Communication, and at the University of Pennsylvania. We are particularly thankful to the following erstwhile members of the Brock laboratory at Ohio State (Dr. Jennifer Garst, Stephen D. Livingston, Phil Mazzocco, and Christian Wheeler). All provided a lively intellectual environment for the progress of the book. Shirley Bostwick, Gloria Puskas, and the Lawrence Erlbaum production staff are thanked for their help.

—*Melanie C. Green*
—*Jeffrey J. Strange*
—*Timothy C. Brock*

December 26, 2001

REFERENCES

Greenwald, A. G., Brock, T. C., & Ostrom, T. M. (Eds.). (1968). *Psychological foundations of attitudes*. New York: Academic Press.

Green, M. C., & Brock, T. C. (2000). The role of transportation in the persuasiveness of public narratives. *Journal of Personality and Social Psychology, 79*, 701–721.

Hovland, C. I., Mandell, W., Campbell, E. H., Brock, T., Luchins, A. S., Cohen, A. R., McGuire, W. J., Janis, I. L., Feirerabend, R. L., & Anderson, N. H. (1957). *The order of presentation in persuasion*. New Haven, CT: Yale University Press.

Petty, R. E., & Krosnick, J. A. (Eds.). (1995). *Attitude strength: Antecedents and consequences*. Mahwah, NJ: Lawrence Erlbaum Associates.

Strange, J. J., & Leung, C. C. (1999). How anecdotal accounts in news and in fiction can influence judgments of a social problem's urgency, causes, and cures. *Personality and Social Psychology Bulletin, 25*(4), 436–449.

1

Power Beyond Reckoning

An Introduction to *Narrative Impact*

Timothy C. Brock
The Ohio State University

Jeffrey J. Strange
Public Insight

Melanie C. Green
University of Pennsylvania

Public narratives—the stories we hear everyday in the news media and the stories that we consume in books, films, plays, soap operas, and so forth—command a large share of our waking attention. Despite the ubiquity of narratives, calls for deeper understanding of their impact are rarely heard from the controllers of public narratives such as censors, school boards, religious leaders, and pundits. Few such calls are issued because these controlling "elders," as well as most parents of school-age children, simply take narrative impact for granted. On the other hand, producers, such as fiction writers, are absolved of responsibility for narrative impact in part via the well-known disclaimer that similarity to real persons and events is coincidental. Other producers, such as journalists, are more accountable for impact but enjoy appropriate First Amendment freedoms. And so both primary controllers and primary producers of public narratives appear to be joined unwittingly in an agnostic conspiracy against understanding the processes that may underlie impact.

Despite the widespread apathy by practitioners and gatekeepers, the impact of public narratives on beliefs and behavior has received substantial scholarly investigation in disciplines such as sociology (e.g., Gamson, 1992), communications (e.g., Bryant & Zillman, 1994; Gerbner, Gross, Morgan, & Signorielli, 1994), humanities (e.g., Booth, 1988), and political science (e.g., Iyengar & Kinder, 1988). The primary aim of the present volume is to provide a coherent understanding of narrative impact by juxtaposing perspectives from these disciplines with perspectives from cognitive/experimental psychology and social psychology. The aim is accomplished by first focusing on individuals' experiencing of narrative (Part I) and then expanding the discussion to important public-narrative arenas (Part II). Finally, theoretical integrations are offered (Part III).

Although narrative impact has long been a focus in some disciplines (see previous discussion), it has been relatively ignored, or even discounted (McGuire, 1986), within psychology. Researchers, particularly social psychologists who claim persuasion processes as their domains, have neglected narratives. Instead, during the second half of the 20th century, *advocacy* messages such as advertising, billboards, sermons, speeches, health campaigns, wartime propaganda, and so forth, have received exhaustive and illuminating scientific study (e.g., Hovland, Lumsdaine, & Sheffield, 1949; Shavitt & Brock, 1994). In contrast, during the same half-century, psychologists have largely overlooked the attitudinal impact of communications whose aim is not advocacy or influence but rather something else, such as entertainment, education, and news reporting. As a result, rhetoric, rather than poetics, has been the focus of the scientific study of persuasion within psychology. This unfortunate imbalance has been the case although, in our everyday world, narrative, in its multifarious manifestations, is far more prevalent than rhetoric. Nonetheless, it is rhetoric that has been the beneficiary of sophisticated theorizing and painstaking empirical inquiry by psychology researchers (e.g., Petty & Wegener, 1998). In the most recent comprehensive graduate-level textbook devoted to the psychology of attitude change (Eagly & Chaiken, 1993), there are more than 2,800 references: None of these thousands of studies addressed the subject of this book, the impact of public narratives, communications that purport to serve functions other than advocacy and propaganda.

Our mandate, to place psychological understanding within the context of a coherent, multidisciplinary approach to narrative impact, stems in part from the magnitude of the effects of such impact. The impact of public narratives can be, and has been, enormous beyond reckoning, as three examples now show. Following these examples, the organization of the book is further delineated, the contributors are introduced, and context for the principal issues and questions is provided.

Uncle Tom's Cabin: The South and Britain

Other than the Bible, *Uncle Tom's Cabin* (Stowe, 1852), a fictional novel, was the best-selling book of the 19th century (Auerbach, 1993, p. 13).

Most Americans are aware that the novel expanded abolitionist sentiment in the years prior to the Civil War, and most Americans may have heard that President Lincoln is alleged to have said to author Harriet Beecher Stowe, "So you're the little lady who wrote the great book that started this great war." However, it is less well known that *Uncle Tom's Cabin* was even more popular in Britain than in America, with British sales of 1,200,000 within 12 months of publication (Johnson, 1997, p. 416).

British schoolchildren had their ideas of America shaped by Eliza, Tom, and Eva. Britain, which had received much preaching about democracy and equality from Webster and Emerson, now viewed America as morally suspect. Johnson (1997) made a strong case that the book's success ensured that the British, whose economic interests were intertwined with the South's (e.g., cotton-based textile industry), remained neutral when the Civil War began. On this view, Stowe's potboiler not only raised abolitionist sentiment sufficiently to enable the recruitment of Northerners into a war against slavery, it also contributed to Union victory by keeping Britain, with its formidable navy and army, from fighting alongside the South. It is very hard to make the case that any rhetorical presentation of the 19th century (Lincoln's Gettysburg Address, say) had an impact that was even remotely comparable to that of the fictional narrative, *Uncle Tom's Cabin*.

Old New Land: Herzl and Israel

Theodor Herzl, a writer and statesman at the turn of the last century, founded national Zionism and the World Zionist Organization. His name and lifework, the political resurrection of the Jewish people, are engraved in the Israeli consciousness. "Death to the Jews," the cry from a Parisian mob at the 1895 Dreyfus trial, imbued Herzl with an idea: "a work of infinite grandeur ... a mighty dream ... if my conception is not translated into reality, at least out of my activity can come a novel" (Potok, 1978, p. 379). The novel was put on hold while more practical steps toward a Jewish homeland were undertaken. These initiatives—all failures—included the enlistment of financial support from wealthy Jewish philanthropists, of political support from the German Kaiser, and of geopolitical support from the Turkish Ottoman empire. The ensuing World Wars and the Holocaust effectively sundered early Zionist organizational efforts. However, in the end, Herzl's inspiring dream, as embodied in his novel, *Altneuland*, prevailed.

> A visionary novel in which Herzl depicted the harsh wasteland of Palestine as seen by a Jew and a non-Jew during their trip to a distant land—and then seen again some decades later by the same travelers after the land had become a Jewish state. People have labored cooperatively with the resources of modern science to transform the land into a green world of canals, farms, gleaming cities, trains, roads. Jericho is a winter resort. Old Jerusalem has been cleaned, its streets and alleys paved with new stones. Around the old city there are modern suburbs, with parks, tree-shaded boulevards, institutions of learning, markets, lovely homes. Wrote Herzl in the epilogue, "All the acts of mankind were dreams once and will become dreams again." (Potok, 1978, p. 386)

Herzl died in 1904, at age 44, but his fictional-narrative prophesy, a Jewish state within 50 years, was realized with the founding of modern Israel in 1948. The novelist's vision prevailed whereas Herzl's considerable practical efforts foundered.

Christopher Columbus: Public Narrative Trumps Historical Truth

Columbus is only one of two persons honored by name with a national holiday in the United States, and Columbus, Ohio is only one of dozens of eponymous cities and towns. In Spain, four disparate sites vie for the honor of Columbus's final resting place, and his six-story statue bestrides a major plaza in downtown Madrid. Columbus is so archpivotal that Western Hemisphere history is demarcated into pre- and post-Columbian epochs.

The collective Columbus story (Nina, Pinta, Santa Maria, etc.), as told in 20th century American schoolbooks (Loewen, 1995, p. 44) is shown in Table 1.1a. There is solid evidence for the upper-case text but no evidence for the lower-case embellishments (arduous journey, not realizing what he had done, died penniless) that comprise the story that is so familiar to generations of schoolchildren (Loewen, 1995, p. 44).

The embellishments (Table 1.1a: lower case) surely seem as harmless improvements to an otherwise prosaic account. However, by strengthening the narrative they help mask the actual history. Embellishments notwithstanding, the real power of myth often lies in omissions.

Representative portions of the historical evidence (e.g., including excerpts from Columbus's diaries, letters) are given in Table 1.1b.

TABLE 1.1a

The Schoolbook Columbus Story: Embellishment Versus Fact

BORN in Genoa of humble parents, CHRISTOPHER COLUMBUS GREW UP TO BECOME AN EXPERIENCED SEAFARER, VENTURING AS FAR AS ICELAND AND WEST AFRICA. His adventures convinced him that the world must be round and that the fabled riches of the East—spices and gold—could be had by sailing west, superseding the overland routes, which the Turks had closed off to commerce. TO GET FUNDING FOR HIS ENTERPRISE, HE BESEECHED MONARCH AFTER MONARCH IN WESTERN EUROPE. After at first being dismissed by Ferdinand and Isabella of Spain, Columbus finally got his chance when ISABELLA DECIDED TO UNDERWRITE A modest EXPEDITION. COLUMBUS OUTFITTED THREE pitifully small SHIPS, THE NINA, THE PINTA, AND THE SANTA MARIA, AND SET FORTH FROM SPAIN. AFTER AN arduous JOURNEY of more than 2 months, during which his mutinous crew almost threw him overboard, Columbus discovered the WEST INDIES ON OCTOBER 12, 1492. Unfortunately, although HE MADE THREE MORE VOYAGES TO AMERICA, he never knew he had discovered a New World. COLUMBUS DIED in obscurity, unappreciated, and penniless. Yet without his daring, AMERICAN HISTORY WOULD HAVE BEEN VERY DIFFERENT, for in a sense he made it all possible.

Note. Untrue or unsubstantiated embellishments are in lower case (Loewen, 1995, p. 44).

In summary, "Columbus revolutionized race relations and the modern world by taking land, wealth, and labor from indigenous people, leading to their *extermination* (our italics), and by initiating a transatlantic slave trade which created a racial underclass" (Loewen, 1995, p. 55). His legacy includes genocide and racism.

The power of the schoolbook Columbus narrative appears enormous beyond reckoning. Imagine that some decades after 1492, a pious and wealthy monarch (Phillip II of Spain, say) decided to pay reparations for the crimes of the Columbus voyages. The magnitude of the heinousness of Columbus's conduct, (Table 1.1b), and, thus, by the same token, the enormousness of the eclipsing power of the schoolbook narrative (Table 1.1a), is seen in the following truth: Even if reparation funds were available and exceedingly generous, by 1555 there was no one left to pay because the targeted indigenous nations had no living survivors! (Loewen, 1995, p. 55).

Public narratives have not only been important engines of major historical transitions and of reconfigurations of peoples' worldviews; narrative impact is a mundane phenomenon and a quotidian issue. For example, censorship has always been ubiquitous: In the United States, one of out of three high school students experiences banning of books (Davis, 1979). A film version of the "fourth best English-language novel

TABLE 1.1b

The Historical Columbus Story: Predator and Racist Slaver

During the return voyage Columbus made false log entries to keep the route to the Indies secret from others. (Loewen, 1995, p. 50)

Columbus's own writing reflects his evolution towards racism. When he was persuading Isabella on the wonders of America, the Indians (e.g., Arawaks) were characterized as "well built" and "of quick intelligence." "They have good customs," he wrote, "the king maintains a very marvelous state, of a style so orderly that it is a pleasure to see it, and they have good memories and they wish to see everything and ask what it is and for what it is used." The next year, when insufficient gold led Columbus to justify his wars and enslavement of the Indians, they became "cruel" and "stupid," "a people warlike and numerous, whose customs and religion are very different from our own." (Loewen, p. 58)

"In the name of the Holy Trinity, we can send from here all the slaves and brazil-wood which could be sold" Columbus wrote to Isabella in 1496. "In Castile, Portugal, Aragon ... and the Canary Islands they need many slaves." Columbus viewed the Indian death rate optimistically: "Although they die now, they will not always die. The Negroes died at first." (Loewen, p. 52)

As soon as the 1493 expedition got to the Caribbean, Columbus was rewarding his lieutenants with native women to rape. Columbus wrote a friend "A hundred castellanoes are as easily obtained for a woman as for a farm, and it is very general and there are plenty of dealers who go about looking for girls; those from nine to ten are now in demand." (Loewen, p. 56)

The slave trade destroyed whole Indian nations. Packed in below deck, with hatchways closed to prevent their escape, so many slaves died that a ship without a compass, chart, or guide, but only following the trail of dead Indians who had been thrown from the ships could find its way from the Bahamas to Hispaniola. Because the Indians died, Indian slavery then led to the massive slave trade the other way across the Atlantic, from Africa. (Loewen, p. 56)

Columbus not only sent the first slaves across the Atlantic, he likely sent more slaves—about five thousand—than any another individual. Other nations—Portugal, England, and France—rushed to emulate Columbus." (Loewen, p. 55)

published this century": *Lolita* (Modern Library Board, 1998) was withheld for 2 years during the 1990s from American audiences. In this volume, we asked contributors to be concerned with the experiences of recipients of public narratives in order to increase understanding of the underlying mechanisms.

OUR QUESTIONS ABOUT NARRATIVE IMPACT

- Are there universal thematic structures that public narratives trade on for their effectiveness?
- What is the role of vicarious emotion; how do we become caught up in the fate of a fictional Anna Karenina?

- What is the role of readers' participatory responses in causing narratives to affect beliefs and conduct?
- How can narratives work together with advanced sensory systems to create a deep sense of presence in a computer-generated virtual environment? What are the enduring effects of such virtual experiences?
- To what do censors attribute the power of fictional narratives? Proponents of banning of books and films are willing to abridge First Amendment rights to protect others from danger; they do not believe that truth and morality will emerge victorious from free exchange in the marketplace of stories and ideas. What evidence do they have for these restrictive policies?
- How can intentional incorporation of educational messages—in such entertainment genres as soap operas, dramas, and comedies, that are disseminated through radio, television, film, theater, popular music, and comic books—be effective in influencing behavior toward socially desirable ends (e.g., family planning)?
- The qualities that are most valued in middlebrow literature include pleasurable absorption, caring about the characters, emotional intensity, immersion in and/or transportation to another world, and sense of connection (*Feeling for Books*, Radway, 1997). How do these qualities mediate changes in readers?
- How do social movements use collective narratives to mask conflicts and create a common story that will mobilize members' energy and commitment?
- In courts of law, how does the narrative of a case (made by the prosecution or the defense) often become a more critical factor in the eventual verdict than the presented facts?
- What criteria must be met by an adequate theory of narrative discourse? With such an adequate theory in hand, how can we use it to predict constraints on the persuasiveness of public narratives?
- How are peoples' beliefs changed by exposure to a story? Is there a human propensity to adjust one's own beliefs to story-implied beliefs?
- Current dual-process theories of rhetorical persuasion can be shown to falter in their handling of narrative persuasion. What new theoretical premises are needed?

To answer these questions, we invited scholars in diverse branches of psychology and media research to explore the subjective experience of stories, the affordances of the narrative environment, and the impact of narratives in public spheres. The book brings together current theory and research on narratives, presented primarily from an empirical psychological and communications perspective, but with contributions from other areas as well: legal (school text censorship), literary theory, and sociology. Within this diversity of perspectives, we attempted to identify sufficient common ground to generate fruitful contributions to an inherently cross-disciplinary field.

ORGANIZATION OF THE BOOK

The chapters encompass three broad themes: the phenomenological and experiential dimensions of story reception (Part I); the uses of narratives in real-world settings (Part II); and theoretical perspectives on narrative impact (Part III).

Part I

Part I deals with the phenomenological and experiential dimensions of story reception. For chapter 2, Victor Nell was asked to break new ground while at the same time reprising and updating his empirical classic, *Lost in a book: The psychology of reading for pleasure* (1988). Professor Nell accomplished this goal by highlighting the role of the thematic content of stories in serving the universal need to maintain a sense of safety and hope in the face of inevitable suffering and death. He addresses mortality salience and narrative from the informed perspective of his expertise in cognitive and neuropsychology as well as from his purview of recent work in social psychology (e.g., Greenberg, Pyszcynski, & Solomon, 1986) and his wide reading in classical literatures. Nell's notion of "lost in a book," or entrancement, is reprised elsewhere in this volume by Melanie Green and Timothy Brock (chap. 13) who present a theory in which being lost in a text, or, in their terms, *transportation*, mediates the impact of experience with a narrative.

For chapter 3, Keith Oatley was asked to extend his previous work (e.g., *The best laid schemes: The psychology of emotions*) in order to confront the concern that "psychologists have shown too little interest in this human capacity to experience emotions vicariously in drama and film" (Lazarus, 1991, p. 821). In addition to postulating mechanisms—such as simulation and the evocation of emotion-laden memories—through which narrative impact is felt in the immediate emotional states of readers, Oatley suggested links between emotional response experienced during reading and potentially long-term changes in the reader's concept of self and of others (e.g., "aspects of the self are enlarged by understandings of people in the imagined world and then, perhaps, also of people in the ordinary world."). Oatley accomplished the aims for his chapter by focusing on narrative structures, narrative experience, and the psychology of emotions, to integrate and extend a model of the processes through which stories gain their power to move readers and to provoke insights into self and society.

In line with the Part I focus on reader experience, chapter 4 (James Polichak & Richard Gerrig) builds on the rich insights of Gerrig's seminal monograph, *Experiencing narrative worlds: On the psychological activities of reading* (1993). Most people have had the experience of watching a suspenseful movie, and at a critical moment, wanting to shout to the hero to "watch out!" Despite the knowledge that the creepy monster on the screen is only a special-effects marvel, the psychological responses of many viewers are made as if they were really experiencing the events. These types of responses have been labeled participatory responses, or p-responses (Allbriton & Gerrig, 1991). The resulting characterization of readers bears more resemblance to a picture of spectators at a sporting event than to one of detached text processors, as found in classical models of story understanding.

Part I ends with a chapter that reflects the rapid advance of technology. It is likely that virtual reality environments will become part of our everyday lives within the first decade of the 21st century. When most people think of virtual reality, the technical aspects of virtual reality machines spring to mind—the goggles, the gloves, and the gigabytes that recreate sensory experience. The goals of virtual reality are not merely technological, however—they are also psychological. People don't merely encounter random virtual stimuli; rather, part of what makes these simulations so powerful is the feeling of presence, of being part of an ongoing story. Chapter 5 (Frank Biocca) concludes Part I by fostering understanding of new forms of technologically mediated storytelling. Biocca builds on his *Communication in the age of virtual reality* (Biocca & Levy, 1995) to provide a framework that covers the forms of interaction facilitated by interactive media and the psychological characteristics of experience in immersive, interactive environments. Written for designers as well as researchers, the chapter sets the stage for distinctive outcomes of interactive narrative experience.

Part II

Part I of this volume zoomed in to focus on empirical study and informed speculation about the responses of individuals as they experience public narratives. In Part II we zoom out to consider the sweeping effects of public narratives in the real world.

Censorship has been ubiquitous for centuries; even Plato's Republic argued that certain stories—those that presented harmful or misleading views of the gods, for instance—should not be permitted to the general public. The desire to ban certain writing is not the sole province of totalitarian leaders; parents and churches often challenge the readings schools have assigned to their children (Davis, 1979). In chapter 6 (Joan DelFattore), the intuitive theories of those who wish to ban or censor books are examined by the author of *What Johnny shouldn't read: Textbook censorship in America* (DelFattore, 1992). To what do censors attribute the power of fictional narratives? What support do they have for these convictions? Joan DelFattore distills the central themes that characterize the legal, legislative, and institutional processes through which U.S. communities determine what their children will and will not read in school. Her chapter illustrates lay theories of narrative impact that emerge in the accompanying school text debates and litigation. A feature of the chapter is consideration of the primordial narrative—where humans come from and what they are supposed to be about—in the context of the perennial textbook controversies surrounding creationist and evolutionary perspectives.

Whereas all stories convey a message of one form or another, social agencies have recently turned to the large-scale use of dramatic narratives as a means to promote changes in health practices and other forms of personal and social behavior. The result, entertainment education, has been defined by one of its pioneers, Everett Rogers, as "the intentional incorporation of educational messages in such entertainment genres as soap operas, dramas, and comedies, that are disseminated through radio, television, film, theater, popular music, and comic books" (Shefner-Rogers & Rogers, 1997, p. 3). Unlike most narratives, edu-tainment stories generally have been written with input from social scientists. Whereas outcome evaluators have continued to ask if and when such story-based persuasion works, psychologists and communication researchers have begun to ask how it works. In chapter 7, Michael Slater (e.g., "Integrating application of media effects, persuasion and behavior change theories to communication campaigns," 1999) examines the evolving use of entertainment education and provides an integrative review of what is known about the processes through which fictional programs can lead to changes in personal practices, interpersonal interaction, and community norms.

In chapter 8, Janice Radway explores the role of narrative in the development of the self-concept in women. Her chapter reiterates her view that "I place more emphasis on the contribution the reader makes to any text-reader interaction; I am much less sanguine about the author's ability to control the effects of a text or to discipline the reader in a predetermined way" (Radway, 1997, p. 393). She uses the emergence of on-line reading communities as exemplified in web-based "Grrrls" magazines, or "zines." In doing so, she reprises her essential work on the ethnography of romance reading (*Reading the Romance: Women, Patriarchy and Popular Culture*; Radway, 1984) and her analysis of criteria and desired effects in middlebrow publishing (*A Feeling for Books: The Book-of-the-Month*

Club, Literary Taste, and Middle-Class Desire; Radway, 1997). Citing examples of girls' reading and of her own reading as a girl, she shows how the experience of reading is situated within a particular social context and how reader response is affected by "variable literacies," that is, divergent ways of reading, using, and evaluating texts.

Whereas chapter 8 is about how public narratives are inevitably, albeit selectively, used by girls in the formation of their identities, chapter 9 (Ronald Jacobs) concludes Part II by making an even larger claim for narrative impact on identity. Jacobs posits that because narrative is basic to the formation of identity, it is the essential resource of social movements. He uses the sociological literature, including his *Race, Media, and the Crisis of Civil Society: From Watts to Rodney King* (Jacobs, 2000), to show that in order to mobilize actual and potential members in a committed and coherent movement, cultural entrepreneurs generate a set of collective narratives that situate the focal groups in time and place. Chapter 9 reviews the increasing scholarly recognition of the role that symbolic resources play during periods of collective action; it shows how narratives are critical in augmenting the individual's sense of belonging to social groups.

Part III

Part I considered the individual's narrative experience and the important roles of thematic structure and of emotion, participation, and presence (in virtual narratives). Part II examined large arenas in which public narratives have enormous impact: school texts, educational entertainment, the self-concept development of girls in the United States, and the role of common stories as engines of effective social movements. The volume concludes with selected theoretical perspectives on narrative impact (Part III).

Chapter 10 (Arthur Graesser, Brent Olde, & Bianca Klettke) describes a constructionist theory of narrative understanding. The models we form of the world around us are derived not only from direct experiences, but also from vicarious ones, from reports about the real or imagined experience of others. Like direct experience, storied experience is driven by a quest to develop a coherent understanding of disparate actions and events and to update prior knowledge about the narrated situation. In order to construct a coherent representation of situations, readers go beyond the information given to draw inferences about the goals, plans and appearances of characters, about the causes of events, the reasons or motives for actions, the intentions of authors, and the story's underlying themes (see Graesser, Singer, & Trabasso, 1994). In making these inferences, readers draw on prior role, event, and action schemas that are instantiated by situations and characters in the story-world. Chapter senior author Graesser (*Structures and Procedures of Implicit Knowledge*, Graesser & Clark, 1985) focuses on the manner in which prior knowledge, expectations, and beliefs influence how narrated situations are construed, remembered, and integrated.

In an important application, Graesser, Olde, and Klettke describe Pennington and Hastie's (1992) "story-model" of juror decision making. Differences among jurors in their judgments of culpability are in large part traceable to differences in the kinds of stories they have fashioned of the same testimonial accounts. In summary, in this chapter, Graesser and his colleagues have provided a state-of-the-art review of cognitive research on the psychology of narrative understanding and impact.

In chapter 11, co-editor Jeffrey Strange (*The Future of Fact*, Strange & Katz, 1998) considers how both historical and realistic fiction might influence our judgments and beliefs about the extratextual world. Strange first examines and challenges common assumptions about what it means to label a text as fiction. He distinguishes different forms of fictional discourse and presents theoretical frameworks aimed to delineate alternative routes through which fictional portrayals interact with prior knowledge to alter the status quo ante of readers' beliefs. In probing the proposed models, Strange describes empirical research designed to account for the processing of two very different kinds of information present in fictional discourse. One study examines how readers might come to accept the real-world validity of direct historical assertions, ones that they "know" to be void of evidential grounding. Another study examines how descriptions of specific characters and events might alter judgments about the urgency, causes and cures of real-world social problems. Given the diversity of story-world experience, Strange argues that no single model can successfully account for the impact of stories. In addition to the models he explicitly tests, the author considers a variety of means through which the readers who depart from the story world come to differ from the ones who entered it.

Chapter 12 (Roger Schank & Tamara Berman) capitalizes on voluminous previous work (*Tell Me a Story*, Schank, 1995; *Dynamic Memory Revisited*, Schank, 1999) to provide an accessible account of the narrative basis of thought and to make the case for story-based models of instruction. The approach is grounded in a fundamental issue of cognitive science: How does our mind organize knowledge?

Recently Schank & Abelson (1995) advanced the intriguing hypothesis that most, if not all, knowledge is stored in the form of narratives. According to these authors, "stories about one's experience and the experiences of others are the fundamental constituents of human memory, knowledge, and social communication ... when it comes to interactions in language, all of our knowledge is contained in stories and mechanisms to construct them and retrieve them" (pp. 1–2). Chapter 12 discusses the "what, how, why, and when" of stories: what a story is, how we learn from stories, and why stories may be more effective than abstract principles, than rhetoric. At the core of Schank's theory is that one's own experiences and the reports of others' experiences constitute cases that exemplify particular lessons and that the mind becomes a repository of thousands of stories.

In the final chapter of Part III, chapter 13, co-editors Melanie Green and Timothy Brock (e.g., "The role of transportation in the persuasiveness of public narratives," 2000) offer an integrative theoretical framework exploring how imagery may interact with transportation into a narrative world to generate enduring effects on individuals' attitudes and beliefs. For many readers, being caught up in a story means that they are not seeing words on a page, but rather, visual images of the story playing out before them. Authors can create vivid scenes through their use of evocative language. These mental pictures formed in the imagination of the reader can play a critical role in the persuasive power of narratives. This chapter presents a unified theoretical model of the way in which transportation into a narrative world and concomitant imagery can affect alterations in real-world beliefs. The chapter addresses issues such as when imagery-laden narratives will be most effective in changing beliefs, the role of individual differences in imagery ability, and the relationship between imagery and narrative. The principal theoretical contribution is to examine the insufficiencies of current dual-process theories (Chaiken & Trope, 1999) and to provide an alternative account of narrative persuasion and persuasion persistence.

READERSHIP

This book is designed to bridge disciplinary divides by drawing together complementary perspectives from diverse fields of inquiry. The need for an integrative volume was confirmed when one of us (Jeffrey Strange) conducted an extensive search of existing publications on this topic while teaching a course on "The Psychology of Stories" to communications students at the University of Pennsylvania. Designed to fill this need, *Narrative Impact: Social and Cognitive Foundations* is intended for advanced undergraduates, graduate students, and researchers from fields including psychology, communications, and literary studies, among others. We expect that each of the constituencies with its special focus—the processes of narrative understanding and thought, synchronous responses to stories, the social functions and long-term influence of story-world experience, and the control of narrative expression—will come away from *Narrative Impact* with a sense of common ground and a set of new explanatory concepts.

REFERENCES

Allbritton, D. W., & Gerrig, R. J. (1991). Participatory responses in prose understanding. *Journal of Memory and Language, 30,* 603–626.
Auerbach, E. (1993). *The courage to write: Women novelists of 19th–century America.* Madison, WI: Board of Regents of the University of Wisconsin.
Biocca, F., & Levy, M. (1995). *Communication in the age of virtual reality.* Hillsdale, NJ: Lawrence Erlbaum Associates.
Booth, W. C. (1988). *The company we keep: An ethics of fiction.* Berkeley: University of California Press.
Bryant, J., & Zillman, D. (Eds.). (1994). *Media effects: Advances in theory and research.* Hillsdale, NJ: Lawrence Erlbaum Associates.
Chaiken, S., & Trope, Y. (Eds.). (1999). *Dual–process theories in social psychology.* New York, NY: Guilford.
Davis, J. (Ed.). (1979). *Dealing with censorship.* Urbana: National Council of Teachers of English.
Del Fattore, J. (1992). *What Johnny shouldn't read: Textbook censorship in America.* New Haven: Yale University Press.
Eagly, A. H., & Chaiken, S. (1993). *The psychology of attitudes.* New York: Academic Press.
Gamson, W. A. (1992). *Talking politics.* Cambridge, UK: Cambridge University Press.
Gerbner, G., Gross, L., Morgan, M., & Signorielli, N. (1994). Growing up with television: The cultivation perspective. In J. Bryant & D. Zillman (Eds.), *Media effects: Advances in theory and research* (pp. 17–42). Hillsdale, NJ: Lawrence Erlbaum Associates.
Gerrig, R. C. (1993). *Experiencing narrative worlds: On the psychological activities of reading.* New Haven: Yale University Press.
Graesser, A. C., & Clark, L. C. (1985). *Structures and procedures of implicit knowledge.* Norwood, NJ: Ablex.
Graesser, A. C., Singer, M., & Trabasso, T. (1994). Constructing inferences during narrative text comprehension. *Psychological Review, 101,* 371–395.
Green, M. C., & Brock, T. C. (2000). The role of transportation in the persuasiveness of public narratives. *Journal of Personality and Social Psychology, 79,* 701–721.
Greenberg, J., Pyszynski, T., Solomon, S. (1986). The causes and consequences of a need for self–esteem: A terror management theory. In R. F. Baumeister (Ed.), *Public self and private self* (pp. 189–212). New York, NY: Springer Verlag.
Hovland, C. I., Lumsdaine, A. A., & Sheffield, F. D. (1949). *Experiments on mass communication.* Princeton, NJ: Princeton University Press.
Iyengar, S., & Kinder, D. R. (1987). *News that matters: Television and American opinion.* Chicago: University of Chicago Press.
Jacobs, R. N. (2000). *Race, media, and the crisis of civil society: From Watts to Rodney King.* Cambridge, UK: Cambridge University Press.
Johnson, P. (1997). *A history of the American people.* New York, NY: Harper Collins.
Lazarus, R. S. (1991). Progress on a cognitive–motivational–relational theory of emotion. *American Psychologist, 46*(8), 819–834.
Loewen, J. W. (1995). *Lies my teacher told me.* New York: New Press.
McGuire, W. J. (1986). The myth of mass media impact: Savagings and salvagings. In G. Comstock (Ed.), *Public communication and behavior* (Vol.1, pp. 173–257). San Diego, CA: Academic Press.
Modern Library Editorial Board. (1998, July 21). Ulysses named best 20th–century novel: The top 100. *Columbus Dispatch,* p. 7E.

Nell, V. (1988). *Lost in a book: The psychology of reading for pleasure.* New Haven: Yale University Press.
Oatley, K. (1992). *Best laid schemes:The psychology of emotions.* New York: Cambridge University Press.
Pennington, N., & Hastie, R. (1992). Explaining the evidence: Tests of the story model for juror decision making. *Journal of Personality and Social Psychology, 62,* 189–206.
Petty, R. E., & Wegener, D. T. (1998). Attitude change: Multiple roles for persuasion variables. In D. T. Gilbert, S. T. Fiske, & G. Lindzey, (Eds.), *The handbook of social psychology.* (4th ed., Vol. 1, pp. 323–390). Boston, MA: The McGraw-Hill Companies, Inc.
Radway, J. (1984). *Reading the romance: Women, patriarchy and popular culture.* Chapel Hill: University of North Carolina Press.
Radway, J. (1997). *A feeling for books: The Book–of–the–Month club, literary taste, and middle–class desire.* Chapel Hill: University of North Carolina Press.
Schank, R. C. (1995). *Tell me a story.* Evanston, IL: Northwestern University Press.
Schank, R. C. (1999). *Dynamic memory revisited.* Cambridge, UK: Cambridge University Press.
Schank, R. C., & Abelson, R. P. (1995). Knowledge and memory: The real story. In R. S. Wyer (Ed.), *Advances in social cognition,* (Vol. VIII, pp. 1–85). Hillsdale, NJ: Lawrence Erlbaum Associates.
Shavitt, S., & Brock, T. C. (Eds.). (1994). *Persuasion: Psychological insights and perspectives.* Boston: Allyn & Bacon.
Shefner–Rogers, C. L., & Rogers, E. M. (1997, May). "Evolution of the entertainment– education strategy." Paper read at Second International Conference on Entertainment–Education and Social Change. Athens, OH.
Slater, M. (1999). Integrating application of media effects, persuasion and behavior change theories to communication campaigns: A stages–of–change framework. *Health Communication, 11,* 335–354.
Stowe, H. B. (1852/1994). *Uncle Tom's cabin.* New York: Norton.
Strange, J. J., & Katz, E. (Eds.). (1998). The future of fact. [Special issue] *Annals of the American Academy of Political and Social Sciences,560,* 8–199.
Strange, J. J., & Leung, C. C. (1999). How anecdotal accounts in news and in fiction can influence judgments of a social problem's urgency, causes, and cures. *Personality and Social Psychology Bulletin, 25*(4), 436–449.

1

The Experience of Stories

2

Mythic Structures in Narrative

The Domestication of Immortality

Victor Nell

Institute for Social and Health Sciences
University of South Africa

> Go, go, go, said the bird: human kind
> Cannot bear very much reality.
>
> (T.S. Eliot, Burnt Norton)
>
> I am Dethe—that no man dredeth—
>
> (Everyman, Anonymous, 1522)

NARRATIVE'S SAFETY

The delight of narrative is its safety: the story-world, unlike dream worlds and the real world, is above all safe and nonthreatening. But how can one traverse the terrifying landscapes of narrative—Grendel the firebreathing dragon, Dr. No's tunnel of terrors—and yet feel safe? Readers are, after all, Spinozans (Gilbert, 1993), automatically believing every assertion they encounter. Whence, then, the reader's invulnerability, the distance readers effortlessly maintain between the narrative world and their own safety—and, at the same time, their absorption and entrancement, their engulfing transportation (Gerrig, 1993) to the narrative world?

Freud's answer (1908/1957; *Lost in a Book*, Nell, 1988, pp. 203–205) is that the hero of all narratives is His Majesty the Ego (1908, p. 180). But this begs the question: Why in narrative is ego immortal when the unequivocal evidence of the world around us is the certainty of death? This is the problem that *Lost in a Book* attempted to address at two levels. Chapter 3, "The Witchery of a Story," considered the phenomenology of narrative, suggesting that a useful metaphor for readers' absorption and entrancement was to consider narrative power as a set of five Chinese boxes nested within one another, each smaller and more delicate than the one before. The insatiable appetite for narrative is contained in the first; the propositions that neither "truth" nor suspense nor an external storyteller is a prerequisite for absorption are in the second, third, and fourth of the boxes; and in the fifth and smallest, the talismanic power of even isolated sentences or single words to transport the listener or reader.

Chapter 10, "Reading, Dreaming, Trance," returned to this central problem of belief, disbelief, and safety by noting that the state of consciousness of the entranced reader "has two principal parallels in the domain of fantasy: dreaming and hypnotic trance" (p. 201). I characterised these two states in terms of cognitive theory. More recent theories have emphasized emotions. Thus, Descartes' error, argued Damasio (1994), was to say that I am because I think; on the contrary—I am because I feel (see also Lang, 1995; Ledoux, 1998; MacLean, 1993). With the wisdom of hindsight, it becomes clear that if reading is not dreaming (*Lost in a Book*, p. 205)—which of course it isn't—it is not so much because of the *cognitive* distinctions between these two states of consciousness, but because their *emotional* tone and content are different.

The major argument in this chapter is that the denial of death is an emotional mechanism that is a necessary condition for animal and human survival; that both animals and humans behave in many situations as if they were invulnerable; that the continuities between animal and human risk-taking suggest that this delusion of invulnerability verging on a sense of immortality has a fitness purpose and has been shaped by evolutionary forces; that the principal cultural manifestation of the immortality delusion is the safety of myth, folktale, and formulaic fiction, in which His Majesty the Ego always survives; that this evolution-to-culture hypothesis is the most parsimonious explanation for the invariance of these forms of narrative; and, finally, that the media no less than the storyteller are constrained to interpret the world in conformity with the boundless optimism of the immortality delusion, thus systematically misrepresenting the world to their audience—who would not, for the same reasons, have it otherwise.

2. MYTHIC STRUCTURES IN NARRATIVE

There is also a minor argument, which is a set of propositions with regard to *knowing* and *feeling*. These are the mechanistic underpinnings for the above structure and hold that the narrative mode, like hypnotic trance and daydreaming, is suspended in a cognitive world in which the reader, listener, or the person in the hypnotic trance may *believe*—which is a cognitive state, a form of knowing. However, despite one's belief in narrative propositions, they remain harmless because believing isn't *feeling*, which is not a cognitive but an emotional state. Knowing and feeling are phenomenologically quite different. This is the fundamental difference between narrative worlds and the dream world. The imperative reality of dreams—I do not have the dream, it is the dream that has me (*Lost in a Book*, p. 226)—arises from the emotional rather than the cognitive mechanisms that drive dreams, in other words from subcortical rather than cortical circuits.

In summary, then, there are three mutually supportive kinds of safety that flow through myth and narrative from a single origin in evolutionary forces: first the immortality delusion that makes risk-taking possible; second, the invulnerability of the hero (and therefore also of His Majesty the Ego, who is none other than His Majesty the Reader), which, third, generates the cognitively driven safety of the narrative world that cannot overwhelm the reader's consciousness.

These are the universal safety modalities that interlock to sweeten death and banish its terror, so that one can live a life replete with real and imaginary risk-taking in the tranquil certainty that death is neither real nor permanent. Freud understood this very well, writing, "One's own death is beyond imagining, and whenever we try to imagine it, we can see that we really survive as spectators ... At bottom, nobody believes in his own death" (Freud, 1915/1985, p. 77).

MYTHIC FORMS

The twofold quality of a folktale, wrote Propp (1928/1986), is "its amazing multiformity, picturesqueness and color, and on the other hand, its no less striking uniformity, its repetition" (p. 21; see also Campbell, 1951/1969). This uniformity is the topic of Frazer's *Golden Bough* (1922/1963), of Jung's studies of archetypes in the collective unconscious (1959), and of Campbell's *Hero with a Thousand Faces* (1949/1973)—which draws on the monumental earlier studies of the thematic coherence of folk narratives by Aarne (1910) and Thompson (1955). Echoing Propp, Campbell writes that "the changes rung on the simple scale of the monomyth defy description" (p. 246): the single hero has a thousand faces.

What is most amazing, Propp and Campbell notwithstanding, is not myth's multiformity but its structural uniformity. The invariant content of this monomyth, as with folktale, is the hero's immortality, which follows a single pattern across time and cultures: the call to adventure, the meeting with a magic helper, crossing the threshold of adventure that is guarded by a shadow figure, where the hero may be dismembered or crucified, continuing in death his descent to the underworld (in Christian mythology, this is the Harrowing of Hell), undergoing a supreme ordeal at the nadir of his journey, and finally re-emerging from the kingdom of dread to redeem the world (Campbell, 1949/1973, pp. 245–246).[1]

This eternal cycle of the call, the descent, and the rebirth is the single most powerful theme in the art of all cultures. It is in itself an endless and pervasive affirmation of immortality—the immortality of the gods, of the mythic hero, and of the world itself, as in the Song of the Sybil in the *Elder Edda* (Taylor & Auden, 1969, p. 152):

> Earth sinks into the sea, the sun turns black,
> Cast down from heaven are the hot stars,
> Fumes reek, into flames burst,
> The sky itself is scorched with fire.
>
> I see earth rising a second time
> Out of the foam, fair and green ...
>
> Unsown acres shall harvests bear,
> Evil be abolished, Baldur return.

The *Edda* is the source of Wagner's *Ring of the Nibelung*. In 1853, the year he began work on *Das Rheingold*, the first of the four operas of the Ring, Wagner wrote to Liszt, "Mark well my new poem—it contains the world's beginning and its end" (in Spencer, 1993, p. ii). In *Götterdämmerung*, the last opera in the cycle, Wotan forsees the fall of the gods, orders Yggdrasil, the World Ash, felled and its wood piled "in a towering heap/ Round the hall of the blessed immortals" (*Götterdämmerung*, Act I). In the opera's closing scene, Brünhilde declares that:

> the end of the gods
> is dawning now:
> thus do I hurl the torch
> into Valhalla's proud-standing stronghold.
> (Spencer, 1993, p. 350)

The stage directions at the end of Act III read: "Bright flames flare up in the hall of the gods, finally hiding them from sight completely. The curtain falls" (Spencer, 1993, p. 351). But the cycle of birth, death, and rebirth continues: "I see earth rising a second time." This mythic cycle of endings as beginnings echoes through Eliot's *Four Quartets* (1949).

The Domestication of Myth

Formulaic narratives appeal to a universal audience. The elite critics who heap scorn on John Grisham and Wilbur Smith can (when they let their guard down)[2] enjoy these potboilers as much as the masses who make them bestsellers: Danielle Steele with her one-syllable words and five-word sentences can touch my emotions as surely as Joyce or Eliot. In what sense might one speak of a motif as lofty as immortality in such materials?

In tamer form, Gerrig's definition (1993) of the reader's transportation[3] recapitulates the hero's journey: As a result of performing certain actions, the narrative "traveller" is transported, going some distance from the world of origin and thus making some aspects of that world inaccessible, then returns to the world of origin, somewhat changed by the journey (Gerrig, 1993, pp. 10–11). At first sight, this is a grievous trivialization of the self- and world-redeeming voyages of Krishna and Odysseus. By what right can the reader, safe at home in an armchair, claim in any meaningful way to have had a transforming experience? But precisely because Gerrig's account of the reader's journey is tamed and domesticated, it captures an exceedingly important aspect of the way in which the everyday use of narrative does indeed recapitulate the most fundamental aspect of grand mythology, which is the endless cycle of death and rebirth that ensures the hero's immortality.

It does so by domesticating immortality as *hope*, which is neither magical nor transformational: on the contrary, hope is a mundane and workmanlike state of mind, and therefore infinitely more usable in day-to-day affairs than immortality. As we shall see in the material that follows, it is this toned-down form of immortality that is an ineluctable aspect of all everyday narrative forms—gossip, anecdotal storytelling, case conferences, newswriting, newsreading, and leisure reading (*Lost in a Book*, chap. 3).

Immortality thus tamed as hopefulness rules folktale and formulaic fiction. The folktale's fecund inventiveness has one end—to devise ever more life-threatening predicaments for the hero, from which time and time again he is delivered. Chapter 3 of Propp's *Morphology* (1928/1986) is given over to the threatening wiles of the villain, the means by which the hero, having been sorely tested, acquires the services of a magical agent, vanquishes the villain, is pursued, rescued, and finally ascends the throne.[4] Morphological analysis of a James Bond adventure or Silhouette romance would yield a near-identical structure of threat and deliverance.

Myth is the rock from which all narrative is hewn, and through narrative, the Homeric bard and the poets of the *Edda* enter our homes and take up residence there, tamed but still powerful. The impact of leisure reading (for which the principal vehicles are the news and formulaic fiction) may be due to the fact that in the shadows behind the hero's predictable evasion of death and misery, however trivial these may be, lurks the power and majesty of primordial myth: these minor salvations reverberate to the deeper beat of mythic resurrection.

The Immortality Delusion in Mimetic Fiction

A strange and indeed quite unexpected phenomenon is that readers are able to preserve their invulnerability quite as well in mimetic narratives (those that mimic life; Cawelti, 1976) as they can in formulaic materials. Let us consider the concluding sections of two prototypical examples of the mimetic genre that do not shy away from misery, dissolution, and death—Joseph Conrad's *Heart of Darkness* (1902/1960), and John Coetzee's *Waiting for the Barbarians* (1980). What might be the reader's state of mind as he raises his eyes from these melancholy passages?

Kurtz, the malevolent antihero of *Heart of Darkness*, is dead, at the end breathing the words, "The horror! The horror!" He is buried in a muddy hole, and Marlow later delivers a bundle of his letters to Kurtz's fiancée. The darkness that had enveloped Kurtz in the Congo follows Marlow to the Intended's home: she speaks adoringly of her beloved's brilliance and integrity, and Marlow, knowing "the colossal scale of his vile desires" (p. 89), feebly agrees. Marlow's tale is done. The frame narrative ends, with Kurtz's dying words and the shame of the lies hanging heavy in the air: "The tranquil waterway leading to the uttermost ends of the earth flowed sombre under an overcast sky—seemed to lead into the heart of an immense darkness" (p. 94).

From Conrad at the beginning of the century to Coetzee near its end: the Magistrate, crippled by the Empire's torturers, dreams of poisoned water, then learns that his love for a Barbarian woman is unrequited. He is blasted by "a wind of utter desolation" (p. 152). Then the icy wind that incessantly tears at the town dies down. It snows, and he watches children build a snowman:

> It is not a bad snowman.
> This is not the scene I dreamed of. Like much else nowadays I leave it feeling stupid, like a man who lost his way long ago but presses on along a road that may lead nowhere. (p. 156)

Why do these glimpses of desolation—a river bearing away to the heart of darkness, a crippled and lonely old man watching the children at play, lost in the cruel new world of the Empire, waiting for his torturers to return—fill me with an immense tranquillity? I have learned from these stories about evil and pain, but beyond this cognitive activity they have also touched me very deeply: I raise my eyes from these books with a lightness in my heart, I am enriched, these deaths and disappointments have indeed touched but not wounded me: because I am present as a witness to these tragedies, they affirm my own survival.[5] As surely as in the endless repetitions of formulaic fiction, these unflinchingly mimetic narratives have worked their magic of hope on me.

The source of this hope is not the death itself but the redemption. This may be explicit, as in the stereotypic love story (boy wins girl, boy loses girl, boy wins girl): it is the mechanisms of the losing-rewinning that thrill, but the walk hand-in-hand into the sunset that brings a tranquil satisfaction (or perhaps tears of joy) to the reader or listener. We are riveted by Beowulf's gushing wound, then lay the saga aside in satisfaction when we read, "His soul passed from his breast to seek the splendour of the saints." Thus also with the death of Heracles: Contemporary icons "showed him bleeding and in agony, as he struggled into the white linen shirt which consecrated him to the Death-goddess.... He tried to rip off the shirt, but it clung to him so fast that his flesh came away with it, laying bare the bones. His blood hissed and bubbled like spring water when red-hot metal is being tempered" (Graves, 1955, pp. 201, 205). Again, it is the manner of dying[6] that engages the reader's emotions but the apotheosis (Zeus bears Heracles up to heaven in a great chariot) that lingers on in satisfaction.

Story hunger and news hunger (that "crying primal want of the mind, like a hunger of the body": Nell, 1988, p. 3) is satisfied not only by the happy endings of formulaic fiction, but also by a peaceable redemption, which in mimetic fiction may be the hero's literal or figurative apotheosis, or the reader's own quiet satisfaction at his or her personal survival.

The Psychological Context of Hope-Creation

If all readers were death-defying optimists, the extraction of hope from narrative would be psychologically redundant. On the contrary, neither tranquillity nor optimism are natural states for human beings. We live in the 21st century with long-established habits of fearful vigilance that were learned by our hunter-gatherer ancestors and their ancestors before them, long before settled civilizations emerged. These habits persist despite the relatively greater safety—and longer life-expectancy—of urban environments. Hyperalertness to threat, which has in children as in adults generalised from physical to psychological dangers, ensures that peace of mind is hard-won, and elusive when achieved.

The hope mechanisms of reading are so powerfully effective because they address an innate human susceptibility to threat. Chapters 4, 10, and 11 of *Lost in a Book* (Nell, 1988) describe the linked processes of attention, absorption, and entrancement that enable narrative to create a psychological context that abstracts readers from the real world, transporting them to a psychological landscape that holds fear at bay because it is ruled by hope.

HIS MAJESTY THE EGO IN EVOLUTIONARY PERSPECTIVE

Is the immortality of His Majesty the Ego an artifact of narrative, or does it have a deeper and more imperative origin? To put the question in terms of the new discipline of evolutionary psychology (Buss, 1999; Cosmides, Tooby, & Barkow, 1992), does this immortality and its reconstruction as hope have a fitness purpose?

Let us approach this question by asking why young people, and young males in particular, routinely take high risks with no thought for the consequences. Not only are they willing to take risks, but they also actively seek them out.[7] Here for example is a story told by Beowulf, the warrior protagonist of a 6th century Old English epic (Gordon, 1926), who presents himself to the Prince of the Danes in order to do battle with the dragon-monster Grendel. Not to be outdone by the Danes' boasting of their exploits, he tells how he and a companion decided

> while we were still youths—we were both then still in our boyhood—that we two should risk our lives out on the sea.... We held naked swords boldly in our hands when we swam in the ocean; we thought to protect ourselves against the whales.... Then we were together on the sea for the space of five nights till the flood forced us apart, the surging sea, the coldest of storms, and a wind from the north, battle-grim, came against us. Wild were the waves. The temper of the sea-monsters was stirred.... A hostile deadly foe drew me to the depths, had me firmly and fiercely in his grip.... Yet it was my fortune to slay with the sword nine sea-monsters.

The joy of youthful risk-taking, the urge to pit one's life against overwhelming odds—here clothed in the wild improbabilities that typify the folktale (Campbell, 1951, p. 30)—are strikingly captured.

Bravery and Terror. There is no fear of death here, only youthful fearlessness and the joy of risk-taking, and the warrior's certainty that even against the odds, he will survive. This fearlessness is not a transient cultural artefact of Old Norse warrior values. On the contrary, risk-taking among humans—and also in the entire animal kingdom—has been shaped by evolutionary forces because it provides a fitness value for the survival of each species. Consider an organism that did in fact correctly appraise risk: for this organism, death would become real and terrifying, and as a result, aggression would be impossible. Fear would triumph and the fearful organism's genes would perish.

Furthermore, the ability to enter combat derives from the conviction of personal invulnerability. If not, fear would reduce the men of the opposing armies to a trembling jelly. Instead of eating his morning meal with peculiar and unfamiliar attention, thinking that it might be his last, the pilot of the Canadian bomber taking off for Kossovo on the morning of April 2, 1999, (Vancouver newspaper *Globe and Mail*, April 3, 1999), would have *known* that it might be his last, and like Ivan Illich (Tolstoy, 1904), knowing that he was dying, would have screamed for three days, and therefore have flown no missions. Evolution has however so arranged matters that for all young males, death has no reality.

The Fitness Purpose of the Immortality Delusion. Attaining social status and winning the most desirable mate thus depend on males' willingness to fight for territorial and dominion privileges. There is overwhelming ethological evidence to support this contention: in species after species, living and extinct, males fight one another for territory and in pursuit of an attractive mate. This is true for insects, reptiles (including dinosaurs), fish, amphibians, birds, and mammals, including primates and humans (Nell, 1998; Wilson, 1975[8]). When young males reach the mating and fighting age, their sense of invulnerability and their level of risk-taking increase even further. In this way, they are prepared for the survival tasks of a ruthlessly competitive social environment. For the heroes of myth and saga, as with today's intoxicated speeding young driver who wears no seat-belt, death has sharply reduced reality.

Sensation seeking—"a trait defined by the seeking of varied, novel, and intense sensations and experiences and the willingness to take physical, social, legal, and financial risks for the sake of such experiences" (Zuckerman, 1994, p. 27) is a correlate of risk-taking, and is also highest in the young and especially in young males. Such evolutionary universals rest on a biochemical platform[9] that humans share with other species.

It may seem preposterous to claim that risk-taking, which can so often be fatal or injurious, has a fitness value. Darwin had a similar problem, writing in his letters that "the sight of a feather in a peacock's tail, whenever I gaze at it, makes me sick." However, "peacock's tails," which are a handicap rather than an asset, abound in the animal kingdom. Their purpose is to signal a mating advantage to females of the species: "any male that has managed to survive despite the handicap of a big tail or conspicuous song must have terrific genes in other respects" (Diamond, 1992). Thus, young men who do crazy things are saying, "See what great genes I have, I have so much strength and skill that I am fearless, I can drink and speed and survive." In other words, "the handicaps convey the message that the male can support these costs" (Cronin, 1991, p. 197).

Knowing, Feeling, Dreaming. The psychological basis for this fearlessness and thus also for the immortality delusion is that *knowing* and *feeling* are separate functions under the control of separate brain systems. Emotions are unconscious and instantaneous, bypassing consciousness (LeDoux, 1998, p. 69). Fear is among the most basic and powerful of the emotions. At its highest intensity, the experience of immobilizing fear is truly dreadful (LeDoux, 1998; Nell, 1999).

LeDoux (1998) makes a useful distinction between *memories of emotions* on the one hand, which are mediated by the declarative hippocampal memory system: These are pale verbal shadows of remembered emotions. *Emotional memories*, on the other hand, emerge from the preverbal amygdala-based implicit memory system, which has no words, only feelings.[10] An ex-prisoner's evidence to an Amnesty International committee of tortures he has endured is a cognitive construction. On the other hand, if the victim were to enter the room in which the torture had taken place, he or she would be overcome by a flood of physical fear, with the nausea, racing heart and dry mouth that accompanied the event itself.

In everyday life, dreams are the most common manifestation of emotional memories. Even a moderately unpleasant dream that falls far short of the terror of a nightmare can unleash emotions that wake the sleeper in a panting cold sweat. It is this flood of emotions, sometimes delightful but more often aversive, that sets dreams so clearly apart from the experience of narrative. Phobias, including posttraumatic stress disorder, are a special case of emotional memory, as in this account by a Vietnam veteran of his reaction to a crack of thunder when he was asleep:

> My hands are freezing, yet sweat pours from my entire body. I feel each hair on the back of my neck standing on end. I can't catch my breath and my heart is pounding.... The next clap of thunder makes me jump so much that I fall to the floor. (in LeDoux, 1998, p. 256)

Because fear is so aversive and potentially disabling, transitions from knowing to feeling are rare, even for the soldier going into battle:

> Our organism is ready to fill the world all alone, even if our mind shrinks at the thought. This narcissism is what keeps men marching into point-blank fire in wars: at heart one doesn't feel that he

will die, he only feels sorry for the man next to him.... *Consciousness of death* is the primary repression, not sexuality. (Becker, 1973, pp. 2, 96)

These states of fearless *knowing*—in storytelling, reading, and daydreaming—and paralysed *feeling* are as old as history. Here in Robert Fagles' translation (Homer, 1990) of the *Iliad* is the strutting Paris, Helen's abductor, all boast and no pith:

A challenger, lithe, magnificent as a god,
the skin of a leopard slung across his shoulders,
a reflex bow at his back and battle-sword at his hip ...
he strode forth, challenging all the Argive best
to fight him face-to-face in mortal combat.

But when Paris sees Menelaus, Agamemnon's brother and Helen's husband, leap fully armed to the ground, his belief that he is invulnerable crumbles:

Paris' spirit shook
Backing into his friendly ranks, he cringed from death
as one who trips on a snake in a hilltop hollow
recoils, suddenly, trembling grips his knees
and pallor takes his cheeks and back he shrinks.

So he dissolved again in the proud Trojan lines,
... magnificent brave Paris

(Homer, c. 800BC/1990, p. 129)

The Cognitive Unconscious

Epstein (1994) provided a useful formalization of this knowing-feeling dichotomy by distinguishing between the rational and experiential systems (that parallel Freud's primary–secondary processes). It is in the experiential system— which Epstein termed the *cognitive unconscious*—that "most information processing occurs automatically and effortlessly outside of conscious awareness ... [and] is far more efficient than conscious deliberative thinking" (p. 710). Among the key differences between the experiential and rational systems are that the experiential system is passive and preconscious: we are seized by our emotions rather than in control of our thoughts; these emotional convictions (what our heart tells us: p. 710) are self-evidently valid, with no need for logic and evidence. Counterintuitively, narratives operate not through the cognitive unconscious but the rational system: they engage our emotions, but under conscious control, ensuring that these emotions are seldom overwhelming—and that if they are, they are at once brought under control by the cessation of reading and learning to avoid emotionally overladen materials.[11]

Tame Deaths [12]

Immortality and hope notwithstanding, death is everywhere present in myth, saga, and folktale; tales of magic never prevent natural deaths from age or illness, nor death as a punishment (Funcke, 1995).[13] Youthful heroes thus enter battle fearlessly, knowing that they may die, but doubly protected, first by the invulnerability with which evolution has endowed the young, and second by the conventions of folktale. So with Beowulf battling the sea-dragons or setting out to confront Grendel:

> I should surely work the will of your people to the full, or fall a corpse fast in the foe's grip. I shall accomplish deeds of heroic might, or endure my last day in the mead hall.... [He] clad himself in warrior's armour; he lamented not his life. (Gordon, 1926, p. 14, 30)

But when old age opens the way to a natural death, it is faced fearlessly. After ruling for 50 years, Beowulf's "mind was sad, restless, brooding on death; fate exceeding near was destined to come on the old man ... to part asunder life from the body" (pp. 48–49). Fate comes in the form of yet another dragon, more fearsome than before, and the aged Beowulf must give battle:

> Beowulf's sword, ancient and grey, failed in the fight.... The bold fire-dragon ... rushed on the mighty man ... hot and fierce in fight; he clutched his whole neck with sharp teeth; Beowulf grew stained with his lifeblood; the gore welled out in surges....
>
> Beowulf spoke, he talked of his wound, of the hurt sore unto death; he knew well that he had ended his days, his joy on earth. Then all his length of days had passed away, death was exceeding close....
>
> Then the warrior spoke.... "Fate has swept all my kinsmen away to their destiny, earls in their might. I must needs follow them." That was the last word from the old man's thoughts, before he sought the pyre, the hot, fierce, surges of flame. His soul passed from his breast to seek the splendour of the saints. (pp. 53–56)[14]

Memento Mori. A curious consequence of this assault on death by the combined forces of the disbelieving emotions and the myriad devices of narrative art is that death becomes more distant than the ethicists of the Judaeo-Christian religions deem fit. In consequence, they continually admonish the faithful to remember death and the moral judgment that follows. From the 12th to the 15th centuries, the most popular form of this admonition was *Memento mori*, "remember death," recalling God's words to the fallen Adam, "Out of [the ground] you were taken; you are dust, and to dust you shall return" (Gen. iii 19). The Catholic liturgy for Ash Wednesday glosses this verse as "Memento homo, quia pulvis est, et in pulverum reverteris." Trappist monks, whose greeting to those they met was "*memento mori*," kept in their gardens an open grave, a warning that death awaits.

But *Everyman* may best reflect the real state of affairs: when Death comes to him, he sharply questions the angel: "I know thee not. What messenger art thou?" to which Death responds: "I am Dethe, that no man dredeth" (Anonymous, 1522/1984).

MORTALITY AND HOPE IMPERATIVES IN THE NEWS

In the late 20th century, the news in all its myriad forms is the most abundant source of narrative—on television and radio, in newspapers and news magazines, on electronic displays above city streets, on the home pages of internet service providers, and in the conversational gossip about the state of the world that acquaintances exchange when they meet.

Is news subject to the same immortality and hope imperatives as other narrative forms? At first sight, given that catastrophe and death are the nature of news, this claim is absurd. In countries at war or with rampant violent crime because of a collapsing civil order—as for example in the former Soviet Union and in South Africa (Nell, 2001)—the newspapers become a litany of horror.

I would nonetheless hypothesize that the content of newspapers and news broadcasts is structured in accordance with the same inexorable emotional laws that determine the structure of myth, folktale, and formulaic fiction. This structure is determined by a fundamental isomorphism between the stories journalists tell and the stories their audience wants to hear (Nell, 1988, pp. 51–54). This isomorphism derives in turn from the identity between the emotional mechanisms of journalists and readers, who equally demand that the news should contribute to the social construction of hope by affirming a metaphoric immortality for the individual, the state, and the world (Nell, 1994).

Although a satisfactory proof of the news-as-hope hypothesis is beyond the scope of this chapter, I draw two points to the reader's attention. The first is that there is a great deal of historical and empirical evidence that perfectly ordinary people are capable of terrible deeds—murder, torture, massacre, or worse—and that these people are untainted by any detectable psychopathology (Arendt, 1963; Browning, 1993; Haney, Banks, & Zimbardo, 1973; Milgram, 1974; Tester, 1997). But rather than deal with the problem of the widespread—perhaps universal—capacity of normal people to commit evil acts, today's media follow age-old distancing techniques that allow a fundamental optimism about the human condition to be maintained: this is to portray individuals—or nations—who commit acts of cruelty as monsters who are less than fully human.

Historically, this is the method followed by Suetonius (100AD/1984) in describing the murderous excesses of the Roman Caesars, and the condemnations of the Arena combats by Rome's elite critics (Seneca, *Epistles*, 7; Tertullian, *Apologeticum*), and of the American press in the late 19th century in dealing with Lizzie Borden's murder of her stepmother and father (Kent, 1992), and the European press in the early 20th on the wave of sexual murders in Weimar Germany (Tatar, 1995). "Monsterisation" continues apace, as for example in the responses of the British and American press to the murder of James Bulger by two 10-year-olds (Nell, 1996), and *Time*'s coverage of the Littleton massacre (Gibbs, 1999), which appeared under the telling headline, "The Monsters Next Door." In this way historians and journalists have been able to maintain a comfortably optimistic view of human nature; if children who torture and murder other children belong to the human race, modernism is wrong, and history cannot be a record of general progress. They must therefore be dehumanised and portrayed as monsters.

The second point is that even the worst of news brings a message of hope and progress: in war, the forces of justice and democracy will triumph; if not, we will have learned a bitter lesson that will stand us in good stead in the future. In disaster, the focus is on the heroism and selflessness of the rescuers. A great leader is assassinated: with pomp and pageantry the machinery of power moves smoothly forward, reassuring the grieving nation that that justice will prevail. If the story is one of unmitigated evil—a baby beaten and burnt, a youth tied to a railway line, a mother drowning her children—the reader does the work: the response is not only to feel one's own survival affirmed, as with the Conrad-Coetzee glimpses of desolation reviewed above, but also to feel an affirmation of one's own greater goodness in relation to these murderous monsters. Narrative has again woven its web of hope.

Narrative in the Service of Terror Management

What links can be forged between this analysis of narrative safety and the robust experimental findings of the terror management paradigm (Arndt, Greenberg, Solomon, Pyszczynski, & Simon, 1997; Greenberg, Pyszczynski, & Solomon, 1986; Simon, Greenberg, Harmon-Jones,

Solomon, Pyszczynski, Arndt, & Abend, 1997)? Three elements of this paradigm, in which a participant is induced to imagine her own death, are especially salient to an understanding of the psychological mechanisms by which narrative confirms immortality: first, that heightened mortality salience is nonanxious; second, that the higher self-esteem, the lower the effects of mortality salience arousal; and third, that the arousal of mortality salience strengthens worldview support.

Mortality Salience is Nonanxious. There is an excellent fit on the one hand between Becker's (1973) claim that consciousness of death is the primary repression, reframed in this chapter as a distinction between knowing death but not feeling it; and on the other with the findings reported by Simon et al. (1997, p. 1143). They found that increases in mortality salience produced no measurable increase in anxiety, either on questionnaire measures or on psychophysiological variables that are sensitive to the increased arousal mediated by anxiety. Here is strong empirical confirmation that mortality salience effects take place outside conscious awareness, in the experiential rather than the rational system, thus maintaining the unreality of one's own death.

Self-Esteem Reduces Mortality Salience. The saga literature cited earlier in this chapter suggests that content analysis of narrative products might confirm the historical and cultural stability of the finding that high self-esteem decreases defensive responses to thoughts of death (Simon et al., 1997). The young Beowulf battling the sea dragons and entering Grendel's lair who "lamented not his life," was supremely confident of his invincibility. With age, mortality salience increases: Beowulf's "mind was sad, restless, brooding on death."

Strengthening of Worldwide Support. In the context of this chapter, the most intriguing finding in the terror management literature is that heightened mortality salience increases support for one's own worldview as well as negative responses to those who do not share that view. From an evolutionary perspective, the mechanism mediating this powerful drive to lock oneself into an ideological support system when danger threatens is Freud's "herd instinct" (1921/1985) or what Tiger (1990) called "the cerebral bridge from family to foe." Tiger argued that the decisive stimulus for aggression and violence is not gonadal, at the lower end of the evolutionary scale, but cortical, at the higher end. Human cognitive and symbolic skills lead to "the construction of the social and ideological boundaries which are the effective prerequisite to large-scale persistent aggressive interaction" (Tiger, 1990, p. 101). The brain evolved to recognise, preserve and through reproduction increase kinship ties—and in today's free agent economic system, the brain anachronistically continues to do what it was evolved to do, to give rise to coordinated group or tribal action through coordinated thought—it "creates ideologies, religions, brilliant certainties.... [the brain is] an instrument of gregariousness, not individualism" (1990, p. 105).

In the laboratory of the real world, wars and disasters—an earthquake, a terrorist bombing—are likely to be the triggers for heightened mortality salience by making death palpable. Because of the threat they pose to individual worldviews of meaning, order and permanence (Arndt et al., 1997), major catastrophes will leave clear traces in the historical record that would take the form of "brilliant certainties" that counter the heightened mortality salience of troubled times. In such times, the scramble to align oneself with those who share one's worldview and persecute those who don't becomes a stampede, and neutrality is impossible.

By way of a history of the magazine, *The New Republic*, Christopher Lasch (1966) offered a brilliant analysis of the war fever that gripped the United States during World War I, and its social outcomes. Founded in 1914 to promote the "scientific solution of social problems," *The New Republic* was rapidly swept into the turmoil of war politics. Bellicosity gripped American liberals. Robert Herrick recanted of "that vague pacifism" he had espoused, returning from a 1915 visit to France to glorify war: "There is not a Frenchman who will not tell you of the immense good that has already come to his people, that will come increasingly from this bloody sacrifice.... A new, larger, and more vital life has already begun" (Lasch, 1966, p. 186). Back home, citizen groups lynched and flogged those whose support for the war was deemed insufficient (p. 178), and the Committee on Public Information forbade speculation about peace with Germany as seditious (p. 203). *The New Republic*'s attitude to the war rested less on the issues, writes Lasch, than "on a powerful emotional abhorrence of neutrality ... [a] fear of neutrality, of political impotence" (p. 191): as an instrument of gregariousness, the brain abhors neutrality.

Allan Rachlin's (1988) analysis of U.S. media responses to the 1983 rocket attack by a Soviet fighter plane on a Korean Airlines Boeing 747, killing all 269 passengers and crew, demonstrates the same impulse to align narrative products in the media against an opposing worldview—in this case, that of the Soviet Union as an evil empire (*Time* magazine, September 12, 1983, p. 11). This alignment took place despite ample and publicly available knowledge that the "strayed" civilian flight had been on a covert intelligence mission for the United States: Many agencies of the U.S. government knew that the plane was headed for intrusion into sensitive Soviet air space and that these agencies had indeed permitted KAL

007 to do so in order to gain a "bonanza" of intelligence information (Tom Wicker in the *New York Times*, in Rachlin, 1988).

The terror management literature thus lends further weight to the argument that, even more than other forms of narrative, the news is constrained to be a vehicle of hope because it expresses worldviews supportive of the society in which it operates; these worldviews are in turn the product of preconscious defences against mortality salience.

MYTH'S RECURSIVENESS

Across time and cultures, the universality of immortality, invulnerability, and hope motifs in myth, folktale, news, formulaic, and mimetic fiction, is to be sought in the universals of human nature set in place through "evolved psychological mechanisms ... constructed by natural selection over evolutionary time" (Cosmides, Tooby, & Barkow, 1992, p. 5). These same forces are the source of Jung's archetypes: Archetypes speak in the language of dreams (Jung, 1959, p. 48), which is the native speech of myth (Campbell, 1951/1969, p. 33), and also the language of the emotions, in which all stories are told and understood.

Myth and life are recursive. Our foundational assumptions about life, death, and hope emanate from myth because myth emanates from the way humankind has evolved. Indeed, if one were to ask, "Does language have a fitness value beyond its uses for communication and as the vehicle of abstract thought?" one might half frivolously and half seriously answer that language was created so that narrative would have a vehicle,[15] because it is stories of the gods and the heroes of fiction, the messages of hope for our nation and our future that we hear in the news, as well as our own daydreams of limitless life and power, that reassure us puffed-up ego machines strutting the earth that we are immortal, and give us the courage to live our lives dangerously—and thus to the full. The final recursion is that language works these wonders in the smallest and most delicate of the five story-magic boxes, in which even a single word can entrance the reader (Nell, 1988, pp. 61–64).

ENDNOTES

[1]The epic quest of Luke Skywalker in *Star Wars* is explicitly derived from Campbell's *Hero* (1949/1973), which George Lucas read as a college student; recursively, the movie's mythic structure engaged Campbell, whose interviews with Lucas became a book about the film (Campbell & Moyers, 1988).

[2]See "The Elitist Fallacy," (Nell, 1988, pp. 4–6).

[3] Nell, 1988 (chap. 10) uses the term *entrancement* to describe this state of profound and world-changing absorption. See especially chapter 13 in this volume.

[4] On the paradoxical nature of suspense in formulaic fiction, see "Scheherezade and the Sultan," (Nell, 1988, chap. 3).

[5] In a perverse echo of the Freud citation on page 5 on the impossibility of believing in my own death, the hero of John Coetzee's *Dusklands* says: "The gun is our mediator with the world and therefore our saviour.... the gun saves us from the fear that all life is within us. It does so by laying at our feet all the evidence we need of a dying and therefore a living world" (Coetzee, 1974, p. 79; Nell, 1990).

[6] In Western culture, Christ's Passion is the archetypical death and resurrection. Heracles' death recalls the sacrifice that immortalised the sacred king, who endured flogging and mutilation until he was laid on the funeral pyre (Frazer, 1922/1963).

[7] What of young females? Except for the first-world nations in the modern era, to become pregnant was to dance with the high risk of death in childbirth. That females experienced, in pregnancy, an unwarranted invincibility, is at this time a speculation that requires further scholarship.

[8] For hercules beetles, see Wilson, 1975, p. 323; frogs, pp. 442–443; *Diplodocus* dinosaurs, p. 447; blue wildebeest, p. 493; hamadryas baboons, pp. 536–537. On the latter, see Wilson, 1978/1995, p. 104: "I suspect that if hamadryas baboons had nuclear weapons, they would destroy the world in a week."

[9] On levels of platelet MAO and the gonadal hormones in relation to gender, age, and risk-taking, see Zuckerman, 1994, pp. 297–298, 314, and Table 11.3.

[10] Located deep within the temporal lobes, the limbic system plays a central role in the encoding and retrieval of memories. The amygdala and the hippocampus are structures within the limbic system that, as LeDoux (1998) indicated, mediate distinctively different memory modalities.

[11] See for example Mary's account of reading Charles Dickens, weeping as she typed a translation of *Oliver Twist*, and avoiding material that upsets her (Nell, 1988, pp. 293–294).

[12] Philippe Ariès' phrase for a death that is anticipated and tranquilly accepted: "Ah, Lord God, help me, for I see and I know that my end has come" (King Ban in *The Childhood of Lancelot of the Lake* in Ariès, 1974, p. 3). The warning was not supernatural but an inner conviction, "something very simple.... There was no way of cheating" (p. 4).

[13] Among other folktale rules for dealing with death are that the hero's violent death caused by evil forces is reversible (it is only persons who are killed violently who can be resuscitated, but no one can be revived without the intervention of a helper-savior; for the hero, death is not final, but an intermediate state between old and new existences.

[14] *Njal's Saga* (Magnusson & Palsson, 1976) precisely parallels this cycle from youthful heroism to a tranquil death.

[15] This idea is Michael Corballis', whom I thank.

REFERENCES

Aarne, A. (1910). *Verzeichnis der Märchentypen* [Index to types of fairy-tales]. Helsingfors: Folklore Fellows Communications.

2. MYTHIC STRUCTURES IN NARRATIVE 35

Anonymous. (1522/1984). *The summoning of Everyman.* Nedlands: University of Western Australia Press.
Arendt, H. (1963). *Eichmann in Jerusalem. A report on the banality of evil.* London: Faber & Faber.
Aries, P. (1974). *Western attitudes toward death: From the middle ages to the present.* Baltimore: Johns Hopkins.
Arndt, J., Greenberg, J., Solomon, S., Pyszczynski, T., & Simon, L. (1997). Suppression, accessibility of death-related thoughts, and cultural worldview defense: Exploring the psychodynamics of terror management. *Journal of Personality and Social Psychology, 73,* 5–18.
Becker, E. (1973). *The denial of death.* New York: Free Press.
Browning, C. R. (1993). *Ordinary men: Reserve Police Battalion 101 and the Final Solution in Poland.* New York: Harper.
Buss, D. M. (1999). *Evolutionary psychology: The new science of the mind.* Boston: Allyn and Bacon.
Campbell, J. (1949/1973). *The Hero with a Thousand Faces.* Princeton: Princeton University Press.
Campbell, J. (1951/1969). *The flight of the wild gander: Explorations in the mythological dimension.* Washington, DC: Regnery Gateway.
Campbell, J., & Moyers, B. (1988). *The power of myth.* New York: Doubleday.
Cawelti, J. G. (1976). *Adventure, mystery and romance: Formula stories as art and popular culture.* Chicago: University of Chicago Press.
Coetzee, J. M. (1974). *Dusklands.* Johannesburg, South Africa: Ravan.
Coetzee, J. M. (1980). *Waiting for the Barbarians.* London: Secker and Warburg.
Conrad, J. (1902/1960). *Heart of darkness.* New York: Bantam.
Cosmides, L., Tooby, J., & Barkow, J. H. (1992). Evolutionary psychology and conceptual integration. In J. H. Barkow, L. Cosmides, & J. Tooby (Eds.), *The adapted mind: Evolutionary psychology and the generation of culture.* New York: Oxford.
Cronin, H. (1991). *The ant and the peacock: Altruism and sexual selection from Darwin to today.* Cambridge, UK: Cambridge University Press.
Damasio, A. R. (1994). *Descartes' error: Emotion, reason, and the human brain.* New York: Avon.
Diamond, J. (1992). *The rise and fall of the third chimpanzee.* London: Vintage.
Eliot, T. S. (1943). *Four quartets.* New York: Harcourt, Brace, & World
Epstein, S. (1994). Integration of the cognitive and psychodynamic unconscious. *American Psychologist, 49,* 709–724.
Frazer, J. G. (1922/1963). *The Golden Bough: A study in magic and religion.* (Abridged edition). London: Macmillan.
Freud, S. (1908/1957). The relation of the poet to daydreaming. In *Collected papers* (Vol. 4). London: Hogarth.
Freud, S. (1915/1985). Thoughts for the times on war and death (pp. 57–90). In *Civilisation, society and religion.* Harmondsworth, UK: Pelican.
Freud, S. (1921/1985). Group psychology and the analysis of the ego. In *Civilisation, society and religion.* Harmondsworth, UK: Pelican.
Funcke, E. W. (1995). The magical tale as mediaeval heritage and its overcoming of death. In L. Viljoen (Ed.), *UNISA mediaeval studies.* Pretoria: University of South Africa.
Gerrig, R. J. (1993). *Experiencing narrative worlds: On the psychological activities of reading.* New Haven, CT: Yale University Press.
Gibbs, N. (1999, May 3). The Littleton Massacre. *Time,* pp. 49–59.
Gilbert, D. T. (1993). The assent of man: Mental representation and the control of belief. In D. M. Wegner & J. W. Pennebaker (Eds.), *Handbook of mental control.* Englewood Cliffs, NJ: Prentice Hall.
Gordon, R. K. (1926). *Anglo-Saxon poetry.* London: Dent.
Graves, R. (1955). *The Greek myths.* Harmondsworth, UK: Penguin.

Greenberg, J., Pyszczynski, T., & Solomon, S. (1986). The causes and consequences of a need for self-esteem: A terror management theory. In R. F. Baumeister (Ed.), *Public self and private self* (pp. 189–212). New York: Springer-Verlag.

Haney, C., Banks, W. C., & Zimbardo, P. G. (1973). Interpersonal dynamics in a simulated prison. *International Journal of Criminology and Penology, 1*, 69–97.

Homer. (1990). *The Iliad* (R. Fagles, Trans.). Harmondsworth, UK: Penguin. (Original work published c. 800BC)

Jung, C. G. (1959). *The archetypes and the collective unconscious*. London: Routledge.

Kent, D. (1992). *The Lizzie Borden sourcebook*. Boston: Branden.

Lang, P. J. (1995). The emotion probe: Studies of emotion and attention. *American Psychologist, 50*, 372–385.

Lasch, C. (1966). *The new radicalism in America (1889–1963): The intellectual as a social type*. London: Chatto and Windus.

Ledoux, J. (1998). *The emotional brain*. London: Weidenfeld and Nicholson.

MacLean, P. D. (1993). Cerebral evolution of emotion. In M. Lewis & J. M. Haviland (Eds.), *Handbook of emotions* (pp. 67–83). New York: Guilford.

Magnusson, M., & Palsson, H. (1976). *Njal's saga*. Harmondsworth, UK: Penguin.

Milgram, S. (1974). *Obedience to authority: An experimental view*. London: Tavistock.

Nell, V. (1988). *Lost in a book: The psychology of reading for pleasure*. New Haven, CT: Yale University Press.

Nell, V. (1990). Oppression, interpersonal violence, and the psychology of colonialism in J. M. Coetzee's "Dusklands." In S. Cooper & L. Nicholas (Eds.), *Psychology and Apartheid* (pp. 125–139). Johannesburg, South Africa: Vision/Madiba.

Nell, V. (1994). All the news that's fit to print and All the news that fits. *South African Journal of Science, 90*, 510, 569.

Nell, V. (1996, March 18). *Bad values, evil emotions*. Presentation to the Institute for the Humanities, University of Michigan.

Nell, V. (1998, October). Why young men drive dangerously: An evolutionary perspective. *The Safety and Health Practitioner (Journal of the Institute for Occupational Safety and Health)*. 19–23.

Nell, V. (2000). An evolutionary perspective on the prevention of youthful risk-taking: The case for classical conditioning. In H. Von Holst, A. Nygren, & A. E. Andersson (Eds.), *Transportation, traffic safety, and health: Human factors* (pp. 163–180). Berlin: Springer.

Nell, V. (2001). Community psychology and the problem of policing in countries in transition. In M. Seedat (Ed.), *Community psychology: Theory, methods and practice. South African and other perspectives*. (pp. 261–291) Cape Town: Oxford University Press.

Propp, V. (1928/1986). *Morphology of the folktale*. Austin: University of Texas Press.

Rachlin, A. (1988). *News as hegemonic reality: American political culture and the framing of news accounts*. New York: Praeger.

Seneca, L. A. (1953). *Ad lucilium epistulae morales*. (R. M. Gummere, Trans.) Cambridge, MA: Harvard University Press.

Simon, L., Greenberg, J., Harmon-Jones, E., Solomon, S., Pyszczynski, T., Arndt, J., & Abend, T. (1997). Terror management and cognitive experiential self-theory: Evidence that terror management occurs in the experiential system. *Journal of Personality and Social Psychology, 73*, 1132–1146.

Spencer, S. (1993). *Wagner's Ring of the Nibelung: A companion*. London: Thames & Hudson.

Suetonius. (1984). *The Twelve Caesars* (R. Graves, Trans.). Harmondsworth, UK: Penguin. (Original work published 100AD)

Tatar, M. M. (1995). *Lustmord: Sexual murder in Weimar Germany.* Princeton, NJ: Princeton University Press.
Taylor, P. B., & Auden, W. H. (1969). *The Elder Edda: A selection.* New York: Random House.
Tertullian. (1977). Apology: De spectaculi. (T. R. Glover, Trans.). Cambridge, MA: Harvard University Press.
Tester, K. (1997). *Moral culture.* London: Sage.
Thompson, S. (1955). *Motif index of folk literature: A classification of narrative elements in folktales, ballads, myths, fables, mediaeval romances, exempla, fablieux, jest books and local legends.* (2nd ed., Six volumes). Bloomington: Indiana University Press.
Tiger, L. (1990). The cerebral bridge from family to foe. In J. Van der Dennen & V. Falger (Eds.), *Sociobiology and conflict: Evolutionary perspectives on competition, cooperation, violence, and warfare* (pp. 99–106). London: Chapman and Hall.
Tolstoy, L. (1904). *The death of Iván Illich.* London: Dent.
Wilson, E. O. (1978/1995). *On human nature.* Harmondsworth, UK: Penguin.
Wilson, E. O. (1975). *Sociobiology: The new synthesis.* Cambridge, MA: Harvard University Press.
Zuckerman, M. (1994). *Behavioural expressions and biosocial bases of sensation seeking.* New York: Cambridge University Press.

3

Emotions and the Story Worlds of Fiction

Keith Oatley
University of Toronto

>Is it not monstrous that this player here,
>But in a fiction, in a dream of passion,
>Could force his soul so to his own conceit
>That from her working all his visage wanned,
>Tears in his eyes, distraction in 's aspect,
>A broken voice, and his whole function suiting
>With forms to his conceit? And for nothing.
>For Hecuba!
>What's Hecuba to him, or he to Hecuba,
>That he should weep for her?
>   William Shakespeare, *Hamlet*, 2, 2, 528–537

Emotion is to fiction as truth is to science. We would no sooner read a novel that did not move us, than an empirical article that did not offer a validly drawn conclusion. Fictional narrative has its impact primarily through the emotions. When an emotion occurs, we experience it as striking. Sometimes a novel can affect a person's whole identity.

Think about it like this: Bruner (1986) proposed that narrative is that mode of mental life in which we understand the actions of people (protagonists) who pursue goals by means of plans that meet vicissitudes. We can contrast it with what Bruner called the paradigmatic mode, which is used to reason about scientific and technical matters. The paradigmatic mode typically involves several kinds of inference used in succession (Oatley, 1996a) and allows conclusions to be exported from one mind to another, without much reference to individuality or relationships.

Within the narrative mode, the vicissitudes that occur to the protagonist-agent tend to elicit emotions of a personal kind. So we can extend Bruner's proposal: fictional narrative is that mode of thinking about, and understanding, people who are somewhat like ourselves, who act purposefully, meet vicissitudes, and as a result experience emotions so that we readers also experience emotions by identification with them, in sympathy with them, or in other ways. A vicissitude is something challenging, a problem to which there is no rehearsed solution. Emotions, therefore, as responses to such events may be seen as prompting the experiencer to some creative response. Creativity is an important aspect of emotions' significance for us (Averill & Nunley, 1992).

This volume is about narrative's impact. Impact is a metaphor of how emotions affect a reader. Here I treat fiction of the kind that is written in novels and short stories, plays, films, and some poetry. Much of what I say applies also to biography, narrative history, and to present-day journalism of the kind that Wolfe (1975) has described. I discuss fiction not to exclude nonfictional genres but because it is the native medium of the emotions of narrative, of both characters in books and the readers of books.

The principal difference between nonfiction and fiction is that in all nonfiction the emphasis will be on empirical truth. Fiction, although it is not necessarily empirically untrue, places the emphasis on two other kinds of truth: coherence truths of interactions among the many elements of a story, and personal truths that relate to concerns of specific readers, and that may also be universal (Oatley, 1999a).

The principal questions of this chapter are: By what means do we experience fiction, and how do we explain its impact? In his book on the psychology of narrative, Gerrig (1993) argued that the experience occurs by the ordinary means of schematic processing that underlies all our ordinary understanding of the world. I think this is correct, but I also believe that there are some special processes underlying the writing and reading of fiction. For Gerrig, fiction has a relation to the understanding of nonfictional truths like that of visual illusions in relation to veridical perception. I propose a different direction of argument.

- Although fiction is often taken to be untruthful, it is a mistake to regard it as defective empirical description. It is not in any necessary conflict with empirical truth, but it prioritizes two other kinds of

truth: the coherence truth of simulation, and the personal truth of insight.
- Fiction is a kind of simulation, but one that runs on minds rather than on computers. As with other simulations, a principal purpose is to understand complex matters, in this case people, their actions, and their interactions, expressed in narrative form. The metaphor of simulation includes the idea of the reader's construction of the story, and it corresponds to older ideas that fiction is imagination, or a kind of dream.
- The impact of fiction is largely emotional. Emotions occur as readers or watchers construct their own versions of the story. As the simulation runs, emotions occur to readers or watchers that depend on psychological processes such as identification with a protagonist, sympathy for story characters, and activation of emotional autobiographical memories that resonate with story themes.

Metaphors of Transportation and Transformation

It has been said that fiction always derives from a wish by author and reader to be somewhere else. Fiction transports the reader to the story world. No longer in this place and time, in this body, or even (sometimes) in this universe, we travel to the place of elsewhere, where strange and exciting things occur. Hilgard (1979) likened the experience of reading to hypnosis: The reader is "transformed or transported by what he reads ... swept emotionally into the experience described by the author." Nell (1988) used this same idea and writes of the reading trance.

When one reads a thriller one wants no more than to be transported (Oatley, 1994). To open such a book is to mount a vehicle, like a Disneyland roller coaster, and take a ride. You get on at the beginning and, apart from a little cardiac consternation, you are the same person when you get off at the end. The Disney Corporation's claim that their theme parks are worlds of the imagination is somewhat disingenuous. There has been extraordinary imagination, but it is the imagination of the Disney designers and engineers. So elaborate are the effects, so carefully laid are the rails through space mountain or underwater fastness, that the opportunity for imagination on the part of the visitor is correspondingly reduced.

Another version of this metaphor is reading-as-package-vacation. A beach, a hotel, acceptable food, excursions, are laid on. In a comparable way, the thriller lays on your identification with a likable protagonist, programs your anxiety in response to a seemingly inescapable threat, and finally offers the relief of safety. One can have an absorbing time, but such experiences can be meager of agency. Although they may be vivid, they typically do not affect the self, or habits of thinking and feeling.

In his discussion of reading as hypnosis, Hilgard (1979) wrote of both transportation and transformation. Both are informative, but the transportation metaphor may be too passive. Fiction can include the sense of entering a new relationship with author and/or characters (Booth, 1988) and, like other personal relationships, it can potentially transform us. Such transformation can occur in two principal ways, the first by means of context (which can have emotional effects), the second by means of emotion directly.

Changes by means of context are best understood in terms introduced by Goffman (1961) in his dramaturgical analyses of the ways in which we all give performances of ourselves, as in the theater. Most social encounters begin by entering a distinctive context: a home, a store, a classroom. But more: Each context is really a psycho-social setting for a particular kind of relationship with another person that, summoning a theatrical metaphor, we can call a role. At home we may enter the role of spouse, or of parent. In a store we take on the role of customer. In a classroom, we become student or teacher. As we enter each contextualized role, it is as if we pass through a semipermeable membrane into a distinctive world, with its own meanings, its own history, its own potential for aspiration, its own opportunities for commentary by others and ourselves on the performances we give. When we enter a store, we know the schema or script of encounters of the shopping kind, and we enter a distinct kind of relationship with the store clerk. Each kind of role-relationship is different, and hence potentially transformative of the baseline self. In each context, we become to some extent a different person: wife-with-husband, shopper-with-clerk, student-with-professor. Encounters are not a bare structure of rules and roles. As Goffman remarked, encounters have "the thickness of reality," and the selfhood in which we engage is vitalizing: "there seems to be no agent more effective than another person in bringing a world for oneself alive or, by a glance, a gesture, or a remark, shrivelling up the reality in which one is lodged" (Goffman, 1961, p. 41).

If encounters transform one by means of their external contexts and the roles they afford, then emotions transform one in comparable ways but, as it were, from within. There is ample evidence for such effects (Oatley & Jenkins, 1996). In happy affection we are kind, understanding, cooperative. In anger—it can be with the same person—we are transformed to become retaliatory, vituperative, resistant.

Metamorphosis, the Greek term for transformation, has been used as a title by several writers, including Ovid, Apuleius, and Kafka. In Apuleius's story, *Metamorphoses*, or *The Golden Ass*, (c. 170/1989), the protagonist is transformed. He becomes a donkey. To start with, his human personality remains intact, but at the end of the story his whole self is transformed. In a kind of rebirth, he becomes an initiate of the goddess Isis. In reading a novel, perhaps including this Roman one, we as readers may also be transformed. William James (1902) linked the core of religious experience to this very idea of rebirth. The term *transformation*, then, also hints at the religious roots of the novel in the ancient world (cf. Doody, 1997) and of our human aspiration to change through experience, and develop within ourselves.

As we assimilate a story, our emotions are our own, not those of the characters. By means of the story our emotions may be transformed by having them deepened or understood better, and they may be extended toward people of kinds for whom we might previously have felt nothing. And when we come to the last sentence, we put the book down, something of the transformation of our identity can remain. As with a love relationship in which something of the loved person continues in us even when the person dies, so when we put a work of narrative art back on the bookshelf, something of it remains as part of the self.

There is a spectrum. At one end is transportation: Fiction can be escape, the pleasurable occupation of time. At the other end is transformation: Fiction can change the self. To increase the chances of transformation the author offers a character with whom one can connect, a certain suggestiveness, dilemmas, a range of ambiguities, something like a set of raw materials and hints at construction, a kit of parts. What the reader or audience member then does is to take part in the relationship that is offered (Oatley, 1999b), and to take up the materials offered by the story, in order to construct them into a personally imaginative result. The result is not just experience but creation (remember that emotions prompt creativity) in which the reader becomes the writer of his or her own version of the story.

In this chapter I examine four distinct aspects of fictional narrative, to help understand the impact of fiction as potential transformation, and I show how the structure of narrative fiction relates to the emotions of the reader or audience member. I depart from the usual practice in psychology, of hanging an explanation solely on empirical findings. Although I will summarize some of my empirical findings later in the chapter, I base much of the argument around a single work of fictional art, William Shakespeare's *Hamlet*, first performed in the Globe Theater in London about 1600. I do this to avoid merely writing *about* the effects and impact of fiction. Instead I would like to offer the reader the possibility of some personal sense of such effects and their impact, and an understanding how they are achieved.

Hamlet has been arguably the piece of fiction with the most widespread impact of any written in English. Shakespeare is the most performed of any playwright, the most widely taught in any course of English literature, and *Hamlet* is still his most popular play. Table 3.1 is a summary of its main events.

TABLE 3.1
Summary of the Event Structure of Hamlet

Hamlet

Scene: the royal court of Denmark, at Elsinore. Time: the North European Renaissance.

Claudius murders the king, his brother. He becomes king and marries Gertrude, the late king's wife and Prince Hamlet's mother. The late king's ghost appears to soldiers of the watch and to Horatio, friend of Hamlet, who tells him of the appearance. Next night, the ghost of his father appears to Hamlet, and demands vengeance for his murder by Claudius. A travelling theater company arrives at court. Hamlet arranges for them to perform a play of the murder of a king. Claudius and his Lord Chamberlain Polonius spy on Hamlet when Ophelia, daughter of Polonius and beloved of Hamlet, is sent to meet him. Hamlet rejects her. The play-within-the-play is staged. When the murder occurs in it, Claudius calls for light, and the play is stopped. Polonius hides behind a curtain in Gertrude's chamber. Hamlet meets Gertrude there. Hearing a voice behind the curtain, Hamlet stabs at it, and kills Polonius. Hamlet pleads with Gertrude to stop sleeping with Claudius. The ghost reappears to Hamlet, to remind him of his task, but is not seen by Gertrude. Ophelia goes mad. Hamlet is sent to England, then in a fight with pirates he escapes, and returns to Denmark. Laertes, son of Polonius, returns from university to the Danish court, and finds his sister Ophelia has drowned herself. He conspires with Claudius to kill Hamlet in a fencing match by using a poisoned rapier. Claudius plans to hold a poisoned chalice in reserve, in case Hamlet is not wounded. After the first pass in the fencing match, Gertrude drinks to her son from the poisoned cup. Hamlet is wounded with the poisoned rapier, which changes hands in a scuffle. Hamlet wounds Laertes with it, then runs Claudius through. Hamlet charges Horatio with telling his story. Fortinbras, the young prince of Norway, arrives on the scene to find many dead.

FOUR FUNDAMENTAL ASPECTS OF NARRATIVE

Since the beginning of the 20th century it has been conventional to divide narrative into two aspects. Russian literary theorists called these *fabula* and *siuzhet*, usually translated as story and plot. In psychology they are more clearly described by Brewer and Lichtenstein (1981) as event structure and discourse structure. For purposes of psychological explanation I propose two more aspects: the constructed realization of a story by a generalized implied reader, and the structure of suggestion that affects each particular reader. These may be regarded as subaspects of the *siuzhet*, although I think it is clearer to see them as separate, in the way I shall describe.

In the following section I discuss these four aspects, which are depicted in Table 3.2.

TABLE 3.2
Four Aspects of Story Structure

Event Structure
The events of the story in the story world. A creation of the author.

Discourse Structure	Suggestion Structure
The text as written by the author, or the drama as performed. Much of this structure is in the form of instructions to the reader or audience as to how to construct the story.	Non-literal aspects, suggested by the text, based on the reader's or watcher's share of knowledge, experience, emotions and ideas, but often having a general quality.

Realization
The enactment in the mind of the reader or watcher, which results from the constructive process and suggestion structure being applied to the discourse structure.

Event Structure

The event structure consists primarily of the happenings of the story world in their order of occurrence. Table 3.1 is a coarse summary of this structure for *Hamlet*. It's not much of a story: Narrative is not simply an account of what happened, not just a representation of events. Table 3.2 shows how this structure stands in relation to the other aspects of narrative.

Components of the event structure include overt actions such as stabbing, intrapersonal mental actions such as Hamlet seeing the ghost when it is not visible to his mother, and interpersonal mental actions such as pleading. They include settings, such as the Court at Elsinore, and furniture of the world such as the curtain in Gertrude's chamber. They also include emotions of story characters, such as Hamlet's jealous disgust of his mother's sexual relationship with his uncle.

The event structure does not occur as such; it is virtual. For nonfictional narrative, such as history or scientific observation, events did once happen. Although they are ineffable, they will have left traces such as people's reports from which an event structure can more or less accurately be reconstructed. Fiction, by contrast, as Aristotle pointed out in *Poetics* (c. 330BCE/1970), is not particular but universal. Its events are what could happen. Its latent events are brought into being only in the simulation of the events as constructed by the writer, and then by each audience member or reader. In *Hamlet*, no actual ghost appears on stage, and the actor who plays Hamlet does not kill a Polonius, any more than the word *ghost* is an apparition or the word *stab* makes blood flow. Rather, the events of the story world have to be told with implicit and explicit instructions to the audience about how to construct them into a simulation, a working mental model (cf. Johnson-Laird, 1983) in the mind of the reader or audience member.

Discourse Structure

A discourse structure corresponds to a specific text, say to the 1623 Folio text of *Hamlet*, or to any particular performance of the play. Event structure and discourse structure of a story correspond, respectively, to two aspects of a computer simulation. The first is a representation of events and objects in the world. The second consists of instructions. I have pointed out this distinction in an example of a simulated conversation partner who gives a human questioner answers to queries about how to travel from one place to another on the Toronto public transit system (Oatley, 1999b). Some pieces of this simulated conversation-partner's code correspond to subway stops in the actual Toronto. They are represented in a list-structured database. Other pieces are directions about how to compute over this database to answer questions.

In a literary simulation, one set of elements such as the words *Hamlet* and *ghost*, corresponds to people and objects in the event structure, the second set is of directions to the reader or audience to make the simulation run. In the event structure of *Hamlet*, the first significant event is the murder of the king. In the discourse structure, the temporal ordering is different: Its beginning is an exchange by the soldiers of the watch on the battlements of the castle at Elsinore. The scene shows Shakespeare's mature mastery: The setting is uneasy. There's a challenge, and a response. There is a military threat to Denmark from Norway. The first really significant event in the discourse structure is Hamlet's friend, Horatio, saying: "What, has this thing appear'd again tonight?" "This thing" is the ghost.

In the discourse structure, it is not until after an interleaved scene of the departure of Laertes for university, that the ghost appears to Hamlet. In general then, the temporal ordering of events in the discourse structure differs from that of the event structure. Its purpose is to boot up and sustain the simulation. The first scenes of *Hamlet* are dominated by the ghost. Emotionally, a ghost is a phenomenon of awe, its origin ambiguous, its intentions mysterious. Shakespeare's discourse structure gives the ghost attentional priority. The simulation starts up, therefore, in mystery-mode, which gives us a feeling of curiosity and apprehension, as if we too might be affected by the ghost's visitation. Resolution comes when the ghost reveals the secret of the murder, and enjoins Hamlet to vengeance. By this time Hamlet has become likeable to the audience. A relationship has begun. We identify with him. A further device of the discourse structure is then brought into play. The engagement of portentous anxiety is transferred to the next aspect of the story (Vorderer, 1996) to make it salient. In *Hamlet* the arousal of our anxiety is transferred seamlessly to concern for Hamlet's predicament: The injustice revealed by the ghost starts the next episode of the plot-simulation, which seems at first to be how vengeance should be exacted.

Realization

The story structure is virtual. The discourse structure, as Iser (1978) has pointed out, is potential: The means by which the effects of fiction are actualized. The realization of the story is what actually occurs, in the mind of an implied reader or audience member. It can be approached in three steps.

Construction. All experience of fiction can be thought of as deriving from readers' constructions of the story. This is common ground for cognitive accounts of understanding narrative, and it derives from Bartlett (1932). In his most famous study, Bartlett asked people to read a Native American folk story that had been collected by Franz Boas, called "The War of the Ghosts," and to return at intervals to the laboratory, to write down what they could remember of it. The story begins like this:

> One night two young men from Egulac went down to the river to hunt seals, and while they were there it became foggy and calm. Then they heard war cries, and they thought "Maybe this is a war-party." They escaped to the shore and hid behind a log. (Bartlett, 1932, p. 65)

The story tells how the two young men were invited by men in a canoe that came up to them, to go and fight with some people up the river. One young man made excuses: first that he had no arrows, then that his relatives would not know where he had gone. He did not go, but the other did. He was wounded in the battle, but did not feel sick. He thought, "Oh, they are ghosts." He returned home. The story ends like this:

> He told it all, and then he became quiet. When the sun rose he fell down. Something black came out of his mouth. The people jumped up and cried.
>
> He was dead.

In their reproductions of the story English readers made many changes. Not only did forgetting occur, but from week to week the remembered story became more like one from English culture: Hunting seals became fishing, and instead of the inconsequential tone of the original, in some hands the story became like a newspaper report. Certain details were well remembered, such as the "something black" that came from the man's mouth. But whereas in the Native American story this event happened as the sun rose, for one subject, it happened when the sun set. In English culture it is more appropriate to die at the end of a day.

Bartlett proposed that the basis for remembering was a schematic outline, based not on fixed and lifeless memory traces, but on a continually operating constructive process. He concluded, from his method of repeated reproduction, that remembering:

> ... is an imaginative reconstruction, built out of the relation of our attitude towards a whole active mass of organized past reactions and experience, and to a little outstanding detail ... It is thus hardly ever really exact ... and it is not at all important that it should be. (Bartlett, p. 213)

Remembering revealed the process. But its site is not just memory. It is a universal principle of mental life: Our every experience is schema-based. I shall use Piaget and Inhelder's (1969) terms: *assimilation* and *accommodation*. We take events, phrases, movements of a story, and assimilate them to a schema of what we already know. They achieve significance for us by becoming parts of our schemas. At the same time schemas may accommodate, just as scientific theories may change with new evidence.

Fiction has its impact, therefore, as people construct their own schematic understandings of a story. We can see how the process of schematic construction yields the effect of transformation. The reader or listener assimilates the material to her or his own schematic processing and thereby transforms the material so that it becomes comprehensible. Then, insofar as the self's knowledge, attitudes, and feelings are involved, the self too may accommodate and be transformed.

Mimesis as Simulation. The single most important term in Western literary criticism is *mimesis*. It was proposed as central to poetry (fiction) by Aristotle in the *Poetics*. The term continued into the Renaissance. To Shakespeare's contemporary, Philip Sidney (1595/1986), it meant "a representing, counterfeiting, or figuring forth" (p. 114). English translations for the succeeding 400 years have mostly followed the same tradition; they include "imitation," and "copying."

I have argued (Oatley, 1992) that such translations are misleading. What a play, novel, or film does is not to offer an empirical description that is inevitably flawed. It offers a parallel, a model. Narrative, especially fictional narrative, is a simulation, like a computer simulation, but one that runs on minds (Oatley, 1992, 1999a).

As far as the distinction between fiction and non-fiction goes, we can say that because fiction prioritizes coherence truth rather than empirical truth (Oatley, 1999a), what is important is how the complex of its elements coheres in a story, and how the Gestalt of the whole may parallel the world. (Empirical truth depends on how individual elements in a description correspond to individual elements in the world.)

In *Hamlet*, Shakespeare (1623/1997) wrote that drama holds, "as 'twere the mirror up to nature," (3, 2, 20). Here he seems to adopt the idea of *mimesis* as representation, but he also had a conception closer to the idea of simulation: *mimesis* not as copy but as imaginative dream, see the quotation at the head of this chapter. This indeed is one of his great and striking innovations. Just as dream parallels waking life, theater is a model that parallels the world. What takes place in his history plays, for instance, is a parallel of the self-serving actions but also some of the idealism, of kings and lords of pre-Elizabethan history. In other plays, of which *Hamlet* is an example, the parallels become wider, to include all humanity. The very name of Shakespeare's company's theater, "The Globe," is a statement of this idea, and in several plays he explicitly explains it to the audience.

In *Hamlet*, this idea is used at several levels: There is the play within the play, which parallels the murder by Claudius of Hamlet's father. Then, more grandly, comes the idea of a person facing the fact that human plans have effects that we must suffer although we do not always will them. In the words of the Player King:

> Our wills and fates do so contrary run
> That our devices still are overthrown
> Our thoughts are ours, their ends none of our own.
> (*Hamlet*, 3, 2, 193–195)

In *Hamlet*, we can see the search for the coherence of *mimesis*-as-simulation in the drafts through which the play passed. It is thought that there may have been an Ur-*Hamlet*, perhaps as Bloom (1999) argued, written by Shakespeare around 1589, soon after he joined the London stage. Most scholars agree that, of the three early surviving texts of the play, the First Quarto is a pirated version, supplied to a printer by a member of Shakespeare's acting company. It was printed in 1603. The Second Quarto was printed in 1604, probably from Shakespeare's own handwritten draft, and was the acting version for his company. The Folio version of 1623 (as used here) was printed from the company's collected stock of plays and is probably Shakespeare's final version, after the plays had been through a number of performances and textual changes by him.

In a simulation, all the components are interrelated. They must cohere, so that everything works together. Here is Aristotle's version of this idea: "A poetic *mimesis*, then, ought to be... unified and complete, and the component events ought to be so firmly compacted that if any one of them is shifted to another place, or removed, the whole is loosened up and dislocated" (330BCE/1970, 1451a, 30–36). Many of Shakespeare's editors, over the last 300 years, have made sure to stuff in as many lines from the Bard as they can, and thus have ignored Aristotle's advice about ill effects of shifting bits about. The result of such ministration in a modern edition of *Hamlet* is, as Jones (1995) put it: "Shakespeare's words but a play he never wrote" (p. 127).

Shakespeare's later thoughts on *Hamlet*, which appear as the Folio version, were to reduce the longer (Second Quarto) version of Hamlet's speech to his mother in her bedchamber to about half its original length. This piece of talk is his most direct in the whole play. It accomplishes the moment that is the play's psychological center, as Hamlet expresses his dread, his jealousy, and disgust, at his mother, and asks her to stop sleeping with his uncle. The moment is achingly delicate. Then, realizing his impertinence, Hamlet speaks with touching respect, and asks his mother's blessing. The eight additional lines that were in the Second Quarto version, but deleted in the Folio edition, are clever, but they dilute the effect and make for too much distance. On reflection Shakespeare gave priority to coherence, so that the simulation would not only run smoothly, but would do so with heightened dramatic impact.

Simulations of the novel and the theater are about fictional people, people we don't know. For reader and audience, one impact of constructing such simulations with all their cohering ramifications, I suggest, is to allow us to practice simulating people we do know, or might know, in their individuality, in the ordinary world. Such simulation in these circumstances has a special name: empathy.

Enactment. Most commentary on reading assumes that the process of interpretation of the text is central. Wittgenstein (1953) said, "all seeing is seeing as." Similarly, all reading is reading as: We read *Hamlet* as tragedy. But the idea, although correct, is too intellectual. Something more active is needed. A metaphor proposed by Sikora, Miall, and Kuiken (1998) is enactment, or as Iser (1978) and Gerrig (1993) called it, performance. The reader, like a Stanislavski-trained actor, enters the story world and offers himself or herself as the source of mind-and-agency from which the narrative takes its life.

The idea of enactment is of each audience member or reader as an actor—although one who does not have to remember all the lines —experiencing interactions and emotions in a play or novel. The writer does his or her job in starting up and sustaining a coherent dream/simulation. Each person's enactment then creates a seamless world and a seamless experience within it. In terms of the three kinds of truth discussed by Oatley (1999a): If nonfiction such as science prioritizes empirical truth, and if simulation prioritizes coherence truth, then enactment prioritizes personal truth.

Games are in many ways like stories. They are primarily about agency, and they thereby illuminate the nature of fiction. Every game offers the agent who enters it a goal (for instance to win in competition with others), some outline plans of how to accomplish the goal, and a set of apparatus, constraints, and rules that must be followed to enact any specific plan within the distinctive world the game affords. Some games are simple. Others are more elaborate and require more creative engagement.

Although games may not be serious, this element of enactment occurs both in fiction and in games, and it can be serious. By engaging fully in what is afforded, the self may be transformed. I have a colleague who is a fine chess player. He gave up competitive chess when held to a draw by a 10-year-old boy. As he recognized, some children do have minds that seem ideally suited to such quasiformal operations as chess. At the same time the transformation of self that further encounters of this kind might offer became unwelcome.

Goffman (1961) pointed out such effects: In a game, as in any other encounter, or in fiction, the question arises of how strongly we engage in the role afforded. Fun only occurs when we engage ourselves fully. Games are those kinds of stylized encounters in which, if we do engage ourselves, we may expect to have emotional experiences that will be fun. And, at the moment in which we immerse ourselves in the role, the role transforms us, makes us into a version of itself. This is why Goffman calls the membrane that surrounds each kind of encounter *semi-permeable*. It lets in persons, but it contains enactments of roles that the encounter affords. In a shop we become the bargain-hunter. In chess we become the player who moves nonchalantly but who by sacrificing a pawn seeks cleverly to invite the other player into an untenable position.

In reading and theater-going we enter, Alice-like, through a looking glass into an imagined world in which the self can become engaged and potentially transformed. We need not be passive. We do not merely receive (as implied by reception studies of art) or respond (as in reader-response). The constructions we make involve enactment: taking an active part in the story in much the same the way as we take part in a game or a social encounter, potentially becoming different from our habitual selves in doing so.

Suggestion Structure

In discussing discourse structure and realization, I hypothesized psychological states of attention, impact, and so forth, as occurring in a general way to an ideal audience member or reader, rather than to someone in particular. In a previous paper (Oatley, 1999b) I called the last-to-be-discussed aspect of narrative the association structure, with associations being based on each individual's personal interpretation, of the novel or play, on his or her culture, preoccupations, thoughts, memories, and emotions, which enter into the constructive process. I now think it better to call the fourth aspect of narrative the suggestion structure; the structure of what is suggested to the reader who is alive to its hints, although these are not directly stated.

This idea has been best expounded by Indian literary theorists who wrote about 1,000 years ago (see, e.g., Hogan, 2000; Ingalls, Masson, & Patwardhan, 1990). The key concepts are the suggestive (*dhvani*) that describe the ways in which a literary text brings to mind ideas that are not in the text itself, and sentiments (*rasas*) which may be thought of as emotions or moods induced by the text. Although these Eastern ideas are of great importance for understanding the impact of narrative, I will approach from a Western psychological direction. First two experiments: Bartlett (1932, discussed above) mentioned that he did his study with the "War of the Ghosts" story toward the end of World War I. For his participants, the issues of separation and the possibilities of no return were vivid. Most of the male subjects had been in the war or faced the prospect of going. For the women, losing relatives and friends was an ever-present threat. Bartlett reported that for one of his groups of participants (13 men and 7 women), only 10 wrote about one excuse of one of the young men in the story, that he had no arrows. But 18 wrote about the second excuse, that the man's relatives would not know where he had gone. Perhaps the excuse of being without arrows was remembered less because it was resolved within the story itself, but Bartlett wrote that participants' anxieties over separation probably contributed to their versions of the story. This second excuse suggested something salient for them. More recently, in one of the studies of our research group, people read "Clay," a story from James Joyce's *Dubliners*. Elise Axelrad (1993) found an effect comparable to that of Bartlett. She had people record autobiographical memories that surfaced as they read "Clay," and found that pieces of these memories became part of what they retold when they reproduced the story.

The argument is that reading a story has effects on the reader that do not just involve understanding the sense that is defined by paraphrases and comprehension tests. There are also effects that are nonliteral and nonparaphrasable. To say that these aspects cannot be paraphrased is not to say one cannot speak of them. One can speak of them a great deal, but they are suggested. They are the reasons why event structures, such as that of Table 3.1, are not stories. Any paraphrase of a story is likely to be tedious. For the medieval Indian literary theorists, it was in the *dhvani* (suggestiveness) that beauty resides, there that occurs any tendency to the sublime.

From a Western approach we would say that suggestion is mediated by the reader's memories, emotions, and thoughts. So here let me interweave another psychological study, in which we can see further how emotions affect the reader of a story. This study, carried out by Seema Nundy with Laurette Larocque and myself (Nundy, 1996; Oatley, 1996b) was of reading Russell Banks's "Sarah Cole." This is a short story about Ron, a New England lawyer, who thinks himself very attractive. At a bar one evening, two women dare a third, Sarah, who is not good looking, to try and pick him up. She succeeds. A sexual relationship begins. After a few months Ron ends it cruelly, and calls Sarah hurtful and degrading names. Only years later did he recognize that he had loved her, and feels he had killed her by acting as he had.

Before they started reading we asked undergraduate participants to complete a structured emotion diary to indicate their current emotions and to rate the intensity of each. We asked for another such diary after subjects had read the story. The story ends in an ambiguous way. After the participants had finished reading we asked them three interpretive questions about the ambiguities.

We sorted into two categories the kinds of reasoning that people showed in response to the interpretive questions, and found 91% agreement between two raters making these categorizations. One category was of what is known in studies of reasoning as backward chaining: first stating a conclusion and then giving reasons to support it. Here is an example, from Participant 1015's response to Question 1, which was: "From the narrator's point of view, why do you think the story says 'She's transformed into the most beautiful woman he had ever seen?'"

> He no longer sees Sarah as belonging to him. She breaks away from him probably more strongly than he tries to separate from her. He is also not truly capable of a true respectful love… and maybe feels guilty and envious that she was giving in the relationship he was never honestly in.

The other category was forward chaining, stating first a set of reasons or premises, then a conclusion. Here is an example: Participant 1006 in response to Question 2 which was: "From the narrator's point of view, why do you think the story says 'It's not as if she has died; it's as if he has killed her?'"

> He knew she knew and everyone else that she was "homely." Perhaps it was perverse or pity that he engaged in a relationship with her. But despite her physical appearance which she struggled with, she had feelings … So out of guilt he might as well have killed emotionally—cut deep into the soul at any rate.

"Sarah Cole" is unusual in that it elicits differing emotions in different readers. Among our participants we found anger, sadness, and, less frequently, disgust. Participants who became sad engaged predominantly in backward chaining. Participants who became angry engaged predominantly in forward chaining. This difference was significant at the $p < 0.02$ level for each of the three interpretive questions. In other words, each reader was emotionally affected by the story, and his or her mode of thinking became different depending on what emotion was experienced. Sadness is a mode in which one starts from the current state and reasons backward to try and understand its causes. Anger is a state in which one reasons forward from the current state about what to do next. Our result is from a single study. We nevertheless think it suggestive that distinctive modes of reasoning were associated with specific emotions. In another study—this time of ordinary life—Grazzani-Gavazzi and Oatley (1999) asked people in Italy and Canada to keep structured diaries of a plan that had been made with someone else and had gone wrong. When the error occurred, anger toward the other person was the most frequent emotion: People were self-justificatory, blaming, and derogatory toward the other. Some people, however, became sorry (an emotion based on sadness). So here again we found a result that suggested a specific, cognitive, effect of an emotion. In this sad emotional transformation of the self, reconciliation with the other person was more likely.

Earlier in this chapter I mentioned that there is evidence that emotion can transform the self, much as can a Goffmanian role-context. In other words, when angry, one is a somewhat different person than when sad or experiencing no particular emotion. What these studies suggest is that when in an emotional state, one thinks and relates to others in ways that are characteristic of the particular emotion. If becoming angry or sad is habitual, or if we do not reflect on it, then nothing will happen when one becomes angry or sad in reading a story except the experience of the emotion. But if the story and its context do allow us to reflect on the emotion together with its meaning, then the reader may reach an insight, and build a new piece of his or her model of the self and its relations. In other words, some cognitive transformation may result.

Thus, people have distinctive personal responses that are suggested by the story, but are not directly caused by it. I have argued (Oatley, 1999b), that literary language that includes tropes—figures such as metaphor and metonymy—has its effects principally by affecting readers' individual associations. If a metaphor works, for instance, it does so because it draws on the reader's own experience of the source of the metaphor, and transforms the reader's experience by assimilating it to something different.

Jacobson (1988) described metaphoric and metonymic poles of language. Metaphor and simile transform by one thing being a model of another, *mimesis* in miniature; the effect is substitutive. So in Hamlet's first scene with Rosencrantz and Guildenstern he says: "Denmark's a prison"

3. EMOTIONS AND THE STORY WORLDS OF FICTION   55

(2, 2, 239). To enter this metaphor, we summon experiences of constraint and apply them. By contrast, metonym transforms by a signifier sliding across adjacent meanings. It works by juxtapositions, and reorderings, based on relations in time and space. A common form is synecdoche: part for whole, or whole for part. So when Marcellus remarks, after the sighting of the ghost in the play's first scene, "Something's rotten in the state of Denmark" (1567), "state" and the situation in Elsinore are close in meaning. He doesn't mean the state generally, he means something much more immediate to the action of the play.

A frequent way of talking about such figures is as defamiliarization, first broached by the Russian formalists at the beginning of the 20th century (see Miall & Kuiken, 1994). The idea is that we have become habituated to our everyday world, so that we are barely conscious of it. The writer makes that world *un*familiar, so that we experience it more consciously. Transformational language (in figures such as metaphor and metonymy) first prompts partial dissolution of aspects of a schema, followed by insightful resolution, which occurs when the schema achieves a new accommodation and readers start to think about the issues in a new way. Some of the impact of narrative fiction, and of lyric poetry, may come about as a result of such changes. My sense is that although the idea of defamiliarization is informative, we are not just affected by shocks of the new. The literary effects work even when we read *Hamlet* for the fifth time. Consider this hypothesis, which is related but different.

Thoughts in literary language need not themselves be unfamiliar. People regularly listen to pieces of music many times, reread favorite poetry, see plays like *Hamlet* over again, and read great novels more than once. Bloom (1994) indeed, proposed that literature is great exactly insofar as it can be read more than once, as far as it stretches us mentally toward formulations that we could not quite have thought up ourselves, or even grasped on the first occasion. This effect is of progressively elaborating the schemas by which we understand works of art. Each enactment is different, each can deepen our personal understanding by bringing the material closer to the self. Hence we can extend ourselves.

The mental effects of transformation, prompted in each specific reader, seldom take place directly. They occur by recruiting conscious or unconscious memories, and emotions (as indicated in the empirical studies mentioned above). They start trains of thought that readers would not otherwise have had, which are not paraphrases of the discourse structure. They prompt new connections within the self, and they elaborate meanings, which can be built into our mental structure as parts of ourselves.

As John Keats wrote in a letter to John Taylor, on 27 February 1818 (1816–1820/p. 113):

> 1st I think Poetry should surprise by a fine excess and not by Singularity—it should strike the Reader as a wording of his own highest thoughts, and appear almost a Remembrance—2nd its touches of Beauty should never be half way ther[e] by making the reader breathless instead of content: the rise, the progress, the setting of imagery should like the Sun come natural natural too him—shine over him and set soberly although in magnificence leaving him in the Luxury of twilight. (p. 46)

The question of what prompts insight has in the West been associated with the idea that literature can be profound. Longinus (1st century CE/1965) introduced the idea that some expressions seem to come from some realm beyond the merely human. They can be sublime thoughts on fundamental issues of existence. Consider, for instance, the very best known of Shakespeare's words, which I give below, but first look at an un-sublime but less familiar version. It comes from the pirated First Quarto of *Hamlet* (1603/1998) 7, 114–118, p. 58).

> To be or not to be, ay there's the point,
> To die, to sleep, is that all? Ay all:
> No, to sleep, to dream, ay marry, there it goes
> For in that dream of death, when we awake
> And borne before an everlasting judge ...

Defamiliarization means disturbing the habitual, and arguably the above does not do this very well, indeed it uses cliché. What I am proposing by citing it is that familiarity–unfamiliarity is not quite the center of the issue. Compare, the lines above with the more familiar version, which is identical in Second Quarto (1604) and First Folio (1623) editions: Shakespeare's own words.

> To be or not to be;[1] that is the question:[2]
> Whether 'tis nobler[3] in the mind[4] to suffer
> The slings and arrows[5] of outrageous fortune, [6]
> Or to take arms[7] against a sea of troubles, [8]
> And by opposing end them. (*Hamlet*, 3, 1, 58–62)

I have numbered each of the figures (tropes). They are as follows.

1. "To be or not to be": metonymic displacement (synecdoche). The phrase means to be alive or to commit suicide.
2. "The question": metonymic displacement (synecdoche). The question means the principal question of human life.
3. "Nobler": metonymic displacement. Noble had an original meaning concerning social class: Noble equals aristocratic. Through wide

usage (as pointed out by Nietzsche) there has been a snobbish sliding of this meaning to honorable, and hence good.
4. "In": metaphor that implies that the mind is a container.
5. "Slings and arrows": metaphor for adversity. This is also a case of the elegant rhetorical figure hendiasis (two for one) in which a doublet of words aims at a single concept. Jones (1995) counted 65 to 70 examples of this figure in *Hamlet*, more than twice the number in any other of Shakespeare's plays.
6. "Fortune": metonymic displacement (synecdoche). Fortune has the principal connotation of good luck. Here it means more generally, chance, which can cause results that are *un*fortunate, and "outrageous," meaning literally "wantonly vicious."
7. "Take arms": combined metonym and metaphor. To take arms is a synecdoche for to do battle. It then becomes a metaphor for "to oppose."
8. "Sea of troubles": metaphor for extensive troubles. As often in Shakespeare this phrase is a quotation; This one is from "*mare malorum*" in Erasmus's (1500) *Adages*, which were Latin translations of Greek classics, which Shakespeare had read. Taking arms against a sea, against waves of confrontation, sounds vigorous, but of course is hopeless.

The effects of fiction depend on tropes and on suggestiveness of other kinds. Literary language, as Sikora, Miall, and Kuiken (1998) found in a study of people asked to read Coleridge's "The Rime of the Ancient Mariner," tended to induce people to experience more affect, and to become more completely engaged in the enactment. The readers found also that boundaries became blurred between the poet and themselves.

Consider now the following, spoken by Horatio, in the final scene of *Hamlet*:

Now cracks a noble heart. Good night, sweet prince,
And flights of angels sing thee to thy rest. (5, 2, 302–303)

Commentators have remarked that the second of these lines is the most beautiful in all of Shakespeare. I agree. First, as Hogan (personal communication) has pointed out the "good night," primes an attachment theme; it is suggestive of the intimacy of a child with parent, before sleeping. Then, if we analyze the figures: "Angels" is prosopopoeia, a form of metonym in which something such as a spirit or idea stands for a person. "Flight" is a metaphorical collective noun that carries the implication of a company with an ethereal quality. "Sing" is a metaphor for the ceremonial of funeral. "Rest" is a metaphor for death, and one of Shakespeare's commonplaces. After Hamlet has tried strenuously to transcend the banality of the revenge demanded by the ghost, it is not just the figures but the whole suggestiveness of the two lines that is tear-promptingly moving. What the lines suggest to me (not fully analyzed) is, that for all of us, imperfect beings as we are, who have struggled and made mistakes, there may be some closely attached friend who will, by continuing our memory, contribute to thinking affectionately of the life that we lived, and affirming it as part of the human community.

Relation of the Four Aspects of Narrative to Criticism and Psychology. Event structure, discourse structure, realization, and suggestion structure; each has a distinctive role in fictional narrative and each has a distinctive mode of explication. Although the event structure is virtual, it can be inferred fairly simply from the text of a novel or play. In terms of linguistics, it is the semantics of the story, the propositional structure around which the plot is formed. In terms of literary criticism, its puzzles are minor. They include the questions of Hamlet's age at the time of the play's events and how Horatio, who is his closest friend, has been in Elsinore for a month since the old king's funeral without Hamlet knowing it. One of its principal effects, therefore, is to provide opportunities for the writer to make mistakes! Psychologically, the event structure is important because, as Bower and Morrow (1990) have shown, in the course of constructing a mental model of places, persons, and events traversed by the narrative, the reader's attention acts as a kind of spotlight that moves through the story world. It defines the focus. It offers a kind of priming that is essential to following a plot, and is also a key process of suggestiveness.

If the event structure is the propositional content, the discourse structure is a set of speech acts addressed to the reader. Sometimes the writer directs such speech acts explicitly to the reader as when Charlotte Brontë (1847/1966) has Jane Eyre saying: "Reader, I married him." At the end of his plays, Shakespeare sometimes addresses the audience via a principal character. In *Hamlet*, for instance, Hamlet says both to watchers on the stage and those in the audience:

> You that look pale and tremble at this chance
> That are but mutes or audience to this act,
> Had I but time—as this fell sergeant, Death,
> Is strict in his arrest—Oh, I could tell you (5, 2, 276–279)

Usually the address of author to reader or audience is indirect; the discourse structure is the transformation of the event structure that creates the plot. It is the main subject of literary criticism. This is why it has usually not been much concerned with the empirical, or with effects of a work on the reader. When Wimsatt and Beardsley (1954) wrote their famous essay "The affective fallacy" they argued that criticism is about the text, not about anyone's feelings when reading. Their argument seems mistaken: The manner in which we run the simulation has huge effects on a work's suggestiveness, and much of literary criticism is about suggestions from the text that we might have missed, by being less sensitive, or less knowledgeable, than the critic.

Properly speaking, the realization (the construction of the story by readers or audience) and the suggestion structure (the nonpropositional emotional tone that contributes to each reader's enactment) are topics of psychology. They are, respectively, the processes of schematic construction, and the set of associative memories, thoughts, and feelings (*rasas*), suggested by the story's language, in readers or listeners. For realization one speaks of the fundamental constructive (modeling, theorizing, schematizing) properties of mind. For the suggestion structure one speaks of connotations and side effects within individual minds, in their enactments.

When I. A. Richards (1929) conducted his famous experiment of asking a group of people for their interpretations of short poems, which he described in his book *Practical Criticism*, he started asking people for their realizations. This was an important step in reader-response psychology. Perhaps prompted by this, a new juncture has been reached at which discourse structure, realization, and suggestion structure can be considered together. Literary critics, such as Rosenblatt (1978) and Iser (1978) have turned to issues of reader-response whereas sociologists and psychologists, who include Scheff (1979) and Graesser, Singer, and Trabasso (1994), have turned to the empirical study of literature. Partnerships have even been formed between literary critics and psychologists, such as that of Miall and Kuiken (1994).

THE PSYCHOLOGY OF THE ELICITATION OF EMOTIONS IN FICTION

In this final section, I indicate three principal psychological processes—memory, identification, and sympathy—by which literary emotional effects occur in readers and audiences of fiction (Oatley, 1994). Each involves entering into the story world and allowing oneself to become engaged in it.

Autobiographical Memory

By offering a mimetic parallel to our own life, a story can resonate with it and bring our own experience into our realization of a story, to create the priming that Hogan (2000) said is essential for a story's suggestiveness. In terms of Jacobson's (1988) distinction this is a metonymic effect:

Readers' memories are juxtaposed with events of the story. The studies of Axelrad, and of Nundy, Oatley, & Larocque mentioned previously, showed examples of this. Comparable effects were found by Larsen and Seilman (1988) who had readers mark the text of a story they were reading when memories occurred. They found that in fictional as compared with expository texts, twice as many memories occurred in which the reader was personally involved as actor. Our research group has extended this method by asking readers to mark an M in the margin when a memory comes to mind, an E when an emotion is prompted and, in some studies, a T when a thought occurs that is not a direct paraphrase of the text. At the end of reading, we can ask our readers to go back over specific Es, Ms, and Ts, and describe their contents.

The most informative theorist of the effects of memory while reading or attending a drama is Scheff (1979), who proposed that in the ordinary course of events we do not always experience our emotions fully. Sometimes we hold these emotions away, keep them overdistanced: We do not allow them to touch us. At other times emotions may be underdistanced: We are overwhelmed by them. In either case we may experience effects of emotions without understanding their meaning or assimilating their significance. Therapy, ritual, and drama, said Scheff, allow renewed opportunities of reliving emotions so that we are better able to understand their meanings.

In a recent study in our research group, Mitra Gholamain (1998) investigated this idea. She asked subjects, who were members of reading groups, to read "Bardon Bus" by Alice Munro. The story is of a woman who recounts the loss of a romantic relationship. Gholamain collected Es and Ms, as described above, then asked the subjects to describe the most significant of the memories prompted by their reading, and also to write an overall response to the story. She categorized the memories into the three kinds described by Scheff. An overdistanced memory is without emotions, whereas an underdistanced memory is raw and unanalyzed—all emotion and no reflection. An optimally distanced memory connects the remembered event to the self and, by implication, to current identity. She found that people who described overdistanced memories tended to give responses that were largely intellectual, or dominated by technical judgments (e.g., about the writing style). Those with underdistanced memories gave summaries of the whole story in a largely emotional way, writing about whether they liked or disliked it, or how they felt what a character was feeling. Those with more optimally distanced memories wrote overall responses that contained both thought and emotion. This result tends to confirm Holland's (1975) theory that in their responses to stories (as indicated in the overall responses), people's own habitual attitudes to the world (as indicated in their memories), are recreated.

Conscious pieces of autobiographical memory are, however, not responsible for the whole effect. From Scheff's idea, one can feel sad at some aspect of a story because of unconsciously elicited memories that have previously not been assimilated. According to this idea, if I feel tearful at Horatio talking of "flights of angels," for instance, it is because it resonates with my own experiences of loss, although these experiences may no longer be conscious to me. When the remembered experiences occurred I may have distanced them, or they may have been too overwhelming. By reliving them in a drama, the chance occurs for me to experience them at a proper distance. That is to say I can both experience the emotion and also reflect on its meaning.

Shakespeare varies emotional distancing in his plays. Sometimes he brings us in close. In *Hamlet*, as I discussed earlier, the emotional center of the play is the intimate conversation between Hamlet and his mother, in her bedchamber. Both here, and at the end of the play during the exchanges with Horatio before Hamlet's death, Shakespeare decreases the emotional distance. At other times he has the audience observe from a distance; his habitual means to increase distance is by humorous passages with rustic characters, in *Hamlet*, the gravediggers. So, in fiction, we let the story take us over and be underdistanced. At other times we hold things at more of a distance. In the one we feel deeply, in the other, we can be thoughtful. Identification and sympathy are the vehicles of these two modes, respectively, as follows.

Identification

When a reader or audience member becomes one with the character in a story or play we talk of identification (Appleyard, 1990; Oatley & Gholamain, 1997).

The emotions of identification derive directly from the theory of simulation (Oatley, 1992, 1999a) discussed previously. In terms of Jacobson's (1988) distinction this is a metaphorical effect; it works by substitution. The part of the mind on which the reader (or audience) runs the simulation of a novel, play, or film, is the planning processor. Ordinarily, we use it in conjunction with our mental models of the world to assemble actions into plans to attain goals, as when planning a journey. In an identificatory reading, a plot may take over (substitute a character's goals into) the planning processor, and the reader then adopts the protagonist's plans. Emotions occur when events become vicissitudes, as actions and their outcomes in the plot are evaluated in relation to the protagonist's goals. Although the goals and plans are simulated, the emotions are not: They are the reader's own.

In one study (see Oatley, 1996a) Angela Biason and I asked 59 high-school students to read one of two short stories about adolescent identity.

One story, by Carson McCullers, had a male protagonist. The other, by Alice Munro, had a female protagonist. We had the subjects record Es and Ms (as described above) as they read. The boys experienced a mean of 3.9 emotions while reading a story, the girls a mean of 6.7, and this difference was significant. There was a similar difference between the number of memories recorded by the boys and girls. We take it that these emotions and memories indicate the degree of involvement in the story. The finding that the girls experienced a larger number of emotions and memories implies that they were able to identify personally and equally with both the male and the female protagonist. The boys not only had fewer emotions and memories overall, but they had the fewest when reading the story with the female protagonist. They were less willing to identify with, become like, a girl. Identification, therefore, involves a factor of likeness to a character, or of wanting to be like that character. Only when the reader wants to make this leap into another mind can identification occur.

In *Hamlet*, as Hazlitt (cit. Bloom, 1999, p. 428) says: "It is we who are Hamlet." But if all that occurred was that we had some selection of Hamlet's emotional experiences —contempt for Claudius, sexual disgust at Gertrude, disdainful rejection of Ophelia, affection toward Horatio—the play would be ordinary. We need to be able to think about such emotions as we feel them, understand them in the scheme of things. The close-up process of identification must be paired with thoughtful modes of sympathy.

Sympathy

Hamlet is a play of observed and observers: Polonius is killed while spying on Hamlet, the play within the play is Hamlet's device for observing the reaction of Claudius, and so forth. The whole plot revolves around who is observing whom. After the play within the play, when Claudius's guilt has been observed by Hamlet and Horatio, Hamlet comes across Claudius, and observes him in the posture of prayer, alone, unarmed, and unguarded. Hamlet could kill him easily.

> Hamlet: Now might I do it pat, now a is praying.
> And now I'll do it. [*He draws his sword*]
>   And so a goes to heaven,
> And so am I reveng'd. (3, 3, 72–75)

This is an intellectual moment for both Hamlet and the audience, more distanced than the scene that follows, between Hamlet and his mother in her bedchamber. We are not so much identified with Hamlet as we observe the tableau. We consider how appropriate it would be for Hamlet to kill Claudius at prayer. There is, however, a double observation, which opens itself to irony, because the audience here knows what Hamlet does not. Although Claudius is kneeling, he cannot pray ("my offense is rank," he says). He is unable to repent because he will not renounce what he has gained from the murder—"My words fly up, my thoughts remain below. | Words without thoughts never to heaven go" (3, 3, 97–98).

The theory of sympathetic elicitation of emotions has been expounded by Tan (1994, 1996). To elicit sympathy, a writer offers patterns of events. The reader substitutes him- or herself into the scene (a metaphorical effect), as something like an observer, but the emotions are more distanced than those of identification because they depend on the imagined predicament of a story character. In ordinary life emotions are caused by appraisal patterns: A pattern of frustration causes anger, a loss causes sadness, and so on. In literary theory, the corresponding idea is T. S. Eliot's, that the "only way of expressing an emotion in art is by finding an objective correlative"(1919/1953, p. 107): A condition, or chain of events, outside the person that would typically cause a particular emotion. It is on the basis of the imagined effect of such appraisal patterns/correlatives on a story character that the reader or audience member feels sympathetic emotions for the character. With Claudius's acknowledgement of his guilt, we feel his loss of the sense of himself. In that moment we become sad for him, more sympathetic than at any time previously. At the same time we feel sympathy for Hamlet in this further instance of his unwillingness simply to behave like a thug.

Emotions in Fiction and Emotions in Life

There are differences between the emotions of fiction and those of life.

The first is that fiction has a laboratory quality. We experience it in a place of safety away from the ordinary world, so that the prompting of emotions is more voluntary than in ordinary life. We choose whether or not to be engaged, we can put down a book, we can leave the theater. In ordinary life we cannot absent ourselves from the sickness of a child, or from the cauldron of an unhappy marriage. If this were not the case (so the argument goes) whenever we experienced the emotion of fear in the theater, we would just get up and leave.

Second, in fiction we are more subject to tears than in ordinary life. Indeed, when we are moved by fiction, the experience is often tearful. Tan and Frijda (1999) suggested that this effect may be a kind of awe, a deference toward something greater than ourselves. Although Tan and Frijda said that the emotions of film are, for the most part emotions of sympathy for story characters (see previous discussion), I have argued that other modes of emotional experience also occur. Whether or not the emotions of real life and those emotions of fiction are different, it really is the self that is touched. These are not counterfeit emotions.

Third, Scheff (1979) proposed, as I discussed earlier, that emotions in fiction can be experienced at different distances, not kept too far away so they do not touch us, nor too close so that they overwhelm us. This effect, therefore, gives fiction the possibility of allowing us to relive, or in other ways to experience, emotion while at the same time reflecting on it.

The Space in Between

In the end, impact may be too violent a metaphor for the effects of narrative fiction. I have argued that being moved is central to the reading of fiction, and insofar as it occurs, for instance in any of the ways just discussed, then transformative insight can occur. The hypothesis is that such insight demands three conditions: First, an emotion must occur at a certain distance, distinctly, but not too overwhelmingly. Second, there must be a reflective context that allows understanding of the emotion's meaning. Third, for any transformative insight, the writer must offer the opportunity of a writerly, rather than a purely readerly, reading (Barthes, 1975). He or she must not merely transport the reader on a set of rails, but offer what Winnicott (1971) called a "space in between" self and the writer. Winnicott's concept was that, to start with, the relation of each of us to our mother (or other caregiver) is symbiotic. Infant and mother are one. Then there grows, as the mother is discovered to be not always available, a beginning of separateness. In this space in between, says Winnicott, human culture develops, built often on playful and affectionate interaction, and always with this primal sense of connection to the other, however slender this connection may later seem.

Books are important in culture. My argument is that rather than authors compelling the reader to think these thoughts, or feel exactly those emotions; they can be, as it were, more suggestive, can allow the reader more playful opportunity, while retaining the link with the other mind. Hence the reader can make his or her own personal construction in this cultural space, in which memories, idiosyncratic emotions, sympathetic impulses, and reflective thoughts can occur.

We cannot always be moved and think about something in an observational way at the same time. What we can more often do is to move in and out along the continuum of emotional distance, be fully engaged emotionally at one moment, and then in the glow of that emotion, think about the experience in a more distanced way. Shakespeare's constant varying of the emotional distance in plays like *Hamlet*, adds to his profundity and suggestiveness.

Is it possible for emotion and meaning to become simultaneously present? The idea of this kind of possibility has been in existence in literary culture for almost a century, from Proust's great novel, *Remembrance of things past* (1913–1927/1981). Proust argued that for the most part experience passes us by—it goes too fast and its sensory basis is dissipated, or our attention moves elsewhere before its meaning can be understood. A novel, therefore, can allow a person to relive some patterns of experience, and at the same time allow the reader to think about its implications. The coming together of a particular experience and its meaning is rare. But if and when it occurs, it can create deeply moving understanding. This was what Proust believed to be the implication of the profound joy he experienced at instants depicted in his novel when he relived a piece of experience and understood it, as with the taste of the Madeleine cake and tea.

The hypothesis is that literature can affect the self and potentially transform identity by suggesting emotions in contexts of understanding. When we are moved by *Hamlet*, we may feel a range of emotions. At the same time our own thoughts go out to some of the great issues of the human predicament, as they affect us personally, and as they affect our fellow beings.

CONCLUSION

I have argued that the impact of fiction occurs mainly via emotions, perhaps especially literary emotions (*rasas*), which are suggested when one reads a novel or short story, or watches a play or film. These emotions occur as the reader/watcher constructs and enacts a version of the story as a simulation that runs on his or her mind.

Reading can transform the self. Emotions have been the core of fiction from the beginning, and in English literature inwardness has been growing at least since Shakespeare's time.

By drawing on our ability to simulate social interaction, and to experience others' emotions, we practice understanding of others in their inwardness and individuality (see Nussbaum, 1995), and normalize this kind of understanding. Shakespeare, George Eliot, Proust, Woolf, and the others, have introduced us by way of fictional literature into the minds of others, and it is likely that the tendency of this movement has spread to everyday life. Who, after all, could now imagine themselves into being a Victorian industrial worker without feeling the inappropriateness of its unhealthiness, dreariness, and long hours?

George Eliot wrote that:

> The greatest benefit we owe to the artist, whether painter, poet or novelist, is the extension of our sympathies. Appeals founded on generalizations and statistics require a sympathy ready-made, a moral sentiment already in activity; but a picture of human life such as a great artist can give, surprises even the trivial and the

selfish into that attention to what is apart from themselves, which may be called the raw material of moral sentiment.... Art is the nearest thing to life; it is a mode of amplifying experience and extending our contact with our fellow-men beyond the bounds of our personal lot. (1856/1963, p. 270)

This is the best manifesto I know for fiction. A recent PhD dissertation from the University of Utrecht, echoes the sentiment with its title: "The moral laboratory: Literature and ethical awareness" (Hakemulder, 1998). There is a corollary that Eliot did not mention in this passage. Fictional identification and empathy are the same process. Both use the self as the means of simulation of the other. Not only, therefore, does the self expand in its sympathetic understanding of others as George Eliot suggested, but in fiction others become more acceptable to the self, even in their otherness.

ACKNOWLEDGMENTS

I thank the members of the research group on emotions and the reading of fiction in the Centre for Applied Cognitive Science—particularly Laurette Larocque, Angela Biason, Elise Axelrad, Seema Nundy, Iliaria Grazzani, and Mitra Gholamain, whose work is discussed previously—and the Social Sciences and Humanities Research Council of Canada for supporting our work. I also thank Patrick Colm Hogan for introducing me to Sanscrit theories of poetics.

REFERENCES

Appleyard, J. A. (1990). *Becoming a reader: The experience of fiction from childhood to adulthood.* Cambridge: Cambridge University Press.
Apuleius (circa 170/1989). *Metamorphoses, or The golden ass* (ed. & trans. J. A. Hanson). Cambridge, MA: Harvard University Press (1989).
Aristotle (1970). *Poetics* (G. E. Else, trans.). Ann Arbor, MI: University of Michigan Press (original work published c. 330BCE).
Averill, J. R., & Nunley, E. P. (1992). *Voyages of the heart: Living an emotionally creative life.* New York: Free Press.
Axelrad, E. (1993). *Repeated recall as a measure of subjective response to literature.* Unpublished master's thesis, University of Toronto, Toronto, Canada.
Barthes, R. (1975). *S / Z* (R. Miller, trans.). London: Cape.
Bartlett, F. C. (1932). *Remembering: A study in experimental and social psychology.* Cambridge, UK: Cambridge University Press.
Bloom, H. (1994). *The Western canon: The books and school of the ages.* New York: Harcourt Brace.
Bloom, H. (1999). *Shakespeare: The invention of the human.* London: Fourth Estate.
Booth, W. C. (1988). *The company we keep: An ethics of fiction.* Berkeley, CA: University of California Press.

Bower, G. H., & Morrow, D. G. (1990). Mental models and narrative comprehension. *Science, 247*, 44–48.
Brewer, W. F., & Lichtenstein, E. H. (1981). Event schemas, story schemas and story grammars. In J. Long & A. Baddeley (Eds.), *Attention and Performance, 9* (pp. 363–379). Hillsdale, NJ: Lawrence Erlbaum Associates.
Brontë, C. (1966). *Jane Eyre*. Harmondsworth: Penguin (original work published 1847).
Bruner, J. (1986). *Actual minds, possible worlds*. Cambridge, MA: Harvard University Press.
Bush, D. (Ed.). (1959). *John Keats: Selected poems and letters*. Boston: Houghton Mifflin Company.
Doody, M. A. (1997). *The true story of the novel*. London: HarperCollins.
Eliot, G. (1963). The natural history of German life. In T. Pinney (Ed.), *Essays of George Eliot*. New York: Columbia University Press (original work published 1856).
Eliot, T. S. (1953). Hamlet. In J. Hayward (Ed.), *T. S. Eliot: Selected prose* (pp. 104–109). Harmondsworth: Penguin (original work published 1919).
Erasmus. (1500). *The adages of Erasmus*. Cambridge UK: Cambridge University Press.
Gerrig, R. J. (1993). *Experiencing narrative worlds: On the psychological activities of reading*. New Haven, CT: Yale University Press.
Gholamain, M. (1998). *The attachment and personality dynamics of reader response*. Unpublished doctoral dissertation, University of Toronto, Toronto, Canada.
Goffman, E. (1961). *Encounters: Two studies in the sociology of interaction*. Indianapolis, IN: Bobbs-Merrill.
Graesser, A., Singer, M., & Trabasso, T. (1994). Constructing inferences during narrative text comprehension. *Psychological Review, 101*, 371–395.
Grazzani-Gavazzi, I., & Oatley, K. (1999). The experience of emotions of interdependence and independence following interpersonal errors in Italy and Anglophone Canada. *Cognition and Emotion, 13*, 49–63.
Hakemulder, F. (1998). *The moral laboratory: Literature and moral awareness*. Unpublished doctoral dissertation, Utrecht University.
Hilgard, E. R. (1979). *Personality and hypnosis: A study of imaginitive involvement*. Chicago: University of Chicago Press.
Hogan, P. C. (2000). *Philosophical approaches to the study of literature*. University Press of Florida.
Holland, N. (1975). *Five readers reading*. New Haven: Yale University Press.
Ingalls, D. H. H., Masson, J. M., & Patwardhan, M. V. (1990). *The Dvanyaloka of Anandavardana with the Locana of Abhinavagupta*. Cambridge, MA: Harvard University Press.
Iser, W. (1978). *The act of reading*. Baltimore, MD: Johns Hopkins University Press.
Jacobson, R. (1988). Linguistic and poetics; and the metaphoric and metonymic poles. In D. Lodge (Ed.), *Modern criticism and theory: A reader* (pp. 31–61). Longman: London.
James, W. (1902). *The varieties of religious experience*. New York: Longmans, Green, & Co.
Johnson-Laird, P. N. (1983). *Mental models: Towards a cognitive science of language, inference, and consciousness*. Cambridge, UK: Cambridge University Press.
Jones, J. (1995). *Shakespeare at work*. Oxford, UK: Clarendon Press.
Keats, J. (1816–20/1951). *Selected poems and letters*. Ed. L. Trilling. New York: Farrar, Straus, & Young.
Larsen, S. F., & Seilman, U. (1988). Personal meanings while reading literature. *Text, 8*, 411–429.
Longinus (1st Century CE/1965). On the sublime. In T. S. Dorsch (Ed.), *Aristotle, Horace, Longinus: Classical literary criticism*. Harmondsworth, UK: Penguin.

Miall, D. S., & Kuiken, D. (1994). Foregrounding, defamiliarization, and affect: Response to literary stories. *Poetics, 22*, 389–407.

Nell, V. (1988). *Lost in a book: The psychology of reading for pleasure*. New Haven, CT: Yale University Press.

Nundy, S. (1996). *The effects of emotion on human inference: towards a computational model*. Unpublished doctoral dissertation, University of Toronto, Toronto, Canada.

Nussbaum, M. C. (1995). *Poetic justice: The literary imagination and public life*. Boston: Beacon.

Oatley, K. (1992). *Best laid schemes: The psychology of emotions*. New York: Cambridge University Press.

Oatley, K. (1994). A taxonomy of the emotions of literary response and a theory of identification in fictional narrative. *Poetics, 23*, 53–74.

Oatley, K. (1996a). Inference and emotions in narrative and science. In D. R. Olson & N. Torrance (Eds.), *Modes of thought*. New York: Cambridge University Press.

Oatley, K. (1996b). Emotions, rationality, and informal reasoning. In J. V. Oakhill & A. Garnham (Eds.), *Mental models in cognitive science*. (pp. 175–196). Hove, UK: Psychology Press.

Oatley, K. (1999a). Why fiction may be twice as true as fact: Fiction as cognitive and emotional simulation. *Review of General Psychology, 3*, 101–117.

Oatley, K. (1999b). Meetings of minds: Dialogue, sympathy, and identification in reading fiction. *Poetics, 26*, 439–454.

Oatley, K., & Gholamain, M. (1997). Emotions and identification: Connections between readers and fiction. In M. Hjort & S. Laver (Eds.), *Emotion and the arts* (pp. 163–281). New York: Oxford University Press.

Oatley, K., & Jenkins, J. M. (1996). *Understanding emotions*. Cambridge, MA: Blackwell.

Piaget, J., & Inhelder, B. (1969). *The psychology of the child*. London: Routledge and Kegan Paul.

Proust, M. (1981). *A la recherche du temps perdu* [Remembrance of things past] (C. K. Scott-Moncreiff, T. Kilmartin, & A. Mayor, trans.). London: Chatto & Windus (original work published 1913–1927).

Richards, I. A. (1929). *Practical criticism: A study of literary judgment*. London: Routledge and Kegan Paul.

Rosenblatt, L. M. (1978). *The reader, the text, the poem: The transactional theory of the literary work*. Carbondale: Southern Illinois University Press.

Scheff, T. J. (1979). *Catharsis in healing, ritual, and drama*. Berkeley: University of California Press.

Shakespeare, W. (1997). Hamlet. In S. Greenblatt, W. Cohen, J. E. Howard, K. E. Maus (Eds), *The Norton Shakespeare Anthology based on the Oxford Edition*. New York: W. W. Norton (Original work published 1623).

Shakespeare, W. (1998). *The first quarto of Hamlet*. Ed. K. O. Irace. New York: Cambridge University Press (original work published 1603).

Sidney, P. (1986). An apology for poetry. In C. Kaplan (Ed.), *Criticism: The major statements*. (2nd ed., pp. 108–147). New York: St Martin's (original work published 1595).

Sikora, S., Miall, D. S., & Kuiken, D. (1998, August). Enactment versus interpretation: A phenomenolgical study of readers' responses to Coleridge's "The Rime of the Ancient Mariner." *Sixth Biennial Conference of the International Society for the Empirical Study of Literature*, Utrecht.

Tan, E. S. H. (1994). Film-induced affect as a witness emotion. *Poetics, 23*, 7–32.

Tan, E. S. H. (1996). *Emotion and the structure of film: Film as an emotion machine*. Mahwah, NJ: Lawrence Erlbaum Associates.

Tan, E. S. H., & Frijda, N. H. (1999). Sentiment in film viewing. In C. Plantinga & G. Smith (Eds.), *Passionate views: Film, cognition, and emotion*. Baltimore, MD: Johns Hopkins University Press.

Tolstoy, L. (1877). *Anna Karenina* (C. Garnett, Trans.). London: Heineman.

Vorderer, P. (1996). Towards a psychological theory of suspense. In P. Vorderer, H. J. Wulff, & M. Friedrichsen (Eds.), *Suspense: Conceptualizations, theoretical analyses, and empirical explorations* (pp. 233–254). Mahwah, NJ: Lawrence Erlbaum Associates.

Wimsatt, W. K., & Beardsley, M. C. (1954). The affective fallacy. In *The verbal icon* (pp. 21–39). Lexington: University of Kentucky Press.

Winnicott, D.W. (1971). *Playing and reality*. Harmondsworth, UK: Penguin.

Wittgenstein, L. (1953). *Philosophical investigations*. Oxford, UK: Blackwell.

Wolfe, T. (1975). The new journalism. In T. Wolfe & E. W. Johnson (Eds.), *The new journalism* (pp. 13–68). London: Picador.

4

"Get Up and Win!"
Participatory Responses to Narrative

James W. Polichak
University of Michigan

Richard J. Gerrig
State University of New York, Stony Brook

In his short story "Sonny Liston was a Friend of Mine," Thom Jones (1997) introduced a very likable main character in the person of Kid Dynamite—a high school student who aspires to be a champion boxer. As the action in the story unfolds, Kid Dynamite is preparing for a rematch with a fighter named Louis Reine, who had defeated him in the previous year's Golden Gloves competition. Kid Dynamite trains obsessively, in the face of long odds. He overhears his stepfather, Cancer Frank, pronounce his doom (p. 85):

> Cancer Frank said, "Not even if you tied one of Reine's hands behind his back does he win.... This other fighter, Reine, has his number. The kid is scared. He isn't going to win. He'll blow it."

The local paper agrees with Cancer Frank's assessment (p. 85):

> ... Louis Reine was now being touted in the Chicago *Sun-Times* as the premier fighter of the tournament. At eighteen, he had won forty-two fights and lost none. He had been fighting stiffer competition from the South Side, and the paper said he was likely to go all the way to the Nationals.

Perhaps these predictions are correct, because early into the rematch Kid Dynamite goes down hard (p. 89):

> It seemed that the floor had flown up and hit him in the mouth. His whole body bounced hard. The canvas was as rough as concrete and his face, elbows, and knees stung with abrasions. He had gone down like he was poleaxed, and the crowd went into a frenzy. Knockdowns, at least spectacular ones, were rare in amateur boxing.

Kid Dynamite is in trouble.

How is the reader feeling at this moment? What is the reader thinking? We would be unsurprised to discover that readers call out mentally, "Get up!" or "You can still win!" These types of responses appear to be very basic to the experience of narratives. How might we characterize these mental contents? Traditionally, cognitive psychologists have had a narrow focus when studying narrative experiences. Theories of text processing have concentrated almost entirely on the inferences readers make to elaborate a narrative world beyond the bare words of a text (Graesser, Singer, & Trabasso, 1994; McKoon & Ratcliff, 1992). Mental responses such as "Get up!" or "You can still win!" are not inferences—they do not fill gaps in the text. Rather, we suggest they are *participatory responses* (*p-responses* for short)—the mental products of readers' participation in a narrative (Allbritton & Gerrig, 1991; Gerrig, 1993). We intend our analysis of p-responses to capture readers' intuitions about their narrative experiences.

In this chapter, we elaborate on the origins of participatory responses. We suggest that p-responses to texts, films, and other forms of media, are produced through the same processes that yield similar effects in conversation and other interactions with people.[1] As such, these p-responses should have similar effects on information processing as are found in conversational settings. We also begin to develop a taxonomy of p-responses and discuss their importance in terms of the effect of narratives on audience response. Finally, we review empirical demonstrations of the role participatory responses play in mediating and moderating narrative impact. Although p-responses are diverse in content and consequence, we suggest they form a coherent category because they have participation at their core.

READERS AS SIDE-PARTICIPANTS

To explore the nature of participatory responses, we begin by considering the theoretical and empirical underpinnings of *participation*. To do so, we embed readers' experience of narratives in the larger context of human interaction, particularly conversational interaction. Most cognitive psychological models of text processing tacitly depict readers as quite *passive*: Readers merely recover meanings that already reside in a text (see Britton & Graesser, 1996). By contrast, an initial focus on conversation will allow us to highlight the *active*, participatory nature of audience response. We suggest that readers can be conceptualized as *side-participants* with respect to their experiences of narratives.

We choose conversation as the basis for our analysis because conversation is the primary form of human communication. Humans developed the ability to speak to each other many thousands of years before they developed systems of writing, which in turn developed thousands of years before film and other visual forms of communication. It seems highly plausible that the core cognitive systems used to understand texts and films are largely the same as those used to interact conversationally. To be sure, text comprehension and film comprehension require specialized subskills such as the ability to translate orthographic and visual codes. We suggest, however, that the core repertory of cognitive skills readers bring to bear on conversational interactions also mediate narrative comprehension.

Consider the goals people bring to conversational interactions. People engage in conversation not just to process information, but to process information for later use. To take a simple example, suppose someone is giving you directions to a party, and your goal is to get to that party with a minimal degree of effort on your part. If you are going to drive to the party with someone who you know has been to the location already, you are likely to pay less careful attention to the directions than if you are going alone. The potential usefulness of the information mediates the degree to which you process the information and the effort you expend to retain it.

We use this example to suggest informally why the modal treatment of listeners as passive recipients of information is incorrect (for a discussion, see Clark, 1997). A more rigorous demonstration of the active nature of listening emerges from empirical analysis of conversational turn-taking. Studies have shown that the process through which a new speaker captures the floor in a multi-party conversation happens very efficiently (Sacks, Schlegoff, & Jefferson, 1974). Conversations often exhibit changes of speakers without gaps in the flow of speech and without the speech streams of the speakers overlapping. A study of telephone conversations found that a third of all transitions between speakers occurred in less than 200 milliseconds (Beattie & Barnard, 1979). This interval is highly salient because 200 milliseconds is about as fast as the quickest voluntary response a human can make. A few hundred milliseconds is clearly insufficient time for an addressee to listen to a speaker's message, process that message, plan a response, and begin to produce it. Instead, addressees must plan their utterances based on their predictions about the content of upcoming speech, when exactly it will end, and what the proper response will be. The data suggest that humans are remarkably accurate at doing this. Such a process would be extremely difficult to characterize as passive. We suggest that readers apply the same active repertory of skills to their narrative experiences.

The conversational circumstances we've described presupposes that one listener is poised to capture the floor. In fact, many instances of conversation include other roles besides a single speaker and addressee. Analyses of conversation and experimental studies have provided much evidence for two other conversational roles, that of *side-participant* and *overhearer* (e.g., Clark, 1992; Clark & Carlson, 1982). As we shall explain, people have ample experience playing these roles as well as those of speaker and addressee, and they play these roles when experiencing a narrative.

Side-participation in a conversation is a common occurrence. Consider a classroom discussion. No one in such a setting would be surprised if a student asked a question of the professor, nor would they be surprised if she responded. At this point, we can assign the role of speaker to the professor and addressee to the student who asked the question. But what of the other students in the class? The professor surely also desires them to understand her response, and may even modify the student's original question to better meet the goal of having the entire class benefit from the exchange. Furthermore, few students would be surprised if they were called on to respond to the professor's response; they have likely expended some energy preparing such responses. Thus, although the professor's response is directed at the student who asked the question, the entire class is being indirectly addressed and included in the exchange. The professor is treating the class as *side-participants* in the conversation—people who are expected to comprehend and potentially participate in the interaction although this is not explicitly indicated in the immediate context.

Not all members of an audience, however, are side-participants. Whereas the class is expected to understand and act in conversation although not directly addressed, we can easily imagine cases in which someone is present but is not expected to understand and act. If a student brings a child to class because of a childcare mishap, few would expect that child to play the role of side-participant. Rather, the child would be present as an *overhearer*—someone to whom utterances are not directed and who may be actively excluded from understanding and participating. People have much experience playing all four conversational roles—speaker, addressee, side-participant, and overhearer—sometimes in the same conversation, and these roles have been shown to produce differences in performance in collaborative settings (Clark, 1992; Schober & Clark, 1989).

We have suggested that the skills people develop in conversation, in terms of generating expectations and preparing to act, are also used in comprehending narratives. However, the nature of narrative places important constraints on the likelihood that an action will be elicited from a person and on the effectiveness of the action. As such, we argue that readers generally are cast in the role of side-participant (see Gerrig, 1993). The narratives they experience engage them in the same way people are engaged when they assume that off-to-the-side conversational role. On some occasions readers will merely be overhearers: They may be excluded from participation by an author who does not wish them to comprehend fully or they may be excluded by their own lack of attention, motivation, or ability. However, when readers assume their more ordinary role as side-participants, they accrue the same privileges and responsibilities as do conversational side-participants.

The analogy of readers to side-participants allows us to suggest that readers bring a well-used repertory of participatory processes to narrative experiences. In that sense, readers are quite prepared not to be mere passive recipients of texts' meanings. Rather, they are active side-participants—fully prepared to play a role in the unfolding of their narrative experiences.

INFERENCE, AFFECT, AND PARTICIPATION

If readers are side-participants, what kinds of mental activities do they perform? We mentioned earlier that the focus of most cognitive psychological research on text processing has been on delimiting the range of inferences that readers make when they experience a text. Consider again the moment at which Kid Dynamite's boxing career is considerably imperiled.

> It seemed that the floor had flown up and hit him in the mouth. His whole body bounced hard. The canvas was as rough as concrete and his face, elbows, and knees stung with abrasions. He had gone down like he was poleaxed, and the crowd went into a frenzy. Knockdowns, at least spectacular ones, were rare in amateur boxing.

These words evoke a scene quite vividly, but the reader is responsible for filling in many of the gaps in the scene. They might, for example, create a mental image of the scene to understand how it would be that Kid Dynamite's "face, elbows, and knees" would all suffer abrasions. A theory of inferencing would attempt to explain when and how that image would come about.

We suggested earlier, however, that readers are also likely to experience participatory responses such as "Get up!" or "You can still win!" In the last section we argued that these types of responses follow from readers' role as side-participants: Within appropriate limits (e.g., they don't yell "Get up!" out loud) readers are having the same sorts of responses they might have if they were genuinely participating as spectators to the match. However, we still need to consider how it is that particular p-responses are engendered. As much as theories of inferences should predict how and when inferences are encoded, we would like to predict how and when p-responses are encoded.

Such an account of participatory responses will require an analysis of the relationship between cognitive and affective responses. Researchers have argued that affective responses to stimuli may be even more basic and efficient than cognitive responses to stimuli (Zajonc, 1980). These affective relationships encode, on a basic level, how individuals feel about a stimulus, and through that, their assessment of its likely effects on them. These affective relationships must be combined for a person to react appropriately to a situation. Through the assembly of these affective relationships, in conjunction with inferencing, we can start to see how participatory responses might arise during moment-by-moment narrative comprehension.

Social psychologists have found a great deal of evidence that affective information is associated with concepts (e.g., Bargh, Chaiken, Raymond, & Hymes, 1996; Murphy & Zajonc, 1993; Vakoch & Wurm, 1997; Wurm & Vakoch, 1996). Furthermore, this affective information is often available sooner than nonaffective information, a finding described as *affective primacy* (Zajonc, 1980). For example, Murphy and Zajonc presented participants with novel Chinese ideographs and asked them to make a series of judgments about them. When the Chinese ideographs were preceded by an extremely brief (4 msec) presentation of an affectively charged prime, the affective ratings of the ideographs were affected by the valence of the prime—people preferred ideographs preceded by smiling faces over those preceded by scowling faces. Nonaffective primes had no effects at brief durations—using large or small shapes as primes had no effects on participants' judgments of the sizes of the referents of the ideographs. In no case could participants report having seen any faces, nor could they make accurate forced-choice discriminations between presented and nonpresented faces. Murphy and Zajonc's results provide strong evidence that affective information is made available very early in the processing of stimuli, is available without conscious awareness, and can affect the processing of subsequent stimuli.

Similar effects of affective associations have been found for verbal materials through studies of priming and word recognition. Bargh et al. (1996) found that otherwise unrelated words primed each other if they were of the same affective valence. For example, *flower* and *knowledge* were found to prime each other, in the absence of any documented association. More impressive is that this priming was found using a naming task, which can be performed with little meaningful processing of a stimulus. Wurm and Vakoch (1996; Vakoch & Wurm, 1997) found that words referring to strong negative emotions (e.g., *rage*) have shorter response latencies in a lexical decision task than words referring to other emotions, whereas for a more general pool of nouns, words referring to very beneficial or fleeting beneficial objects (e.g., *food, blanket*) had shorter lexical decision times than other words. Affective associations have an impact on basic word recognition and priming processes.

These types of research strongly suggest that affective responses are readily available to guide readers' participatory responses to narratives. By accessing and combining basic affective components, people are able to assess the potential of a situation to affect them and able to prepare to respond appropriately. Through further elaboration—making predictions about the likelihood and desirability of possible outcomes, and so on—people select potential responses. When the concepts to be combined are presented in narrative form, such preparations and responses provide the content of participatory responses.

Let us now begin to examine the kinds of participatory responses that might arise as a consequence of involvement in a narrative, focusing on Kid Dynamite's fight. The main preconditions for comprehending and experiencing a narrative are the accessing of affective and conceptual representations of the individual elements in the narrative, whether written words in texts or spoken words and visual objects in films. To understand Kid Dynamite's story, the reader must access affective and conceptual representations of the words in the text and combine them to achieve a mental representation of the larger situation, one that contains both cognitive components detailing the content of the situation and affective components detailing the reader's emotional relationship to this content and the situation as a whole. Readers not only mentally represent the details of the ultimate boxing match between Kid Dynamite and Louis Reine, but also how they feel about the match.

We suspect that most readers have, by this point in the story, developed at least a moderate liking for Kid Dynamite: He appears to be a nice young man who is respectful of his grandmother and kind to his girlfriend; he is also portrayed strongly as an underdog who needs the readers' support. When a mental representation of Kid Dynamite is incorporated into the larger representation of the boxing match, that representation makes note of the readers' positive affect. As a consequence, when Kid Dynamite goes down hard, we would expect readers to emit a p-response such as "Oh no!" This basic expression of an affective stance toward narrative objects or outcomes is a type of p-response we call an *as if* response. We label such responses *as if* responses because these responses resemble the kinds of basic emotional and verbal responses a person would experience if they were observing the scene as a participant, with little influence of more complex and strategic thought processes. Consider the difference between immediately thinking "Who is it?" in response to a doorbell and generating a mental list of potential candidates and evaluating how likely each is to be at the door. These kinds of immediate thoughts may be considered relatively reflexive responses elicited by a situation. Thus, although all participatory responses can in an important sense be characterized as 'as if' responses, *as if* participatory responses, in our taxonomy, are limited to more immediate and basic thoughts that are generated by a situation. We take it to be the case, for example, that readers will quite often encode—and mentally express—preferences for outcomes in this unreflective *as if* fashion.

Readers, however, often participate in more elaborate ways. Two of the most common strategies that readers develop when they have gone beyond *as if* responses to the situation are *problem-solving participatory responses* and *replotting participatory responses*. Both of these responses are highly dependent on people's ability to mentally simulate alternatives to a situation: The generation of both predictive and retrospective counterfactual representations of situations is a basic human thought process that has demonstrable effects in the formation of people's representations of real-world and narrative situations (Kahneman & Miller, 1986; Roese & Olson, 1995). *Problem-solving p-responses* occur when readers process a narrative with a goal in mind and focus their attention on ways that goal might be achieved. As such, the content of these p-responses, and their impact on a person's narrative experience, will differ with the reader's individual goals. Consider the reader who would like Kid Dynamite to win the fight. This reader will likely pay careful attention to elements of the story that might indicate whether the Kid can do so. At a minimum, for the Kid to win he must get up by the count of eight. Thom Jones, of course, drags this scene out in the story for far longer than that, allowing much time for the reader to wonder what will happen and make predictions. As the Kid is lying on the floor and the count is advancing, he notices that a man in the audience is about to lose a button, and expresses a desire to warn him about it. Readers who like Kid Dynamite and want him to win are likely trying to think of some way for the Kid to regain his focus, to get up, and still overcome his opponent. Conversely, readers who dislike the Kid might find satisfaction in his distraction, and perhaps support for their negative assessment of him. Their problem solving may take the form of mentally searching for evidence that the Kid will remain down and will lose. *Problem-solving p-responses* are a reader's attempts to strategically gather evidence from a narrative that will allow them to more confidently predict outcomes, particularly those they favor.

Replotting p-responses are elicited by similar situations as are problem-solving responses, but are retrospective. As the count advances and Kid Dynamite is lying distracted and hurt on the floor, it grows less and less likely that he will rise in time, much less win. Readers who want the Kid to win are likely experiencing growing discomfort at this situation. Their attempts at problem solving are probably failing to identify any way for the Kid to win. These readers may be prompted to mentally undo the Kid's situation through replotting earlier events. In particular, they will likely focus on the start of the fight, when the Kid sees his Grandmother in the audience, who hasn't otherwise left her shop in years except to go to church, and is distracted by her presence. As a result, Kid Dynamite fails to block Reine's first punches, and is soon down for the count. We can easily imagine the reader thinking "If only the Kid didn't see his grandmother," or "If only he saw Reine's punch in time to block it," to find some way, even retrospectively, to reduce their discomfort with the unlikeliness of a Kid Dynamite victory.

The p-responses discussed so far are limited to the experience of the narrative itself. Participation in a narrative can have effects beyond this, having an impact on people's beliefs about the world and the way they themselves ought to behave. We label these types of p-responses *evaluatory responses* because these responses reflect readers' evaluation of a narrative's specific or general "messages." For example, after reading Kid Dynamite's story, with its vivid depictions of the Kid's injuries, the reader might come away less sure that boxing is a reasonable form of entertainment and an appropriate activity for high school students. These thoughts may influence the reader's later decisions to view the sport or participate in it.

It is important to note that inferential processes often provide the critical link from one type of p-response to another. Consider three readers who have all mentally represented Kid Dynamite lying on the floor, one who likes the Kid, one who (despite the author's best efforts) dislikes him, and one who just doesn't care about the Kid. These readers would likely emit different *as if* responses: "Get up!" "Stay down!" "Oh well." As such, the reader who likes the Kid will be inclined to formulate predictive inferences about possible outcomes, along the lines of "If the Kid doesn't get up, he'll lose the fight," and "If the Kid can just get up, he can still win." These inferences will create a context in which problem solving p-responses such as "Get up!" will arise. The reader who dislikes the Kid will be inclined to make similar predictions for outcomes, but those inferences will lead to different problem solving p-responses, such as "Just stay down!" The reader who doesn't care about the Kid may forgo all this mental activity. We see here the critical interrelationships among inferences and p-responses: *as if* p-responses ("I want Kid Dynamite to win") lead to inferences ("If the Kid doesn't get up, he'll lose") which lead to problem solving p-responses ("Ignore the audience!").

We have reviewed a number of categories of p-responses: We believe these types of reader participation to be critical to a person's experience of a narrative. We have also tried to give a sketch of how and when some of these p-responses might arise and why some p-responses may require different types of focused effort on readers' parts. Some responses, like the development of an affective association to a character, are likely to occur with relatively minimal involvement in a narrative, while problem solving, replotting, and evaluation are likely to occur only with a reasonable degree of commitment to a narrative. We now turn to a detailed examination of the psychological evidence for these participatory responses and of the effects they have on readers' experiences of narratives.

PARTICIPATORY RESPONSES AND NARRATIVE IMPACT

What might the consequences be of reading Kid Dynamite's saga? That is, what lasting impact might Jones's brief story have on its reader? In this section, we will define three experiential categories in which a narrative might have an impact on a reader, and describe how p-responses mediate and moderate those categories of impact. We consider, in turn, the manner in which p-responses affect readers' emotional experiences, their memory structures, and their real-world beliefs.

Readers' Emotional Experiences

Consider this narrative situation (Walton, 1978, p. 5):

> Charles is watching a horror movie about a terrible green slime. He cringes in his seat as the slime oozes slowly but relentlessly over the earth destroying everything in its path. Soon a greasy head emerges from the undulating mass, and two beady eyes roll around, finally fixing on the camera. The slime, picking up speed, oozes on a new course straight toward the viewers. Charles emits a shriek and clutches desperately at his chair.

Here, we are concerned with the way in which p-responses affect the emotional impact of narratives. Much of Charles's emotional response to the slime precedes any p-responses; it is physiological, resulting from the accessing of affective and conceptual information associated with the objects on the screen and their combination into a representation of the situation. We can ask, however, in what way p-responses transform Charles's ultimate emotional experience (Lazarus, 1995).

To address this issue, we offer two variations on the scenario with the terrible green slime:

1. Moments before the slime approaches, a young girl is shown playing with her doll in the yard in front of her ramshackle home. In its path toward the viewer, the slime will also engulf this child.
2. A loathsome murderer is escaping on foot from the scene of his most recent crime. In its path toward the viewer, the slime will also engulf this criminal.

It seems likely that p-responses will alter the way in which readers experience emotions for each scenario. For scenario 1, we might imagine that viewers would p-respond "Watch out!" Their inability to protect the little girl from the slime would heighten the negative emotionality of the scene. For scenario 2, we might imagine that viewers would p-respond (to the slime), "Get him!" In this case, the arousal that might originate as fear to the approaching slime would be transformed into a more positively tinged emotional experience by virtue of the slime's compliance with the viewers' mental request. Note that, in both cases, we are assuming that the viewers' responses are *as if* p-responses (and these *as if* p-responses are dependent on prior mental simulation of alternate outcomes and differences in preferences for these outcomes). The emotional impact of the scenes are determined, in part, by the viewers responding as if their mental voices could really be heard.

Consider an empirical demonstration of the role *as if* responses play in readers' emotional experiences (Gerrig & Prentice, 1996). In another of Thom Jones's (1992) stories, "The Pugilist at Rest," Jones describes the actions of a bully (Hey Baby) against a less gung-ho marine (Jorgeson), who is the narrator's close friend (p. 125):

> And then, about two weeks before boot camp was over, when we were running out to the parade field for drill with our rifles at port arms, all assholes and elbows, I saw Hey Baby give Jorgeson a nasty shove with his M-14.... Jorgeson nearly fell down as the other recruits scrambled out to the parade field, and Hey Baby gave a short malicious laugh.

Participants in an experiment read a longer passage adapted from Jones's story that fleshed out the bullying relationship between Hey Baby and Jorgeson and ended with this act of aggression. The passage was intended to prompt readers to encode a preference that the narrator punish Hey Baby on Jorgeson's behalf.

After reading this passage, participants were asked one of two questions. One question was *neutral* with respect to the putative p-response, "Avenge Jorgeson": From what you've read so far, do you think Jorgeson will make an effective marine? A second question assessed readers' *commitment* with respect to the p-response: Would you like to see the narrator help Jorgeson get back at Hey Baby? The two groups of participants answered their questions on a scale ranging from 1 (definitely no) to 9 (definitely yes). Participants were largely neutral with respect to Jorgeson's fitness (mean = 5.06); they were somewhat more sure that they wanted revenge (mean = 6.47).

After making their ratings, participants read a second passage adapted from Jones's original. In this latter passage, the narrator goes well beyond evening the score. Here are excerpts from that passage:

> I set my body so that I could put everything into it, and with one deft stroke I hit him in the head with the butt of my M-14.... Hey Baby dropped into the ice plants along the side of the company street.... Blood was leaking from his right ear. Did I see skull fragments and brain tissue? It seemed that I did.

The magnitude of the narrator's revenge was, presumably, more than that which readers hoped for in their p-response request to "Avenge Jorgeson." As a consequence, readers might be feeling guilty—*as if* they had played some role in bringing about this harsh outcome. If this prediction is correct, we would expect that readers who committed themselves to revenge (i.e., those who answered the commitment question) would feel more guilty than those who had not (i.e., those who had answered the neutral question). The data bore out this prediction. When asked "How much do you hope that Hey Baby will recover?", participants who had committed themselves to revenge gave mean ratings of 6.24 (1 = not at all; 9 = very much) versus mean ratings of 4.97 for those who had not. The important conclusion from this demonstration is that *as if* p-responses have an impact on how readers are feeling at the end of their narrative experiences.

Emotional experiences are also affected by other types of p-responses. Consider the types of responses we characterized earlier as problem-solving p-responses. Recall that we suggested that, at the moment Kid Dynamite is lying on the floor of the boxing ring, readers would likely struggle to find a way to get Kid Dynamite off the ground and spur him on to victory. By generating a range of possibilities—"Maybe he could..."—and then rejecting some or all of those possibilities, readers thereby contribute greatly to their own sense of how distant a desired outcome might be. As a consequence, readers' p-responses can rapidly increase their own feelings of distress and helplessness. However, let's focus on a somewhat less intense emotion, suspense.

Readers' experiences of suspense suggest an important role for participatory responses. It is quite easy to define the type of text structure that will initiate feelings of suspense (Brewer & Lichtenstein, 1982, p. 481):

> In a suspense discourse organization the initiating event occurs early in the discourse. The initiating event causes the reader to be-

come concerned about the consequences for the relevant character and this produces suspense. Typically, additional discourse material is placed between the initiating event and the outcome event, to encourage the build up of suspense. The suspense is resolved when the outcome is presented in the discourse.

Note that this definition of a *discourse organization* for suspense already tacitly includes mention of p-responses in the sense that readers must "become concerned about the consequences for the relevant character." The content of this concern, as we have suggested, are p-responses such as "I hope Kid Dynamite wins." We might predict, therefore, from this definition that the more mental concern a reader expresses with respect to an outcome, the more suspense the reader will feel (cf. Brewer, 1996; Zillmann, 1996).

Problem-solving p-responses, however, take readers beyond mere concern to an active process of trying to mentally undo obstacles to the outcome. We can see this most clearly when writers manipulate readers' evaluations of the solutions available to characters who have become imperiled. Consider this passage from Ian Fleming's novel, *Casino Royale*, which occurs after James Bond has been captured by his enemy, Le Chiffre:

> He [Bond] felt thoroughly dispirited and weak in resolve as well as in his body. He had had to take too much in the past twenty-four hours and now this last stroke by the enemy seemed almost too final. This time there could be no miracles. No one knew where he was and no would miss him until well on into the morning. The wreck of his car would be found before very long, but it would take hours to trace ownership to him. (1954, p. 105)

Fleming has put the reader inside Bond's head. The narration models a process in which paths to escape are mentioned, but then swiftly eliminated. To the extent that the readers' attempts at problem solving—alongside Bond—are thwarted, they should experience a proportional increase in feelings of suspense.

The claim here is that readers' efforts at producing problem-solving p-responses will contribute to their ultimate feelings of suspense. To test this view, Gerrig and Bernardo (1994) asked readers to read story excerpts about James Bond and report on their feelings of suspense. In one experiment, Le Chiffre had captured Bond. As Bond attempted to escape, some readers encountered a version of the story that mentioned Bond's pen:

> As he crashed to the ground, Bond rolled agilely and, with a motion that he hoped went unnoticed, moved his fountain pen deeper into his breast pocket.

This sentence should prompt an inference that Bond planned to use the pen to escape with consequent p-responses. A second group of readers encountered a control sentence:

> As he crashed to the ground, Bond rolled agilely and, with a motion in which he took great pride, he righted himself with minimal damage.

Later in the passage, some of the people for whom the pen had been mentioned read that Le Chiffre took it away ("he crossed the room and snatched the pen away"). Readers were subsequently asked "How suspenseful do you find this passage to be?" (1 = not very suspenseful; 7 = extremely suspenseful). Suspense ratings were reliably higher when Bond's pen had been removed (mean = 4.38) than when the pen had not been mentioned (mean = 3.78).

This result may not be particularly dramatic, but it makes an important contrast to accounts of suspense that focus largely on discourse structures. The removal of Bond's pen does not have any effect on the elements of the suspense discourse structure. The initiating event (Bond's capture) and the desired outcome (his escape) remain the same. What's changed is the types of thoughts—p-responses—readers will endure: "Now how will Bond get away?" Readers who have been encouraged to take on the role of problem-solver will already experience less efficacy and more suspense. An account of suspense that only makes reference to discourse structures can say little more than suspense will be present or absent. By attending to p-responses, it is possible to make predictions about the relative magnitude of suspense.

A second experiment adds weight to this argument. Gerrig and Bernardo (1994) created a textual analog to the problem-solving phenomenon of *functional fixedness*. In a classic experiment, Duncker (1945) demonstrated that people were less likely to find a solution to a problem when the solution required them to overcome their fixation on the ordinary function of an object. In this second experiment, Le Chiffre once again relieved Bond of an object, his pocket comb. However, some readers first encountered the comb being put to its ordinary use:

> [Bond] noticed that his hair was just the least bit mussed, so he extracted his comb from his pocket and smoothed his wandering locks back into place.

Other readers saw only a control passage:

> [Bond] noticed that he had a white thread on his lapel, and removed it.

Finally, Bond's comb was removed:

> Le Chiffre pulled out Bond's pocket comb and ran his finger down its teeth.
> He smiled broadly, and flipped the comb well out of Bond's reach.

If functional fixedness applies here, readers should only have produced problem-solving p-responses when they had not read the passage in which the comb served its ordinary function: If the comb is just a comb, it has no relevance to the readers' task at hand—to "help" Bond escape. In fact, readers' reports of suspense confirmed a role for textual functional fixedness. Readers' self-reports of suspense were reliably higher when they had not encountered the comb in its usual role (mean = 3.96) than when they had (mean = 3.41). In this experiment, Bond is in the same objective state at the end of each version of the story: He has no comb. We attribute readers' different experiences of suspense to the p-responses provoked by one version but not the other.

In this section, we have suggested generally how p-responses may contribute to the emotional impact that narratives have on readers. Our empirical examples reinforce the claim that readers' p-responses play an important role in specifying the identity and intensity of those feelings. In the next section, we turn to another manner in which the impact of p-responses on narrative experiences may be reckoned: What do readers remember from the narratives they encounter?

Memory for Narratives

Part of the impact of Kid Dynamite's tale is that it is memorable. The story unfolds in such a fashion that it engages lingering involvement. Within cognitive psychology, the goal of many theories of narrative processing has been to explain and predict exactly that sort of impact: What aspects of stories become rigorously encoded in long-term memory (cf. Britton & Graesser, 1996)? These theories, however, have excluded consideration of the types of narrative experiences that we have characterized as participatory responses. We suggest here that p-responses, in fact, can have important effects on readers' memory representations.

Cognitive psychological theories of text representation have most often focused on the propositions conveyed by a text, the inferences licensed by those propositions, and the more general mental model suggested by those propositions and inferences (e.g., Kintsch, 1998). Consider this scene from "Sonny Liston Was a Friend of Mine," when Kid Dynamite wakes his mother up after winning the boxing match that presages his rematch with Reine (p. 84):

> "I won. I got him good," [Kid Dynamite] said.
> Her face was covered in a luminescent green mask. "Did you knock him out?" she said wearily. There was a bath towel on her pillow.

Let's focus on "Her face was covered in a luminescent green mask." This sentence relates a proposition—COVERED (face, luminescent green mask)—as well as an inference—the mask must be something that's intended to preserve youthful skin tone. If readers generate somewhat more of a mental model, they'll also have an easier time interpreting, "There was a bath towel on her pillow." Any adequate cognitive psychological model of text processing would need to account for each of these elements of a representation of this textual moment. Suppose, however, that in response to "Did you knock him out?" readers produce the p-response, "Give the kid a break!" This type of mental content has not appeared in theories of text representation. We suggest that it should.

Consider once more the readers' (modal) preference that Kid Dynamite win his fight. As we suggested at this chapter's outset, after inspiring this preference, the story provides ample reason to believe that Kid Dynamite will *not* win—neither his stepfather nor the local paper have much hope. What happens when readers encounter the passages that lay out the evidence that violates their preference? Research suggests that people are likely to devote considerable effort to argue against statements that are inconsistent with their prior attitudes (e.g., Edwards & Smith, 1996). As a function of this counterarguing, people often become more entrenched in their beliefs after encountering disconfirming evidence (e.g., Lord, Ross, & Lepper, 1979). In that light, it seems likely that readers would produce a large number of p-responses when they encounter narrative information that is inconsistent with their preferences.

For example, when Kid Dynamite's stepfather, Cancer Frank declares, "Not even if you tied one of Reine's hands behind his back does [Kid Dynamite] win." We might expect readers to begin to p-respond, "Of course, the *stepfather* doesn't like the kid." This type of mental activity is likely to leave readers more secure in their preferences—if the stepfather is a villain then they probably have even more empathy for Kid Dynamite—but it is also likely to have an impact on their memory representations. Suppose we were to ask readers to recall what exactly transpired when Cancer Frank made his prediction about Kid Dynamite's prospects. We suggest that the swirl of mental activity surrounding readers' evaluations of Cancer Frank's statements would lead to a memory representation that departed from a mere representation of the gist of the narrative. Our general claim is that p-responses will direct readers' attentional resources to focus on parts of texts that come to matter most to them.

These considerations lead to a specific prediction: For some narrative experiences, participatory responses may interfere with readers' ability to recall what actually happened in a narrative. Allbritton and Gerrig (1991) suggested that one such set of narrative experiences arises when a story prompts readers to prefer nonnormative outcomes, like preferring that a bomb explode rather than be disarmed. This suggestion arose from an application of Kahneman and Miller's (1986) *norm theory*. Kahneman and Miller reviewed a body of evidence that exceptional events are more likely than unexceptional events to evoke thoughts about counterfactual alternatives. For example, to identify the cause of an automobile accident, readers were likely to focus on the driver's departures from his or her normal routine rather than on standard features of the journey (Kahneman & Tversky, 1982).

With respect to narratives, Allbritton and Gerrig suggested that there is a normal preference for positive outcomes. In the abstract, for example, readers would prefer that a main character such as Kid Dynamite win his boxing match. However, stories can also establish preferences for negative outcomes: Jones's story could be changed so that Kid Dynamite has cheated, leading most readers to prefer that he lose the fight. Norm theory suggests that *negative preferences* (i.e., exceptional preferences for negative outcomes) should lead to more replotting p-responses—in the form of counterfactual alternatives—than do *positive preferences*. The greater range of replotting p-responses, in turn, should interfere with readers' ability to remember the actual outcome of a narrative.

To test this prediction, Allbritton and Gerrig (1991) wrote brief stories that manipulated readers' preferences about story outcomes. Each story began with a statement of the outcome, which for some readers was positive and for some readers negative. For example, the story, "The Pharaoh's Tomb," told of a man in search of the Pharaoh Atman's lost tomb. The positive outcome version began with "When he entered the tomb, Jack was astounded by the treasures it held," while the negative version began with, "When Jack entered the tomb, he found it completely empty." The story continued in versions that created preferences with respect to this outcome. Some readers were led to develop a preference in favor of the positive outcome:

> He [Jack] planned to bring rare artifacts back to the Smithsonian Institute. He only hoped that a band of looters would not beat him to the tomb.

Others were led to a preference for the negative outcome:

> It would be Jack's most profitable grave robbing yet if he found it. He only hoped he could beat the museum's archeologists to the loot.

Pilot testing ensured that these preference sentences had their intended effects. The rest of the story was the same for all readers, and ended with the events that led up to the outcome:

> Jack's men had been digging for hours. Finally, they found the entrance to the tomb. As Jack approached the entrance, he wondered whether they had found it in time.

Participants in the experiments read stories that contained all four combinations of positive and negative outcomes and positive and negative preferences: Preferring that the tomb be empty when it was empty, preferring that the tomb be empty when it was full, preferring that the tomb be full when it was full, and preferring that the tomb be full when it was empty.

In the first experiment, participants read a series of 32 stories. After reading the series of stories, participants were asked to verify the outcomes of each story. They were, for example, asked to say "true" or "false" to the statement "The tomb was empty." The participants' response times revealed a reliable effect for positive versus negative preferences. When the stories had created negative preferences with respect to either type of outcome, participants took 319 msec longer to verify the outcome. In a second experiment, Allbritton and Gerrig asked participants to verify the outcome of each story as soon as they had finished reading it. This pattern of testing provides a more daunting test of the hypothesis because it both minimized memory load and potentially allowed participants to ignore all story information except the story-initial statement of the outcome. Even so, negative preferences reliably slowed verification, by 237 msec. This result suggested that, even under adverse conditions, participatory responses can become sufficiently encoded as part of the memory representation of a story to interfere with readers' ability to confirm the "real" content of the story.

A final experiment confirmed that the negative preferences exerted their effect specifically on readers' ability to remember the outcomes of the stories. Allbritton and Gerrig asked readers to confirm or disconfirm information from the stories unrelated to the outcomes, such as "The tomb was that of Pharaoh Atman." The participants were no more likely to make errors on this type of information: The percent correct was 84.4% for outcome information in the first experiment and 83.6% for nonoutcome information in this final experiment. However, there was a 153 msec *advantage* for stories that created negative preferences. These results suggest that the p-responses generated by readers' preferences for nonnormative outcomes interfered specifically with their ability to remember those outcomes.

These experiments were intended as strong demonstrations of why adequate predictions about memory representations for texts require theorists to attend to participatory responses. The data suggest that theories will fail to make correct predictions about, for example, representations of narrative outcomes if they do not make reference to reliable noninferential responses. If some part of a narrative's impact depends on the traces it leaves behind in memory, we once again see why participatory responses are critical to gauging that impact. A final point about memory representations is that the structures a narrative establishes in memory become an important part of the database against which readers make subsequent judgments. We turn now to the impact narratives, particularly fictional narratives, can have on readers' real-world attitudes and beliefs.

Real-World Judgments

We haven't yet revealed whether Kid Dynamite ultimately wins his fight. Suppose he does. We could then take his story as evidence in favor of the hypothesis that determination and hard work can overcome all obstacles. Suppose he loses his fight. We could then take his story as evidence in favor of the hypothesis that people should not be allowed to persevere when it will cause them physical and psychological damage. Either way, the story is likely to add to the storehouse of experiences that readers use to make choices about their own courses through life. Can they overcome obstacles? Should they persevere? Should they cut their losses? A final way to assess the impact of a narrative is by the breadth of the effects it has on readers' subsequent judgments.

We can see from the alternative lessons that Kid Dynamite's story might generate how participatory responses could play a role with respect to this type of narrative impact. We suggested earlier that the modal reader would prefer greatly that Kid Dynamite win and would, therefore, produce p-responses that encourage him in various ways. If Kid Dynamite wins, those p-responses are rewarded; if Kid Dynamite loses, those p-responses are punished. In each case, the reader's participation in the unfolding story works to amplify the story's message. If, for example, the reader is left thinking "I really wanted this guy to win, and he didn't," that may prompt the story's conclusion, "People should not be allowed to persevere," to be represented in memory in a particularly vivid form. This conclusion drawn from the narrative may then be generalized to real-life situations, changing long-term belief structures.

To demonstrate the impact of evaluatory p-responses on real-world judgments, Prentice, Gerrig, and Bailis (1997) wrote a story in which the characters drew conclusions about topics that were false with respect to the real world. One passage, for example, addressed the probability of catching cold after being doused in a downpour:

> Brad interrupted, "In fact, in some ways, getting totally soaked will help you avoid getting a cold. When you get soaked, your body has to pump itself up to help keep you warm. When you increase your body's internal temperature, that also makes it harder for viruses to live within you. So, by getting soaked you can help kill the virus that might cause a cold—how does that sound? Getting soaked actually helps prevent colds."

The narrative element that made external perspectives relevant to the experience of the overall story was the college Brad and the other characters attended. For some readers, Brad and his peers were Yale students; for others, the characters attended Princeton. In the experiments, half of the readers were themselves Yale students and half were Princeton students. Researchers in social psychology have demonstrated that readers tend to evaluate more critically information relevant to issues that are of personal importance (for reviews, see Cacioppo, Petty, Kao, & Rodriguez, 1986; Johnson & Eagly, 1989). Prentice et al. (1997) hypothesized that readers of stories set at their home school (e.g., a Yalie reading about Yale students) would appraise information more carefully. Accordingly, Prentice et al. predicted that belief change in the direction of the counterfactual arguments would be more likely for the away school.

The data supported this prediction. Readers indicated their agreement with statements such as "Getting soaked in a rainstorm decreases your chances of catching a cold" on a 9-point scale (1 = strongly disagree; 9 = strongly agree). The readers' ratings assumed different patterns of interaction as a function of their home school and the story setting. However, as a simple summary, after reading the stories set at an away school, readers' agreement with the assertions in the story went up by an average of .52 rating points (with respect to the ratings of a control group who read an unrelated story). Home school readers' agreement with story assertions fell by .12 rating points. What is important here is that both Yale and Princeton students read exactly the same texts, word for word. The differences Prentice et al. (1997) found in changes in attitudes cannot, therefore, be attributed to the texts. They can only be attributed to the cognitive activities the students carried out with respect to the texts. Presumably evaluatory p-responses to the home school version (e.g., "A Yalie wouldn't believe that") focused scrutiny on the counterfactual arguments. In that way, readers' perspectives had a major impact on the effect the text had on the reader.

Experiments by Wheeler, Green, and Brock (1999), however, suggest that the effects of external perspectives might be rather fragile. Wheeler et al. had Ohio State University students read modified versions of the Prentice et al. (1997) story set at OSU and Princeton. The OSU students showed persuasion by narrative arguments, but were no more persuaded by those contained in stories set at Princeton than those set at OSU. Although this result is discrepant with the original Prentice et al. result, it does not necessarily reflect negatively on Prentice et al.'s original suggestion that the effect of home versus away schools is mediated through participatory responses. We have suggested that not all readers will experience the same participatory responses. Thus, it is not particularly damaging to our account to suggest that there are some p-responses Yale and Princeton students experience that OSU students do not. Wheeler et al. ruled out a role for one individual difference variable, Need for Cognition (Cacioppo & Petty, 1982) in explaining their failure to replicate Prentice et al.'s home versus away school effect. We suspect, however, that a different type of individual difference measure, *working memory span*, might be more relevant to the contrast between the two studies. Working memory span is a measure of the processing resources readers bring to text comprehension (Daneman & Merikle, 1996).[2] It is quite possible that readers who are relatively overburdened by the processes required to understand a complex text might not have sufficient resources to engage in strategic p-responses of the problem solving, replotting, or evaluatory types. We believe this is a hypothesis worth pursuing. In the next section, we turn to another direction research on participatory responses might take.

The Specific Content of Participatory Responses

We have argued that readers' participation in narratives arises out of the same basic mental operations and emotional responses evolved for comprehending and responding to conversation. People generally respond to narrative as side-participants, aware that they are expected to understand and potentially act on the situation represented. Narratives differ in the degree to which they elicit these participatory responses. In turn, as we have just reviewed, these participatory responses have effects on the evaluation and long-term impact of a narrative.

However, all these empirical demonstrations have been indirect. Although we have made guesses at the forms specific p-responses might take (e.g., "Get up!"), we have not provided any evidence about that specific content. To do so, we could turn to the types of methodologies researchers have developed to study the time course with which inferences are encoded. For example, McKoon and her colleagues (e.g., McKoon, Gerrig, & Greene, 1996; McKoon & Ratcliff, 1992) often use a recognition probe technique to track the availability of discourse objects within a mental representation of a text. This technique is quite straightforward: Experimental participants are most often asked simply to indicate whether a particular word has appeared in a text. This measure has allowed, for example, McKoon et al. (1996) to demonstrate quite abrupt changes in the accessibility of particular characters as a function of episode boundaries within brief stories.

Many of our claims about p-responses could similarly be couched as claims about changes in the availability of certain categories of discourse information. Recall the stories in the set of experiments by Allbritton and Gerrig (1991). Readers were informed about outcomes at each story's outset. We could test directly for the content of a p-response by determining how hard it would be for readers to *reject* words consistent with their preference but not the already revealed outcomes. For example, if readers found it difficult to reject the word "empty" when they read that Jack the grave robber is exploring the tomb of the Pharaoh Atman—which reflects their preference—rather than "full" which reflects the actual outcome, we could take that as more direct evidence in favor of the specific content of a participatory response.

CONCLUSIONS

In this chapter, we have explored the origins of participatory responses to narratives. These responses, which are crucial to the experience and enjoyment of a narrative, arise from the same basic cognitive processes that people use to engage in active conversational interactions. In particular, we have suggested that readers generally adopt the role of side-participants with respect to their experiences of narratives. It is this side-participant role that ensures the high-level coherence of the category of participatory responses. We believe that each type of participatory response requires some type of reader participation.

As when they engage in conversations, people process a narrative with respect to various goals. The desire to fulfill these goals leads to the various forms of participatory responses we have described, such as mentally simulating alternative outcomes and evaluating the larger meaning of a narrative. The different kinds of p-responses, and the differences in their specific content, have been shown to have important effects on the experiences of readers in a number of ways. Participatory responses help define the emotional experiences of readers (e.g., heightening feelings of suspense and guilt). They can also shape readers' long-term mental representations of a narrative (e.g., interfering with the ability to recall story outcomes). And, moving beyond the scope of the individual narrative, they can also influence the degree to which readers change their beliefs as a consequence of experiencing that narrative.

If we have done our job well, we have made our own readers participate in Kid Dynamite's story, and aroused a desire to know his ultimate fate in his match with Reine. We are happy to reveal that although the victory was not glamorous, Kid Dynamite ultimately succeeded (p. 89):

> "Seven," cried the referee. Kid Dynamite was on one knee.... "Eight!" He was standing....
>
> In the next round Kid Dynamite withstood an onslaught—everything Reine had. But as Reine started to tire and lost more and more of his composure Kid Dynamite set out to box him carefully and methodically. As Reine started winging punches, Kid Dynamite found a home for his right uppercut. By the end of the round, Reine's fair skin was marked with red welts.
>
> The referee announced a split decision in Kid Dynamite's favor ... the ring doctor jumped into Kid Dynamite's corner and pressed a

gauze bandage under his eye ... now the doctor shook his head, looked at him gravely and said, "You won the fight but your tournament is over. That's a twelve-stitch cut."

ACKNOWLEDGMENTS

This material is based upon work supported by the National Science Foundation under Grant No. IRI-9711974. Please address correspondence to Richard J. Gerrig, Department of Psychology, State University of New York, Stony Brook, Stony Brook, New York, 11794-2500 (e-mail: rgerrig@notes.cc. sunysb.edu).

ENDNOTES

[1]For convenience, we will use reader and text throughout this chapter rather than viewer, films, and so on. However, our account of participatory responses is intended to span different media.

[2]Wheeler et al. (1999) gave a subset of their participants a portion of the verbal SAT and found a tendency for those who scored more highly to show greater levels of persuasion. However, working memory span provides a more direct measure of the resources readers bring to moment-by-moment comprehension of the text. Our hypothesis, which clearly requires supportive evidence, is that the working memory span measure of moment-by-moment resources will prove more relevant to readers' capacity to formulate p-responses alongside ordinary comprehension.

REFERENCES

Allbritton, D. W., & Gerrig, R. J. (1991). Participatory responses in text understanding. *Journal of Memory and Language, 30,* 603–626.

Bargh, J. A., Chaiken, S., Raymond, P., & Hymes, C. (1996). The automatic evaluation effect: Unconditional automatic attitude activation with a pronunciation task. *Journal of Experimental Social Psychology, 32,* 104–128.

Beattie, G. W., & Barnard, P. J. (1979). The temporal structure of natural telephone conversations (directory assistance calls). *Linguistics, 17,* 213–229.

Brewer, W. F. (1996). The nature of narrative suspense and the problem of rereading. In P. Vorderer, H. J. Wulff, & M. Friedrichsen (Eds.), *Suspense: Conceptualizations, theoretical analyses, and empirical explorations* (pp. 107–127). Mahwah, NJ: Lawrence Erlbaum Associates.

Brewer, W. F., & Lichtenstein, E. H. (1982). Stories are to entertain: A structural-affect theory of stories. *Journal of Pragmatics, 6,* 473–486.

Britton, B. K., & Graesser, A. C. (Eds.). (1996). *Models of understanding text.* Mahwah, NJ: Lawrence Erlbaum Associates.

Cacioppo, J. T., & Petty, R. E. (1982). The need for cognition. *Journal of Personality & Social Psychology, 42,* 116–131.

Cacioppo, J. T., Petty, R. E., Kao, C. F., & Rodriguez, R. (1986). Central and peripheral routes to persuasion: An individual difference perspective. *Journal of Personality & Social Psychology, 51,* 1032–1043.

Clark, H. H. (1992). *Arenas of language use.* Chicago: University of Chicago Press.

Clark, H. H. (1997). Dogmas of understanding. *Discourse Processes, 23*, 567–598.
Clark, H. H., & Carlson, T. B. (1982). Hearers and speech acts. *Language, 58*, 332–373.
Daneman, M., & Merikle, P. M. (1996). Working memory and language comprehension: A meta-analysis. *Psychonomic Bulletin & Review, 3*, 422–433.
Duncker, K. (1945). On problem solving. *Psychological Monographs, 58*, whole no. 270.
Edwards, K., & Smith, E. E. (1996). A disconfirmation bias in the evaluation of arguments. *Journal of Personality & Social Psychology, 71*, 5–24.
Fleming, I. (1954). *Casino Royale.* New York: Maximillian.
Gerrig, R. J. (1993). *Experiencing narrative worlds.* New Haven, CT: Yale University Press.
Gerrig, R. J., & Bernardo, A. B. I. (1994). Readers as problem-solvers in the experience of suspense. *Poetics, 22*, 459–472.
Gerrig, R. J., & Prentice, D. A. (1996). Notes on audience response. In D. Bordwell & N.Carroll (Eds.), *Post-theory: Reconstructing film studies* (pp. 388–403). Madison: University of Wisconsin Press.
Graesser, A. C., Singer, M., & Trabasso, T. (1994). Constructing inferences during narrative text comprehension. *Psychological Review, 101*, 371–395.
Johnson, B. T., & Eagly, A. H. (1989). Effects of involvement on persuasion: A meta-analysis. *Psychological Bulletin, 106*, 290–314.
Jones, T. (1992). The pugilist at rest. In *The best American short stories 1992* (pp. 121–139). Boston, MA: Houghton Mifflin Company.
Jones, T. (1997, November 11). Sonny Liston was a friend of mine. *New Yorker,* pp.84–89.
Kahneman, D., & Miller, D. T. (1986). Norm theory: Comparing reality to its alternatives. *Psychological Review, 93*, 136–153.
Kahneman, D., & Tversky, A. (1982). The simulation heuristic. In D. Kahneman, P. Slovic, & A. Tversky (Eds.), *Judgment under uncertainty: Heuristics and biases* (pp. 201–208). New York: Cambridge University Press.
Kintsch, W. (1998). *Comprehension: A new paradigm for cognition.* New York: Cambridge University Press.
Lazarus, R. S. (1995). Vexing research problems inherent in cognitive-mediational theories of emotion—and some solutions. *Psychological Inquiry, 6*, 183–196.
Lord, C. G., Ross, L., & Lepper, M. R. (1979). Biased assimilation and attitude polarization: The effects of prior theories on subsequently presented evidence. *Journal of Personality & Social Psychology, 37*, 2098–2109.
McKoon, G., Gerrig, R. J., & Greene, S. B. (1996). Pronoun comprehension and memory based text processing. *Journal of Experimental Psychology: Learning, Memory, and Cognition, 22*, 919–932.
McKoon, G., & Ratcliff, R. (1992). Inference during reading. *Psychological Review, 99*, 440–466.
Murphy, S. T., & Zajonc, R. B. (1993). Affect, cognition, and awareness: Affective priming with optimal and suboptimal exposures. *Journal of Personality and Social Psychology, 64*, 723–739.
Prentice, D. A., Gerrig, R. J., & Bailis, D. S. (1997). What readers bring to the processing of fictional texts. *Psychonomic Bulletin & Review, 4*, 416–420.
Roese, N. J., & Olson, J. M. (Eds.). (1995). *What might have been: The social psychology of counterfactual thinking.* Mahwah, NJ: Lawrence Erlbaum Associates.
Sacks, H., Schlegoff, E. A., & Jefferson, G. (1974). A simplest systematics for the organization of turn-taking in conversation. *Language, 50*, 708.

Schober, M. F., & Clark, H. H. (1989). Understanding by addressees and overhearers. *Cognitive Psychology, 21,* 211–232.
Vakoch, D. A., & Wurm, L. H. (1997). Emotional connotation in speech perception: Semantic associations in the general lexicon. *Cognition and Emotion, 11,* 337–349.
Walton, K. L. (1978). Fearing fictions. *Journal of Philosophy, 75,* 5–27.
Wheeler, S. C., Green, M. C., & Brock, T. C. (1999). Fictional narratives change beliefs: Replications of Prentice, Gerrig, and Bailis (1997) with mixed corroboration. *Psychonomic Bulletin & Review, 6,* 136–141.
Wurm, L. H., & Vakoch, D. A. (1996). Dimensions of speech perception: Semantic associations in the affective lexicon. *Cognition and Emotion, 10,* 409–423.
Zajonc, R. B. (1980). Feeling and thinking: Preferences need no inferences. *American Psychologist, 35,* 151–175.
Zillmann, D. (1996). The psychology of suspense in dramatic exposition. In P. Vorderer, H. J. Wulff, & M. Friedrichsen (Eds.), *Suspense: Conceptualizations, theoretical analyses, and empirical explorations* (pp. 199–231). Mahwah, NJ: Lawrence Erlbaum Associates.

5

The Evolution of Interactive Media

Toward "Being There" in Nonlinear Narrative Worlds

Frank Biocca
Michigan State University

FROM THE PHOTOPLAY TO THE HOLODECK

The original narrative medium was the body and the spoken word. The body and the word were used to simulate narrative worlds: physical spaces, social interactions, and mental states of characters. But increasingly the body, the word, and all the elements of the narrative world are experienced through various media: books, video, and interactive virtual environments. In her book on *Computers as Theatre*, Brenda Laurel implored her engineering oriented readers to, "think of the computer, not as a tool, but as a medium" (Laurel, 1991, p. ix). This chapter considers the narrative implications of the computer medium.

What is striking about the early 21st century is the many ways new media alter the nature of narrative experience. A claim can be made that the computer seeks to become a 3-D stage instead of a dreary drone. In the early 1990s, cognitive scientist and human–computer interaction guru, Donald Norman, pointed to the number crunching box and asked: "Do you enjoy the experience of using these new technologies? If not, why not? Perhaps it never occurred to you that the concepts of 'enjoy' and 'experience' could apply to the new devices ..." (D. Norman in Laurel, 1991, p. x).

With the arrival of advanced multimedia, narrative virtual environments, and the Internet, the computer may now be the leading edge vehicle for artistic expression in our culture. With higher quality audio, video, and embodied interaction the computer has become more expressive, more pliable, and it has increased its ability to mimic the sensory qualities of other media. It can now mimic the capabilities of all past narrative media—the canvas, the book, the radio, the television, the arcade ride, and, maybe, even the live theater (Roehl, 1999).

Why should technology play a role in narrative experience? Significant changes in technology have altered the sensory experience and representational codes that structure narrative. We can see a steady progression of expressive forms from the pre-writing, iconic representational codes of Lascaux Caves to the coordinated multisensory codes of the latest virtual reality system. Innovations in technology or technique can go the heart of narrative experience. For example, computer simulation technologies can alter representational techniques and simulate physical spaces, social interactions, and the mental states of characters (Cassell, Sullivan, Prevost, & Churchill, 2000; Foley, Dam, Feiner, Hughes, & Philips, 1999; Magnenat-Thalmann, Kalra, & Escher, 1998; Sims, 1994).

New media technologies and narrative also share a common goal: the transformation of experience. Narrative has played a role in expanding our experience of other lives, other spaces, and other ways of being. High interactive media such as immersive virtual reality technologies (Biocca & Levy, 1995; Durlach & Mavor, 1994) are designed to be engines of experience. Interactive media transform the audience member into an *interactor* (Laurel, 1991). The very term suggests a new role, a sense of agency and activity. If older narrative structures are a set of train cars steaming down a linear, predictable track, this new agent, the interactor, is a conductor steering the train off the track and into a field of dreams. But the term *interactor* just as easily suggests a body twitching appropriately to stimulation, yanking levers, transformed into a kind of piston in some narrative engine. Some see the possibility of immersive, sensory-intensive experiences rich in personal transformation and insight (e.g., Murray, 1997). Others see a random bouncing around of a nonlinear series of episodes and scenes, the narrative equivalent of the pin ball machine. For example, consider the biting observations of Brian Ferren, executive vice president for creative technology and research at Walt Disney Imagineering:

> You know, when it comes to storytelling, people suspect that, 'oh well, I'm just as qualified to tell a story as anyone else is.' It is not true. When you saw Schindler's list ... if you had at home a little box with a knob that let you dial in "Happy Nazis," "Mean Nazis," "Nazis that speak Portuguese," a whole collection of different options, it wouldn't make it a better film. The reason Steve Spielberg is paid a great deal of money is because he is a master storyteller." (Ferren, 1997)

Only few aspects of computer-generated narrative experience can be called "new, " or better still, "adapted." Interactive technologies share a lot of techniques with earlier media. This chapter focuses on what is different about narrative experiences involving interactive media. This emphasis on *what is different* will tend to take us toward the more advanced forms of interactive media, such as hypertext, and more multisensory, such as virtual reality. We avoid focusing on specific technologies, but rather treat interactive media as a family of evolving forms of narrative media. Our discussion focuses on:

- The *evolution of interactive media* and how the dimensions of this evolution affect the qualities of narrative experience.
- *Dramatic narratives* in interactive media, and only to a lesser degree, more mundane representations of everyday narrative sequences.
- The *experience of presence* (e.g., "being there" in the story) in multi-sensory interactive media, especially the families of evolving immersive media.
- And, finally, the application of computer intelligence to narrative form, especially in the dimensions of nonlinear interactive narrative forms.

Munsterberg and the Photoplay: A Short Story About New Media, Psychologists, and "Laws of the Mind"

Before we step onto a stage cluttered with technologies like virtual reality, let me briefly tell a cautionary tale. To do this I take you to a backstage area, to the prop room, to recreate a narrative involving a much older technology. In this more comfortable, familiar place, I can tell you a brief story that illustrates the dilemma of analyzing the psychology of any young medium.

The date is 1916. The location Harvard yard. Our protagonist is the head of the experimental psychology lab at Harvard, Hugo Munsterberg (Munsterberg, 1916). He is sitting in lab watching flickering patterns of light on a wall, puzzled by a new technology, the "fashion" on the streets of Boston. Munsterberg complains to his close friend, William James, that some of the youth of Harvard are mesmerized by a new technology. It was just a "gimmick" that seemed to be mimicking the theater. From the salons of Paris to the offices of Edison, there were attempts to use a new technology to tell stories. Gears, celluloid, and the electric light had given birth to this new narrative vehicle, the Photoplay. For Munsterberg, there was something very interesting psychologically about the relationship of the viewer to the experience of film. Munsterberg was conducting research, of course. As a Harvard professor, he would be loathe to admit that so plebian an offering as a Photoplay could be enjoyable. But in the spirit of Pragmatism, he sat in the dark observing, exploring, and analyzing the curious psychological devices of the new medium. The collection of notes and observations gave birth to a book called *The Psychology of the Photoplay*, probably the first substantial psychological study of the new electric media. The book appeared in 1916, the year Munsterberg died.

Like the author of this chapter almost 100 years later, Munsterberg did not have many examples of outstanding narrative in the newly emerging medium. But early narrative films like *The Life of an American Fireman* (1902) and *The Great Train Robbery* (1903) displayed early forms of film language. The year Munsterberg was writing his book on the psychology of the photoplay, a classic film, the *Birth of a Nation* (1915) was released.

There were certainly no experimental studies of the psychology of narrative in film. Nonetheless, Munsterberg could discern the simulation of psychological processes like attention, the devices that stimulated semantic associations, and mechanisms that stimulated arousal and emotions. He observed that the closeup and zoom simulated the movement of attention in the environment (e.g., "zoom" theories of attention, Johnston & Dark, 1986).

Although the photoplay and stage play shared many conventions, especially in 1917, emerging techniques foreign to the theater such as the cut, zoom, and other emerging film conventions suggested that there was something fundamentally different about the way the narrative world of the photoplay was constructed and experienced. Observing the curious structure of imagery in this "realistic" medium, he concluded "The photoplay obeys the laws of the mind rather than those of the outer world" (p. 15). In the new medium Munsterberg could see a stimulus that generated a rich environment that modeled not so much the "real world," as the way the mind experienced the world.

Here we are again at the turn of the century, almost 100 years after Munsterberg began his observations. Sitting in the multi-university, networked Media Interface and Network Design (M.I.N.D.) Lab we can observe the latest generation of students gathering in cyberspace to experience various interactive media such as MUDS, Moos, virtual environments, interactive games, and so forth. These environments are the descendants of 1962's Spacewar, the first interactive computer game. Like Munsterberg we share a suspicion that these narrative virtual environments have less to do with the reproduction of world and more with "objectification" of thought processes. In these cognitive artifacts rich in multisensory stimuli, there lies a pathway to mental simulation. If these emerging narrative media are cognitive artifacts, they must be defined in relation to cognition. What is most critical to the structure of a new medium is not the silicon, plastic, fiber optics, and copper that form the technology, but the way the medium is coupled to the human mind and body. It is in this coupling of medium, body, and mind that the explanation of the fuzzy concept of *interaction* lies.

Interactive Media Along the Road to the "Holodeck"

Interactive narrative may be experienced through small, hand held computer game consoles, online hypertext, or highly immersive virtual reality systems. Because computer interfaces are constantly evolving, it is important not to dwell on a specific technology. Rather, in our quest to better understand how narrative experience may be altered by technological change, we first examine research on the experience of "presence" or "telepresence" inside interactive narrative worlds. We then outline some basic dimensions that array the families of interactive media and their evolution, and explore how each dimension potentially influences qualities of narrative experience.

INCREASING THE INTERACTOR'S SENSE OF BEING INSIDE THE NARRATIVE SPACE: THE LEVEL OF PRESENCE

Media, especially those high in perceptual realism, can engage the user with multiple sensory cues and elicit a strong sense of a perceptual space (Hochberg, 1986). Indeed, when engaged with a compelling medium or story, we may sometimes experience a sense of being transported to a different place (Gerrig, 1993), so much so we seem to be inside the mediated space. For a brief moment or longer, we may forget that the experiences flashing across a screen (the artificially generated light arrays) are being presented through technology. At some moment we become aware just of the experience, and not the medium. We somehow feel present "there" in the narrative world created by the medium: behind the steering wheel of a flame-red convertible racing down a dusty desert road; floating on a red blood cell through an artery; or clinking a wine glass at a small outdoor café table on the left bank of Paris. Our awareness of the virtual environment may be clear and our mental model vivid, while our awareness of our physical environment may be diminished. We may feel as if the characters conjured up in this medium are copresent in this world, as much "here" with us as any living person.

Our reactions to objects and beings in the virtual environment might compel us to flinch and duck when something "jumps" out at us, to cry at a "sad scene," or to stand silently in awe as the images and sounds saturate our senses. In rare instances these virtual places may give us a deep sense of understanding about the world in which we live, a sense of "being in someone else's shoes," or allow us to comprehend something about ourselves. These are moments when *a narrative is most powerfully connected to the user*, moments that users often remember, moments when the distinction between a mediated experience and a direct experience becomes blurred.

Narratives can be seen as a form of simulation, the product of representational techniques and cognitive artifacts that allow us to extend the range of our experience to other physical and social environments. Simulations are most often used for training (e.g., Ramesh & Andrews, 1999), for scientific exploration and physical modeling (e.g., Bryson, 1996), and, of course, for entertainment (Hawkins, 1995). Simulations can vary from high-end, immersive flight simulations used to train military fighter pilots to simulations of social environments such as those found in the SimCity series (Barfield, Zeltzer, Sheridan, & Slater, 1995; Durlach & Mavor, 1994; Hays & Singer, 1989; Neyland, 1997; Sutherland, 1965).

In the late 1980s and increasingly in the 1990s advanced media and interface design research centers in universities, the military, and corporations became interested in the role of what came to be called "the sensation of presence" while using different kinds of simulation technologies (Hays & Singer, 1989; Minsky, 1980; Sheridan, 1992; Short, Williams, & Christie, 1976). The preoccupation with the theoretical concept of *presence* emerged, and the concept became central to a discussion of human experience in high performance interactive media, like virtual reality (Biocca & Delaney, 1995; Durlach & Mavor, 1994). The engineering and human–computer interaction community of MIT spawned a journal with the nonengineering name of "Presence." It focused on advanced virtual environment design ("Teleoperators and Virtual Environment Design"). Presence, a psychological goal, came to define the design focus of a hardware and software engineering community. A research program was launched that focused on the phenomenological qualities of experience in advanced interactive media. To design media that push the limits of mediated experience, be it in narrative or in military training, it became necessary to understand "being there," moments when our awareness of the medium disappears and *we are pushed through the medium* to sensations that approach direct experience.

Most researchers in this community acknowledge that that experience of presence predates any advanced media. This acknowledgment is bound up with the theoretical conundrum we call the *book problem*. A theory of presence derived for work in advanced media must also be able to explain how the sensation of "being there" can occur not just in a virtual reality system, but with any medium, including much older noniconic, "low-tech" media such as books (e.g., Gerrig, 1993). But presence research, using advanced media, seeks not just to explicate a theoretical concept, but to better control presence, to more consistently and reliably evoke the experience of presence in the user. By immersing the sensorimotor system into coordinated mediated stimuli such as those found in advanced virtual reality interfaces, designers can generate compelling sensations of leaving behind our unmediated physical body and environment and entering the virtual environment. The key to optimizing human performance and experience in these "mind machines" may lie in understanding how the machine interacts with the mind to create this deep sense of what has come to be called *presence*. One goal of interactive narrative experience is to immerse the mind of the "interactor" into the narrative world, and the achievement of presence is one way to define the psychological impact and success of a narrative environment.

Let us offer a working definition of presence. To capture some of the dimensions, we use the concepts of telepresence, social presence, and self-presence. A definition and explication of these is provided in Table 5.1.

Definitions of the concept of presence take a number of overlapping forms (Barfield et al., 1995; Lombard & Ditton, 1997; Loomis, 1992; Sheridan, 1992; Steuer, 1995). The "short hand" definition of presence most commonly defines it as the illusion of "being there" in the virtual environment. Some theorists acknowledge that the sensation of presence is not unique to media use and may define a quality of being in any environment or experience. Loomis (1992), Steuer (1995), Biocca (1992) and others consider presence, generally, as a phenomenological state, a mental model and awareness of the physical environment experienced through the senses. For Steuer (1992) it is almost the same as consciousness when he defines it very simply as the "experience of one's physical environment."

Loomis (1992) provided a more subtle argument grounded in perceptual psychology. For Loomis, the experience of telepresence, the mediated form of presence (see Table 5.1) is just a form of externalization or distal attribution, the basic psychological process by which stimulation of the senses (proximal stimulus) leads the individual to attribute the sensation (distal attribution) to an external environment (distal stimulus) as opposed to the sensory organ itself. For example, sight is not experienced as patterns of light stimulating our retina; rather, we experience a room "out there."

> The perceptual world created by our senses and the nervous system is so functional a representation of the physical world that most people live out their lives without ever suspecting that contact with the physical world is mediated; moreover, the functionality of perception impedes many reflective individuals from appreciating the insights about perception that derive from philosophical inquiry. Oddly enough, the newly developing technology of teleoperator and virtual displays is having the unexpected effect of promoting such insight, for the impression of being in a remote or simulated environment experienced by the user of such systems can be so compelling as to force a user to question the assumptions that the physical and perceptual world are one and the same. (Loomis, 1992, p. 113).

Some theorists feel that a definition of presence may be premature (Durlach & Mavor, 1998). Some take a rather restricted view that focuses solely on human performance and seeks to ignore presence as an

TABLE 5.1
Three Dimensions of the User's Sense of Presence in Mediated Environments

Three constructs that define presence in mediated environments	Definition of the construct	Related definitions
Telepresence (Physical Presence)	Telepresence is the sense of "being there," the level of vividness of a remote or simulated place experienced via a communication technology. The sensation of telepresence arises out of the effort by the user to construct a mental model of the space in the mediated environment. The sensation of telepresence is characterized by temporary suspension of attention to the physical environment, a dominant spatial mental model of the mediated environment, and some level of behavioral response or acceptance ("suspension of disbelief") of the mediated environment. When the illusion of telepresence is broken, subjects often report a sense of having been "transported" to another place and momentary disorientation as they readjust to the physical space they are in.	• "Mediated perception of an environment" (Steuer, 1995, p. 36) • "Being there" (Heeter, 1992; Reeves, 1991; Sheridan, 1992) • "Form of out-of-the-body experience" (Rheingold, 1991, p. 256) • "Feeling like you are actually 'there' at the remote site of operation" (Minsky, 1980, p. 120) • "Sense of transportedness" (Gerrig, 1993; Kim & Biocca, 1997)
Social Presence (Mediated Co-presence)	Mediated co-presence is the level of phenomenal vividness of a remote or simulated intelligent being experienced via a communication medium. Co-presence is the sensation of the presence of another intelligence or consciousness (Sartre, 1956) and, usually, the other's awareness of you. The sensation of copresence arises out of the effort by the user to construct a mental model of other intelligent actors in the environment who are capable of intentionality and action. The inference of a human or artificial intelligence is extracted from the experience of the other's mediated embodiment, voice, virtual body, body movement, etc. The level of co-presence is variable and higher levels are characterized by an increased sense of access to the other's existential states: others' perceptions of the environment, emotional states, intentional and goal states.	• "Social presence" (Heeter, 1992; Short, Williams, & Christie, 1976) • "Co-presence" (Goffman, 1963) • "Closeness" of others (Muhlbach, Bocker, and Prussog, 1995; Perse, et al., 1992) • Sense of "togetherness" (Ho, et al., 1998) • Presence of "the other" (Sartre, 1956)

Mediated Self-presence

Mediated self-presence is the experience of self as situated and active in a mediated environment, especially when characterized by an increased sense of self-awareness, self-mastery, or creativity.

The mental model of the self is a cognitive construct, not unlike the construction of the copresent other or the perceived space surrounding the self and the other. Mediated environments are often designed to engage mental models of the self; they are created to alter the self in some way: Change skill sets, mood states, or attitudes.

While the self has sometimes been conceptualized as a relatively stable, rarely changing, unitary mental structure (Allport, 1955; Snygg & Combs, 1949), there is also a tradition descendant from the symbolic interaction perspectives (Cooley, 1902; Gergen, 1971; Mead, 1934) that sees a more fluid, multiple role model version of the self that emerges in interaction of the self with others and in different environments (Rosenberg & Gara, 1985; Rosenberg, 1986, Cantor & Kihlstrom, 1987). In the latter perspective and in hybrid hierarchical models of the self (Kihlstrom & Cantor, 1984; Kihlstrom & Klein, 1994; Klein & Loftus, 1990). There are moments when the individual self-consciously observes his or her behavior to form a network of traits and behaviors that compose a mental model of the self (Markus & Ruvolo, 1989). Some of these moments are characterized by an increased sense of insight and accessibility to the self. We call such moments of self-awareness, self-presence. The level of self-presence is variable across individuals, media, and time. Some tasks or encounters may make us more-or-less aware of our own consciousness. Higher levels of self-presence may be characterized by increased awareness and insight into one's own bodily states (e.g., spatial position, movement, etc.); intentional states, cognitive processes, and mood states. For Kant, this self-consciousness was called the *transcendental consciousness*, an awareness of the stream of experience as a representation, a kind of insightful observation of one's self, thinking, and acting. Csikszentmihalyi's (Csikszentmihalyi, 1990; Csikszentmihalyi, 1996) concept of "flow" appears to describe a level of self presence associated with task mastery, creativity, and positive affect, a mental state purportedly associated with higher levels of creativity and human performance.

- "Self-schema" (Markus & Ruvolo, 1989)

epiphenomenon (Ellis, 1996; Ellis, Dorighi, Menges, Adelstein, & Joacoby, 1997). Part of the problem is that the early users of the concept were mainly grounded in engineering and, in some cases, perceptual psychology (Loomis, 1992). Both communities tended to be uncomfortable focusing on the "soft" and illusive phenomenological tendencies of the concept, a problem that required an exploration of the subtle properties of consciousness. For example, some theorists, especially engineering-oriented researchers, tended to make the mistake of defining a momentary phenomenological state (a cognitive dependent variable) by extensive reference to its causes (engineering independent variables; e.g., Sheridan, 1992; Zeltzer, 1992).

In the context of narrative environment, the concept of presence and its dimensions attempt to tap into the user/reader/viewer's sense of being inside the narrative space and the feeling of insight into the intelligence of the characters. For an anecdotal insight of how social presence and telepresence are intertwined consider Murray's description of her sensation of being looked at by a character in a 3D IMAX film:

> Sitting in the theater with the 3D-goggles on, I felt myself begin to blush, as if I were actually meeting his gaze. There is a discomfort in not knowing the limits of the illusion. (Murray, 1997, p. 120)

The intensity of the sense of presence can vary considerably within and across individuals. Higher levels of presence are characterized by a strong awareness of the physical space including one's position in space, the objects in the space, and other intelligent beings in the space. Presence is experienced during the processing of the everyday physical environment, of sensory stimuli of mediated environments, and from purely internal representations, such as in dreams.

THE EVOLUTION OF INTERACTIVE TECHNOLOGIES AND SOME IMPLICATIONS FOR NARRATIVE EXPERIENCE

The 21st Century Proscenium: The Computer Interface

In Greek theater the narrative unfolded in proscenium, the space in front of the backdrop. Architectural technologies allowed unobstructed views of the actors and used large urns to amplify the sound in the theater. The proscenium connected the play to the senses of the audience, the eyes and ears, and created a narrative space.

In the world of interactive computer narratives, the interface is the modern proscenium. Interfaces are the devices such as telephones, computers, and television sets that allow the human user to transmit or absorb information. The word interface is conventionally defined as "The point of interaction or communication between a computer and any other entity, such as a printer or human operator" (American Heritage Dictionary, 1992). But this misses key dimensions of the concept that are important to understanding how media work and how they will evolve. There are a number of different ways to conceptualize the idea of an interface (Shneiderman, 1998). We choose a more psychological approach to defining the interface.

To understand the interface, one must begin with the body, the primordial communication medium. The senses are the locus for the reception of all information, and the motor systems are means of transmitting information, emotional states, and so on. Approached fundamentally with the body, we can conceptualize not just past interfaces, but all current and evolving interfaces. The interface is that part of the medium that is directly coupled with the body of the user to send information to the user or to receive information from the user by registering user actions. Effectors or output devices (e.g., monitors, motion platforms) interface with the senses to deliver sensory stimuli (i.e., energy arrays). Whereas codes such as spoken and written language continue to carry much information, other representational codes and conventions, such as the "windows" interface, organize information, guide user perceptual processing, and goad user action. Interactive technologies differ from noninteractive technologies primarily in the sophistication of devices and the way data from the devices is mapped to sensory stimuli to create the illusion of "interaction." The computer's sensors track bodily movement (e.g., the mouse) and uses this information to deduct goals and map sensory feedback.

In short, the interface is always at an information transformation point *where narrative structure is changed into narrative experience* as it moves from one form to another, from one system to another system, as from the "bits" inside the computer to the "meanings" interpreted by the user, from the analog world to the digital world, from cyberspace to physical space, or from one code (e.g., spoken language) to another code (e.g., written language).

Finally, all media must store and transmit narrative content to the user, and they differ on how this is done. Narrative content has been distributed via physical channels by transporting physical storage objects such as paper, CDRoms, and tapes, but increasingly information is stored electronically and is transported to the user via telecommunication channels (e.g., WWW).

Four Dimensions of the Evolution of Communication Technologies

If all interfaces can be considered as points in the evolution toward some ideal transparent interface, then we could array narrative media on the key dimensions that distinguish one from another (Steuer,

1995). Most of evolutionary patterns of media interfaces and transmission systems can be captured by four simple dimensions. The dimensions of mediated embodiment, sociability, intelligence, and ubiquity of access capture the main thrusts in the current evolution of media interfaces. Figure 5.1 arrays the dimensions into one four-dimensional plot. The figure allows us to locate media along these four dimensions and to see how they cluster. This figure includes traditional telecommunication interfaces such as the telephone, but also more general media interfaces such as books and television. We use these four dimensions to organize our discussion of how interactive narrative interfaces influence the experience of narrative.

Mediated Embodiment: Getting More of the User's Body Into the Narrative Experience

Interactive media vary as to their level of mediated embodiment, or how much of the body is immersed into the narrative environment. The user's level of mediated embodiment is defined as the degree to which the body is coupled to the interface, or the degree to which sensorimotor channels are immersive (See Biocca, 1997; Biocca & Delaney, 1995; Durlach & Mavor, 1994). In a Gibsonian sense (Gibson, 1966, 1979) the user's body is linked

Four Dimensions of Media Interface Evolution

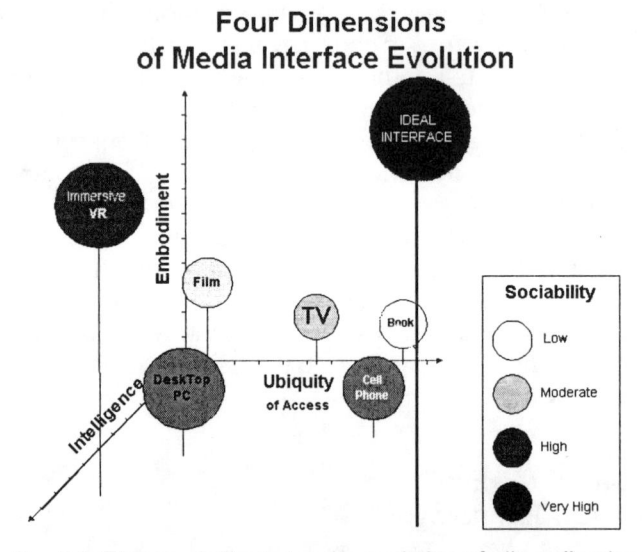

Fig. 5.1. The graph illustrates the evolution of all media along four dimensions towards an ideal medium positioned at the end point of the graph. All existing media are characterized by a location along the four dimensions.

to the environment. Once motor action and sensory feedback are linked, the user is embodied in the virtual environment (Biocca, 1997). To make the user perceptually aware of his or her actions, interactive environments give the user some form of "body" that is linked to the user's motor action and "represents" the user in the virtual environment. This bodily representation of the user can be as small and impoverished as a mouse arrow that, like a hand, moves over and "touches" objects in the virtual environment. It can also be as rich as a full 3D graphic "avatar," a bodily representation of the user, inside the virtual environment.

Media interfaces vary in how many sensory channels are supported. For example, audio, visual, tactile, and sensory cues may be provided in each channel. They might vary in how much the sensory channel is im-

TABLE 5.2
Four Dimensions of Evolution of Telecommunication Interfaces

Dimension	Definition
Level of Mediated Embodiment	Mediated embodiment is defined as the degree to which the user's body is connected to the telecommunication system. Level of mediated embodiment is a combination of: (1) the number of sensory, motor, and autonomic channels engaged (e.g. vision, hearing, taste, hand motion, heart rate), (2) display or sensor fidelity for each channel, and (3) amount of channel bandwidth filled with stimuli from the mediated environment versus stimuli from the physical environment (e.g., field of view, 1-100%), and (4) level of coordination of stimuli across sensory and motor channels.
Level of Interface Intelligence	Interface intelligence refers to the ability of the interface to interact, to sense, respond, and adapt to the user's behavior. Intelligent response to user behavior includes the interface's ability to simulate both the interactive properties of: (1) physical environments (i.e., space and objects), and (2) intelligent beings (i.e., simulated animals, humans, and other sentient beings).
Ubiquity of Access	Ubiquity refers to how many physical locations the interface can be accessed. Ubiquitous access can be achieved by having many interfaces in the physical space (e.g., TV sets) or by making interfaces more portable (e.g., satellite phone).
Sociability	Sociability is defined as a combination of: (1) the number of mediated and non-mediated simultaneous users, and (2) the quality of interpersonal interaction of these users that the interface can support remotely. Sociability is not exclusively a property of the interface. It is more dependent on other properties of the telecommunication system, such as the quality of the network and the nature of the application, than the other interface dimensions.

mersed in the mediated environment (e.g., small screen versus IMAX screen). They also might vary on the input side, how much of the user's body's motions and responses (motor behaviors) the computer can sense. For example, input devices for an interface might sense a user's motor channel activity, such as how a user is moving his hand in 2D space (e.g., a mouse) or where the user is looking (e.g., head tracker or eye camera). In some interfaces input sensors also pick up a user's autonomic responses such as heart rate, blood pressure, etc.

When we array all narrative media interfaces along the dimension of embodiment, we can see a high degree of variance. On one end of the extreme are noninteractive narrative media such as the book, which utilizes only a small part of the visual channel with noniconic stimuli. When there are no pictures, the book uses a small part of the sensory cues detectable by the visual channel to carry information. Closer to the other end of the embodiment dimension among noninteractive media we find the visual iconic extremes of widescreen, IMAX theaters. These saturate the visual channel with information, filling all that the eyes can see with information from the virtual as opposed to the physical environment. But still, the viewer cannot interact with virtual environment on the film screen.

At the absolute other end of the dimension are narrative media that not only provide a lot of sensory information to a large number of senses, but they are interactive (intelligent) as well and make real time use of more of the user's actions and responses. For example, immersive VR bathes the visual, aural, and sometimes the tactile senses, but also tracks every fine movement of the head, the hands, and other parts of the body to increase the ways in which the body can interact with the objects and characters inside the narrative virtual world . To be able to sense and meaningfully use the user's motor behavior, a medium must have some minimal intelligence.

Looking at the graph, we see a clear trend where advanced media like virtual and augmented reality are steadily increasing the mediated embodiment of the user both in terms of improved sensory displays and greater and more intelligent sensing of motor behavior. This trend means media involve more the sensory, motor, and autonomic channels; it further means that sensors and displays increase steadily in their fidelity; and that media use more of the bandwidth of each channel.

The most compelling media interfaces found with advanced telecommunication systems such as virtual reality can be further classified according to their level of media embodiment. Table 5.3 briefly lists various classes of virtual environments according to the degree of mediated embodiment, that is the degree to which they are coupled to the user's body. All of these have been used for the experience of narrative environments.

TABLE 5.3
Classes of Narrative Interfaces Arrayed According to the Level of the User's Mediated Embodiment

Classification	Level of Mediated Embodiment	Description	User Sensorimotor Experience	Example Narrative Applications
Window Interface	Very Low	The basic personal computer where only the window display, monitor, and mouse connect the user's body to the virtual environment.	Limited field-of-view and limited sensorimotor interactions provide a modest experience of presence.	Internet narrative worlds. Moos, consumer computer games.
Mirror Interface	Low	An image of the user's body is captured by video equipment. The image of the user's body is superimposed on the computer environment, which is projected onto a screen in front of the user.	Users see a video image of themselves on a large screen often with other people. Cutout images interact with the environment. Can be compelling, but sense of presence is modest.	Walk-through museum or narrative art experiences. Some arcade gaming applications.
Panoramic Interface	Medium	Large wide-screen projection system fills the user's visual field. Often includes 3D stereographic glasses and tracked, hand-held input devices, and high-end audio systems.	One or more users stand in front of large 3D window on the virtual world. Motion effects and sense of depth can deliver higher levels of presence.	Corporate product visualization. Scientific and medical visualization.
Virtual Rooms	Medium	Takes panoramic portals to their logical extreme. Users walk into a physical room that is a large display system. The motion and perspective of the user are continuously updated by tracking devices as the user interacts with the virtual environment seamlessly projected on at least three walls and the floor.	Sense of space can be quite compelling. The virtual environment immerses the user's visual sensory system. Usually viewed through 3D glasses. Expensive system ideal for multiple users.	Scientific visualization. Corporate product and design visualization.

(continued on next page)

TABLE 5.3 (continued)

Vehicular Interface	High	Users enter a mock vehicle (i.e. cars, planes, submarines, tanks, flying carpets, etc.) where they are allowed to operate input devices that control their vehicle inside the virtual environment. The vehicles often include motion platforms to simulate physical movement, and the computer graphics based world is projected onto the 'windows' of the vehicle.	Sense of presence and motion can be quite compelling. The interface can faithfully reproduce a lot of detail, and a feeling of being inside the "real" vehicle.	Military and corporate training, simulation. High-end location-based entertainment rides.
Immersive VR Interface	Very High	Users wear displays that fully immerse a number of the senses in computer generated stimuli (e.g., vision, hearing, and touch). These systems often use the distinctive head-mounted, stereographic display, 3-D spatial audio. Input devices (sensors) immerse the motor actions of the user into the virtual environment. Trackers may register head and hand location. Data gloves may sense finger movement. Other sensors may track eye movement, walking, etc. It is primarily the much higher levels of sensorimotor integration; the linking of sensory feedback to body movement that distinguishes immersive systems most from other VR systems.	Arguably provides a significant 'jump' in the level of 'presence' because of the tight sensorimotor integration and the full immersion of at least the key senses of vision and hearing. Some purists argue that immersive environments are the only true VR systems because they are the only systems that attempt to completely immerse the sensorimotor system into a virtual environment.	Scientific and medical visualization. Corporate product and design visualization. Military training. Some low quality systems used for gaming.
Augmented Reality Interface	Medium to High	The most advanced augmented reality systems use hardware similar to that found in immersive VR. But rather than fully immerse the user in a virtual world, augmented reality systems overlay 3-D virtual objects onto real world scenes. The goal here is to enhance the user's experience with reality.	Few systems yet achieve a truly convincing integration of a stable 3D virtual object and the real world, but many of these show promise with less compelling implementations and schematic virtual displays.	Medical imaging. Battle display systems. Manufacturing and equipment maintenance. Facilitating navigation with the natural environment.

Implications of Increased User Embodiment for Narrative Experience

As the user's body is more and more immersed in the virtual environment, does this change some aspect of the narrative experience? There is widespread belief among interface designers, and some research support, for the proposition that increasing levels of mediated embodiment (sensory immersion, motor immersion, and sensorimotor coordination) in the medium will influence user's sense of presence (Akiyama, et al.,1991; Barfield & Furness, 1995; Biocca, 1997; Durlach & Mavor, 1998; Hatada, Sakata, & Kusaka, 1980; Hays & Singer, 1989; Heilig, 1992/1955; Held & Durlach, 1992; Hendrix & Barfield, 1996; Ijsselseijn, 1998; Ijsselseijn, Ridder, Hamberg, Bouwhuis, & Freeman, 1998; Lombard, Ditton, Gabe, & Reich, 1994; Lombard & Ditton, 1997; Loomis, 1992; Pausch, D., Proffitt, & Williams, 1997; Reeves & Nass, 1996; Sheridan, 1992; Steuer, 1995; Tromp, 1995; Witmer & Singer, 1994). Some findings suggest that immersing the body of the user in the virtual environment (sensorimotor immersion) increases the sense of presence, all other things being equal. Increasing the number of sensory channels receiving stimuli from the virtual environment (e.g., Gilkey & Weisenberger, 1995), increasing immersion of the visual channel (Arthur, 2000, Hatada et al., 1980; Hendrix & Barfield, 1996; Prothero, Hoffman, Parker, Furness, & Wells, 1998), or providing some key sensory cues such as motion of the visual field appears to increase the level of telepresence. Systems such as immersive virtual reality tightly couple motor action and sensory feedback. This tight coupling appears related to the sense of presence in these systems, and presence is disrupted when delays are introduced between action and perception (e.g., Welch, Blackmon, Liu, Mellers, & Stark, 1996). Fidelity defined as image resolution, on the other hand, has an inconsistent effect on presence and expected correlates such as learning and memory (Alessi, 1988; Christel, 1994; Hays & Singer, 1989; Welch et al., 1996).

Reality Testing

Extending the evolution of existing interfaces, over time we can expect higher levels of embodiment with each medium, what we call "progressive embodiment" (Biocca, 1997; Biocca & Nowak, 2001). With each increase in the level of immersion or the arrival of any new immersive medium, commentators speculate euphorically about the medium or, on the other hand, complain about the confusion between direct experiences in the physical world and mediated experiences in virtual environments (Heim, 1993; Lanier & Biocca, 1992; Lauria, 1997; Murray, 1997; Rheingold, 1991). The history of media shows interesting occurrences of users' confusion about the "reality" of mediated, fictional experience (See Shapiro & McDonald, 1995, for a discussion in the context of virtual reality). Immersive technologies have long been presented as sources of powerful illusion in utopian or dystopian hues in science fiction: for example, Orwell's "feelies," Bradbury's "televisors," the Star Trek "holodeck" and Gibson's "simstim." Anxiety about the powers of "mimesis" has often greeted technologies that increase presence, a concern that at high levels of presence physical, fictional, and imaginal become "almost" indistinguishable. But, as yet, in studies of the current generation of virtual reality systems there is little evidence of "reality testing" confusion (e.g., blurring the boundary between direct and virtual experience; Hullfish, 1986). Although it may seem far away and out of reach, making the virtual, mediated perception, indistinguishable from the "real," direct perception, has been the goal of virtual environment engineering since its birth (Sutherland, 1965).

The goal of full perceptual immersion in a narrative illusion, an absolutely "transparent" medium, has not yet been achieved, of course. Confusions in perceptual reality judgments do occur, but only in highly constrained settings (i.e., stationary monocular viewing) or for very short periods of time. A certain level of perceptual realism has been achieved in film special effects in that many viewers are unable to distinguish between computer generated simulations of physical reality and filmed physical events and scenes. But such judgments are made in a highly constrained environment, as it is an illusion within the film medium and not a "real time" interactive medium. During the richly rendered boat scenes from the movie *Titanic*, for example, few in the theater believe they are riding on the Titanic, and in film, none can take the helm.

Arousal

With increased mediated embodiment, more contact between the body and the medium, there arise the issues of the increased arousal of the user. When the narrative space surrounds the body of the user, some believe that emotional arousal may be intensified (e.g., Laurel, 1991; Murray, 1997). For example, the highly subtended field-of-view of wide screen IMAX, interactive motion rides, and high-end virtual reality systems can produce physiologically arousing illusions of vection during motion sequences (Boothe, 1994; Casali & Wierwille, 1986; Hettinger, Berbaum, Kennedy, Dunlap, & Nolan, 1990; McCauley & Starkey, 1992).

A significant amount of narrative interactive media are (1) designed to heighten arousal through direct physiological stimulation or arousing content, and (2) used by interactors to regulate mood states. Research on media underlines how media content, including the experience of narrative, is often used for "mood management," the user seeks to use the content to alter or maintain a mood state (Kubey & Csikszentmihalyi, 1990;

Zillmann & Bryant, 1994). Much of the research on arousal has been concerned with the effects of pornography, violence, or fear inducing content on children and adolescents and, especially, transfer of emotional effects to behavior or mood states outside the mediated environment (e.g., Cantor, 1994; Gunter, 1994). So it appears that arousal and interactive media appear to be systemically linked both by design goals of producers (e.g., "twitch" games, violent games, interactive adventure) and by user intentions when using them (e.g., the design for stimulation, diversion, etc.).

Some theorists and critics have voiced concern about the effect of advanced interactive media on interactor emotion and arousal. Many argue some variation on the following: as interactive media immerse more of the body in narrative experience (i.e., increased the level of mediated embodiment) and as users gain more control over the pacing and unfolding of the narrative, that:

(a) with unlimited narrative paths, emotional effects and control of the user become harder to design weakening narrative emotional effects and/or

(b) arousal and mood states in interactors may become more intense or extreme than with media lower in embodiment and intelligence (i.e., less vivid and interactive), and/or

(c) interactors become more susceptible to the effects of content category (e.g., violence, pornography, etc.) on social cognition and behavior.

For example, consider the following in a recent review of the video game and violence literature:

> If the latest three dimensional video games have more potential to build the aggressive behavior repertoires of consumers than television shows and movies, then violent virtual reality games constitute another step forward into the danger zone (Dill & Kill, 1998, p. 414).

But it appears that most of the research on video games and violence (see reviews by Dill & Kill, 1998; Griffiths, 1998) has sought only to reproduce the findings from early television research. We can find little research on whether any of the variables that distinguish interactive media from passive media increase postexposure aggressive thoughts and behavior as compared to television or other media with lower levels of mediated embodiment or intelligence (or versions of these concepts confounded in the notions of "interactivity" and "vividness").

Narrative designers tend to be more concerned with modulating and controlling states of arousal during exposure to the narrative experience. For example, Murray, an MIT instructor in interactive narrative design:

> if a participatory immersive experience is not to be pornographic
> and if it is not to lead to frustration or to inappropriate explosion
> ... then the participant's arousal must be carefully regulated. The
> trance should be made deeper and deeper without the emotions
> becoming hotter and hotter. (Murray, 1997, p. 119)

Murray seems to want to achieve high levels of presence (the "trance should be made deeper and deeper") but somehow dampen arousal effects. But there is some preliminary evidence that presence and arousal are linked. Lang has found that high levels of physiological arousal measured by skin conductance and heart rate are related to higher levels of presence (A. Lang, personal communication, March 24, 2000). Decoupling presence effects from arousal effects may not be easily achieved. There is not yet enough research showing that higher levels of mediated embodiment interact with the "same" content to intensify arousal and its related effects as compared to traditional media.

Can Interactive Narrative Worlds Distort Users' Sense of Their Body?

Media mediate our perception of the physical and social environment. They substitute mediated stimuli (e.g., a video image of a room) for unmediated stimuli (direct perception of the room). Most interactive media interpose themselves between the motor actions of the user and the sensory feedback afforded by the physical world. For example, head motion in an immersive virtual reality system is coupled to a change in the virtual scene visible in a head-mounted display. Sensory experience can change the user's internal representation of the body's morphology and the relationship between motor actions and sensory feedback (Welch, 1978; Welch, 1998; Welch & Warren, 1986). The body schema is more labile and unstable than most people would believe. Myers & Biocca (1992) found changes in young women's perception of the shape of their bodies following exposure to no more than ½ hour of programming that emphasized a thin ideal body image.

When a narrative world substitutes mediated perception for direct perception, it is almost certain that some aspect of the mediated stimuli will not match the characteristics of unmediated stimuli. For example, perceptual cues in traditional media such as film and video are distorted (Hochberg, 1986). It is unlikely that virtual reality will successfully match the perceptual characteristics of the sensory environment any time soon (Durlach & Mavor, 1994).

Distorted perceptual cues in an interactive narrative, especially in an immersive environment, can take the form of competing cues within a sensory channel (e.g., vergence and accommodation within vision) or competing cues across sensory channels (i.e., intersensory conflict, for example conflict between the seen and felt position of the arm). Most commonly there may be competing cues across and within the senses as to the location, depth, and characteristics of an object or scene coming to the senses. Welch (1998) listed a number of cues that can be different in virtual environments, including:

1. inadequate sensory resolution
2. an absence of certain sensory cues or entire sensory modalities
3. constricted range of stimuli (e.g., fields of view)
4. sparse, ambiguous, or distorted object, motion, and depth cues from computer graphics
5. delayed, faulty, variable, or absent sensory feedback from the user's movements, and decorrelations between sensory cues or systems, and
6. distortions of visual size, shape, and spatial orientation.

Distortions in these sensory cues mean that interaction with the virtual environment is different than interaction with the physical environment. To the degree that the virtual body is that part of the sensorimotor system interacting with the virtual environment, we might describe the condition as a mismatch between the virtual body and the physical body. The virtual body in mediated perception is inevitably composed of a distorted subset of the dynamic perceptual range of the physical body in direct perception (see Barfield et al., 1995; Ellis, 1996).

What is the effect when the interactor's virtual body does not match the range and properties of the physical body? Or more precisely, what is the effect when mediated sensorimotor cues do not precisely match unmediated forms of those cues? There is some evidence of more noxious effects as perceptual distortions become more visible. In conditions of high user embodiment the potential for noxious effects increases. A widely reported side-effect of the use of highly immersive virtual reality systems is simulation sickness (e.g., Baltzley, Kennedy, Berbaum, Lilienthal, & Gower, 1989; Barret, 1968; Biocca, 1992; Casali & Wierwille, 1986; Ebenholtz, 1992; Hettinger, Berbaum, Kennedy, Dunlap, & Nolan, 1990; Kolasinski, 1995; Stone, 1993). Simulation sickness is best classified as a syndrome with a variety of causes and symptoms (Kennedy & Fowlkes, 1992). Users experiencing simulation sickness report various symptoms such as stomach awareness, sweating, ataxia (postural stability), and vomiting (Kennedy et al., 1987). Simulation sickness is believed to be a form of motion sickness (Reason, 1975) caused by intersensory cue conflict between visual and vestibular cues in the virtual environment. Lag between head motion and visual feedback in some virtual systems is believed to be a key source of problems (Meyer, Applewhite, & Biocca, 1992).

Can time spent in an interactive narrative alter the interactor's sense of their own body? The effects of a mismatch between the virtual and physical body can be more disturbing. Humans tend to adapt to some degree to a wide range of changes in the perceptual environment (Welch, 1978). Cue conflict in the virtual environment can temporarily alter the way the individual perceives and interacts with the virtual world, and aftereffects can carry this effect into the user's interaction with the physical world (Biocca & Rolland, 1998). Biocca and Rolland (1998) found that when users entered a virtual environment that significantly altered the users' sense of their felt and seen hand position, users adapted their hand–eye coordination to fit the relationship in the virtual world. But when the users left the virtual environment and returned to the unmediated physical environment, they continued to show evidence of perceptual adaptation. The users' hand–eye coordination had been altered so that their reaching and pointing actions were no longer accurate, but distorted and adapted to the distortions found in the virtual environment. To put it another way, the configuration of the users' virtual body altered their mental representation of their body, and this altered representation continued into the physical environment. In summary there is widespread speculation and some narrow evidence that interactive narratives inside media high in embodiment may increase arousal, presence, and expose the user's body to possible sensorimotor disturbances.

Sociability: Interacting With Others in an Interactive Narrative Environment

Interactive narrative environments can be very sociable worlds, especially in advanced virtual environments. We define a medium (especially the interface) as sociable when two or more individuals interact with each other *through* the mediated environment represented in the interface (e.g., networked games, collaborative virtual environments) or *around* the interface (e.g., multiple viewers of a TV set sharing/commenting on the experience), especially when that interaction is synchronous and in real time. The more individuals can interact with each other at the same time, the more sociable the medium. It should be noted that the medium's contribution to the quality of the interaction is usually a function of the level of the mediated embodiment and/or the intelligence of the interface. So sociability in interactive technology is related to the (1) number of interacting users, and (2) level of synchronicity.

Media may be sociable when people interact *around* the use of the medium, such as in film, although clearly this is passive interaction. When you are at a film you are in a social setting around the medium. You are a member of an audience and you are made aware of the others' emotions and responses to the narrative experience (i.e., their laughter, silence, applause, etc). But you do not interact with the people on the screen (inside the medium) or through the medium to some remote individual. Whereas film and video may be viewed in groups, individual interaction is rare and very rarely occurs inside the narrative space, with some notable exceptions such as the elaborate costumed rituals that audiences to *The Rocky Horror Picture Show* created in the 1970s (*The Rocky Horror Picture Show*, 1998).

Multi-user virtual environments allow multiple users to experience the narrative world both through and around the media interface. In fact, some systems can support more than a thousand simultaneous users interacting synchronously as a character inside some large, quasinarrative virtual environment.

The property of sociability is one of the key defining features of interactive narrative. In older noninteractive media such as books and television, most dramatic narratives have held a clear boundary between the author, actor, and audience. In interactive media this becomes a fuzzy boundary. The crossing of this boundary is a both a source of pleasure and problems for narrative.

To become an interactor in a narrative experience is to have a role. Highly social interactive narrative experience most resembles other human pursuits involving role playing. It is perhaps not surprising that the first quasinarrative interactive mediated experiences evolved from role playing games such as Dungeons and Dragons (Cook, Tweet, & Williams, 2000).

Implications of Increased Sociability on Interactive Narrative Experience

A highly sociable interface presents problems for narrative structure. If the interactors have a certain amount of freedom, then each contributes to the plot and to characterization; the two key components of narrative, plot and character, must be negotiated. As a result, rule structures, often similar to games, control certain aspects of the narrative such as character motivation, the relative "powers" of a character (i.e., social status, work role, gender, physical power, and "otherworldly" attributes) and the setting for the action, among other constraints. One of the problems of such a design is the need to sometimes jump in and out of character to arbitrate, remove an obstacle, or communicate an understanding. This movement in and out of the narrative space tends to interfere with the sense of presence; the movement is "a constant negotiation of the story line and also of the boundary between the consensual halluncination and the actual world" (Murray, 1997, p. 115).

Narrative often portrays life at the extremes. Turkle's (Turkle, 1984, 1997) interviews with role players suggest that role playing environments allow individuals to express thought, feel emotion, and engage in behaviors that are not easily accessed in everyday life (see also Murray, 1997). Observing and playing roles may have an important formative role in social cognition (Bandura, 1985). Role playing narrative virtual environments have some potential value in socialization, training, and counseling. In the past, narrative forms such as the "morality play" have been used to instruct about right behavior as well as to entertain. The more sophisticated the system, the more likely that the role playing has some organizational function such as training or collaborative work. For example, immersive virtual reality systems are often used in military simulations and "team building" environments (Crane, 1999; Dacunto & Prybyla, 1997; Neyland, 1997; Singhal & Zyda, 1999).

Does occupying a social role in a virtual environment give you significant insight into the existence of another? Does it support empathy (Zillman, 1991)? Jaron Lanier, a pioneer of virtual reality technology, believed that interactive virtual environments could give insight into other people's realities (Lanier & Biocca, 1992), a classic function of narrative. He used to demonstrate his pioneering system to male Silicon Valley executives. When they passed a strategically placed mirror in the virtual environment, the blue suited executives were often shocked to find that their virtual body was that of a chubby, homeless, bag lady! As suggested by this example and the work above on distortions of the body in highly embodied systems, one's virtual body, the interactor's "avatar" inside the virtual environment, may influence both judgments of others and of oneself (Nowak, 2000).

In summary, the evolution of interactive technologies toward higher levels of sociability has significant implications for the psychology of narrative. From a design viewpoint, the sudden crowding of the virtual stage by audience members-turned-interactor presents significant challenges to producing recognizable and satisfying narratives. Turning the audience into role playing interactors strikes at the very heart of human identity exploration, experimentation, and formation. As environments increase in their level of mediated environment, the psychological impact of role playing may be heightened. The intelligence of the environment can also interact with sociability, so we now turn to this aspect of interface evolution.

Interface Intelligence: Responding Meaningfully to the Interactor's Actions

Consider the dimension of interface intelligence. Over time, computer interfaces are evolving to incorporate progressively higher levels of intelligence. The interface has intelligence ("interactivity"), when it can sense its environment (usually the user), process the information within some representational or logical scheme, and respond in physically or socially appropriate and varied ways to the environment (i.e., user behavior). The interface is perceived as "more intelligent" when its responses are more varied, quicker, and perceived as more physically or socially appropriate or effective.

For the purpose of illustration, let's again contrast the book interface with evolving families of interactive interfaces. It is true that books are written by intelligent people and filled with intelligent information. But considered as interfaces and our definition of intelligence, books are very unintelligent. Why? Books do not sense, respond to, or adapt to the user.

Now let's consider intelligence in an interface. Because early computer interfaces were text-based, there has been a historic tendency to think of the computer as a "talking brain" (Pratt, 1987). This is one form of interface intelligence. But it misses many other ways in which an interface displays intelligence. The "talking brain" view of computer intelligence only emphasizes one aspect of the simulation of intelligent beings, and misses the application of intelligence to the computer simulation of the physical dynamics of the nonvirtual world. For example, an intelligent virtual environment may simulate a virtual room where objects obey the rules of gravity. In virtual worlds, gravity is produced by intelligence, not physics!

Intelligence lies at the very heart of the idea of interactivity, a unidimensional concept that is best replaced by reference to multidimensional patterns of sensorimotor interaction. Whether simulating a talking agent or the laws of gravity, the machine intelligence must link its sensor inputs intelligently to its effector outputs (displays) in physically and socially appropriate and meaningful ways. Desktop computers can display moderate to high levels of intelligence depending on the way they sense the user and make use of that information to alter the display. Immersive virtual environments, especially those with sophisticated agent technologies, incorporate comparatively higher levels of interface intelligence. Virtual environments are continuously recalculated, with the user's perspective tracked. The display is continuously updated to account for the user's motions and actions in the environment.

In summary, in narrative virtual environments interface intelligence is used to:

1. Link interactor's motor inputs (e.g., head movements) perceptually and meaningfully to sensory displays or outputs (e.g., a change in the translation or rotation of the user's visual perspective on the virtual room) (e.g., Barfield & Furness, 1995; Durlach & Mavor, 1994).

2. Simulate the physics and dynamics of virtual inanimate objects and process (e.g., gravity, object deformation, fluid dynamics of water wave action), biological entities and process (e.g., simulated plant growth), as well as animate body motion (e.g., Foley et al., 1999).

3. Animate the physical and social behavior of intelligent agents in response to the virtual environment and interactor behavior (Cassel et al., 1999; Chorafas, 1997; Magnenat-Thalmann et al., 1998; Reeves & Nass, 1996).

4. Provide an "intelligent playwright," i.e., the control of narrative storylines and the meaningful unfolding of events (Laurel, 1991).

Implications of Increased Intelligence for Narrative Experience

Of the many applications of intelligence to interactive narratives, none has more compelling psychological implications then the interactors' perception and response to embodied agents. The engineering design and specification of embodied agents relies very strongly on psycholinguistic, social psychological, and communication research (e.g., Cassell et al., 2000; Picard, 1997; Reeves & Nass, 1996). Although there are a number of interesting psychological issues in the engineering of agents, we focus on the interactor's psychological responses to their interactions with agents in virtual environments, especially narrative virtual environments.

Three key sets of issues have been the focus of research: (1) what minimum stimuli are needed for an interaction to be perceived as social and intelligent (i.e., to be a "believable agent"), (2) what differences are there between an interactor's social perceptions of virtual humans who are intelligent agents (i.e., controlled by a computer program, versus those that are avatars, i.e., controlled by a human intelligence), and (3) what is needed to make interaction with an intelligent artificial intelligence indistinguishable from an interaction with a human intelligence?

Research from earlier work in film animation suggests that very impoverished stimuli can elicit perceptions of emotion and personality (Bordwell, 1985). It appears that a similar principle applies to the interactive realm. A program of research by Cliff Nass and Byron Reeves (Reeves & Nass, 1996) suggests that interactants tend to respond socially to computers in general, and more important, appear to apply the same social cognitive rules to any stimuli that behave socially. Replicating various social psychological studies in which two humans are interacting, but substituting a computer for one of the human interactants, they consistently find the same results. It appears that human interactants apply the same social rules to artificially intelligent agents, including being polite to them. Furthermore, some of these social responses have been achieved with either primitive stimuli and/or primitive programmed intelligence (e.g., a linear fixed set of text responses). Reeves and Nass' work suggests that users will respond to stimuli "as if it were human" even when they know they are interacting with an artificial intelligence.

This has important implications for responses to agent characters in interactive narratives. It suggests that the same kind of strong emotional responses that are found in film and animation can be easily achieved in interactive settings. But, furthermore, the interactant is likely to use and ascribe highly complex mental models of intentionality, personality, and person perception to interactive agents, even in cases when the cues of intentionality and personality are minimal, and when there is clearly no personality or intelligence present other than in the most primitive programming use of such terms.

The larger question of long term interaction with artificial characters has not been adequately studied. The research on parasocial interaction with film and television characters, anthropomorphization of interactions with animals, as well as perceived "relationships" with noncorporeal agents such as "gods" and "spirits" suggests that the tendency to apply human mental models to all manner of interactions is widespread and ancient. Work by Turkle (Turkle, 1984, 1997) suggests possible concern with "interpersonal relationships" with agents in which the interactant exercises inordinate amounts of control, especially concern about the generalization of inappropriate interaction patterns to "real" human interactions.

Ubiquity of Access: Connecting Users to Narrative Virtual Environments Anywhere in Space and Time

When we consider ubiquity of access, we consider when and where users have interactive narrative experiences, the spatial and social context of narrative experience. Consider an interface as a window or port to the narrative world. When and where is the port attached to the senses to trigger a narrative experience? There are two ways in which an interface can facilitate more ubiquity of access: (1) we can have copies of the interface in many locations, or (2) it can be mobile and portable. Film theaters carry narrative experiences but have very low ubiquity of access. We can only access their information in a few places in each town, and they are not easily or practically portable. TV sets can display the same information as film (at lower levels of embodiment) in more places, almost every home in America. Satellite phones also have very high levels of ubiquity. Although there are few of them, each user is able to access the telecommunication network from any place on earth. In general, ubiquity of access and level of mediated embodiment are negatively correlated. The user usually has to surrender some level of embodiment (e.g., the small screen size of a portable TV) to gain great ubiquity of access.

Effect of Ubiquitous Computing on Narrative Experience

All narrative experience is situated. There is an interaction of narrative experience and the physical and social setting in which the medium is located, and the experience is "consumed." When this issue is studied, the issue of attention is usually of central concern (Hancock & Meshkayi, 1988; Johnston & Dark, 1986) although there have been some studies looking at the effect of properties of the physical environment on the sense of presence in the mediated environment (e.g., Kim & Biocca, 1997). Books and portable radios have been ubiquitous, but these media have minimal intelligence and are not social; they are "unaware" of their physical setting and are noninteractive.

Ubiquity becomes particularly important when the user is connected to a system that is mobile, has higher levels of mediated embodiment, intelligent awareness of some aspects of physical environment, and, finally, is social. This is true of some mobile systems, such as wearable computers, and media that mix virtual environments and physical environments, such as augmented reality (Barfield & Caudell, 2000). In a wearable computing augmented reality system, the narrative characters and objects can appear superimposed in the physical environment. Perceptually and psychologically there is a tight interaction of the physical and narrative worlds. At the time of this writing, there were only a few systems in place and, certainly, to our knowledge no empirical studies of narrative experiences using such systems.

CONCLUSIONS

We have presented a view of interactive technologies and some potential consequences of interactive narrative experience. We have stressed the importance of looking not at the specific configuration of computer interfaces, but at the evolutionary trends in interactive technologies. One fundamental goal of media technologies and some narrative environments is the elimination of the perception of mediation, and the creation of simulation environments that deliver very high levels of presence. Embedded in the evolution of media is the goal of ubiquity and sociability, that is that the interfaces are eventually to be used anywhere to interact not only with fixed narrative but with many other users in worldwide, interactive quasiritualistic narrative environments. If the reader has followed this argument closely, you may have noticed that the endpoint of the evolution appears to be the embedding of narrative structures into everyday life; and kinds of interaction in environments in which interactors enact a series of "roles" that steadily blur the boundaries between social roles and "real" action and between narrative roles and play. In some ways this portrayal of the evolution of interactive narrative is like a vision of the past: a world of ritual where narratives are enacted by participants in a ritualistic environment. For example, consider the dancing shaman wearing an eagle mask as he attempts to cure a sick child by enacting a tale of "eagle and the fish." Is this an enactment of narrative or a medical procedure? Where is the boundary between the narrative environment and the physical environment? Now transpose this possibility to a worldwide telecommunication system supporting mobile, immersive augmented reality systems, and this observation by Murray takes on additional meaning:

> We are all gradually becoming part of a worldwide repertory company, available to assume roles in ever more complex participatory stories. Little by little we are discovering the conventions of participation that will constitute the fourth wall of this virtual theater, the expressive gestures that will deepen and preserve the enchantment of immersion. (Murray, 1997, p. 125)

ACKNOWLEDGMENTS

I gratefully acknowledge the help of the following people in the preparation of earlier stages of this manuscript: Duncan Rowland, Eric Maslowski, and Jin Kim. This work was funded in part by a grant from the MSU Foundation.

REFERENCES

Akiyama, K., Tetsutani, N., Ishibashi, M., Ichinose, S., Hiorshi, Y. (1991). Consideration of three-dimensional visual communication systems. *IEEE Journal on selected areas in communications, 9*(4), 555–560.

Alessi, S. M. (1988). Fidelity in the design of instructional simulations. *Journal of Computer-based Instruction, 15*(2), 40–47.

Allport, G. W. (1955). *Becoming*. New Haven, CT: Yale University Press.

Arthur, K. (2000). *Effects of field of view on task performance with head-mounted displays*. Chapel Hill: University of North Carolina.

Baltzley, D. R., Kennedy, R. S., Berbaum, K. S., Lilienthal, M. G., & Gower, D. W. (1989). The time course of postflight simulator sickness symptoms. *Aviation, Space, and Environmental Medicine, 60*, 1043–1048.

Bandura, A. (1985). *Social foundations of thought and action: A social cognitive theory*. New York: Prentice Hall.

Barfield, W., & Caudell, T. (2000). *Fundamentals of wearable computers and augmented reality*. Mahwah, NJ: Lawrence Erlbaum Associates.

Barfield, W., & Furness, T. A. (1995). *Virtual environments and advanced interface design*. New York: Oxford University Press.

Barfield, W., Zeltzer, B., Sheridan, T., & Slater, M. (1995). Presence and perfomance within virtual environments. In W. Barfield & T. A. Furness (Eds.), *Virtual environments and advanced interface design* (pp. 473–513). New York: Oxford University Press.

Barret, G. V., & Thornton, C. L. (1968). Relationship between perceptual style and simulator sickness. *Journal of Applied Psychology, 52*(4), 304–308.

Biocca, F. (1992). Will simulator sickness slow down the diffusion of virtual environment technology? *Presence, 1*(3), 258–264.

Biocca, F. (1997). The cyborg's dilemma: Embodiment in virtual environments. *Journal of Computer-mediated Communication, 3*(2), www.ascusc.org/jcmc

Biocca, F., & Delaney, B. (1995). Immersive virtual reality technology. In F. Biocca & M. Levy (Eds.), *Communication in the age of virtual reality* (pp. 51–126). Mahwah, NJ: Lawrence Erlbaum Associates.

Biocca, F., & Levy, M. (1995). *Communication in the age of virtual reality*. Mahwah, NJ: Lawrence Erlbaum Associates.

Biocca, F., & Nowak, K. (2001). Plugging the body into the telecommunication system: Mediated embodiment, media interfaces, and social virtual environments. In C. Lin & D. Atkin (Eds.), *Communication technology and society: Audience adoption and uses of new media* (pp. 407–447). Mount Waverly, V.I.: Hampton Press.

Biocca, F., & Rolland, J. (1998). Virtual eyes can rearrange your body: Adaptation to visual displacement in see-through, head-mounted displays. *Presence: Teleoperators and Virtual Environments, 7*(3), 262–277.

Boothe, R. G. (1994). Biological Perception of Self-motion. *Behavioral and Brain Sciences, 17*(2).

Bordwell, D. (1985). *Narration in the fiction film*. London: Methuen.

Bryson, S. (1996, May). Virtual reality in scientific visualization. *Communications of the ACM, 39*(5), 62–72.

Campbell, J. (1998). The body image and self-consciousness. In J. L. Bermudez, A. Marcel, & N. Eilan (Eds.), *The body and the self* (pp. 29–42). Cambridge, MA: MIT Press.

Cantor, J. (1994). Fright reactions to mass media. In J. Bryant & D. Zillmann (Eds.), *Media effects: Advances in theory and research* (pp. 505–540). Hillsdale, NJ: Lawrence Erlbaum Associates.

Cantor, N., & Kihlstrom, J. K. (1987). *Personality and Social Influence.* Englewood Cliffs, NJ: Prentice-Hall.

Casali, J. G., & Wierwille, W. W. (1986). Vehicular simulation-induced sickness, Volume III: Survey of etiological factors and research facility requirements. [*FOR Technical Report No. 8503. NTSC TR 86-012.* Orlando, FL: Naval Training Systems Center.]

Cassell, J., Bickmore, T., Billinghurst, M., Campbell, L., Chang, K., Vilhjalmsson, H., & Yan, H. (1999, May). *Embodiment in conversational interfaces.* Paper presented at the CHI99 Conference Proceedings: Human factors in computing systems, Pittsburgh, PA.

Cassell, J., Sullivan, J., Prevost, S., & Churchill, E. (2000). *Embodied conversational agents.* Cambridge, MA: MIT Press.

Chorafas, D. N. (1997). *Agent Technology Handbook.* New York: McGraw Hill.

Christel, M. G. (1994). The role of visual fidelity in computer-based instruction. *Human-Computer Interaction, 9,* 183–223.

Cook, M., Tweet, J., & Williams, S. (2000). *Dungeons and dragons players handbook.* San Francisco, CA: Wizards of the Coast.

Cooley, C. (1902). *Human Nature and the Social Order.* New York: Scribner.

Crane, P. (1999). Implementing distributed mission training. *Communications of the ACM, 42*(9), 90–94.

Csikszentmihalyi, M. (1990). *Flow: The psychology of optimal experience.* New York: Harper Perennial.

Csikszentmihalyi, M. (1996). *Creativity, flow and the psychology of discovery and invention.* New York: Harper Perennial.

Dacunto, L. J., & Prybyla, D. J. (1997, December). Combat simulations in U.S. Army training and testing. *Proceedings of the conference on winter simulation* (pp. 896–902). Paper presented at the WSC '96. Coronado, CA.

Dill, K., & Kill, J. (1998). Video game violence: A review of the literature. *Aggression and violent behavior, 3*(4), 407–428.

Durlach, N., & Mavor, A. (1994). *Virtual reality: Scientific and technological challenges.* Washington: National Research Council.

Durlach, N., & Mavor, A. (1998, September 9). *Presence in shared virtual environments and virtual togetherness.* [On-line], Available: http://www.cs.ucl.ac.uk/staff/m.slater/BTWorkshop/durlach.htm

Ebenholtz, S. M. (1992). Motion sickness and oculomotor systems in virtual environments. *Presence, 1*(3), 302–305.

Ellis, S. R. (1996). Presence of Mind: A Reaction to Thomas Sheridan's "Further Musings on the Psychophysics of Presence." *Presence, 5*(2/Spring), 247–259.

Ellis, S. R., Dorighi, N. S., Menges, R. M., Adelstein, B. D., & Joacoby, R. H. (1997). In search of equivalence classes in subjects scales of reality. In M. Smith, G. Salvendy. & R. Koubek (Eds.), *Design of computing systems: Social and ergonomic considerations* (pp. 873–876). Amsterdam, Netherlands: Elseveir.

Ferren, B. (1997). *Keynote speech.* Paper presented at the SIGGRAPH, division of the Association for Computing Machinery, Orlando.

Foley, J. D., Dam, A. V., Feiner, S. K., Hughes, J., & Philips, R. (1999). *Computer graphics.* New York: Addison Wesley.

Gergen, K. J. (1971). *The concept of self.* New York: Holt, Rinehart and Winston.

Gerrig, R. (1993). *Experiencing narrative worlds.* New Haven, CT: Yale University Press.

Gibson, J. J. (1966). *The senses considered as perceptual systems.* Boston, MA: Houghton-Mifflin.

Gibson, J. J. (1979). *The ecological approach to visual perception.* Boston, MA: Houghton-Mifflin.

Gilkey, R. H., & Weisenberger, J. H. (1995). The sense of presence for the suddenly deaf adult: Implications for virtual environments. *Presence, 4*(4), 357–363.
Goffman, E. (1963). *Behavior in public places: Notes on the social organization of gatherings.* New York: The Free Press.
Griffiths, M. (1998). Violent video games and aggression: A review of the literature. *Aggression and violent behavior, 4*(2), 203–212.
Gunter, B. (1994). The question of media violence. In J. Bryant & D. Zillmann (Eds.), *Media effects: Advances in theory and research* (pp. 163–211). Hillsdale, NJ: Lawrence Erlbaum Associates.
Hancock, P. A., & Meshkayi, N. (Eds.). (1988). *Human mental workload.* Amsterdam, Netherlands: North-Holland.
Hatada, T., Sakata, H., & Kusaka, H. (1980). Psychophysical analysis of the "sensation of reality" induced by a visual wide-field display. *SMPTE Journal, 89*(560–569).
Hawkins, D. G. (1995). Virtual reality and passive simulators: The future of fun. In F. Biocca & M. Levy (Eds.), *Communication in the age of virtual reality* (pp. 159–190). Mahwah, NJ: Lawrence Erlbaum Associates.
Hays, R. T., & Singer, M. J. (1989). *Simulation fidelity in training system design: Bridging the gap between reality and training.* New York: Springer-Verlag.
Heeter, C. (1992). Being There: The subjective experience of presence. *Presence, 1*(2), 262–271.
Heilig, M. (1992/1955). El cine de futro: The cinema of the future. *Presence, 1*(3), 279–294.
Heim, M. (1993). *The metaphysics of virtual reality.* New York.
Held, R. M., & Durlach, N. I. (1992). Telepresence. *Presence, 1*(1), 109–112.
Hendrix, C., & Barfield, W. (1996). Presence within virtual environments as a function of visual display parameters. *Presence, 5*(3), 274–289.
Hettinger, L. J., Berbaum, K. S., Kennedy, R. S., Dunlap, W. P., & Nolan, M. D. (1990). Vection and simulator sickness. *Military Psychology, 2*(3), 171–181.
Ho, C. B. C., Slater, M., Durlach, N., & Srinivasan, M. A. (1998, September). An experiment on the influence of haptic communication on the sense of being together. Paper presented at the Presence conference. London. Available: http://www.cs.ucl.ac.uk/staff/mslater/BTWorkshop/TouchExp/index.htm [1998, September 9].
Hochberg, J. (1986). Representation of motion and space in video and cinematic displays. In K. R. Boff, L. Kaufmann, & J. P. Thomas (Eds.), *Handbook of perception and human performance* (Vol. 2, pp. 22/21–22/64). New York: Wiley.
Hullfish, K. (1996). *Virtual Reality Monitoring: How Real is Virtual Reality?* Unpublished master's thesis, University of Washington, Seattle, Washington.
Ijsselseijn, W., & de Ridder, H. (1998, September 9). Measuring Temporal Variations in Presence, [On-line], Available: http://www.tue.nl/ipo/people/ijsselseijn/btpapter.htm
Ijsselseijn, W., de Ridder, H., Hamberg, R., Bouwhuis, D., & Freeman, J. (1998). Perceived depth and the feeling of presence in 3DTV. *Displays, 18*, 207–214.
Johnston, W. A., & Dark, V. J. (1986). Selective Attention. *Annual Review of Psychology, 37*, 43–75.
Kennedy, R. S., Allgood, G.O., Van Hoy, B.W., & Lilienthal, M. G. (1987). Motion sickness symptoms and postural changes following flights in motion-based flight trainers. *Journal of Low Frequency Noise and Vibration, 6*(4), 147–154.
Kennedy, R. S., & Fowlkes, J. E. (1992). Simulator sickness in polygenic and polysymptomatic: Implications for research. *International Journal of Aviation Psychology, 2*(1), 23–38.
Kennedy, R. S., Hettinger, L. J., & Lilienthal, M. G. (1987). Simulator sickness. In G. Crampton (Ed.), *Motion and space sickness,* (317–341). Boca Raton, FL: CRC Press.

Kihlstrom, J. K., & Cantor, N. (1984). Mental Representations of the Self. *Advances in Experimental Social Psychology, 17*, 1–48.
Kihlstrom, J. F., & Klein, S. B. (1994). The self as a knowledge structure. In R. W. Wyer, Jr. & T. K. Srull (Eds.), *Handbook of Social Cognition: Vol. 1. Basic Processes* (pp. 153–208). Hillsdale, NJ: Lawrence Erlbaum Associates.
Kim, T., & Biocca, F. (1997). Telepresence in television. *Journal of computer-mediated communication, 3*(2), http://www.ascusc.org/jcmc/vol3/issue2/).
Klein, S. B., & Loftus, J. (1990). The Role of Abstract and Exemplar-based Knowledge in Self Judgements: Implications for a Cognitive Model of the Self. *Advances in Social Cognition, 3*, 131–139.
Kolasinski, E. M. (1995, May). *Simulator Sickness in Virtual Environments*. Alexandria, VA: U.S. Army Research Institute for the Behavioral and Social Sciences, Department of the Army.
Kubey, R., & Csikszentmihalyi, M. (1990). *Television and the quality of life: How viewing shapes everyday experience*. Hillsdale, NJ: Lawrence Erlbaum Associates.
Lanier, J., & Biocca, F. (1992). An insider's view of the future of virtual reality. *Journal of Communication, 42*(4), 56–83.
Laurel, B. (1991). *Computers as theatre*. Reading, MA: Addison-Wesley.
Lauria, R. (1997). Virtual reality: An empirical-metaphysical testbed. *Journal of computer-mediated communication, 3*(2), (http://www.ascusc.org/jcmc/vol3/issue2/).
Lombard, M., Ditton, T. B., Grabe, M. E., & Reich, R. (1994, July). Direct reponse to television: The role of screen size. Paper presented at the annual conference of the International Communication Association. Sydney, Australia.
Lombard, M., & Ditton, T. B. (1997). At the heart of it all: The concept of presence. *Journal of Computer-Mediated Communication, 3*(2), (http://www.ascusc.org/jcmc /vol3/issue2/).
Loomis, J. M. (1992). Distal attribution and presence. *Presence: Teleoperators and Virtual Environments, 1*(1), 113–119.
Magnenat-Thalmann, M., Kalra, P., & Escher, M. (1998, May). *Face to Virtual Face*. Proceedings of the IEEE, Volume 86(5), 870–883.
Markus, H., & Ruvolo, A. (1989). Possible selves: Personalized representations of goals. In L.A. Pervin (Ed). *Goal concepts in personality and social psychology*, (pp. 211–241). Hillsdale, NJ: Lawrence Erlbaum Associates.
McCauley, M. E., & Sharkey, T. J. (1992). Cybersickness: Perception of self-motion in virtual environments. *Presence, 1*(3), 311–318.
Mead, G. H. (1934). *Mind, self, and society*. Chicago: University of Chicago Press.
Meyer, K., Applewhite, H., & Biocca, F. (1992). A Survey of Position Trackers in Virtual Reality Systems. *Presence, 1*(2), 173–201.
Meyers, P., & Biocca, F. (1992). The elastic body image: An experiment on the effect of advertising and programming on body image distortions in young women. *Journal of Communication, 42*(3), 108–133.
Minsky, M. (1980). Telepresence. *Omni, 2*, 44–52.
Mulbach, L., Bocker, M., & Prussog, A. (1995). Telepresence in videocommunications: A study on stereoscopy and individual eye contact. *Human Factors, 37*(2), 290–305.
Munsterberg, H. (1916). *The Photoplay: A Psychological Study*. New York: D. Appleton & Co.
Murray, J. (1997). *Hamlet on the Holodeck: The future of narrative in cyberspace*. New York: Free Press.
Neyland, D. L. (1997). *Virtual Combat: A Guide to Distributed Interactive Simulation*. New York: Stackpole Books.
Nowak, K. (2000). *The influence of anthropmorphism on mental models of agents and avatars in social virtual environments*. Unpublished dissertation, Michigan State University, East Lansing.

Nowak, K., & Biocca, F. (1999, August). *"I THINK THERE IS SOMEONE ELSE HERE WITH ME!": The Role of the Virtual Body in the Sensation of Co-presence with Other Humans and Artificial Intelligences in Advanced Virtual Environments.* Paper presented at the Cognitive Technology Conference, San Francisco, CA.

Pausch, R., Proffitt, D., & Williams, G. (1997). *Quantifying immersion in virtual reality.* Paper presented at the Computer Graphics Proceedings, Annual conference series/ACM Siggraph, Los Angeles.

Perse, E. M., Burton, P. L., Kovner, E. S., Lears, M. E., & Sen, R. J. (1992). Predicting computer-mediated communication in a college class. *Communication Research Reports, 9*(2), 161–170.

Picard, R. (1997). *Affective computing.* Cambridge, MA: MIT Press.

Pratt, V. (1987). *Thinking machines: The evolution of artificial intelligence / Vernon Pratt.* Oxford, UK: Basil Blackwell.

Prothero, J. D., Hoffman, H. G., Parker, D. E., Furness III, T. A., & Wells, M. J. (1998). *Foreground/Background manipulation affect presence.* Seattle, WA: Human Interface Laboratory, University of Washington.

Ramesh, R., & Andrews, D. H. (1999). Distributed mission training: Teams, virtual reality, and real-time networking. *Communications of the ACM, 42*(9), 64–67.

Reason, J. T. (1975). *Motion sickness.* London: Academic Press.

Reeves, B. (1991). *"Being There": Television as a natural versus symbolic experience.* (Unpublished manuscript). Stanford, CA: Institute for Communication Research.

Reeves, B., & Nass, C. (1996). *The media equation: How people treat computers, telelevison, and new media like real people and places.* Cambridge, UK: Cambridge University Press.

Rheingold, H. (1991). *Virtual reality.* New York: Summit Books.

The Rocky Horror Picture Show (1998/2000, May 5). [On-line], Available: http://www.rockyhorror.com/

Roehl, B. (1999). Multi-user virtual environment systems. *VRNews, 5*, 10–16.

Rosenberg, M. (1986). Self-concept from middle childhood through adolescence. *Psychological Perspectives on the Self, 3*, 107–135.

Rosenberg, S., & Gara, M. A. (1985). The Multiplicity of Personal Identity. *Review of Personality and Social Psychology, 6*, 87–113.

Sartre, J. P. (1956). *Being and Nothingness.* New York: Washington Square Press.

Shapiro, M., & McDonald, D. (1995). I'm not a real doctor, but I play one in virtual reality: Implications of virtual reality for judgements about reality. In F. Biocca & M.Levy (Eds.), *Communication in the age of virtual reality* (pp. 323–346). Mahwah, NJ: Lawrence Erlbaum Associates.

Sheridan, T. (1992). Musings on telepresence and virtual presence. *Presence, 1*(1), 120–126.

Shneiderman, B. (1998). *Designing the user interface: Strategies for effective human-computer interaction.* Reading, MA: Addison-Wesley.

Short, J., Williams, E., & Christie, B. (1976). *The social psychology of telecommunications.* London: John Wiley & Sons.

Sims, K. (1994, July). Evolving Virtual Creatures. Orlando, FL: ACM SIGGRAPH.

Singhal, S., & Zyda, M. (1999). *Networked virtual environments: Design and implementation.* New York: Addison-Wesley.

Snygg, D., & Combs, A. W. (1949). *Individual Behavior.* New York: Harper & Row.

Steuer, J. (1995). Defining virtual reality: Dimensions determining telepresence. In F. Biocca & M. Levy (Eds.), *Communication in the age of virtual reality* (pp. 33–56). Mahwah, N.J.: Lawrence Erlbaum Associates.

Stone, B. (1993). Concerns raised about eye strain in VR systems. *Real Time Graphics, 2*(4), 1–3, 6, 13.

Sutherland, I. (1965, May). *The ultimate display.* Paper presented at the Proceedings of the International Federation of Information Processing Congress. New York, NY.

Tromp, J. (1995, December). *Telepresence and immersion: The cognitive factors of embodiment and interaction in virtual environments.* Paper presented at the First Annual conference of the Fieve Group, Framework for Immersive Virtual Environments, London, UK.

Turkle, S. (1984). *The second self: Computers and the human spirit.* New York: Simon and Schuster.

Turkle, S. (1997). *Life on the Screen: Identity in the Age of the Internet.* New York: Touchstone.

Welch, R. B. (1978). *Perceptual modification: Adapting to altered sensory environments.* New York: Academic Press.

Welch, R. B. (1998). *Adapting to telesystems.* Unpublished manuscript. Moffett Field, CA: NASA -Ames Research Center.

Welch, R. B., Blackmon, T. T., Liu, A., Mellers, B., & Stark, L. (1996). The effects of pictorial realism, delay of visual feedback, and observer interactivity on the subjective sense of presence. *Presence, 5*(3), 263–274.

Welch, R. B., & Warren, D. H. (1986). Intersensory interactions. In K. R. Boff, L. Kaufmann & J. P. Thomas (Eds.), *Handbook of perception and human performance* (Vol. 1, Chapter 24, pp. 1–36). New York: John Wiley.

Witmer, B. G., & Singer, M. J. (1994). *Measuring immersion in virtual environments (1014).* Alexandria, VA: U.S. Army Research Institute for the Behavioral and Social Sciences.

Zeltzer, D. (1992). Autonomy, interaction, and presence. *Presence, 1*(1), 127–132.

Zillmann, D. (1991). Empathy: Affect from bearing witness to the emotions of others. In J. Bryant & D. Zillmann (Eds.), *Responding to the screen: Reception and reaction processes* (pp. 76–87). Hillsdale, NJ: Lawrence Erlbaum Associates.

Zillmann, D., & Bryant, J. (1994). Entertainment as a media effect. In J. Bryant & D. Zillmann (Eds.), *Media effects: Advances in theory and research* (pp. 437–461). Hillsdale, NJ: Lawrence Erlbaum Associates.

II

Real-World Impact of Narratives

6

Controversial Narratives in the Schools

Content, Values, and Conflicting Viewpoints

Joan DelFattore
University of Delaware

The selection of narratives for inclusion in elementary and secondary school textbooks often gives rise to intense ideological debates involving social or cultural content, moral values, and political viewpoints. This chapter discusses several such controversies, all of which reflect at least three overarching questions:

Given that narratives convey not only facts but also attitudes, ideals, and philosophies, what kinds of material should be included in schoolbooks and why? If disagreements arise, who should make the final decision?

- Does exposure to certain types of narrative content influence students' beliefs and behavior? If so, how should that consideration be taken into account in the selection process?
- What types of evidence are needed to demonstrate that a given narrative or set of narratives would have a particular behavioral impact on the students?

To suggest just one example for the sake of illustration, is it important for students to be exposed to narratives that show people of different racial groups? If so, why? There are many possible responses to this question, such as the contention that depicting white European-Americans to the exclusion of all other ethnicities would, in and of itself, assert the superiority of that group. Because this book deals with the impact of narratives, however, let us focus on the frequently made allegation that reading multicultural narratives will influence students toward a more positive attitude toward diversity. How do we know that that is true? Is the contention self-evident or does it require proof?

To many scholars, such an association between narratives and attitudes could not be taken for granted but would have to be supported by studies showing that the inclusion of multicultural narratives does indeed have the alleged effect on students' values. Appendix A lists a variety of works that set out to demonstrate, in one way or another, that students' attitudes toward race are affected either by certain narratives *per se* or by some particular method of presenting them. Purely for the sake of argument, however, suppose that there were no studies demonstrating the relationship between diversity in the selection of literature and students' responses to race. What then? Would the absence of such proof make it acceptable to exclude narratives about anyone other than white European-Americans, at least until someone did a controlled scientific study demonstrating the behavioral or attitudinal impact of greater diversity?

Or should other considerations, such as appeals to social justice, common sense, or political expediency, prevail? This chapter explores such questions by considering the types of narrative content that are most often challenged for ideological reasons, the justifications offered by protesters who want certain materials removed, and the standards employed in resolving these disagreements.

May It Please the Court

If English professors were polled about the way we think disputes over controversial narratives should be settled, we would probably raise such questions as whether the narrative is of high literary quality, whether it occupies an important place in the historical development of its genre, and whether it does in fact have the alleged negative impact on students' values and behaviors. The courts, however, almost never approach a disagreement about the inclusion of a particular narrative in the elementary or secondary school curriculum by trying to evaluate the intrinsic merit, importance, or impact of the work itself. Instead, the emphasis is on *who* has the right to make curricular decisions, not on *what* choice is the best one. Typically, legal challenges to instructional materials focus not on literary excellence or historical significance but on such issues as free speech, free exercise of religion, freedom from government establishments of religion, the right of parents to control their children's upbringing, and the power of school boards to determine curriculum. This is not to say that no objective evidence is required in lawsuits that deal with the ideological content of narratives, but the evidence in such cases is directed toward questions of constitutional rights and locus of control, not toward determining whether a given narrative does in fact promote certain values or exercise particular influences over student behavior.

Perhaps the best example of this type of lawsuit is a Tennessee case entitled *Mozert v. Hawkins County Public Schools* (1987), which is notable for the range of narratives it covered and for the unusually extensive mass of testimony and exhibits that documented the protesters' arguments. Space does not permit a detailed discussion of this lawsuit, but a few examples may serve to illustrate the concerns the protesters raised, the kinds of evidence they offered, and the grounds on which the two courts that heard the case based their decisions.[1]

Mozert was filed in 1981 by a Washington-based conservative advocacy group, Concerned Women for America (CWA)[2], on behalf of 10 conservative Christian families from a mountainous rural area in Church Hill, Tennessee. Although the name of a local preacher, Bob Mozert, headed the list of plaintiffs, the protest was organized and led by Vicki Frost, a full-time homemaker and mother of six children. It began when the Hawkins County school district adopted the then-new Holt, Rinehart, and Winston Basic Reading Series for Grades 1 through 6 (Weiss et al., 1980). Frost went through the books brought home by her children and concluded that they contradicted her religious beliefs. She discussed the matter with other members of her fundamentalist Christian church, and nine other families joined her in challenging the books on the grounds that the series promoted a world view they called *secular humanism*. Their definition of the term included such values as independence, critical thinking, nontraditional gender roles, pacifism, evolution, globalism, world unity, tolerance for diversity, religious tolerance, imagination, creativity, vegetarianism, disrespect for authority, acceptance of the occult, multiculturalism, and self-reliance. In their view, secular humanism, thus defined, was a rival religion that represented the polar opposite of their own conservative Christian beliefs.

At first, Frost and the other protesters demanded that the school district stop using the Holt books because, they said, promoting secular humanism over Christianity violated governmental neutrality toward religion. When this attempt failed, they contacted CWA, which provided legal representation for a lawsuit. On the advice of CWA lawyers, the plaintiffs stopped trying to ban the books and sought instead to remove their own children from reading classes while leaving them in school for the rest of the day. Under Tennessee law, they could have taken their children out of the public schools altogether and educated them either in religious schools or at home, and some of them did so for the duration of the lawsuit. They did not, however, accept this option as a long-term solution. The state, they maintained, had an obligation to provide their children with a public education that did not violate their religious beliefs, which could be accomplished either by creating a separate reading program or by excusing their children from reading classes and allowing the parents to find another means of teaching them to read.

In response, the Hawkins County school officials vigorously denied that the Holt books promoted religious views of any kind. They refused to provide separate reading instruction for the plaintiffs' children, arguing that developing and implementing a reading curriculum that was hand-tailored to fit certain religious beliefs would impermissibly entangle the school with the tenets of a particular faith. With regard to the plaintiffs' desire to keep their children out of reading classes, the school officials protested that reading instruction in elementary school, particularly in Grades 1 through 3, is interspersed throughout the entire school day. Indeed, the officials claimed, elementary school children spend so much time learning to read that removing them for that much of the school day would grossly interfere with their education.

The One Right Answer

Because *Mozert* was directed against an entire reading series, the list of complaints was much too long and detailed to be covered here, but a few examples may serve to convey the general sense of the protesters' objections. Among the better known of the challenged narratives was Jack London's short story "To Build a Fire," in which a nameless protagonist decides to go on a long journey alone during a brutal Yukon winter. He accidentally gets his feet wet, and desperate to keep them from freezing, he imprudently builds a fire under a tree bearing a load of snow. The snow falls onto the fire, dousing it and condemning the man to a death that the story describes as a pleasant sleep. According to the Holt teachers' manual, the man's fatal flaw is his lack of imagination, because he neither recognizes his own vulnerability nor envisions what will happen if he builds the fire under the snow-laden tree. The manual also suggests that the man could have saved his own life if only he had exercised more forethought.

According to the plaintiffs, "To Build a Fire" conflicted with their religious beliefs and advanced what they termed the religion of secular humanism by promoting imagination and self-reliance as positive values. "Man's survival," Frost testified, "does not depend upon man's ability to create in his imagination solutions to problems. Man's survival is determined by God."[3] She also objected to the death scene, arguing that its failure to mention heaven or hell was yet another indication that the story focused only on human endeavor and the present world. Moreover, the absence of an eschatological element was, in her view, a way of promoting belief in evolution because it made a man's death resemble that of an animal. "And of course," she said, "when the Christian dies, the born again Christian, he or she goes to be with the Lord.... For those who believe, their security is secured by Jesus Christ in heaven, but for the non-believer, those who have rejected the Lord Jesus Christ, that they will go to hell.... [T]he humanist believes that there is no God, no hereafter, no hope of the eternal, that maybe it's like in this story, you drift off into a sleep, good night, goodbye forever, you're gone."[4]

Frost's main concern, which was shared by the other plaintiffs in *Mozert*, was that "To Build a Fire" and similar stories might have what they considered a negative influence on their children. Among other things, they feared that the children would become disobedient, substituting their own will and judgment for submission to their parents and to God. As Frost pointed out, themes such as independence and critical thinking were not confined to any one story but pervaded the entire reading series, beginning with the primary grades. The teachers' manual for Grade 2, for example, explicitly advocated "teaching the child to become independent and self-reliant." "And the philosophy on this page," she said, "is a religious violation of how that I teach my child from a biblical standpoint. My child is to-my children are to listen to the ways of their mother and their father as unto the Lord, and they are to receive my instruction and my guidance, not to rebel and want to go their own way."[5]

Asked whether her children's behavior had changed as a result of reading the Holt stories, Frost testified that her 7-year-old daughter, Sarah, whom she described as "the meekest of my children," had begun to "demand her way"[6] and to complain if she did not like what her mother served for dinner. Another plaintiff, Alice Mozert, said that her 7-year-old, Sundee, had also shown uncharacteristic willfulness. She had, for example, eaten a candy bar without permission and had then defended herself by stating that she had bought it with her own money. Anecdotal evidence of this kind, based on the unproven assumption that a cause-and-effect relationship existed between the stories and the children's behavior, were the closest the plaintiffs came to demonstrating that the stories had the alleged effects. To them, the fact that the books presented material of this kind was *a priori* evidence that the children's behavior was intended to change in accord with those ideas and would in fact do so.

Good Fences Make Good Neighbors

In addition to opposing stories that promote self-reliance and rational approaches to problem-solving, the *Mozert* plaintiffs challenged the Holt series' emphasis on tolerance and diversity. Among the items to which they objected was a piece by Archibald MacLeish entitled "Fitting Parts into a Whole," which states, "To see the earth as it truly is, small, blue, and beautiful in that eternal silence where it floats, is to see ourselves as riders on the earth together, brothers on that bright loveliness in the eternal cold—brothers who know they are truly brothers."[7] Frost's response was, "All men are not brothers. In the Christian belief, brothers are those who have received Jesus Christ as their Savior, who have been born again, are of the family of God. That's what makes us brothers. We are not brothers of every religion."[8]

For the same reason, Frost objected to a short story entitled "A Visit to Mars," by John Kier Cross. The story includes Martian characters who are able to understand all languages—or rather, to transcend language entirely—by means of mental telepathy. To Frost, presenting universal communication as a positive value contradicted the biblical account of the Tower of Babel, which she interpreted to mean that God had chosen to use linguistic differences to protect American Christians from the false ideas of other cultures. "If all the people in the world speak the same language," she explained, "my child is still a part of the world, but it's the philosophy of the one world language which brings all the people together. And to the Christian, he cannot be enjoined with other peoples in the world in the same way. To the Christian, he is a separate people unto God.... Heathen nations and nations which honor God are not to come together in a one world government. Nations which reject God, according to God Himself, will be turned into hell. He will separate the sheep nations from the goat nations, those who honor him and those who do not."[9]

The plaintiffs' conviction that global unity was a violation of God's will also played a role in their opposition to stories that taught children to be kind to animals. Among other things, they argued that promoting what they saw as a sentimental attitude toward animals contradicted the biblical verses that give humans dominion over the earth and all that moves on it. Moreover, because animals are different from humans, the plaintiffs maintained that teaching children to be kind to things that are "other" might lead to tolerance for false religions, thus ending religious strife. This, they feared, would increase global unity until at last a one-world government would be established. According to their interpretation of the Bible, a one-world government under any rule but that of Jesus would be the reign of the Antichrist and would precipitate the end of the world.

As the foregoing examples illustrate, Frost and the other *Mozert* plaintiffs raised a host of objections to the narratives in the Holt readers. However, the single underlying message was that they did not want their children to be exposed to ideas with which they disagreed. To them, such exposure was a competing influence that contradicted their own teachings and thus confused their children. They regarded as self-evident the premise that presenting such ideas as self-reliance, tolerance, and world unity in a positive way was a form of indoctrination that would affect their children's thinking and behavior. When the school board's lawyer challenged this assertion, the plaintiffs retorted that they had an absolute right to bring up their children as they saw fit. Neither courts nor school officials, they maintained, had any legitimate authority to second-guess their judgment as parents about what would or would not affect their children.

So What Did the Courts Say?

Mozert was heard by a federal district court judge, Thomas Hull, in a nonjury trial. In his decision, he wrote, "The plaintiffs believe that, after reading the entire Holt series, a child might adopt the views of a feminist, a humanist, a pacifist, an anti-Christian, a vegetarian, or an advocate of a 'one-world' government. Plaintiffs sincerely believe that the repetitive affirmation of these philosophical viewpoints is repulsive to the Christian faith—so repulsive that they must not allow their children to be exposed to the Holt series" (*Mozert v. Hawkins County Public Schools*, 1986). Out of deference to these sincere beliefs, he ordered the school district to allow the plaintiffs to teach their children reading at home while sending them to school for the other classes. He also awarded the plaintiffs approximately $50,000 to reimburse them for the cost of sending their children to private schools while the lawsuit was in progress. Clearly, Hull was not primarily concerned with determining whether the plaintiffs had proven their claims about the alleged behavioral impact of the challenged narratives. Indeed, any attempt at an objective analysis of the narratives' influence and value would have been irrelevant, because the central question of the lawsuit was not whether any particular narrative should be taught in the schools but who had the authority to decide what the plaintiffs' children should read.

Dismayed, the school officials turned to the Sixth Circuit Court of Appeals, asking that Judge Hull's ruling be overturned. A year later, in August 1987, a panel of three judges handed down a decision in favor of the school authorities. The appeals court agreed with Hull that the courts' main responsibility was to determine locus of control, but they concluded that he had arrived at the wrong answer to that question. Chief Judge Pierce Lively pointed out that the plaintiffs had failed to show that their children were required to express agreement with the ideas presented in the narratives. "What is absent from this case," he wrote, "is the critical element of compulsion to affirm or deny a religious belief or to engage or refrain from engaging in a practice forbidden or required in the exercise of a plaintiff's religion" (*Mozert v. Hawkins County Public Schools*, 1987). Judge Cornelia Kennedy agreed with Lively that the Hawkins County reading program did not burden the plaintiffs' free exercise of religion, but she found that even if a burden had existed it would have been justified by the school district's interest in promoting critical reading skills. The third judge, Danny Boggs, disagreed with his colleagues' reasoning but voted in favor of the school board as a matter of local control. In his view, the school district could and should have provided alternate readers but federal courts did not have the authority to force it to do so (*Mozert v. Hawkins County Public Schools*, 1987).

This is not to say that no objective evidence is required in lawsuits that deal with the ideological content of narratives, but the evidence in such cases is directed toward questions of constitutional rights and locus of control, not toward determining whether a given narrative does in fact promote certain values or exercise particular influences over student behavior.[10]

Politics, Never Pure and Seldom Simple

Not all disputes about curricular content are decided in courtrooms, and those that are not adjudicated almost always fall within the purview of elected or politically appointed officials, such as state and local school boards, state legislators, governors, and the U.S. Congress. Here, as in the courts, the decision-making process rarely includes scholarly studies involving control groups, double-blind designs, and analyses of dependent variables. On the contrary, it is assumed as a matter of common sense that if, for example, a story shows a happy homosexual couple raising a well-adjusted child, then students reading that narrative will be influenced toward thinking that homosexuality is normal and acceptable. Indeed, if anyone were to suggest designing a study to find out whether reading such stories does in fact have the expected effect on children's attitudes toward homosexuality, that proposal would be derided by populist politicians and grassroots activists as a pointless attempt by ivory-tower elitists to prove something that is obvious. Worse, such a suggestion might be denounced as a cynical effort by prohomosexual effetes to obfuscate the plain truth with intellectualist gobbledygook. To many politicians and grassroots activists, the silliness of academic projects such as these is self-evident. Of course, to scholars who see the rules of evidence differently, it makes perfect sense to question whether popular assumptions are in fact true. From this perspective, it is well worth analyzing the extent to which presenting a certain value in a narrative actually affects the students' attitudes and behaviors. Nevertheless, the reality is that disputes over the ideological content of narratives are far more likely to be resolved according to such principles as "majority rules," "the squeaky wheel gets the grease," and so-called "common sense" (which is sometimes neither) than by means of double-blind controlled studies.

Another characteristic of curriculum controversies that are conducted outside of the courts is that they do not always reach any clear, definitive conclusion. Even if school boards do not remove a book from the schools, either because they decide not to do so or because they do not take up the question, teachers or principals may decide against retaining a text that has become—or may become—the focus of disruption. Alternatively, school officials may try to make a controversy go away by using stalling tactics designed to delay any decision until the protest has lost momentum. Examples of such techniques include the use of parliamentary procedures to delay school board action from month to month; personnel transfers in controversies that center on the actions of a particular teacher, principal, or librarian; and the appointment of a committee to study the issue, after which nothing more is publicly announced unless the protesters return to the fray and demand a response.

Potting Potter

The preceding generalizations about the ways in which curriculum disputes are resolved—or left unresolved—outside of the courts may best be understood by examining two well-publicized recent controversies. The first of these is the uproar that arose when protesters in several states attempted to eliminate J. K. Rowling's highly acclaimed Harry Potter stories from elementary school classrooms. In the series, Harry is a lovable little orphan who patiently bears the ill treatment he receives from Vernon and Petunia Dursley, the aunt and uncle with whom he lives. Although the Dursleys shower their cloddish son, Dudley, with gifts and food, they force Harry to live in a barren attic room and often send him to bed without his supper. His fortunes turn when he discovers that he is in fact a young wizard gifted with impressive magic powers. He delights in attending Hogwarts, a boarding school for student wizards, although he must still spend the summers with his unsympathetic relatives. In an updated version of classic fairytale plots and themes, Harry foils the machinations of the archvillain, Lord Voldemort, with the help of wise counselors, a flying broom, a cloak of invisibility, and other conventions of fantasy literature.

The Harry Potter books, of which there are now four, have become phenomenally popular on both sides of the Atlantic; at one point, all of them appeared together on the *New York Times* best-seller list. They have won several prestigious prizes, notably the Whitbread Children's Book of the Year Award (1999). Rowling was also named Author of the Year at the British Book Awards ceremony in February 2000. The books have become a favorite of children worldwide, causing parents, teachers, and librarians to rave about Rowling's ability to engage the attention of youngsters who are normally reluctant to read. Nevertheless, the series has encountered determined opposition from conservative Christians who claim that it promotes witchcraft, disrespect for authority, depression, rebellion, dishonesty, and violence. Because space does not permit a discussion of each charge, this chapter focuses on the most prevalent one: that the books present satanic elements in a favorable light, thus violating the biblical declaration that all witches are evil.

Parental complaints about the magic elements in the Harry Potter series have met with a mixed reception from school officials in different parts of the country.[11] One reaction is, of course, to remove the books either in response to a local controversy or in the hope of preventing one. According to a story in the *Star Tribune* of Minneapolis, Minnesota, for example, a teacher in nearby Lakeville stopped using the Potter books because of what the principal described as "'less than a handful'" of protesters (Draper, 1999). Similarly, the principal of a school in Tampa, Florida, announced in January 2000 that the school library would retain the one Potter book it already owned[12] but would not order any more. In a press interview, the principal explained why the decision had been made. "It was because of the witchcraft themes," [she] said. "We just knew that we probably had some parents who wouldn't want their children to read these books" (Wynne, 2000). Based on this statement, it appears that not only were Potter foes in Tampa not required to prove their allegations, they did not even have to show up. By the time the principal made that announcement, the nationwide Potter controversy was already well-publicized, and either she was taking preemptive action on the assumption that some of her students' parents were among those who disliked the books, or she had heard from complaining parents privately and was willing to give them what they wanted without requiring them to come forward to justify their views in public.

A controversy that reached a very different outcome took place in the Clarence school district near Buffalo, New York, where parents decried the use of a Potter book on the grounds that "'Cover to cover, it's all about witchcraft'" (Hutchinson, 1999a). Carol Poliner, leader of the protesting parents, argued that witchcraft is a religion that contradicts Christianity, from which it follows that reading the Potter books in public school classes violates governmental neutrality toward religion. Unlike the Lakeville teacher and the Tampa principal discussed above, the Clarence school board refused to ban the book, although it agreed to excuse individual students from the readings. A lawyer whom Poliner consulted then wrote a letter to the Superintendent of Schools calling on the district to cease "'the unlawful and unconstitutional promotion of these religiously oriented books in the classroom" (Hutchinson, 1999b). According to news reports, Poliner is determined to continue opposing the series, which, she fears, could leave children vulnerable to satanistic influences because it "presents witchcraft in a very appealing light" (Hutchinson, 1999b).

Although such disputes routinely include references to "community" values, it is not in fact necessary for the majority of the parents in a school district, or even for a substantial number of them, to raise an outcry before a book is likely to be removed. On the contrary, it takes a very small number of squeaky wheels—and sometimes only one—to bring about the banning of a challenged narrative.

Although many protests of this kind arise spontaneously from the parents' world view, others are generated by newsletters, radio programs, and other communications from advocacy groups warning parents about objectionable material that may be circulating in their schools. Chief among the organizations that took up the crusade against the Potter novels was a Colorado-based group called Focus on the Family.[13] "'This book contains some powerful and valuable lessons about love, courage and the ultimate victory of good over evil,' said Paul Hetrick, spokesman for the organization. 'But these positive elements are packaged in a medium—witchcraft—that is specifically denounced in Scripture.... Other books do what the Harry Potter books do, but from a Christian world view,' he said" (DeVine, 1999). Within days after Focus on the Family began criticizing the Potter novels, a school librarian who had heard the complaints posted a notice on the Internet to warn other librarians against purchasing the books. In this situation, as in the others mentioned here, there was no recourse to scholarly studies about the alleged impact of the books, nor was there a majority vote or a legislative fiat. The books were excluded either because school personnel agreed with the complaints or because they wanted to avoid controversy (Kurtz, 1999).

Unpacking the Protest

No one can deny that the Potter foes are entirely correct in stating that a favorable view of magic permeates the entire series of novels. To be sure, magic can be used for evil purposes or can inadvertently go awry, as it does when one of Harry's friends accidentally turns herself into a cat, but wizardry *per se* is a highly positive value in the series. It is this overall assumption that magic can be both virtuous and fun, rather than any particular scene or event, that rouses the ire of the protesters. Indeed, many of the most outspoken Potter foes see no reason why they should even read the stories, because in their view the undisputed fact that the books make wizardry appear attractive is sufficient to condemn them regardless of any other content they may include. To the protesters, the more virtuous the actions of Harry and his wizard friends are, the more they defy the Bible and encourage children not to fear or avoid witchcraft. They would be far *less* disturbed by stories that depict magic figures as wholly evil than they are by the suggestion that wizards and witches, who are so evil in the sight of God that the Bible tells us not to suffer a witch to live, are really warm friendly people whom one would be proud to know.

Before concluding this summary of the Potter controversy, it should be noted that opposition to magic elements in children's literature is by no means unique to this dispute. A review of past issues of the American Library Association's *Newsletter on Intellectual Freedom* or a scan of the websites listed in the footnote below[14] reveals numerous objections to Halloween stories, fairy tales, *The Wizard of Oz*, Maurice Sendak's books, and other examples of fantasy literature. This issue has also arisen in several lawsuits, including the Hawkins County controversy discussed earlier in this chapter. Among the works challenged in that case was *The Wizard of Oz*, which, as the references in Footnote 14 illustrate, has figured in several controversies. Among other things, Vicki Frost and the other plaintiffs maintained that the workaday real world of Kansas was made to appear inferior to the colorful magic world of Oz. This contrast would, they feared, promote not only satanism but also the use of hallucinogenic drugs that students might perceive as a means of escaping bleak reality.

Room Enough for All

Although *Mozert* and the Harry Potter controversy are based on conservative Christian views, other recent challenges to classroom materials reflect different sensibilities. In the fall of 1998, for example, approximately 60 African-American parents in Brooklyn, New York, vehemently objected when a white teacher used a critically acclaimed children's story, *Nappy Hair* (Herron, 1997), in her third-grade class. The story centers around a little African-American girl whose wise old uncle teaches her to appreciate her African features, especially her hair. The author of *Nappy Hair*, an African-American college professor named Carolivia Herron, said that the book was inspired by her own uncle who had encouraged her to revel in her fluffy, tightly curly hair. As Herron explained, she wrote the book in the belief that people of African descent should celebrate their racial characteristics. Nevertheless, the parents protested that the word "nappy" was derogatory. Expressing suspicion of the motives that might impel a white person to use such a book, they accused the teacher of trying to undermine the self-esteem of her minority students.

Most of the parents who complained about *Nappy Hair* had not read it but were responding to photocopied excerpts, mostly pictures rather than text, that had been distributed by a parent who had found the story among her daughter's school materials. According to the president of District 32's school board, "'When the pages were copied from the book and there was no background information explaining how it was meant, it looks like pictures to degrade African-Americans,' he said. 'The way it looks in black and white is different from the way it looks in the book'" (Holloway, 1998). Other protesters said that they were reacting to the word "Nappy" in the title. The most comprehensive explanation of why the book was offensive came from Cathy Wright, one of the leaders of the group. "'As I began to look through the material and I read different things about how the hair sounds like crunching snow and a lot of different things, it didn't make me feel good about myself,'" she told a *New York Times* reporter. "'And I don't think it really made my daughter feel good about herself.'"

Herron's defense of her book was backed by several New York City school administrators, many of whom are African-American. Among these was Rudy Crew, the Chancellor of Schools, as well as several members of the New York City School Board. Although conceding that *Nappy Hair* could easily be misunderstood and that teachers were not supposed to introduce new material into the curriculum without the principal's permission, the book's defenders argued that some parents had overreacted to the title and to out-of-context pictures without understanding the point of the book as a whole. Nevertheless, *Nappy Hair* remains controversial. A year after the dispute, teachers in Brooklyn and Queens invited Herron to discuss her book with their classes, but the invitation was withdrawn when school officials refused to approve the visit.

Orthodoxy and Revolution: How Textbooks Change

Having considered a few examples of recent disputes over the selection of narratives for classroom use, it might be appropriate to step back and consider the larger context in which such controversies take place. Broadly speaking, the viewpoints and perspectives that underlie the current generation of American instructional materials—in other words, the orthodoxy that today's protesters are struggling either to reverse or to intensify—grew out of a reaction against pre-1970s textbooks that reflected a cultural construct known as "the American way of life." Among these were the widely used Dick and Jane readers. Daddy went to work every day dressed in a white shirt and a business suit while Mommy wore a frilly apron and baked cupcakes and Baby Sally cooed in her cradle. Their little boy, Dick, ran and ran ("Run, Dick, run!") while "See Dick run" described a major activity of his sister Jane. The family had the obligatory cat and dog, and they all lived in a suburban house with a nice lawn and a garden on a quiet street with no traffic. Everyone was happy: Mommy and Daddy never quarreled, Dick and Jane were models of juvenile courtesy, and the pets never misbehaved on the rug. All of the human characters were Caucasian; indeed, their coloring, body build, and facial features appeared to suggest northern European ancestry, with no beaked noses or raven locks among them.

Clearly, the world of the Dick and Jane readers had little to do with the real-life experiences of many students, but that was not seen as a disadvantage. The series was based on the belief that education should present students with an ideal world, thus providing them with models of a normative lifestyle for which they were to strive. Naturally, no one suggested that students of other races or ethnic groups could become ectomorphic blondes if they tried hard enough; the message was that non-Caucasians and ethnic-looking brunettes were not in the foreground of the American ideal as presented in schoolbooks.

Rumblings of discontent with this Eurocentric and Panglossian approach to education were discernable as early as the 1920s, but it was not until the 1970s that changing social values, an increasingly diverse population, and new attitudes about the role of minorities led to a noticeable alteration in the assumptions underlying textbook content. Today, people of different races and ethnic backgrounds are consistently, although not extensively, included in elementary and secondary school textbooks. Similarly, history, social studies, and literature curricula have begun to reflect the experiences and perspectives of people who are neither white, European, Christian, nor male.

As progressive textbook protesters are quick to point out, these changes are by no means all-pervasive. Even today, most of the stories in elementary school readers and secondary school literature anthologies could have been—and in many instances were—included in the books of the 1950s. Among these traditional materials, however, there appears a sprinkling of stories about people of diverse backgrounds who live in cities, in apartments, and in nontraditional families. Women have jobs outside the home, fathers share in child care, and some people experience serious problems. Underlying these changes in textbook content is a philosophy of education that focuses on two goals: ensuring that every student is exposed to instructional material reflecting his or her own cultural identity and real-life experiences; and teaching all students to think of the world in terms of a wide range of ethnic, religious, economic, and social backgrounds. Just as the earlier textbook orthodoxy suggested that certain kinds of people, experiences, and lifestyles were "American" and normative while others were not worthy of consideration, this new orthodoxy promotes such values as knowledge of other cultures and tolerance for diversity. In that sense, the current textbooks encourage students to think in terms of an ideal world as much as the earlier ones did, but the ideal has changed from homogeneity to heterogeneity and from cultural absolutism to a more relativistic system of values.

In addition to emphasizing cultural inclusiveness, the new textbook orthodoxy opens the door to critical thinking about historical figures and movements, political and fiscal policies, and theories of human nature that had previously been considered sacrosanct. Since the 1970s, for example, textbooks have begun to suggest, however tentatively, that free-market capitalism may not be the solution to all social and financial problems, that American militarism may have disadvantages, and that overpopulation and pollution have the potential to destroy the planet. Furthermore, although American textbooks long ago lost the overtly religious character of their 18th- and 19th-century predecessors, the viewpoints and assumptions underlying instructional materials have become increasingly secularized in recent decades. As a result, the current treatment of such topics as evolution, human sexuality, racial and social justice, and gender roles sometimes conflicts with traditional, conservative religious views to which previous generations of textbooks had deferred.

Inevitably, these changes in the content, philosophy, and tone of instructional materials have led to the next stage in the textbook-evolution cycle: the two-pronged backlash. On one side are activists who revile modern textbooks for contributing to what they see as the secularization, moral relativism, social decay, and "political correctness" that are destroying this nation. On the other side are critics who argue that the movement away from pre-1970s textbook orthodoxy has never gone far enough and is now in retreat because of the publishers' timidity in the face of conservative protesters. Protesters in California, for example, routinely rise during the "public comment" portions of state school board meetings to accuse publishers of giving brown faces and ethnic names to characters who represent essentially white, middle-class values and lifestyles. In that way, critics assert, publishers try to get credit for "minority representation" without providing genuine cultural diversity that might offend traditionalists.

Somewhere Over the Rainbow

The current movement toward multicultural instructional materials, together with its resulting backlash, was graphically illustrated by a controversy that arose in New York City in the spring of 1990. In an effort to meet the needs of the city's highly varied population, Chancellor Joseph Fernandez and the New York City Board of Education endorsed an unusually progressive, experimental elementary school reading program entitled "Children of the Rainbow," more commonly known as the "Rainbow Curriculum." Among other things, this curriculum assumed that classroom instruction should reflect the real world, be inclusive of diverse cultural groups, promote respect for a variety of lifestyles, and reflect the students' own interests and experiences. Moreover, like other innovative reading programs of that period, it replaced traditional made-for-the-classroom textbooks with the kinds of children's books that are available in bookstores—an approach that has caused contention because such books sometimes deal with sensitive topics that are ignored or watered down in textbooks.

The books that are included in any given reading program may, of course, be more or less controversial depending on the editors' selection. Some of those recommended in the Rainbow Curriculum were particularly troubling to critics because they placed an unusual emphasis on unconventional lifestyles, such as single-parent families and people living in poverty. Of greatest concern to the Rainbow Curriculum's opponents was the fact that some of its materials promoted tolerance for disfavored groups, including homosexuals. Although only two of the hundred-plus books on the reading list—*Daddy's Roommate* (Willhoite, 1990) and *Heather Has Two Mommies* (Newman, 1989)—focused on homosexuality, they became the flashpoint for all of the discomfort that some people felt with the program as a whole. Neither story spells out the physical mechanics of homosexuality, but both of them strongly promote the view that homosexual couples can form perfectly ordinary families that are as loving and normal as any other family.

Heather Has Two Mommies is the story of a lesbian couple—although the word "lesbian" is never used—who have a child through artificial insemination. Mama Kate does the housework, Mama Jane works as a carpenter, and Heather plays with the dog and the cat. Heather and her mommies go to the beach, bake cookies, and do all the things ordinary families do. Indeed, Heather's world is as ideal as that of Dick and Jane, and that sense of rightness and peace is the whole point of the story. When Heather attends a play group and realizes that some of her playmates have daddies and she has none, the teacher reinforces the theme of normality by inviting other children, including those from single-parent and blended families, to tell their varied stories. One little girl lives not with two mommies but with two daddies, while other children live in traditional two-parent heterosexual families. The overarching message is that all of these permutations are perfectly normal and equally acceptable.

The other pro-homosexual children's story in the Rainbow Curriculum (1992), *Daddy's Roommate*, is narrated by a little boy whose parents are divorced and whose father now shares an apartment with another man. The child lives with his mother but spends weekends with Daddy and Frank. They go to ballgames, work in the garden, and eat peanut butter and jelly sandwiches. Unlike *Heather Has Two Mommies*, *Daddy's Roommate* uses the word "gay." The child's mother, who wears an apron saying "World's Best Mom," tells him that his father is gay, that being gay is simply another way of loving people, and that love is the true source of happiness. The book includes pictures of Daddy and Frank doing such things as watching television, cooking, shopping, hugging, and sharing a bed. Both men dress in conservative clothing, are fully covered at all times, and do not touch or even face each other in bed, but physical contact is unquestionably more explicit here than it is in *Heather Has Two Mommies*. More troubling to some critics, however, is the fundamental similarity of the messages conveyed by both books: that it is entirely normal to have one or more homosexual parents, and that the homosexual couple is doing nothing that is wrong or even remarkable.

In order to understand the controversy that erupted over the use of the Rainbow Curriculum, it is necessary to be aware that the New York

6. CONTROVERSIAL NARRATIVES   147

City schools have a two-tiered governance structure. At the top is the New York City Board of Education and a Chancellor of Schools who serves as the chief executive officer of the citywide school system. The board and the chancellor are responsible for overseeing citywide educational matters, such as instructional standards, transportation, and food services.[15] Under the citywide board are more than 30 local school boards, each of which is responsible for implementing all of the necessities of an educational system at the local level. Inevitably, this arrangement engenders considerable overlap, confusion, and disagreement about where the line should be drawn between the responsibilities of the citywide board and those of the local school districts, and it is in this gray area of authority that the Rainbow Curriculum controversy arose.

Despite rumblings of discontent from some New York City school districts, the city school board and Chancellor Fernandez ordered local boards to incorporate the Rainbow Curriculum into their elementary school reading programs. Local officials had some flexibility in selecting books from a list of titles, but Fernandez was insistent that all of the curriculum's goals—including promoting tolerance for homosexuality—had to be met in some fashion. Conservative local school boards in Brooklyn, Queens, and Staten Island refused to comply, and their stand was vigorously supported by Pat Robertson's Christian Coalition, the Roman Catholic Archdiocese of New York, and the Reverend Al Sharpton. These groups campaigned vigorously for the repeal of the Rainbow Curriculum, the resignation of Chancellor Fernandez, and the victory of anti-Rainbow school board members in the election of 1990. Homosexual activists and their supporters responded by running their own candidates for the city school board and for various local boards. The outcome of the election was close to a draw, with a slight advantage to the homosexual community, and the fight over the Rainbow Curriculum continued unabated.

After 3 years of discord, during which school board meetings erupted into disorder, Chancellor Fernandez altered the Rainbow Curriculum to remove some of its most controversial elements, including the presentation of prohomosexual material in the primary grades. Nevertheless, when some of the local school boards that had held out against the original Rainbow Curriculum approved the modified version in 1993, disruptions again broke out at meetings. Fernandez's contract was not renewed, and the curriculum faded into obscurity except for a heavily revised version that continues to be used in the city's first-grade classes. The city school board attempted to perpetuate some of the curriculum's goals by adopting a general policy statement favoring multicultural education and tolerance for diversity, but this recommendation is not tied to any specific requirement for action.

Obviously, the Rainbow Curriculum's recommendation of overtly prohomosexual books for students as young as first-graders was far out on the cutting edge of nontraditional instruction. Nevertheless, arguments over the use of such materials with small children beg the question, because antihomosexual activists reject nonjudgmental treatments of homosexuality in textbooks at any level, including those intended for high school seniors, many of whom are legally adults.[16] Perhaps better than any other topic, the debate over how, or whether, homosexuality should be presented in the curriculum illustrates the division between protesters who want to return to an earlier textbook orthodoxy and those who want to press forward with changes that are, in their view, still inadequate. To prohomosexual activists, nothing less than unequivocal acceptance of homosexuality beginning in Grade 1 would provide sufficient protection against discrimination, second-class citizenship, and violence. In the view of traditionalists, however, the mere mention of homosexuality—especially in the absence of explicitly condemnatory language—normalizes immorality and undermines the religious views their children are taught at home.

Up From the Dust or Out of the Sea: The Debate Over the Origins of Life

Another prominent example of the tension that has resulted from today's largely secularized textbook orthodoxy is the dispute over what students should be told about the origins of life. Obviously, the controversy over the teaching of evolution in the public schools does not involve narratives in the narrow sense of the term—a genre of writing based on plot, characterization, and other elements of storytelling. When the origins of life are discussed in terms of carbon dating, fossil reconstruction, and DNA retrieval, the subject tends to be characterized as *factual* and *scientific*, as if that disqualified it from being the stuff of which narratives are made. Nevertheless, even a cursory review of world literature shows that descriptions of the origin of life, usually called "creation myths," appear in the literatures of most cultures. It seems that accounts of how life began are classified as narratives when they are seen as factually inaccurate and as science when they are presumed to be true. All the same, the stories scientists construct from fossil remains and other evidence are, in the broad sense of the term, the narratives of a technological culture. In that sense, the conflict described in this section of the chapter reflects a clash between the origin-of-life stories told by two different groups of contemporary Americans: evolutionists and creationists.[17]

For all practical purposes, the first volley in this battle was fired in the 1920s, when the State of Tennessee forbade the teaching of evolution. The American Civil Liberties Union (ACLU), which had just been formed, advertised for a teacher who was willing to violate the law and thus provide a test case. John Scopes offered his services, and the local sheriff was invited to attend his class and listen to him read a chapter on evolution from a textbook. The sheriff later testified that he was not sure whether what he had heard was evolution or not, but the teacher said it was, so he arrested him. The jury found Scopes guilty (*Scopes v. State*, 1925) although his conviction was later overturned because of a procedural error by the judge (*Scopes v. State*, 1926).

Other states followed Tennessee's example, passing anti-evolution laws that were challenged in lawsuits filed by the ACLU and other groups. In one of these cases, *Epperson v. Arkansas* (1968), the U.S. Supreme Court ruled that the state's anti-evolution law was unconstitutional because it had no secular basis but was designed to prevent the science curriculum from conflicting with certain religious beliefs. Because *Epperson* effectively prevented any state from banning the teaching of evolution, its opponents were forced to shift their ground. If evolution could not be eliminated from the curriculum, they reasoned, perhaps creationism could be added.

The primary architect of this new strategy was the Institute for Creation Research, a think tank near San Diego, California, that describes itself as "a Christ Focused Creation Ministry."[18] Staff members, aided by outside consultants, developed a proposed new law called the Balanced Treatment Act and sent it to anti-evolution legislators in several states. The Act provided that if either evolution or creationism were taught in the public schools, then both approaches would have to be presented. Because creationism was rarely if ever included in the science curriculum, this proposal could have only two possible effects: injecting creationism into science classes, or stopping teachers who were unwilling to teach creationism from teaching evolution. The Act was passed in Arkansas and Louisiana, and opponents promptly filed lawsuits to prevent its implementation. In 1987, it was struck down by the U.S. Supreme Court in *Aguillard v. Edwards* (1987). The Court stated that creationism is religion, not science, and there is no secular reason for requiring teachers to present it in conjunction with evolution.

Faced with the reality that state laws against the teaching of evolution were unlikely to be upheld in court, creationists once again sought another means of achieving their goal. This time, they turned to the textbook adoption process. Even if states could not pass laws banning evolution from the curriculum or inserting creationism into it, there was still a chance that the topic could be made so controversial that publishers would eliminate or at least downplay it.

The creationists' textbook strategy has been partially successful, although support for evolution from school officials in California, New York, New Jersey, Illinois, and other states guarantees that the topic will not vanish from textbooks. Nevertheless, because of unremitting pressure from anti-evolution forces in Texas, Alabama, Oklahoma, Arizona, Idaho, and other states, publishers are experimenting with several compromises. One approach is to divide science materials into two parts: a textbook that does not mention evolution and a separate "evolution supplement" that is provided on request. In other science programs, evolution is mentioned only in discrete chapters that can be skipped over or sliced out of the books. A third approach has been to insert prominent disclaimers, usually at the front of science books, suggesting that evolution is no more or less valid than other theories about the origin of life.

Like most compromises, the publishers' attempts to reduce controversy over evolution have satisfied neither side. Creationists continue to seek more extensive and respectful treatment of what they see as scientific evidence that the universe was created by intelligent design, in more or less its present form, only a few thousand years ago. Meanwhile, scientists who support evolution maintain that all the testable evidence shows that the Earth is millions of years old. They also assert that evolution is an important organizing principle of modern science and cannot be shunted off into a separate section or dismissed as merely one theory among many. Finally, they accuse creationists of confusing the term *theory* as it is used in science with the common meaning of the word. Gravity is as much a scientific theory as evolution is, they argue, and teaching biology without discussing evolution makes as much sense as teaching physics without mentioning gravity.

Among the most recent attempts to limit the teaching of evolution was a policy enacted by the Kansas State School Board in 1999.[19] A committee of 27 scientists had spent a year developing new standards for science instruction in the state, and their proposal included substantial coverage of evolution. By a vote of 6 to 4, the state school board deleted that topic from the standards and excluded it from the science tests given to students throughout the state. The new policy does not forbid the teaching of evolution, but it allows teachers and local school officials to exclude it from the curriculum if they wish to do so. Conversely, if teachers or local boards choose to continue teaching evolution, the policy gives their opponents a basis for challenging them for wasting valuable class time on material for which the students will not be held accountable. Throughout the controversy, people who wanted to retain evolution in the standards emphasized such values as scientific evidence and the testability of the facts on which evolution and creationism were based. Because of this focus, they rejected many of the considerations that were important to their opponents, such as local control, majority rule, and equal treatment of differing views. According to a spokesman for the National Center for Science Education,[20] "Teachers are so susceptible to the argument that we should have kids debate both sides.... It sounds so sensible. But it's like debating whether the Earth is flat or spherical" (Simon, 1999).

CONCLUSION

As this chapter has shown, the selection of narratives for use in elementary and secondary schools is a thorny and troubled issue. Controversies that arise from the use of certain narratives involve not only differences of opinion about what content is appropriate for children of various ages but also disagreements about the bases on which such decisions should be made. The horror expressed by some scientists after the Kansas board's ruling, for instance, appeared to reflect not only dismay at the decision itself but also shock and frustration at the process. In that situation, the year-long efforts of a committee of scientists and the closely reasoned, research-based standards developed by a coalition of highly prestigious national science organizations were overruled on a vote of 6 to 4 by an elected board whose members are not required to have even a high school diploma. Similarly, scientists who supported the teaching of evolution were appalled by the notion that decisions about how science is taught—or even *what* science is taught—should be left up to the general population of each local district.

Clearly, the Kansas dispute and the other controversies discussed in this chapter reflect a tension between populism and intellectualism. On one side are people, not all of whom are academics, who believe that objective, research-based data are, although not foolproof, the best means we have to determine what should be taught. On the other side are people, some of whom are academics, who believe that public schools should not contradict the values and beliefs that are passed on by parents to their children. A discussion of how all this fits into the notion of a diverse yet cohesive society could easily fill another chapter—or another book. For now, dramatic as this sounds, it is not much of an exaggeration to say that disputes over the teaching of narratives in the public schools form at least a small part of an ongoing cultural battle for the soul of the nation.

APPENDIX A

Burch, C. W. (1995). *Increasing awareness and appreciation of cultural diversity among fourth graders through integrated curriculum experiences*. Ed.D. Practicum Report, Nova Southeastern University.

Friedland, S. (1994). Bridging the gap. *Executive Educator, 16*(10), pp. 26–28.

Lankard, B. A. *Cultural Diversity and Teamwork*. ERIC Digest No. 152. Columbus, OH: ERIC Clearinghouse on Adult, Career, and Vocational Education, 1994.

Logan, J. *Teaching Stories*. Plymouth, MN: Minnesota Inclusiveness Program, 1993.

Marvis, B. J. *Contemporary American Success Stories: Famous People of Hispanic Heritage*. Volumes I– IV.

McIntosh, P. (1990). *Interactive Phases of Curricular and Personal Re-Vision with Regard to Race*. Working Paper No. 219. Wellesley, MA: Center for Research on Women.

Mitchell L. (1997). Multicultural Biography Series. Childs, MD: Mitchell Lane Publishers.

Moore, T. L., & Reeves-Kazelskis, C. *Effects of formal instruction on preservice teachers' beliefs about multicultural education*. Paper presented at the Annual Meeting of the Mid-South Educational Research Association, Knoxville, TN: November 10–13, 1992. Available through ERIC.

Slavin, R. E. *Cooperative learning: Theory, research, and practice*. Boston: Allyn and Bacon, 1995.

Toombs, W., & Tierney, W. (1992). *Meeting the Mandate: Renewing the College and Departmental Curriculum*. ASHE-ERIC Higher Education Reports. Washington, DC: ERIC Clearinghouse on Higher Education and George Washington University School of Education and Human Development.

Tubbs, J. (1992, August). *Cultural Diversity and Creativity in the Classroom*. Paper presented at the Meeting of the World Organization for Early Childhood Education, Flagstaff, AZ. Available through ERIC.

Vilscek, E. (1994, March). *Dialoguing on the interactions between racially/ethnically identifiable characters in children's books*. Paper presented at the Annual Spring Conference of the National Council of Teachers of English, Portland, OR. Available through ERIC.

Walker-Dalhouse, D. (1992). Using African-American literature to increase ethnic understanding. *Reading Teacher*, 45(6), 416–22.

APPENDIX B

Suing school officials for using certain textbooks has proven to be one of the most effective ways for activists to influence instructional content, despite the fact that the plaintiffs almost always lose because the courts are strongly inclined to defer to the authority of education officials. Given such a low probability of success, filing these lawsuits may seem quixotic if not perverse, but there is a method to the apparent madness. For one thing, if a case includes any novel element, there is always an outside chance of victory. Moreover if the plaintiffs lose in court, they have an excellent chance of achieving their goal if they can make a book so controversial that the publisher will either withdraw it or revise it heavily. Alternatively, a book may become so "hot" that school officials will hesitate to purchase it, and it will then go out of print for lack of sales. Several lawsuits of this type are analyzed in *What Johnny Shouldn't Read* (DelFattore, 1992), and perhaps a brief list of sample decisions may provide a general sense of this type of litigation.

Brown v. Woodland, 27 F. 3d 1373 (9th Cir. 1994). Parents sued a school board for using the Impressions Reading Series published by Holt, Rinehart, and Winston, claiming that the books contradicted Christianity and promoted secular humanism and devil worship. The court upheld the board's authority to select textbooks.

Fleischfresser v. Directors of School District 200, 15 F. 3d 680 (7th Cir. 1994). Another unsuccessful challenge to the Impressions Reading Series. Following a spate of such lawsuits, the publisher discontinued the series.

Gheta v. Nassau County Community College, 33 F. Supp. 2d 179 (1999). Taxpayers sued a community college for offering a sex education course which, they alleged, contradicted Judeo-Christian ethics. The court rejected their claim that the course violated the First Amendment by promoting hostility toward religion.

Smith v. Board of School Commissioners of Mobile County, 827 F.2d 684 (11th Cir. 1987). Parents and teachers alleged that all of the history, sociology, psychology, and home economics books used in the county advanced secular humanism in opposition to Christianity. The district court ruled in their favor, but the appeals court found no evidence that the books promoted or hindered any religion.

Virgil v. School Board of Columbia County, 862 F.2d 1517 (11th Cir. 1989). Parents and teachers sued a school board for discontinuing the use of a humanities textbook following a clergyman's protest against what he considered immoral works by Chaucer and Aristophanes. The appeals court upheld the board's authority to stop using the book.

ENDNOTES

[1] Fuller analyses of this lawsuit may be found in DelFattore (1992) and in Bates (1993).

[2] According to CWA's website, its purpose is "to restore the family to its traditional purpose and thereby allow each member of the family to realize their God-given potential and be more responsible citizens" (http://www.cwfa.org/about/). The organization engages in lobbying, litigation, and grassroots activism; among other things, it supports school prayer and an isolationist foreign policy and opposes abortion and acceptance of homosexuality.

[3] Deposition, April 15, 1986, p. 163.

[4] *Ibid.*, pp. 166–67.

[5] Deposition, March 19, 1986, pp. 133–34.

[6] *Ibid.*, p. 251.

[7] Quoted in Frost's deposition, April 15, 1986, p. 58.

[8] *Ibid.*

[9] Deposition, April 3, 1986, pp. 378–79.

[10] Appendix B provides a summary of several other lawsuits involving challenges to curricular material. Readers might also wish to consult book-length discussions of disputes over narratives taught in elementary and secondary schools; examples include *Storm in the Mountains: A Case Study of Censorship, Conflict, and Consciousness* (Moffett, 1988), *Stifled Laughter: One Woman's Story About Fighting Censorship* (Johnson, 1994), and *Anatomy of a Book Controversy* (Homstad, 1995).

[11] In the controversies discussed here, decisions about using the Potter books are sometimes made by teachers and school librarians, sometimes by principals, and sometimes by local or state school boards. In case this is confusing to some readers, it should be noted that the most common pattern is for the voters of a particular school district to elect a local school board that has overall authority to determine curriculum, subject to any guidelines or standards that may have been imposed by either the state board of education or the state legislature. Local school boards often delegate the authority to select textbooks, li-

brary books, and supplemental reading materials to principals, library specialists, and teachers. For that reason, the identity of the decision-maker may vary from one situation to another.

[12] A U.S. Supreme Court decision, *Board of Education v. Pico* (1982), makes it difficult for school libraries to remove controversial books once they have been included in the collection.

[13] Focus on the Family offers the following statement of its mission: "To cooperate with the Holy Spirit in disseminating the Gospel of Jesus Christ to as many people as possible, and, specifically, to accomplish that objective by helping to preserve traditional values and the institution of the family" (http://www.family.org). The group advocates corporal punishment and stay-at-home mothers and opposes divorce, abortion, and homosexuality.

[14] Up-to-date summaries of current challenges to instructional materials may be found in the *Newsletter on Intellectual Freedom*, a bimonthly publication of the American Library Association; and on several websites, including those of People for the American Way (www.pfaw.com), Banned Books Online (www.cs.cmu.edu/People/spok/banned-books.html), the Thomas Jefferson Center for the Protection of Free Expression (www.tjcenter.org), and the American Library Association (www.ala.org). Among the websites offering links to a variety of Internet resources dealing with challenges to books are www.booksatoz.com/censorship/banned.htm and www.clairscorner.com/censorship/default.htm.

[15] An organizational chart giving more detail is available at http://www.nycenet.edu/offices/orgchart.pdf.

[16] In 1994, for example, the Texas State School Board decreed that all sex education textbooks purchased with state funds had to include little if any information about homosexuality. If the topic was mentioned, the board demanded, the books had to include the full text of Texas's laws against oral and anal intercourse. See, e.g., Dillon (1994), Rugeley (1994), and Smith (1994). Although this dispute did not involve narratives *per se*, it is relevant because attitudes about homosexuality tend to affect any mention of that subject, whether in a senior high school sex education textbook or in *Heather Has Two Mommies*.

[17] Space does not permit a full discussion of the differences between these approaches to the origins of life, but among the many recent works explaining the subject for general audiences are *The Triumph of Evolution—and the Failure of Creationism* (Eldredge, 2000), *Summer for the Gods: The Scopes Trial and America's Continuing Debate Over Science and Religion* (Larson, 1998), *Intelligent Design: The Bridge Between Science and Theology* (Dembski & Behe, 1999), and *Refuting Evolution* (Sarfati & Ham, 1999).

[18] http://www.icr.org/

[19] At the time of this writing, New Mexico has adopted Kansas's policy, and other states are considering it.

[20] This group defines itself as "a non-profit, tax-exempt membership organization working to defend the teaching of evolution against sectarian attack" (http://www. natcenscied.org/).

REFERENCES

Aguillard v. Edwards, 482 U.S. 578 (1987).
Bates, S. (1993). *Battleground: One mother's crusade, the religious right, and the struggle for control of our classrooms*. New York: Poseidon Press.

Board of Education v. Pico, 457 U.S. 853 (1982).
Brown v. Woodland, 27 F. 3d 1373 (9th Cir. 1994).
"Children of the Rainbow" Curriculum. (1992). New York City Public Schools: Office of the Chancellor.
DelFattore, J. (1992). *What Johnny shouldn't read: Textbook censorship in America.* New Haen, CT: Yale University Press.
Dembski, W. A., & Behe, M. J. (1999). *Intelligent design: The bridge between science and theology.* Downers Grove, IL: InterVarsity Press.
DeVine, A. (1999, November 10). Teachers told not to use "Potter": Parents complain about mysticism. *Denver Post*, p. B2.
Dillon, S. (1994, March 17). Publisher pulls a textbook in furor on sexual content. *New York Times*, p. B10.
Draper, N. (1999, September 30). "Harry Potter" in Hot Water. *Star Tribune*, p. 1B.
Eldredge, N. (2000). *The triumph of evolution—and the failure of creationism.* New York: W. H. Freeman & Co.
Epperson v. Arkansas, 393 U.S. 97 (1968).
Fleischfresser v. Directors of School District 200. 15 F. 3d 680 (7th Cir. 1994).
Gheta v. Nassau County Community College, 33 F. Supp. 2d 179 (1999).
Herron, C. (1997). *Nappy Hair.* New York: Knopf.
Holloway, L. (1998, November 25). School officials support teacher on book that parents call racially insensitive. *New York Times*, p. 10B.
Homstad, W. (1995). *Anatomy of a book controversy.* Bloomington, Indiana: Phi Delta Kappa Educational Foundation.
Hutchinson, B. (1999a, October 26). Content of fifth-grade book sparks protest. *The Buffalo News*, p. 5B.
Hutchinson, B. (1999b, November 9). Mother presses for removal of Potter books. *The Buffalo News*, p. 4B.
Johnson, C. (1994). *Stifled laughter: One woman's story about fighting censorship.* Golden, CO: Fulcrum.
Kurtz, H. (1999, November 6). Harry Potter expelled from school. *Denver Rocky Mountain News*, p. 6A.
Larson, E. J. (1998). *Summer for the gods: The Scopes trial and America's continuing debate over science and religion.* Cambridge, MA: Harvard University Press.
Moffett, J. (1988). *Storm in the mountains: A case study of censorship, conflict, and consciousness.* Carbondale: Southern Illinois University Press.
Mozert v. Hawkins County Public Schools, 647 F. Supp. 1194 (6th Cir. 1986).
Mozert v. Hawkins County Public Schools, 827 F.2d 1058 (6th Cir. 1987).
Newman, L. (1989). *Heather has two mommies.* Boston, MA: Alyson Publications.
Rugeley, C. (1994, January 2). Religion, sex education keep Texas schools in turmoil. *Houston Chronicle*, p. A1.
Sarfati, J., & Ham, K. (1999). *Refuting evolution.* Green Forest, AR: Master Books.
Scopes v. State, 152 Tenn. 424; 278 S.W. 57 (1925).
Scopes v. State, 154 Tenn. 105; 289 S.W. 363 (1926).
Simon, S. (1999, July 12). Creationists use new tactic to challenge evolution. *Los Angeles Times*, p. A1.
Smith v. Board of School Commissioners of Mobile County. 827 F. 2d 684 (11th Cir. 1987).
Smith, M. (1994, February 11). Education panel orders text revisions: Most changes pertain to sexual references. *Houston Chronicle*, p. A29.
Virgil v. School Board of Columbia County, 862 F.2d 1517 (11th Cir. 1989)
Weiss, H. J., Rosenbaum, P. S., Shaw, A. M., & Tolbert, M. J. (Eds.), (1980). *Holt Basic Reading: Kindergarten -8.* New York: Holt, Rinehart, & Winston.
Willhoite, M. (1990). *Daddy's roommate.* Boston, MA: Alyson Publications.
Wynne, S. K. (2000, January 30). School ends Harry Potter adventures. *St. Petersburg Times*, p. 4B.

7

Entertainment Education and the Persuasive Impact of Narratives

Michael D. Slater
Colorado State University

Exhibit one: a typical AIDS education effort in Africa, featuring posters showing patients wasting away and radio spots exhorting the use of condoms. Exhibit two: a long-running Tanzanian radio soap opera in which a man who, espousing many of the beliefs and attitudes characteristic of those who resist monogamy or safe sex practices, loses a daughter to prostitution, his wife to a desire for a better future, and eventually his own life to AIDS.

Which of these might we expect to have a greater impact on attitudes and behavior, and why? Obviously, these are profoundly different types of messages. The first approach is overtly persuasive. The second tells a story, from which various lessons may be vicariously learned. This chapter explores reasons why story-telling may in many cases prove a more effective way to influence attitudes and behaviors than conventional persuasive efforts.

This issue is important from a theoretical as well as from an applied point of view. Persuasion researchers have focused almost exclusively on the study of explicitly persuasive messages. Theorists of media effects, in contrast, have been concerned with the incidental but substantively important impact of popular culture, especially television and film, on beliefs, values, and behavior. Communication practitioners in health and social development have adopted narrative techniques—most notably broadcast series melodramas, but also comic books and text-based narratives—to change attitudes and behaviors. In so doing, they have in effect bridged the theoretical domains of media effects and persuasion processes. Understanding processes by which these persuasive narratives influence behavior should also help us understand mechanisms underlying possible incidental persuasive effects of entertainment programming.

ENTERTAINMENT AS PERSUASION: CONTEMPORARY EXAMPLES

Telenovelas and Entertainment-Education: A Brief History

The use of story-telling to influence behavior is at least as old as Aesop and is deeply ingrained in Western as well as non-Western cultures—the book of Job and the parables of the New Testament being perhaps the most prominent examples in the Judeo-Christian tradition. The potential for television and film to promote antisocial behavior has been a matter of considerable debate since the 1950s. However, attempts to systematically use story-telling to promote socially desirable behaviors, based on social science principles, originated in Latin America in the 1970s (see Singhal & Rogers, 1999, for a detailed description and discussion of these and subsequent entertainment-education efforts).

Latin America provided fertile soil for the nurturing of this new approach. A reasonable degree of consensus existed on the social value of promoting a variety of behaviors, including participation in adult education and training and family planning. Television and radio were widely available even among the poor. The number of channels was limited, reducing information clutter and increasing attention to any given set of broadcasts. Series melodramas—soap operas—were enormously popular. The use of such broadcast melodramas, or *telenovelas*, for explicitly persuasive purposes was pioneered by Miguel Sabido, of Televisa, the Mexican network that is the dominant force in television production in Latin America. In 1969, a Peruvian telenovela, *Simplemente Maria*, had inadvertently led to a remarkable upsurge in sales of sewing machines wherever it had been shown in Latin America. Maria, the central character in this series, is an impoverished country girl who comes to the city to work as a domestic, but quickly runs into trouble as she is seduced, becomes pregnant, and is subsequently fired by her employer. Maria acquires a sewing machine, learns to use it, strives to educate herself, sets up in a clothing-design business, and then sews her way to economic and romantic success. The engagement of the public with this story was remarkable: For example, tens of thousands of people turned out to view the filming of her happy-ending wedding, to provide their good wishes for her future!

Sabido recognized the potential of telenovelas to support economic and social development efforts. Sabido was familiar with Bandura's social learning theory (Bandura, 1977) and understood that the application of these principles might influence viewers to adopt socially desirable behaviors (Institute for Communication Research, 1981). For example, he sought to instantiate Bandura's suggestion to script attractive characters who were similar to the target audience and to use vicarious reinforcement, whereby characters who engage in the desired target behaviors achieve positive outcomes, whereas characters who fail to do so suffer negative consequences.

Sabido was responsible for the design of six development-oriented telenovelas from 1975 to 1981 (Institute for Communication Research, 1981; Rogers & Antola, 1985), several of which received some empirical evaluation. The year that Televisa aired *Ven Conmigo (Come with Me)*, a series intended to promote adult literacy, enrollments in adult literacy programs increased 63 % (Berrueta, 1986, cited in Singhal & Rogers, 1989). *Acompaname (Come Along with Me)*, whose dramatic plot centered around family-planning issues, was associated with a 32% increase in visits to state-run family planning clinics (Institute for Communication Research, 1981). Although evaluations of these programs could not control for other, simultaneous efforts to promote the targeted behaviors, increases of this magnitude were unlikely to be attributable to the more conventional promotional efforts. Increases in years subsequent to the year the programs aired were nominal, suggesting that the telenovelas were primarily responsible for these changes in behavior.

Since that time, several development and international education organizations have spearheaded efforts to air such programs, now commonly referred to as *entertainment education*. Two of the leading advocates for entertainment education are the Center for Communication Programs' Population Communications Services (PCS), at Johns Hopkins University, and Population Communications International (PCI), in New York. Family planning lends itself especially well to the series melodrama format: Issues such as sexuality, women's roles, and marital conflict offer a wealth of engaging story opportunities.

During the 1980s, PCS developed dramatic series for three Islamic nations—Turkey, Pakistan, and Egypt—in which discussion of family planning was particularly sensitive. In some cases, scenes were as explicit as a couple discussing family planning in bed. Evaluations of the four TV dramas shown in these countries (two were shown in one country) indicated that the programs reached 37% to 78% of the targeted audiences. Across the four programs, 15% to 63% of these viewers said that the programs led them to discuss family planning with their spouses or friends. Between 20% and 49% said they intended to visit a family planning clinic or counselor, and, in the two instances where behavioral outcomes were measured, 6% to 9% said they actually had visited a planning provider as a result of viewing the programs (Kincaid, 1993; Kincaid, Yun, Piotrow, & Yaser, 1993). It is not possible to assess the accuracy of these self-reported outcomes or to ascertain whether other family-planning initiatives contributed to these behaviors. However, even when discounted substantially, impact of this magnitude is quite impressive for a communication intervention. PCS has also promoted entertainment education efforts in other popular media. For example, they contributed to the production of the popular hit song *Cuando Estemos Juntos (When We are Together)*, which was designed to promote sexual responsibility among teens in Mexico (Piotrow, Kincaid, Rimon, & Rinehart, 1997).

Entertainment-Education: A Closer Examination

The social learning principles used to construct entertainment-education stories are fairly simple. The task of creating stories and characters that resonate with audiences is rendered particularly challenging when audience members hold traditionalist values that are at odds with the conveyed message. Similarly, characters and situations must be constructed to ensure they are believable and easy to identify with, and efforts must be extended to ensure that the message audiences take away from a story is the message its designers intend to convey. Extensive audience research and message pretesting is essential to achieve such effective character and story construction (Piotrow, et al., 1997).

These lessons were underscored in the development of *Hum Log*, one of the first efforts to transfer the Mexican experience to another culture. Developed with the aid of PCI, the 156 episodes of *Hum Log* were broadcast by the public broadcasting system in India. Following a model used in the Televisa telenovelas, each episode of *Hum Log* concluded with a 30 to 50 second epilogue featuring a popular actor summarizing the key message of each episode. Positive role models included the strict but supportive grandfather and Badki, a plain but self-sufficient young woman who becomes an advocate for women's rights. Negative role models included the chauvinistic and often-drunk father and the passive mother. Topics included women's rights, family planning, problems of urbanization, and alcohol. The program was extremely popular, especially after writers deemphasized the family planning message (which was initially a relatively hard-sell message resisted by many viewers) in favor of the more general lessons surrounding gender equality and family life. *Hum Log* reached between 65% and 90% of the potential audience in Hindi-speaking North India, and between 20% and 35% of the urban audience in major South Indian cities, in which Hindi is not the primary language used.

Viewers sent over 400,000 letters to the show's producers, actors, and actresses. It was by far the most successful program shown up to that time on Indian television (Singhal & Rogers, 1989).

Survey results suggest that the series was effective in influencing attitudes but not behavior relating to family planning and gender equality. The absence of behavioral effects may be due to the fact that producers toned down the family planning message to conform to strong countervailing values in Indian culture. Singhal and Rogers (1989) also examined identification with the positive and negative role models in the program. More than half of the viewers said they identified with the intended positive role models. On the other hand, almost a quarter said they identified with an intended negative role model, such as the long-suffering wife and mother. Whereas producers intended viewers to criticize this character for her ineffectuality, many instead appreciated her for her forbearance. Singhal and Rogers compare this problem to that identified in studies of the American situation comedy *All in the Family*, in which prejudiced viewers perceived the parodied bigot, Archie Bunker, as a sympathetic character who espoused legitimate positions (Vidmar & Rokeach, 1974).

With increasing international experience in entertainment education, sophistication regarding conceptual development, formative research, production, and dissemination has grown apace (Brooke, 1995; Piotrow, et al., 1997). A 204-episode radio melodrama, *Twende na Wakati* (*Let's Go with the Times*) focused on gender issues and AIDS education in Tanzania. Developed with technical assistance from PCI, this series avoided some problems associated with prior efforts, such as the widespread identification with an intended negative role model that occurred in *Hum Log*. Formative research intended to insure acceptance of the message, story lines, and appropriate identification with characters was exceptionally thorough: 4,800 personal interviews and 160 focus groups were conducted. Research indicated, for example, that a major route for HIV infection was long-distance truck drivers, who frequently had sex with prostitutes en route. The key negative role model, then, became a long-distance trucker, Mkwaju, a promiscuous and chauvinistic fellow who contracts AIDS and loses his marriage. Other negative and positive role models were developed, as were characters whose ideas and behaviors were shown to evolve in the desired direction over the course of the drama, and who were shown to benefit accordingly (also called *transitional* characters). Female positive and transitional characters achieved a degree of security and success through education and use of family planning services. Thirty-second epilogues were used in this programming, as well (Rogers, Vaughan, & Shefner-Rogers, 1995; see also Singhal & Rogers, 1999).

The drama was evaluated using field experiment methodology, in which the interior of Tanzania (which could only receive the program by shortwave radio) served as a comparison group. Results focused on behavior change, as pretest knowledge and attitudes proved to be already very consistent with the program's message. During the period that the program aired, self-reported family planning adoption increased almost 10% in parts of Tanzania receiving the broadcasts and decreased slightly in the comparison region. More than 20% of persons interviewed at family planning clinics reported that they had adopted a family planning method due to exposure to the program. Although an equivalent decrease in number of sexual partners was found in treatment and control communities, condom distribution increased 600% in treatment communities, compared to 140% in the control region (Rogers et al., 1995). Despite methodological problems that are typical of field experiments (differences between the interior and other regions, other communication programs, including entertainment-education, also taking place in Tanzania), these are impressive effects. It is possible that the apparent behavioral effects were so large precisely because relevant attitudes were already consistent with program objectives.

Epilogues: Adding a Traditional Persuasive Element to the Narrative

The inclusion of epilogues to emphasize the program's message has become well-accepted as part of the entertainment-education strategy. A typical epilogue might include rhetorical questions asking what the viewer would do in the character's position, and statements emphasizing reasons for the advocated behavior, all presented by an actor or actress from the program (see Singhal & Rogers, 1999, for more details on the use of epilogues).

Apparently, without such epilogues it is too easy for viewers or listeners to focus on character and not engage with the message's persuasive subtext. Unfortunately, like much in the realm of entertainment-education, the empirical foundation for using such epilogues appears to be largely unpublished, presumably being buried in agency files describing message pretesting efforts. One exception is found in Singhal and Rogers' (1989) discussion of a survey finding positive responses to the epilogues used in the *Hum Log* series. What is intriguing is that it seems that such epilogues do not disrupt viewer or listener involvement with the characters and story. The epilogues blend the narrative and the persuasive or didactic—they are communicated by the actors and actresses playing the dramatic roles. This raises some interesting questions. To what extent do viewers or listeners respond to the actors in the epilogue as actors or as story characters? Does the appearance of the actors in the epilogue in any way reduce the subjective engagement with and believability of the story, either in retrospect or in subsequent episodes? Exploring these questions empirically would not only clarify issues concerning entertainment-education, but would help clarify important theoretical issues regarding the boundaries between the narrative, fictional world, and the social world as experienced by the narrative's audience. The use of the epilogue does suggest that the boundary is both permeable and to some extent one-way—that the audience is willing not only to draw social information from the narrative (Prentice & Gerrig, 1999; Slater, 1990), but can be asked to do so explicitly without compromising involvement with that fictional world.

Evaluation Issues. It should be recognized that a great deal remains to be done in the evaluation and analysis of entertainment-education efforts. The rigor of outcome evaluations, as noted previously, is limited (see Yoder, Hornik, & Chirwa, 1996, for a more in-depth discussion of evaluation issues). Moreover, detailed examination of the elements of entertainment-education programs, such as responses to varying characterizations (positive, negative, transitional, same and cross sex) and epilogues as noted previously, are rare and overdue. One exception is a recent study of a PCS entertainment-education radio drama in Nepal. This study found that the more key role-model characters were seen as central to the story line, the greater was the behavioral intention or behavior in the advocated direction (Storey, Boulay, Karki, Heckert, & Karmacharya, 1999). These findings underscore the desirability of assessing identification with key characters and their perceived importance to the story as part of formative research efforts.

Entertainment as Education and Persuasion in the United States

Each of the entertainment education efforts discussed to this point has taken place in developing nations. The uncluttered nature of the media landscape in these countries allows a single program to gain substantial visibility and reach. Government has control or considerable influence over the content of broadcast media. To what extent are such efforts and approaches transferable to the industrial West, in which many different messages compete?

The most direct application has been with transplanted Latin Americans—migrant farmworkers—in the U.S. Novela Health Education (based at the University of Washington) has developed video and radio dramas and *fotonovelas* (comic-book type melodramas using, in most cases, photographic still images) on topics such as AIDS prevention and agricultural safety. Research indicates that the Novela programs have led to many of the cognitive, attitudinal, and behavioral changes they were designed to promote (Mishra, Conner, & Lewis, 1996).

However, the most significant equivalent applications have been various dramas and situation comedies that, based on the convictions of their producers, have promoted various beliefs, attitudes, and behaviors. Although these programs are not as deliberately designed to induce change as are prototypical entertainment education programs, they do appear to have influenced viewer attitudes. For example, during the 1970s, both the ABC miniseries *Roots* and the CBS situation comedy *All in the Family* did, on the whole, sensitize viewers to racism and bigotry in America, despite the boomerang effect of *All in the Family* on some prejudiced viewers as noted previously (Ball-Rokeach, Grube, & Rokeach, 1981; Vidmar & Rokeach, 1974; Wander, 1977).

Media Advocacy: Influencing the Content of Entertainment Programming

Another major strategy has been media advocacy: efforts by public health professionals and other public interest advocates to influence the content of entertainment programming as well as news coverage. The Harvard Alcohol Project, for example, during the late 1980s successfully convinced studio executives, writers, and producers to include content that promoted designated drivers and other safety-oriented practices related to drinking and driving. Unlike the entertainment-education programs developed in developing nations, the Harvard project did not attempt to develop whole series. They instead sought to model appropriate behavior by adding bits of dialogue where protagonists decline a drink before driving, or identify themselves as the designated driver, although in some cases full episodes focused on drinking and driving issues. Over a 15-month period, 62 television episodes aired with dialogue or scenes reinforcing the inappropriateness of drinking and driving. In addition, three situation comedies and two dramas featured programs plotted around drinking and driving topics. Poll results suggested increases in self-reported use of designated drivers over this time frame; however, it is not possible to separate effects of this media advocacy effort from other education efforts ongoing at the same time (Montgomery, 1993).

The Harvard Alcohol Project is but one of numerous efforts to influence the content of Hollywood's entertainment programming. Public health officials and advocates have long been urging responsible portrayals in television and film (Montgomery, 1989). The Office of National Drug Control Policy (ONDCP) in the White House has successfully negotiated with television networks to air popular dramas and situation comedies with scripts written to reflect drug prevention messages using social learning principles. ONDCP allowed networks to provide such programming as an alternative to free advertising spots otherwise required to match ONDCP's advertising spending (Forbes, 2000). Considerable controversy erupted when such arrangements were publicized, underscoring the difficulties of planned entertainment education efforts in the United States, at least when government is involved. The effects of these programs have not been gauged empirically. From a theoretical perspective, of course, the potential of such portrayals to influence behavior is substantial.

Narrative Simulations and Interactive Technology

Several other approaches to utilizing narrative for persuasive and educational purposes have been explored in recent years. Henry Cole, a psychologist working in the area of occupational safety, has developed what he calls *narrative simulations*. Narrative simulations are short stories that illustrate possible negative consequences such as agricultural injury and the resulting economic damage to one's family. These consequences arise from mistaken choices that are nonetheless typical of what happens in work settings such as farms or mines, given the pressures and demands of such work. The narrative becomes a simulation through the incorporation of an interactive element: Participants may review options at each decision point, and receive feedback regarding the problems associated with selecting the wrong option. Evaluations suggest the method is effective in increasing knowledge and influencing intended behaviors (Cole, 1997; Cole, Vaught, Wiehagen, Haley, & Brnich, 1998).

As Cole points out, simulations are widely used in technical training (e.g., aviation and emergency response) to develop decision-making skills in realistic contexts (Cole, 1994; Giffen & Rockwell, 1984). One can conceptualize behaviors such as family planning, safe sex, and avoiding substance abuse as successful decision-making processes. Role-playing, of course, has been popular in some training programs as a means of simulating appropriate decisions and practicing the skills needed to implement those decisions (such as refusing a joint or asking a partner to use a condom). A number of projects are currently underway to use interactive CD-ROMs or websites to provide such simulations regarding substance abuse prevention and other health topics, with evidence emerging for positive impact on outcomes such as knowledge, self-efficacy (one's confidence that one can successfully undertake the behavior), and behavior (Lieberman, 1997).

THEORETICAL FOUNDATIONS FOR THE ROLE OF NARRATIVE ENTERTAINMENT IN PERSUASION AND BEHAVIOR CHANGE

Entertainment education efforts, from their inception, have been informed by social psychological theory, primarily by Bandura's social learning (now called *social cognitive* theory; Bandura, 1977; Bandura, 1986; Institute for Communication Research, 1981). Social cognitive theory emphasizes the effects of vicarious experience, such as the positive or negative reinforcement of our own behavior that occurs when we watch the behavior of others, particularly those similar to ourselves and those we would like to be like (role models). According to social cognitive theory, vicarious experience may alter behavior by changing beliefs about our competencies in successfully performing a behavior (i.e., "self-efficacy beliefs"), and by providing vicarious practice in carrying out a desired behavior.

However, social cognitive theory alone is not sufficient to account for all entertainment education effects or to inform all communication design decisions. Persuasion theory, for example, has traditionally been concerned with how communication can influence beliefs and attitudes that may precede behavior change (Ajzen & Fishbein, 1980; McGuire, 1989). In Ajzen & Fishbein's theory of reasoned action, communication might lead to behavioral change by influencing expectations about the outcomes (positive or negative) of engaging in a target behavior, or by changing perceptions about the social norms surrounding that behavior. In recent years, key persuasion and behavior change theorists such as Ajzen as well as Bandura have implicitly recognized that the social influence process is a continuum embracing both persuasion and social learning and self-efficacy processes. Ajzen, for example, incorporated a version of the self-efficacy construct in his Theory of Planned Behavior (Ajzen, 1991), and Bandura incorporated what he called *outcome expectations* (Bandura, 1986), which are similar to Ajzen and Fishbein's (1980) attitudinal beliefs and subjective norms, in social cognitive theory. In this section, I develop a cross-theoretical model for the persuasive influence of entertainment education that reflects this understanding of persuasion and social influence as an integrated process. Later, I explore processing issues that may help explain underlying reasons for this persuasive influence, and that may explain possible incidental persuasive effects of entertainment narratives.

Hierarchy of Effects and Stages of Change. The importance of such a cross-theoretical perspective was suggested by both Kincaid (1993) and Rogers et al. (1995). Both discuss impact of entertainment education efforts across what they call a hierarchy of effects: effects on awareness, attitudes, and interpersonal communication behavior that precede behavioral change. Such a hierarchy is characteristic of information-processing models of persuasion (Hamilton, 1997; McGuire, 1989). Social cognitive theory is primarily concerned with more proximal factors leading to behavior change such as self-efficacy, and tends to assume the necessary awareness and consonant attitudes (although more recently Bandura has emphasized the more attitudinal construct of outcome expectations). In addition to incorporating Bandura's theory, Kincaid draws on McGuire's (1989) information processing model and on models that emphasize the role of affect in persuasion (Zajonc, 1980), the dynamics of social influence processes (Farr & Moscovici, 1984), and media influences on the perception of social norms (Gerbner, Gross, Morgan, & Signorielli, 1994). Rogers et al. (1995) referred briefly to both McGuire's information processing model and the stages-of-change model (Prochaska, DiClemente, & Norcross, 1992) as the basis for their thinking regarding a hierarchy of effects.

The *stages-of-change* model is particularly useful in thinking crosstheoretically about the persuasive effects of entertainment education. This model was developed originally as a clinical framework, intended to identify appropriate therapeutic interventions for patients with addictive problems such as tobacco, alcohol, or substance abuse (McConnaughy, DiClemente, Prochaska, & Velicer, 1989). The central concept was that different kinds of interventions, often based on different theoretical models, were appropriate depending on the readiness of the patient to change behavior. Empirical work suggested four or five stages, depending on the analysis. The five stage version begins with *precontemplation*, consisting of those who have no intention to change, deny any need to change, or, in the communication campaign context, are simply unaware of any reason to change. In the *contemplation* stage, people acknowledge the issue and consider the pros and cons of behavior change. *Preparation* is the transition between contemplation and action (sometimes combined with the contemplation stage) in which people have accepted the desirability of behavior change and are beginning to plan for or experiment with such change. In the *action* stage, people have implemented behavior change and in the *maintenance* stage have succeeded in sustaining the change (Prochaska, et al., 1992).

The stages of change model is also called the *transtheoretical* model by its authors, because it is used to facilitate integrating a range of theoretical approaches in a systematic way for clinical purposes. In the same way, it can be used to integrate theories of attitude and behavior change, and theories of media effects, in the context of persuasive communication campaign efforts (Maibach & Cotton, 1995; Slater, 1999).

The Persuasive Impact of Entertainment Narratives Across Stages of Change: A Cross-Theoretical Perspective. Here, I present a brief survey of the role of various theoretically specified social, interpersonal, and intrapersonal processes across the stages of change (see Slater, 1999, for a more detailed examination of these issues). This survey highlights social and psychological mechanisms through which entertainment education might influence behavior, and also provides prescriptive insights into design and implementation strategies.

For example, a variety of media theories address the development of awareness concerning issues, and their legitimization in the minds of individuals and within communities—the prerequisites for the move from precontemplation to contemplation, in stages-of-change parlance. Research in agenda-setting and multistep flow (Katz & Lazarsfeld, 1955; Shaw & McCombs, 1977; Tichenor, Donohue, & Olien, 1980) has focused on the role of news coverage. In particular, agenda-setting research indicates that news coverage makes a given topic or issue salient to members of the public. Multistep flow research emphasizes how the impact of news on opinion is mediated by conversations with friends and acquaintances, particularly opinion leaders or persons with particular credibility regarding that topic. However, it is probable that highly visible entertainment programming, emphasizing issues such as family planning and safe sex, will have a similar impact in raising the salience of issues and stimulating discussion among friends, family, and neighbors (Chaffee & Mutz, 1988; see Strange & Leung, 1999, for an experimental study illustrating narrative effects on beliefs about social problems and issues). In fact, it is likely that entertainment narratives, with their suspenseful story lines and viewers' identification with characters, will result in in-depth and quite personal discussions (Rouner, 1984; Rubin & Perse, 1987).

Such discussions, in turn, are likely to influence perceptions of community norms, and should play an important role in the contemplation stage. Viewing the behavior of socially similar others is likely to provide another source of beliefs about social norms, particularly on topics that tend not to be directly observable, such as sexual behavior and contraception use. At the same time, influence may take a more conscious route, as viewers deliberately accept attitudes and positions that the characters espouse. Moreover, viewing outcomes of characters' behavior, if perceived as credible, might influence perceptions of the costs and benefits associated with the behavior—e.g., the expectancy-value equation (Fishbein & Middlestat, 1989). See Figure 7.1 (adapted from Slater 1999) for an illustration of these relationships.

Exposure to these entertainment narratives, then, might influence the process of contemplation through both social influence and more cognitive routes. The potential impact of entertainment narratives is even greater in the next stage, preparation. The weakness of the theory of reasoned action is that it is much better at predicting behavioral intention than behavior. One of the strengths of social cognitive theory (Bandura, 1986) is that it provides both an explanation of and a remedy for slippage between intention and behavior: the lack of confidence in undertaking the behavior (i.e., lack of self-efficacy) and the related lack of necessary skills and experience. Lack of confidence and skills, according to social cognitive theory, can be addressed by providing socially similar models who successfully model the necessary skills (or even better, model acquisition of those skills) in realistic social situations—something that can

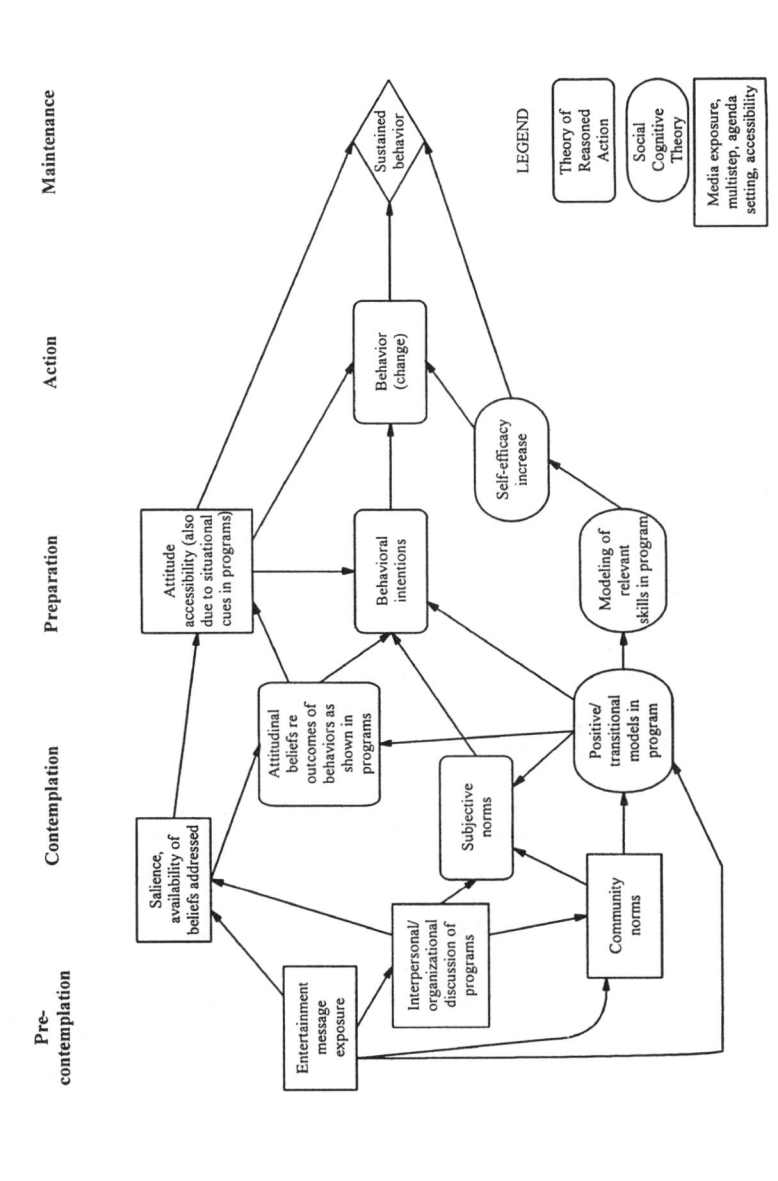

Fig. 7.1. Persuasive impact of entertainment-education across stages of change: A cross-theoretical model (adapted from Slater, 1999).

more effectively be accomplished in an entertainment narrative than in any other communication genre.

The slippage between attitudes and beliefs is also addressed by *attitude accessibility* theory (Fazio, Powell, & Williams, 1989). This theory suggests that attitudes are more likely to predict behavior when they are accessible in the appropriate context: Attitudes consistent with safe sex and condom use are of little use if they are espoused in the living room but are replaced by more hedonistic perspectives in the bedroom. Attitude accessibility can potentially be increased when messages incorporate social cues that occur with the behavior. In other words, it is more effective when attitudes regarding family planning are being conveyed by a couple shown in a bedroom than when mouthed by a "talking head."

Clearly, then, entertainment messages have substantial potential to influence behavior. It is difficult to imagine another communication genre that can communicate beliefs, model behavior, teach skills, provide behavioral cues, and simulate consequences of behaviors over time in as compelling and involving a fashion. This analysis also suggests some strategic approaches in developing entertainment education as a function of the stages of change of one's intended audience. For example, when there is considerable lack of awareness or resistance regarding the topic of the message—as there was with family planning in India—a key objective should be building support for alternative norms, with less expectation of behavior change. In hindsight, the need to softsell the family planning message in *Hum Log* is unsurprising. Similarly, emphasizing positive or negative role models, which may tend to polarize viewers or be misinterpreted, may not be as effective as portraying the evolution of key sympathetic characters as they come to accept new norms and new behaviors. In other words, resistant audiences might best be addressed by modeling the process of attitude change itself. For example, the traditionalist mother in *Hum Log* might have been portrayed as a transitional character, in the difficult process of adapting to new values. Conversely, this analysis suggests that many Tanzanians who viewed *Twende na Wakati* were already in the preparation stage, having already accepted the value of the AIDS-related behaviors proposed by the series. The emphasis of this series on characters who modeled and reinforced appropriate behaviors appears to have resulted in the higher self-efficacy and appropriate behavioral skills required for actual behavioral change.

One of the attractive aspects of entertainment messages for the persuasive communicator, then, is that it is possible to simultaneously address audience members at each stage of change—something nearly impossible in most messages. Some characters can model skills; some can model the process of accepting new values and norms. Narrative allows the complexity of the social world, and the range of beliefs and values of audiences members, to be plausibly reflected and addressed in the message.

THE PROCESSING OF THE PERSUASIVE CONTENT OF ENTERTAINMENT NARRATIVES

That people seek out communication that provides entertainment is obvious. Massive industries—film, television, publishing— generate stories to meet the seemingly insatiable demand for pleasure, such as vicarious social relationships (Rubin, Perse, & Powell, 1985) or excitement and distraction (Zillmann & Bryant, 1994), available from immersion in narrative. But what does the seeking out of pleasure from a narrative imply from a persuasion processing perspective?

Here we immediately encounter a dilemma. From the traditional persuasion perspective, involvement in entertainment narratives should be relatively low. If we use, for example, Johnson and Eagly's (1989) typology of outcome-relevant, value-relevant, or impression-relevant involvement, we would conclude that there are typically no personally relevant outcomes at stake, no direct implications of the message for the recipient's time, money, or other resources. Readers or viewers are unlikely to be concerned with impression management associated with resulting social interactions (except perhaps for book discussion club members!). Stories may or may not impinge on recipients' values in a way that recipients would notice. However, if this impingement is too blatant, it reduces rather than increases involvement with the entertainment message: Recall how *Hum Log* did not obtain widespread viewer acceptance until its writers toned down the family planning subtext in the episodes.

On the other hand, the viewers or readers of an entertainment narrative typically appear to be far more engrossed in the message than are readers or viewers of news stories, speeches, ads, or social science book chapters. After all, narratives tell of love and loss, birth and death, conquest and defeat; these tales escape traditional persuasion definitions of involvement because they do not directly bear on the reader, viewer, or listener as an individual, except insofar as he or she is vicariously engaged. This vicarious form of involvement has been referred to as *absorption* (Graesser, 1981) or *transportation* (Green & Brock, 1996; see also Nell, 1988). Absorption is a particularly dramatic example of the different kinds of cognitive arousal and attention that comprise involvement. It is characterized not by the increased cognitive effort associated with high involvement in a persuasive message, but by a nearly complete focusing of attention, and an automaticity that reflects our innate propensity for processing social information (Bower, Black, & Turner, 1979; Graesser, 1981; Mandler & Johnson, 1980).

Possible psychological and structural factors that lead to greater absorption or involvement in a narrative are reviewed elsewhere in this volume. Several points, however, are worth emphasizing for this discussion of persuasion processes. Elements of plot structure that increase absorption can be expected to include drama, the impact of the action on the lives of story characters, and suspense, the sustained uncertainty concerning the direction of the dramatic action. Identification or empathy with story protagonists, then, is a necessary condition for effective drama and suspense: If one doesn't care about the protagonists, the impact of and uncertainty regarding action will be much less likely to compel attention. *Identification*, in this sense, may be based on perceived similarity to oneself based on personal qualities and life situation (oneself as one is), on the attractiveness and social desirability of the protagonist (oneself as one would like to be or would like to have as a friend), and on the creative skill with which the character is portrayed and the resulting ease with which one can experience the tale through the eyes and ears of the key characters. Such identification may cause cognitive rehearsal of the beliefs and values expressed or embodied by the character, leading to reinforcement or movement toward those beliefs and values. Social cognitive theory suggests, however, that viewers should not be prompted to identify with characters whose characteristics and skills are beyond their attainment. It is useful in this context to recall *Simplemente Maria*, in which the protagonist climbs her way out of poverty into wealth and success through adult education and her skill as seamstress, designer, and entrepreneur.

Complicating this picture, however, is the relative lack of conceptual clarity in the literature regarding what it means to identify with a character. For example, in a recent study of a short story excerpt featuring alcohol misuse as a subplot, Donna Rouner and I (Slater & Rouner, 1999) found two identification factors—perceived similarity to (or identification) and liking of (or sympathy with) story characters (see also Zillmann & Bryant, 1994, regarding sympathy with characters). These factors operated somewhat differently for male and female readers, and effects of same-sex versus opposite-sex identification also operated differently in some cases for both genders. In other words, patterns of identification demonstrated some of the richness and complexity of human social relations.

There is also an interesting tension between drama and persuasive subtexts. If persuasive subtexts are too obvious and come to conscious awareness, they may interrupt the absorption in the narrative that is essential to a successful narrative. The more controversial the persuasive topic, then, the more subtle must be its incorporation into the story line so as to minimize its intrusiveness. On the other hand, persuasive subtexts often do address issues that inherently matter to most human beings, and thus become legitimate vehicles to move a plot along. Sexuality, family politics, and social class, for example, are both addressed in many social interventions and are fundamental narrative themes.

Not all persuasive uses of narrative need revolve around fundamental human issues. Superficial persuasive effects may result from techniques such as product placement, which is the use of various products by story protagonists on payment from the manufacturer in film and TV (the bidding by automotive manufacturers to determine what sports car James Bond would drive comes to mind, as does the anecdotally reported increased market share of Reese's Pieces after being shown in the film *ET*). However, it seems likely that both intended and incidental persuasive effects of entertainment messages may occur whenever such fundamental themes are systematically and effectively developed by writers and producers with a clear point of view, whether the attitudes or behaviors modeled are positive or negative.

Involvement in an entertainment message, then, should be governed by the extent of identification with characters and by the narrative interest of the plot for the viewer or reader. Involvement in the entertainment message, however, should increase message impact on beliefs, attitudes, or behavior only to the extent that the portrayals and events bearing on those beliefs and behaviors are seamlessly integrated into plot and characterization. After all, when a viewer is seeking entertainment, there is no reason to attend to information relevant to one's own social and economic circumstances unless such information is inextricably part of an engaging story line. If, however, persuasive content is effectively imbedded in well-received plot and characterizations, what are the implications for subsequent processing of that content? How does processing of entertainment messages of this kind differ from processing overtly persuasive messages? What persuasive effects might be expected given such processing differences?

Entertainment Narratives and Inhibited Counterarguing. The most important difference regards the inclination and ability to cognitively resist or counterargue the persuasive content. Generating thoughts that counter a persuasive message, according to both theory and empirical findings, is central to discounting and resisting a persuasive message (Petty & Cacioppo, 1986; Roberts & Maccoby, 1973). Counterarguing tends to increase to the extent that the communication is discrepant with the audience member's attitudes and also may be influenced by the extent to which the message's intent to persuade is apparent (e.g., Brock, 1967). However, various context factors can decrease counterarguing. For example, when distraction makes it too difficult for a message recipient to discount message content, even a didactic message previously known to be inaccurate and untrue will influence recipient beliefs (Gilbert, 1991). We might expect that the distraction provided by a gripping narrative tends to inhibit discounting and counterarguing. After all, such counterarguing would fundamentally disrupt the suspension of disbelief that is essential if one is to be absorbed in a narrative. In addition, the persuasive intent of the message is not salient in the same way it is for a traditional persuasive message.

The study of cognitive responses to the short story excerpt mentioned above (Slater & Rouner, 1997, 1999) provides some preliminary data regarding the hypothesis that counterarguing will be relatively infrequent in response to implicitly persuasive messages imbedded in a narrative. College-student participants read an excerpt from a short story about a blind date, in which the use of alcohol results in the young woman's intoxication and (in various versions) difficulties such as getting sick on the date or causing a fender-bender. In a replication, they also read a story about a minor boating mishap in which drinking played a role. These incidents remained secondary to the overall plot, concerning the relationship between the two protagonists. Despite the fact that this brief excerpt was not likely to deeply engage readers to the extent that a novel, television program, or film might, we found that there were virtually no counterarguments made regarding the implicit persuasive content of the message concerning difficulties associated with social alcohol use (Slater & Rouner, 1997). Typically, with this college-student population, counterarguments to persuasive content negatively portraying alcohol use are quite common (e.g., Slater & Rouner, 1996). Although our results certainly demand replication with more engaging narrative materials, they are consistent with our expectations given the arguments presented here.

Other data from the same studies (Slater & Rouner, 1997, 1999) also supported the importance of narrative interest in predicting cognitive responses regarding alcohol use. More conventional involvement constructs such as personal involvement with alcohol or value-based involvement with alcohol did not serve a consistent mediating role, as would be expected when processing explicitly persuasive messages (see Petty & Cacioppo, 1986). In other words, narrative interest, and to a lesser extent, involvement, functioned as the key involvement variables in this narrative context, not issue- or value-related involvement as is found in studies of overtly persuasive messages (see Slater, 1997, for a full discussion of differences in types of involvement across message genres, including narrative). Since issue- or value-relevant involvement is considered a key mediator in traditional elaboration likelihood approaches (Johnson & Eagly, 1989; Petty & Cacioppo, 1986), it is clear that such traditional models are inadequate for characterizing the persuasive processing of entertainment messages (see also Prentice & Gerrig, 1999 and Slater, 1997 regarding problems with applying the Elaboration Likelihood Model to narrative messages and alternative theoretical strategies; these problems are also noted by Wheeler, Green, & Brock, 1999).

The lack of cognitive resistance associated with reduced counterarguing should enhance persuasive effects (see also Prentice, Gerrig, & Bailis, 1997; Prentice & Gerrig, 1999; Slater, 1990; Wheeler et al., 1999 for more experimental data regarding persuasive effects of fictional narratives). Use of narratives, in fact, may be one of the only strategies available for influencing the beliefs of those who are predisposed to disagree with the position espoused in the persuasive content. Normally, if persuasive message content is counterattitudinal, message recipients will ignore such content, counterargue it, or belittle the source of such information in a process Petty & Cacioppo (1986) called *biased processing*. However, the tendency of narrative-type information to suppress counterarguing may be quite strong.

In another study that dealt with attitudes toward drinking, we simply added one-paragraph anecdotes to an otherwise didactic advocacy message (Slater & Rouner, 1996). The inclusion of these anecdotes substantially increased receptivity to the persuasive appeal among those who initially disagreed with the message. Among these "counterattitudinal recipients," the inclusion of the anecdote indirectly influenced attitude change by altering perceptions of the quality and believability of the message. In contrast, the counterattitudinal recipients counterargued statistical evidence provided in the other experimental condition. These anecdotes, however, were not presented as being fictional.

The effectiveness of such anecdotes with counterattitudinal recipients suggests another possible reason for the persuasive effectiveness of narrative. It may be that lived experience of others is intrinsically difficult to counterargue: One may dispute the relevance or generality of another's experience, but not its substance. Perhaps, in vicariously living the experience of fictional characters, audience members accept such experiences in a similar way. It may be, on a primitive level, that people do not readily distinguish between accounts of real and fictional experience (consistent with Gilbert, 1991). A reader or viewer's visceral experience of "realness" may be more a function of emotional and physical arousal to the narrative than a consequence of the knowledge that a story is fiction, or even whether or not a story corresponds to known reality. The *Star Wars* world, in that sense, is probably more "real" to many pre-adolescents than many historical worlds to which they have been exposed in school. The relative contribution of subjective realism (see for example Potter, 1988) and fictional versus factual attribution remain largely unanswered empirical questions.

IMPLICATIONS FOR INCIDENTAL PERSUASIVE EFFECTS OF ENTERTAINMENT NARRATIVES

Intentionally persuasive narratives such as those found in entertainment-education provide a prototype for investigating and understanding persuasive effects from any entertainment narrative. The principal way in which entertainment-education differs from other entertainment narratives is in the explicit intention and care with which persuasive effects are sought. There is no reason why similar effects would not be found resulting from narratives not explicitly intended to influence attitudes or behavior.

For example, several decades of studies on violent television programming and violent films have led to the conclusion that such mediated violent portrayals do have a small but significant impact on violent behavior (see Gunter, 1994 for a review). However, the mechanisms by which such effects take place have not always been well elucidated, and it is difficult to use this research to develop general models of how entertainment messages influence individuals in society.

Potential for incidental effects of entertainment narratives may be greatest (a) when the topic of the message is unfamiliar, (b) when behaviors previously invisible in a media environment are favorably portrayed, or (c) when consistent information is portrayed across multiple messages. The first case can be understood intuitively: If one reads a historical novel or sees a historical movie such as *Shogun* and has no scholarly background regarding the time period portrayed, one's beliefs about that time and place are likely to be shaped by that fictional message. A study manipulating excerpts to have either fictional or nonfictional attributions, and to be about either familiar or unfamiliar social groups, found effects on beliefs about social groups to be equal or greater for excerpts with fictional attributions when the groups were unfamiliar (Slater, 1990).

The second case has been the focus of considerable public debate, although little empirical examination has been done. Considerable controversy has accompanied appealing examples of unmarried motherhood (*Murphy Brown*) and lesbian relationships (Ellen DeGeneres) on prime-time television. The furor may result from an intuitive lay recognition of an interesting theoretical possibility. Portrayal of a behavior previously perceived as deviant, by an attractive, socially desirable protagonist who receives largely positive or neutral reinforcements for the behavior in the portrayal, may lead those who identify with the protagonist to redefine the behavior as nondeviant. This strategy was also used by the pioneering public relations expert, Edward Bernays, to, as he put it, "break the taboo" against women's smoking. He arranged for attractive, socially prestigious debutantes to smoke while walking in New York's Easter Parade—a behavior that appeared the next day on the front page of the *New York Times* (Moyers, 1986).

The third case is the most commonplace one. As suggested earlier, instances of portrayals of people, social groups, social attitudes and social behaviors are likely to be well-remembered from engaging entertainment narratives. Such instances may serve cognitively as exemplars, and provide a basis for estimating social norms and social realities (Kahneman & Miller, 1986; Tversky & Kahneman, 1973). As Shrum and O'Guinn (1993) point out, this is a likely mechanism for the cultivation effect found in some sociological analyses, in which higher media-exposure is related to shared and inaccurate beliefs about social phenomena such as the frequency of criminal victimization (Gerbner, et al., 1994). Indeed, their study showed that heavier viewing of action programs, dramas and movies was associated with faster response times to questions regarding incidence of various kinds of crime and violence—a result consistent with the notion that such viewing resulted in relevant beliefs being more salient and more accessible to the viewer (Shrum & O'Guinn, 1993).

The incidental and cumulative effect of entertainment narratives on beliefs, values and behaviors is one of the most important issues facing communication scientists. Critical and cultural scholars have long emphasized the importance of such effects in understanding the impact of media on contemporary society. This chapter has summarized theoretical explanations and supportive empirical evidence regarding persuasive effects of narrative. Few areas of study in communication offer so much potential for understanding how communication influences individuals in society.

Entertainment education also highlights moral and ethical challenges associated with the persuasive potential of such stories. There is substantial, but by no means complete, consensus accepting use of such techniques to promote AIDS prevention, family health, substance abuse prevention, and gender equity. Nonetheless, questions may be raised about the rights of government or nonprofit organizations to attempt to influence personal, social, and cultural values by manipulating the content of popular culture such as broadcast entertainment programming. How far should such attempts go? What kinds of values and behaviors are appropriate and inappropriate to influence? What ideologies are implicitly supported through such efforts?

My own position on these issues rests on the conclusion that stories inevitably exert some form of influence on attitudes, beliefs, and/or behavior. In the absence of deliberate attempts to utilize the power of such communication for what can reasonably be argued to be public goods, the content of such programming is in most cases driven instead by either inertia or ratings. Certainly, in the United States, the drive to attract television and film audiences often appears to result in sensational content that is hardly likely to model behaviors that will improve the lives of viewers. Debate over the appropriateness and accountability of efforts to influence entertainment content is healthy—especially if such debate increases attention to the possible larger effects of entertainment content. Unwillingness to consider such interventions may well be irresponsible.

REFERENCES

Ajzen, I. (1991). The theory of planned behavior. *Organizational behavior and human decision processes, 50*, 179–211.

Ajzen, I., & Fishbein, M. (1980). *Understanding attitudes and predicting social behavior.* Englewood Cliffs, NJ: Prentice-Hall.
Ball-Rokeach, S. J., Grube, J., & Rokeach, M. (1981). "Roots: The Next Generation": Who watched and with what effect. *Public Opinion Quarterly, 45,* 58–68.
Bandura, A. (1977). *Social learning theory.* Englewood Cliffs, NJ: Prentice-Hall.
Bandura, A. (1986). *Social foundations of thought and action.* Englewood Cliffs, NJ: Prentice-Hall.
Berrueta, M. (1986). The soap opera as a reinforcer of social values. Unpublished master's thesis, IberoAmericano University, Mexico City, Mexico.
Bower, G., Black, J., & Turner, T. (1979). Scripts in text comprehension and memory. *Cognitive Psychology, 11,* 177–220.
Brock, T. (1967). Communication discrepancy and intent to persuade as determinants of counterargument production. *Journal of Experimental Social Psychology, 3,* 269–309.
Brooke, P. (1995). *Communicating through story characters.* Lanham, MD: University Press of America.
Chaffee, S. H., & Mutz, D. C. (1988). Comparing mediated and interpersonal communication data. In R. P. Hawkins, J. M. Wiemann, & S. Pingree (Eds.), *Advancing communication science: Merging mass and interpersonal processes* (pp. 19–43). Newbury Park, CA: Sage.
Cole, H. P. (1994). Embedded performance measures as teaching and assessment devices. *Occupational Medicine, 9*(2), 261–281.
Cole, H. P. (1997). Stories to live by: A narrative approach to health behavior research and injury prevention. In D. S. Gochman (Ed.), *Handbook of Heath Behavior Research IV* (pp. 325–349). New York: Plenum Press.
Cole, H. P., Vaught, C., Wiehagen, W. J., Haley, J. V., & Brnich, M. J. (1998). Decision making during a simulated mine fire escape. *IEEE Transactions on Engineering Management, 45*(2), 153–162.
Farr, R., & Moscovici, S. (1984). *Social representations.* Cambridge, MA: Cambridge University Press.
Fazio, R. H., Powell, M. C., & Williams, C. J. (1989). The role of attitude accessibility in the attitude-to-behavior process. *Journal of Consumer Research, 16,* 280–288.
Fishbein, M., & Middlestat, S. E. (1989). Using the theory of reasoned action as a framework for understanding and changing AIDS related behavior. In V. M. Mays, G. W. Albee, & S. F. Schneider (Eds.), *Primary prevention of psychopathology* (pp. 93–110). Newbury Park, CA: Sage.
Forbes, D. (2000, Jan. 13). Prime time propaganda. *Salon.* http://salon.com/news/feature/2000/01/13/drugs/index.html.
Gerbner, G., Gross, L., Morgan, M., & Signorielli, N. (1994). Growing up with television: The cultivation perspective. In J. Bryant & D. Zillmann (Eds.), *Media effects: Advances in theory and research* (pp. 17–42). Hillsdale, NJ: Lawrence Erlbaum Associates.
Giffen, W. C., & Rockwell, T. H. (1984). Computer-aided testing of pilot response to critical in-flight events. *Human Factors, 26,* 573–581.
Gilbert, D. T. (1991). How mental systems believe. *American Psychologist, 46*(2), 107–119.
Graesser, A. C. (1981). *Prose comprehension beyond the word.* New York: Springer-Verlag.
Green, M. C., & Brock, T. C. (1996). Mechanisms of narrative persuasion. *International Journal of Psychology, 31,* 13–14.
Gunter, B. (1994). The question of media violence. In J. Bryant & D. Zillmann (Eds.), *Media effects: Advances in theory and research* (pp. 163–212). Hillsdale, NJ: Lawrence Erlbaum Associates.
Hamilton, M. A. (1997). The phased interface omnistructure underlying the processing of persuasive messages. In F. Boster & G. Barnett (Eds.), *Progress in Communication Science* (Vol. 13, pp. 1–42). Norwood, NJ: Ablex.

Institute for Communication Research. (1981). *The social use of commercial television.* Strasbourg, France.
Johnson, B. T., & Eagly, A. H. (1989). Effects of involvement on persuasion: A meta-analysis. *Psychological Bulletin, 106,* 290–314.
Kahneman, D., & Miller, D. T. (1986). Norm theory: Comparing reality to its alternatives. *Psychological Review, 93*(2), 136–153.
Katz, E., & Lazarsfeld, P. F. (1955). *Personal influence: The part played by people in the flow of mass communications.* New York: The Free Press.
Kincaid, D. L. (1993, May). Using television dramas to accelerate social change. Annual conference of the International Communication Association, Health Communication Division. Washington, DC.
Kincaid, D. L., Yun, S. H., Piotrow, P. T., & Yaser, Y. (1993). Turkey's mass media family planning campaign. In T. E. Backer & E. M. Rogers (Eds.), *Organizational aspects of health communication campaigns: What works?* (pp. 68–92). Newbury Park, CA: Sage.
Lieberman, D. A. (1997). Interactive video games for health promotion: Effects on knowledge, self-efficacy, social support, and health. In R. L. Street Jr., W. R. Golds & T. Manning (Eds.), *Health promotion and interactive technology* (pp. 103–120). Mahwah, NJ: Lawrence Erlbaum Associates.
Maibach, E. W., & Cotton, D. (1995). Moving people to behavior change: A staged social cognitive approach to message design. In E. W. Maibach & R. L. Parrott (Eds.), *Designing health messages: Approaches from communication theory and public health practice* (pp. 41–64). Newbury Park, CA: Sage.
Mandler, J. M., & Johnson, N. S. (1980). Remembrance of things parsed: Story structure and recall. *Cognitive Psychology, 9,* 111–151.
McConnaughy, E. A., DiClemente, C. C., Prochaska, J. O., & Velicer, W. F. (1989). Stages of change in psychotherapy: A follow-up report. *Psychotherapy, 26*(4), 494–503.
McGuire, W. J. (1989). Theoretical foundations of campaigns. In R. E. Rice & C. K. Atkin (Eds.), *Public communication campaigns* (2nd edition, pp. 43–66). Newbury Park, CA: Sage.
Mishra, S. I, Conner, R., & Lewis, M. (1996, July 10). *AIDS prevention among Latino migrant workers: Evaluation of a prevention program.* XI International Conference on AIDS, Abstract We.D. 482.
Montgomery, K. C. (1989). *Target: Prime-time—Advocacy groups and the struggle over entertainment television.* New York: Oxford University Press.
Montgomery, K. C. (1993). The Harvard Alcohol Project: Promoting the designated driver on television. In T. E. Backer & E. M. Rogers (Eds.), *Organizational aspects of health communication campaigns: What works?* (pp. 178–202). Newbury Park, CA: Sage.
Moyers, B. (1986). *Imagemakers.* Broadcast March 3rd by the Public Broadcasting System.
Nell, V. (1988). *Lost in a book.* New Haven, CT: Yale University Press.
Petty, R. E., & Cacioppo, J. T. (1986). *Communication and persuasion: Central and peripheral routes to attitude change.* New York: Springer-Verlag.
Piotrow, P. T., Kincaid, D. L., Rimon, J. G., & Rinehart, W. (1997). *Health communication: Lessons from family planning and reproductive health.* Westport, CT: Praeger.
Potter, W. J. (1988). Perceived reality in television effects research. *Journal of Broadcasting and Electronic Media, 32,* 23–41.
Prentice, D. A., & Gerrig, R. J. (1999). Exploring the boundary between fiction and reality. In S. Chaiken & Y. Trope (Eds.), *Dual-process theories in social psychology* (pp. 529–546). New York: Guilford.
Prentice, D. A., Gerrig, R. J., & Bailis, D. S. (1997). What readers bring to the processing of fictional texts. *Psychonomic Bulletin & Review, 4,* 416–420.
Prochaska, J. O., DiClemente, C. C., & Norcross, J. C. (1992). In search of how people change: Applications to addictive behaviors. *American Psychologist, 47,* 1102–1114.

Roberts, D. F., & Maccoby, N. (1973). Information processing and persuasion: Counterarguing behavior. In P. Clarke (Ed.), *New models for mass communication research* (pp. 269–307). Newbury Park, CA: Sage.

Rogers, E. M., & Antola, L. (1985). Telenovelas in Latin America: A success story. *Journal of Communication, 35*, 24–35.

Rogers, E. M., Vaughan, P., & Shefner-Rogers, C. L. (1995, May 27). *Evaluating the effects of an entertainment-education radio soap opera in Tanzania: A field experiment with multi-method measurement*. International Communication Association. Albuquerque, NM.

Rouner, D. (1984). Active television viewing and the cultivation hypothesis. *Journalism Quarterly, 61*, 168–174.

Rubin, A. M., & Perse, E. M. (1987). Audience activity and soap opera involvement: A uses and effects investigation. *Human Communication Research, 14*, 246–268.

Rubin, A. M., Perse, E. M., & Powell, R. A. (1985). Loneliness, parasocial interaction, and local television news viewing. *Human Communication Research, 12*, 155–180.

Shaw, D. L., & McCombs, M. E. (1977). *The emergence of American political issues*. St. Paul, MN: West Publishing.

Shrum, L. J., & O'Guinn, T. C. (1993). Processes and effects in the construction of social reality. *Communication Research, 20*, 436–471.

Singhal, A., & Rogers, E. M. (1989). Prosocial television for development in India. In R. E. Rice & C. K. Atkin (Eds.), *Public communication campaigns* (pp. 331–350). Newbury Park, CA: Sage.

Singhal, A., & Rogers, E. M. (1999). *Entertainment-education: A communication strategy for social change*. Mahwah, NJ: Lawrence Erlbaum Associates.

Slater, M. D. (1990). Processing social information in messages: Social group familiarity, fiction vs. nonfiction, and subsequent beliefs. *Communication Research, 17*, 327–343.

Slater, M. D. (1997). Persuasion processes across receiver goals and message genres. *Communication Theory, 7*, 125–148.

Slater, M. D. (1999). Integrating application of media effects, persuasion and behavior change theories to communication campaigns: A stages of change framework. *Health Communication, 11*, 325–354.

Slater, M. D., & Rouner, D. (1996). Value affirmative and value protective processing of alcohol education messages that include statistics or anecdotes. *Communication Research, 23*(2), 210–235.

Slater, M. D., Rouner, D. (1997, May). *The processing of narrative fiction from the persuasion perspective: An exploratory study*. International Communication Association, Information Systems Division, Montreal, Canada.

Slater, M. D., & Rouner, D. (1999, May). *Identification, evaluation, and persuasion in the processing of narrative fiction*. International Communication Association, Information Systems Division, San Francisco, CA.

Storey, D., Boulay, M., Karki, Y., Heckert, K., & Karmacharya, D. M. (1999). Impact of the integrated Radio Communication Project in Nepal, 1994–1997. *Journal of Health Communication, 4*, 271–294.

Strange, J. J., & Leung, C. C. (1999). How anecdotal accounts in news and in fiction can influence judgments of a social problem's urgency, causes, and cures. *Personality and Social Psychology Bulletin, 25*, 436–449.

Tichenor, P. J., Donohue, G. A., & Olien, C. N. (1980). *Community conflict and the press*. Newbury Park, CA: Sage.

Tversky, A., & Kahneman, D. (1973). Availability: A heuristic for judging frequency and probability. *Cognitive Psychology, 5*, 207–232.

Vidmar, N., & Rokeach, M. (1974). Archie Bunker's bigotry: A study in selective perception and exposure. *Journal of Communication, 24*(1), 36–47.

Wander, P. (1977). On the meaning of "Roots." *Journal of Communication, 27*, 64–69.

Wheeler, S. C., Green, M. C., & Brock, T. C. (1999). Fictional narratives change beliefs: Replications of Prentice, Gerrig, & Bailis (1997) with mixed corroboration. *Psychonomic Bulletin & Review, 6,* 136–141.
Yoder, P. S., Hornik, R., & Chirwa, B. (1996). Evaluating the program effects of a radio drama about AIDS in Zambia. *Studies in Family Planning, 27*(4), 188–203.
Zajonc, R. B. (1980). Feeling and thinking: Preferences need no inferences. *American Psychologist, 35,* 151–175.
Zillmann, D., & Bryant, J. (1994). Entertainment as media effects. In J. Bryant & D. Zillmann (Eds.), *Media effects: Advances in theory and research* (pp. 437–462). Hillsdale, NJ: Lawrence Erlbaum Associates.

8

Girls, Reading, and Narrative Gleaning

Crafting Repertoires for Self-Fashioning Within Everyday Life

Janice Radway
Duke University

I was born in 1949. This makes me a member of the baby boom generation. Like hundreds of thousands of others, I was a girl in the 1950s, a teenager in the 1960s, and a young adult in the 1970s. Throughout, I was desperately trying to figure out what I might make of myself with the materials I had been given during the years of my coming of age. Of course this accident of birth also made me a middle-aged adult in the 1990s. Like many women of my generation, I am the mother of a daughter who is also trying to discern, as I once did, who she might be and where she might travel in the future. Wanting very much to ease Kate's progress through girlhood and into female adolescence, I have cast about, just as many others have, for advice and recommendations, for the perfect guidebook to a girl's coming of age. What I have found, to my dismay, is a series of disturbing narratives about girls at risk.

GIRLS AT RISK?

Our public discourse about girls is dominated these days by worried stories about how girls lose their sense of self as the culture transforms them into female teens whose only project is their own body. This ominous narrative paints a picture of girls bombarded by the redundant messages of titillating teen television shows, by the sexually explicit lyrics of pop music, by print and video images of anorexic models, and by endless quizzes about heterosexual mating and dating in teen magazines. Girls, the story goes, can only respond by taking up the singular place prescribed for them in these narratives that are often patriarchal (a social system where women are constituted only in and by their relationships to more powerful men). They can do nothing but absorb the monotonous and uninflected messages such forms supposedly convey. Participants in this discourse imply that if girls are to be liberated from depression and a destiny of enclosure, adult intervention will be necessary to protect girls from the surrounding culture so as to enable them to discover their deepest, most "authentic" selves.

In *The Body Project* (Brumberg, 1997), for instance, a much-discussed history of sexual maturation among girls in the United States, historian Joan Brumberg admitted that "The umbrella of protection created by the Victorians to shelter sexually maturing young girls had many problems, to be sure" (p. 25). Yet, in the interest of indicting contemporary culture for its obsession with bodily appearance, she went on to claim that the strictures of Victorian culture actually "eased the rite of passage in ways that adolescents today greatly need—and only rarely receive." Brumberg continued, "Instead of beginning an interlude of special guidance and support from other women, menarche today is just another step that moves girls deeper into a consumer culture that seduces them into thinking that the body and sexual expression are their most important projects." She then traced the ways in which this consumer culture mendaciously sells girls cosmetics, undergarments, clothes, and popular magazines by persuading them that their own flawed bodies not only should be, but can be, remade in the image of a prescribed ideal.

Joan Brumberg's principled reflections about how differently girls come of age now from the ways they did in the past were first expressed in more alarmed tones by Mary Pipher in the best-selling *Reviving Ophelia* (1994). There, she suggested that we must save the selves of adolescent girls because, in her words, "Something dramatic happens to girls in early adolescence" (p. 19). Pipher threateningly warned, "Just as planes and ships disappear into the Bermuda Triangle, so do the selves of girls go down in droves." She continued, "In early adolescence, studies show that girls' IQ scores drop and their math and science scores plummet. They lose their resiliency and optimism and become less curious and inclined to take risks. They lose their assertive, energetic and 'tomboyish' personalities and become more deferential, self-critical and depressed. They report great unhappiness with their own bodies." Although Pipher focused much more on contemporary family structure than Brumberg did as a factor in girls' depression, she also indicted the surrounding culture for its misogyny and its constraining effect on girls' sense of themselves.

As a mother, of course, I find these narratives about girls extremely troubling. As a feminist, I also recognize the truth of their depiction of contemporary culture. Consumer culture is, after all, still obsessively preoccupied with policing women's bodies; not merely with brushing, buffing, shaving, and adorning them, but also with rendering them uniformly thin and pretty through the devices of the diet, orthodonture, the work-out, and the knife. Yet something about these narratives also strikes me as significantly misguided. As a student of reading and media consumption, as a researcher interested in what people actually do with the stories they encounter in the context of a socially complex everyday life, I wonder about the picture of the girl reader or viewer that the girls' at-risk narratives implicitly construct. Not only are girls rendered entirely passive in these alarmist narratives, that is, as defenseless recipients of external, all-powerful cultural messages. At the same time, they are presented in isolation, as if all they do is watch television, read books, or flip through magazines. Gone are their families, their girlfriends, their schools, and their relationships with a multitude of others. Gone are the many creative activities they engage in around their media consumption. Girls are depicted in these at-risk narratives as incapable of a selective, critical response to narrative structures that, theoretically at least, could be subjected to scrutiny, dismantled and decomposed into a miscellany of parts, gleaned for usable images, ideas, and concepts, that is, for materials applicable to the process of self-fashioning.

READING PRACTICES VARY

My previous research leads me to ask, then, how girls actually make use of the narratives they encounter in the ordinary environment of the everyday. It seems important to ask whether girls *are* so successfully managed by the narratives they encounter? Can they imagine nothing more for themselves than the sexualized position of the girl heroines depicted in "Dawson's Creek," say, or in *Seventeen* and *Glamour*, or in the various titles of The Babysitters' Club series? Do girls identify so completely with the textually inscribed protagonist's point of view in the narratives they are given that when such stories conclude, their own, real-life desires have been remade to match the reduced satisfactions offered to their imagined counterparts in those stories? Are readers always fully subjected to the narratives they read? My previous work on romance readers (Radway, 1984) and the kind of middlebrow reading promoted by the Book-of-the- Month Club (Radway, 1997) suggests that girl readers may not be so thoroughly disciplined as their worried advocates might think.

In my work with readers of mass market romance, for instance, I have discovered that although women tend to accept the romance's recommendation of heterosexual coupling as the only route to happiness, some readers also take up highly selective, critical positions with respect to the romances they read. As I discussed at length in *Reading the Romance: Women, Patriarchy, and Popular Literature* (Radway, 1984), women do not necessarily approve of all romances they read, nor do they assent in any simple way to the way romantic heroines are depicted. They sift and select from the huge corpus of romance fiction published every month, relying on familiarity with favorite authors, recommendations from family and friends, and even on reviews to assist them in finding books that will provide the kind of pleasurable reading experience they seek. They constantly compare the heroine's experiences and perceptions to their own as a way of thinking critically about gender expectations and the relation between the sexes. Although romances do seem to reiterate the inevitability of heterosexual coupling in the end, they also appear to function as an occasion for meditation on the particular factors that make certain couplings more successful than others. There seems to be a certain variability, then, in how individual women take up a particular relationship to the patriarchal tale told by the romance.

Similarly, I have discovered that in making their way through the formulaic and highly structured romance narrative, women readers demonstrate significant variety in their manner of response to the developing story. Some read from beginning to end, straight through, waiting for the contentment that the narrative resolution promises to provide. Such readers seem deeply invested in being told yet again that romance is possible, that marriage won't destroy it, and that therefore men really can supply the emotional sustenance women need. In cases like this, romance reading seems to function as a necessary, perhaps even somewhat desperate, reassurance in the face of suspicion that something is deeply wrong with the gender order as we know it. Other readers, however, check out the ending first just to ensure that the desired resolution will present itself. Once they have done so, they suggest, they give themselves over more intensely to the welter of conflicting emotions that their engagement with the full range of textual characters and events incites. In these cases, it seems that some romance readers are more invested in the erotic tension and sexual desire generated by the bulk of the romance narrative than in the achievement of that state of narrative hypnosis and contentment provided by the heterosexual closure of the marriage plot. If this is true, it seems possible that the romance narrative may in fact be generating emotions and desires within the duration of the reading process that its own structured resolution cannot contain. In that case, reading may not suture women ever more tightly into the patriarchal fabric of contemporary culture, but rather may be generating dissatisfactions and longings that could conceivably promote change among the women who so faithfully return to the romance form again and again. Reading, in this case, may not always be a closed process of taking up an already prescribed textual and cultural position but rather more like a practice of exploration, a practice of trying on new roles and experimenting with new emotions in the safe space of the imaginary.

I have attempted to address the question of whether romance reading could alter women in unpredictable ways in two articles entitled, "Identifying Ideological Seams: Mass Culture, Analytical Method, and Political Practice," (Radway, 1986) and "Romance and the Work of Fantasy: Struggling with Female Subjectivity and Sexuality at Century's End" (Radway, 1993). The former focuses on the ways in which the private, isolated experience of habitual romance reading often leads to the impulse to write a romance, thus transforming some women from readers to writers, from consumers to producers. Sometimes this leads subsequently to the formation of romance writing groups that enable women to come together in new ways around interests other than private, domestic concerns. In the second article, I pursued a related line of thinking by examining recent changes to the romance plot in the context of a discussion of certain psychoanalytically based theories about narrative engagement.[1] These theories suggest that readers never simply identify with a single character in a narrative, that is, with the protagonist of the plot. Rather, they argue that readers' investments in fictional structures may be more promiscuous. They may be multiple, mobile, and fluid. Readers may wander in their investments, now identifying with the heroine or the hero, now with minor characters, now with the narrator. Identifications, it would seem, can cross gender and color lines.

Indeed there is a certain amount of evidence to suggest that romance readers' identifications are not solely with the romance heroine. For some, in fact, the actual target of interest and meditative energy is the hero. Conventionally, one might suggest that such an investment implies only that female readers imaginatively desire the hero. However, it may also be the case that such readers are in fact imagining what it would be like to *be* that hero. In this view of narrative engagement, readerly interest is not fixed to a single character. In fact, it may not always be channeled in and through character at all, but may range more freely. It may be dispersed across a landscape, a scene, or through the depiction of a certain feeling tone. Reading, in this view, is an interactive, even interpersonal process between text and reader, an intersubjective engagement that is infinitely more complex, more contradictory, more at odds with itself than traditional views of reading as consumption or even interpretation would suggest.[2] As such, reading is much more difficult to track and to describe. Similarly, its effects are more difficult to discern and to explain. Readers may indeed be affected and changed by the narratives that engage them, but not always in predictable, controlled, even detectable ways. Reading, in some cases, may be genuinely prospective, that is, it may propel the reader into the future in new ways. In that case, reading's effects may not be realized for years.

THE QUESTION OF READING'S EFFECTS

I have taken up the question of reading's impact on the reader in another investigation of reading as a social practice, that is, in *A Feeling for Books: The Book-of-the-Month Club, Literary Taste and Middle Class Desire* (Radway, 1997). Initially conceptualized as a way to get at the variability of reading practices or literacies, this project was changed significantly by my gradual discovery that despite the apparent variety of books on offer through The Book-of-the-Month Club, club editors and officials actually selected that diverse collection of titles with an extraordinarily consistent set of aesthetic criteria in mind as well as with clear expectations about why and how people read. Through interviews with club officials, participant observation at editorial meetings, and careful analysis of the multiple reader's reports generated for every title considered at the club, I was able to delineate the particulars of what I called the middlebrow aesthetic. The Book-of-the-Month Club chose books that were neither too technical nor too superficial, neither too ponderous nor too lightweight. They aimed to distribute "serious books" for the general reader, for those who want to be informed and yet entertained as they read.

Fiction, popular histories, handbooks and guidebooks, nonfiction, even reference works—all were evaluated at the Book-of-the-Month Club for their ability to inform the reader in a warm-blooded, human, "personalist" way. According to the club's judges, their readers don't want to know technical details about the physiology of the heart. That sort of book is for physicians and other medical experts. Their general readers want to know rather, how to avoid a heart attack, what to do when you suspect you may be having one, or, perhaps more imaginatively, what it feels like to recover from one. *A Feeling for Books* (Radway, 1997) attempts to explain the appearance of this particular way of reading, this middlebrow "personalism," by placing it within a history of cultural production and the development of the middle class. I suggested that middlebrow readers longed for cultural mastery and informational expertise yet demanded from the books they read a sense that both could be had without losing one's affective, emotional investment in the human and the particular. Although I can't summarize the complexities of that argument here, it is important to note in this context that I do suggest that middlebrow reading helped to produce certain emotional capacities and modes of perception among readers that were congruent with a developing middle class perspective on the world. As the romance underscores the value of compulsory heterosexuality, so middlebrow reading teaches the naturalness of a view of the world that values the individual and the particular over the structural and the abstract, the value of an individual's affective life over his or her intellectual distance.

Even as *A Feeling for Books* (Radway, 1997) attempts to explain how middlebrow literature and middlebrow reading practices may have helped to produce certain forms of middle-class desire, however, it also makes an effort to show how the effects of reading are not everywhere thoroughly disciplined and controlled. Although I had wanted to interview Book-of-the-Month Club subscribers in some depth about their individual reading habits and experiences as a way of getting at this kind of readerly variability and excess, I could not gain the kind of access to subscribers that would have made this possible. As I was about to concede that the project would not be able to take up the question of reading at all except in a speculative way, I discovered that a collection of books I had read as a home-bound, teen-aged girl under treatment for curvature of the spine were, in fact, Book-of-the-Month Club books. I decided to offer my own experience with them, then, as an instance of one person's history with the Book-of-the-Month Club. I aimed to discuss some of the books I had read in detail by juxtaposing my own memories of how I had read them then with my interpretations of them now as instances of middlebrow narrative and thought. Throughout these discussions, I aimed to maintain a tension between the ways in which such texts acted on me, thereby producing certain kinds of discernibly middle-class desires, and a description of the idiosyncratic details I somewhat perversely gleaned from the texts and stored within my developing repertoire of memorable fictional characters, readerly experiences, and bookish perceptions.

Yet, now, as I look back on the project in the context of my thoughts on girls' reading and media use, it seems to me that *A Feeling for Books* (Radway, 1997) does not go far enough in its effort to trace a double movement. That is, it doesn't adequately capture both the way in which my middlebrow reading inscribed me into a dominant, middle-class way of thinking and provided the occasion for my selective investment in peculiar details of characterization, scenic description, and feeling tone. The trajectory it describes, even as it attempts to pay attention both to a modal and a particular way of reading, is still too unified, too coherent, too closed off, as if the narrator, "Janice Radway," knows definitively who the girl, "Janice Stewart," became and exactly what role her reading played in that process. This history pragmatically assumes (at least for the purposes of this particular volume) that there was only one way I used the peculiar details I drew from the books I read. In fact, in the process of meditating on why our approaches to girls and reading may be seriously limited, it has occurred to me that I might narrate my reading history in an entirely different way. In fact, I made of the materials I gleaned from my reading not only the inspiration for, and tools with which to craft, a middle class professional life, but something else as well. The texts discussed in *A Feeling for Books* might be connected with a longer reading history, one that, for me, started somewhat earlier. They might be treated therefore as later contributions to an already assembled fund of images, ideals, and promises. That fund developed in a manner that was deeply entwined with incidents from everyday life. Together, that reading and the quotidian life within which it proved meaningful, constituted an imaginative and emotional storehouse that supplied both the resources for a distinctly middle-class desire *and* the materials for a very different and specifically gendered, self-fashioning.

I want to extend my reading history backward in time a bit in order to provide an alternative account of it for two reasons. I hope to provide a compelling account of the idiosyncratic way in which reading can sometimes proceed despite the fact that a reader always engages with an already structured text. In addition, I hope this account will cast doubt on a certain understanding of how selfhood develops, the kind of understanding that I believe grounds the recent girls at-risk narratives. Those narratives, it seems to me, in their obsessive concern for the lost, "authentic" selfhood of girls implicitly construes selfhood as somehow external to culture. In these narratives, in fact, culture—in the form of books, films, and television shows—seems to exist outside girls and beyond them. It impinges on them only as an alien, controlling force. The girls themselves seem to have no agency or power to transform the cultural materials they take in from outside. In opposition to this, I want to suggest that action and agency are misconstrued if they are seen as coming only from within a supposedly authentic self that is set somehow in opposition to an imprisoning culture. Selves are intertwined *with* culture. Children are not born with their resources intact. They can't speak, they can't express themselves, and they can't even move their bodies about in space. Children gradually develop resources by taking up *particular* languages, objects, gestures, and habits, those that are presented to them as they emerge always *within and through* culture. Children make and remake themselves with materials ready to hand. What I am interested in here is how that making proceeds when it is abetted by reading and how the results of that reading and making can sometimes be remade in the future through the re-use of materials gleaned from earlier reading experiences.

READING AND WRITING AS PRACTICES OF SELF-FASHIONING

I grew up in the 1950s and 1960s in Cresskill, New Jersey, a middle-class suburb of New York City, during a time of relative prosperity, when the consumer culture we are so familiar with today was taking off with a vengeance. I can remember when we got our first television, how much I wanted a Revlon doll (one of the precursors to Barbie), the birthday I got my first nylon stockings and a garter belt, and my relentless demand for a particularly large, black purse displayed in the window of the Florence Shop in Bergenfield just before Christmas in 1961. Clearly, I was conventionally ushered into the culture of girlhood and femininity by the movie and teen magazines I read so faithfully and by the sexy, pounding rock n' roll issuing from my first bedside radio. But interspersed with these memories that were evoked recently when I read those handbooks I bought to advise Kate during her adolescence, are other memories, memories I have carried for a long time, recollections I have often returned to in the effort to tell myself or another who I take myself to be. In the past, I have narrated this history as the source for emergent class desires that enabled me to escape traditional, 1950s-style gender expectations for girls. Now, however, I see also that the materials I derived from this reading-inflected history may have subsequently become useful in quite a different response to traditional gender arrangements.

The first recollection from this familiar memory fund comes from the third grade. I remember that I absolutely adored my teacher, Miss Guardiano, who was tall, thin, and beautiful. She had short, black hair—shorter than I had ever seen on a woman before. I remember liking her intensely, desperately wanting her to like me, and wanting even more to be like her. The 200-odd days I spent in her company are gone, however, represented only by the recollection that it was in her class that I learned what a French seven was. When Miss Guardiano began teaching us addition and subtraction and elementary division, she wrote her sevens on the board with a weird, insouciant little cross through the stem. I don't recall whether she told us that that was how they did it in France, but I do know that ever since then, I have written my sevens in that odd, affected, different way. Who can tell what I thought I was doing? I must have been no more than 8 or 9 years old. But it seems clear to me now that I was trying to create an identity through a particular act of writing, to inscribe a self like that of the much-admired, loved, and longed-for Miss Guardiano.

That does seem clear, I suppose, because this third-grade memory is followed in my narrative of self-development by several from the fourth grade that specifically connect writing with reading. It was in the fourth grade that I first began to read "whole books," as I called them then, "on my own." I began to check out an endless stream of stories and biographies aimed at young readers from our grade school library after discovering a novel called *The Boxcar Children*. I no longer remember any of the details of this story nor why I liked it so much. I *can* recall my absorption and enthrallment, however. These recollected emotions call up in my imagination a fuzzy, indistinct image of a line drawing of a group of young children running out of the railroad boxcar they were living in, "on their own." Reading, this association suggests, was connected for me with independence, with a way to be "on my own" yet in the company of appealing fictional others.

The other things I remember checking out of the Bryan School Library after *The Boxcar Children* (Warner, 1977) was Louisa May Alcott's *Little Women* and every title in the Nancy Drew series written to that point. I was fascinated by Jo March *and* by Nancy, by Jo's cropped hair and by her desire to write, by Nancy's sporty blue coupe and by the fact that she had a girlfriend named George. I loved the fact that she could solve mysteries "on her own" with only a little help from her largely absent father, Carson Drew. Alcott's novel and the Nancy Drew books are forever merged in my mind because it was also during this year that I used some of my birthday money to buy a pack of loose-leaf paper the size of a 5 × 7 inch book. I bound that packet together with scraps of red yarn and a cardboard and yellow construction paper cover on which I inscribed the title, *The Secret under the Stairs*. It was accompanied by a crudely drawn illustration that was an imitation of the predominantly blue and yellow paintings of secret corners and dark places that graced the covers of the books by Carolyn Keene.

I remember taking my lovingly crafted blank book out to the patio one late summer afternoon, my version of Jo March's garret, to begin writing, as she once had. Unlike Jo, however, I never got past the first paragraph. Why, I don't know. Perhaps it was because I was intimidated by all that blank paper. Perhaps because I couldn't yet imagine what a girl heroine might do. I only know now that, then, I wanted to be a writer, an author like the women I was reading, a character like the girls they were writing about. I imitated the things I admired in them as I had imitated Miss Guardiano. I was worried that this was stealing, that I didn't have a self of my own. I didn't advertise my acts of love and theft therefore, I didn't call attention to my mimicry. But I presented myself to the small world of Heather Hill Court and Bryan School as a girl who wrote French sevens, as a curious reader of signs and clues like Nancy, and as someone who wanted someday to be a writer like Jo.

One final scene will clarify the point I am trying to make here about the nature of self-fashioning with these fragments from my past. This particular fragment comes from my sixth-grade year, the year that my class was taught by an exchange teacher from England, by the fastidious, prim, and superior Mr. Maw. Mr. Maw was contemptuous of the America he discovered in 1960, a country infatuated with television, still mesmerized by Elvis and rock 'n roll, and newly preoccupied with putting a man in space. He hectored my friends and me about how inferior we were to English children and about how poor our schools were compared to those he had known in his home country. "Why, children your age in London would be reading Shakespeare," he told us, "they would be familiar with Dickens." He was going to acquaint us with "literature," he lectured, he was going to ask us to live up to a higher, *European* standard.

You can imagine, I suppose, what this must have meant to that snobbish girl who had already declared herself to be both bookish and different in some sort of cosmopolitan way. She threw herself into the business of acquiring culture with zeal and devotion. I still don't know if the passion was for Shakespeare and high culture or for the paunchy but oh-so-cultivated Mr. Maw himself. But I read my *Hamlet* and *Romeo and Juliet* diligently although I couldn't understand very much of the language of either. Still, I asked my grandfather to give me a volume of Shakespeare's collected plays for Christmas and enthusiastically participated in the Elizabethan pageant that Mr. Maw concocted for our parents. He required all of us to dress for the gala performance as a character from the plays. I insisted in going in drag—not as Romeo or Mercutio, or as Hamlet or Polonius, but as Shakespeare himself. To my parent's eternal credit, they never once expressed misgivings or worried that I wanted to cross dress. They simply indulged my desire to carry out this impersonation by finding a theatrical supplier who would sell us greasepaint and a wig, a mustache and the glue to put it on. Indeed my mother crafted breeches and a doublet on the sewing machine in my bedroom and she made a smashing hat complete with plume and an enormous sweep of a blue brim.

My unabashed effort at self-fashioning in this instance crossed gender boundaries and historical limits. I made myself the subject of a ridiculously expansive and ambitious desire by playing at being the world's most famous poet and dramatist from the 16th century. This form of mimicry clearly grew out of, and built on, the longings and desires I had already experienced by identifying so strongly and somewhat promiscuously with Miss Guardiano, the Boxcar children, Jo March, and Nancy Drew. Although I never again cross-dressed, at least in so ostentatious and exuberant a manner, nor ever tried my hand at poetry, I continued to nurture a desire to write, not as a novelist but as a journalist. The middlebrow, middle-class desire to master the process of information production, which was promoted by the Book-of-the- Month Club books I encountered then at age 14, fit right into this developing configuration of selfhood.

In recounting these vignettes here, I don't mean to celebrate the wants and desires they attest to, nor even to recommend them. Now, in fact, they appear not only deeply ideological but also distinctly narcissistic, too individualist, too bound up with capturing the gaze and attention of admiring others. What I do want to point to, however, is to their existence in the midst of a traditionally gendered girlhood, one that included party dresses, a first pair of heels, the desire to be a cheerleader, hundreds of movie and fashion magazines, and a contradictory passion for Broadway musicals, especially for the mouthy, loud and brassy women who starred in them. Not for me the sweet and lyrical Julie Andrews of the film version of "The Sound of Music." I preferred my Maria in the person of Mary Martin, who played her first on Broadway, and much more audaciously, to my eyes. I admired Carol Channing, Ethel Merman, Liza Minelli and Carol Burnett. I can conjure them even now; mouths wide open, belting out their songs, arms thrown wide to the world.

SELFHOOD AS COLLAGE

My point is to suggest that growing up is not a process of gradual realization, of cultivating an already existent, singular, authentic self sitting passively and in anticipation, like the seed of a daffodil, awaiting the warmth and light of the spring. Nor is it a simple process of inhabiting certain *culturally* constructed desires, whether they are middle-class or traditionally gendered in a patriarchal sense. Rather, it is much more like wandering through an enormous attic filled with the cast-offs and hand-me-downs of others, rushing from dusty thing to thing, imagining how they might be put to work differently, gleaning from that miscellaneous collection those few tattered and worn habiliments and treasures that might be adapted for use in one's own bedroom, in one's own ordinary life. I believe that we make ourselves with and through materials that are ready-to-hand, presented to us by those people and institutions with whom we inevitably live. To be sure, then, we make ourselves with materials and in conditions that are *not* of our own making. Thus, those materials and conditions inevitably exert their own kind of force and constraint on our acts of fabrication. Still, we do manage to alter the materials we work with if only by contextualizing them differently, by inserting them into somewhat different narratives. We make ourselves out of the very stories, songs, objects, performances, and characters that people our daily lives and point us and our imaginations toward an only dimly discerned future.

Now I realize you may be thinking to yourself that this narrative of self-construction may well be idiosyncratic. After all, I eventually did make myself into a mouthy professor and a writer, albeit of a different sort from Jo March, Carolyn Keene, or Will Shakespeare. You might also be thinking, and justifiably so, I believe, that this is a class-specific narrative about a privileged child. After all, my parents and grandparents had enough resources to save enough money to take me occasionally to Broadway musicals, to buy me a few original cast albums, to abet my promiscuous desires by taking me to the library. They themselves were privileged enough to want an education for me, to hold it out to me as a goal, to provide the means and encouragement to go after it. As Susan Miller (1998), a theorist of composition studies, literacy, and writing observed in an important book about commonplace writing in 17th century America, entitled *Assuming the Positions*, "individuals do not have equal access to the subject positions or the power or passivity they entail, in specific cultural settings" (p. 3). Constraints always structure what we are given and how we might take them up just as the weight of those constraints are felt more heavily by some than by others.

Not everyone, clearly, had equal access in the 1950s to Jo March or even to Dolly Levi. Nor was every girl enabled by the prospects embedded in her class position to ignore Jo's eventual marriage to Professor Baehr in the service of remembering her only as the tomboyish writer of hair-raising sensation stories. More girls were taught to admire Jo's conventional sisters, Meg and Beth, or to imitate the ingratiating, melodic tones of Julie Andrews rather than the insurgent, guttural, growl of Carol Channing and Ethel Merman. Still, it seems to me that those processes of imitating more authorized models are not different in kind from the identification and mimicry I have tried to detail here from my own history of self-construction. Nor are they different from those engaged in by my students in the 80s and 90s who tried to dress like Madonna or Queen Latifah, or from the efforts of their younger sisters who bounce along now in their rooms to the tunes of the Spice Girls or who learn to step in church groups, community centers, and school sororities.[3] They are equally related to the strenuous efforts of many thousands of girls and young women who labor diligently to produce the toned, tanned, and taut bodies that they see garner all the attention in ads, television shows, and at the movies. These acts of self-construction—however we evaluate them—are generated by the same impulse, by the desire to project a self that might move about in the world and among particular kinds of people in specific, intensely desired ways. As such, they are mixes of creation and constraint. They are the products of inchoate, genuinely prospective desires, of a willed determination to make something of what has been offered by a contradictory, contested cultural environment that cannot, for all its trying, either predict or determine the future.

What the privilege of my particular story suggests is that we ought to be preoccupied with providing a range of disparate, even contradictory materials to all girls in order to aid and abet them in their processes of self-dramatization and self-construction. And, in the present environment, when so much of cultural production is controlled by only a few corporations that want to turn out only those stories or objects that will attract the largest, most generalized and usually white audience, this is becoming increasingly difficult to manage. Similarly, at a time when our schools—especially in the lower divisions—are still charged with deploring the pleasures of popular culture and teaching only the value of a "serious," legitimate cultural tradition, it is "the restricted possibilities for articulating desire," (p. 3) as Susan Miller (1998) put it, that deserves our attention. Girls need to be presented with all kinds of narrative materials, materials that engage them and capture *their* interest, not ours.[4] Stories, songs, styles of dress, games, sports, and occasions for performance, all of these sketch out manifold possibilities for imagining the body in space and in relation to captivating others. Girls need to read, watch, and listen to all kinds of narratives, both popular and legitimate. Equally importantly, however, they need to be encouraged to wander about within all those narratives, to glean from them just the materials they want to write, create, and produce their own. Reading, in the broadest sense—that is, the taking in of significant experiences and observations through narrations of both—must be connected to writing, to active creation and production, to the process of renarration. For it is in the space between these two fundamental practices that all of us, girls included, manage to gesture toward the world and the future in genuinely prospective, unpredictable ways.

THE UNPREDICTABILITY OF PLAYFUL GLEANING

I want to stress the importance of the word, unpredictable, here, to suggest that it is very important that we not assume that we know what will be made, or is being made, of any particular story, book, or object we provide for young girls. Indeed I am certain that if my parents thought at all about my early acts of reading and writing or about my odd tastes for certain kinds of performances, they undoubtedly thought of them as good preparation for achievement in school and for a professional career. That is certainly how I myself have construed the incidents I have just related here in the past, that is, as the first steps on the road to that middle-class subjectivity abetted in its construction by the next stage in my reading history, that encounter with the middlebrow books of the Book-of-the-Month Club. In that sense, these were the occasion for my ideological inscription into a familiar and dominant cultural narrative about the worth of bourgeois individualism and the value of middle-class achievement and professionalism. But when I tell the story now I aim to evoke in it the distinct intimations of a different history, the history of the construction of a lesbian self with desires to have a butch girlfriend named George, to soar through the world like Mary Martin cross-dressed as Peter Pan, to sing loudly to the world of a woman's desire in the voice, no less, of Ethel Merman, and not for life busting out all over or for a man, but for another woman who might, just might, resemble one's beloved third-grade teacher. This, too, is my history, although I could only claim it and tell it as such relatively recently.

Pleasure reading, it would seem, can be a way of imagining possible ways of occupying social space and relating to the world. It can be a way of actually inhabiting other subjectivities, other ways of gesturing toward the world with words. For me, certainly, it was decidedly *not* a hermeneutic practice of explicating what Louisa May Alcott or Carolyn Keene had to say to me about that world, a practice I was first taught in my high school English classes when I was instructed to ask, "what does the red sun symbolize at the end of *The Red Badge of Courage?*" Nor was my pleasure reading a simple matter of submitting myself to Alcott's and Keene's superior authority and intelligence. Reading was sometimes more of a form of itinerant poaching for me—to use Michel de Certeau's (1984) terminology—a way of raiding texts for what I could use to project a future.

Those raids were incited by particular affective identifications and emotional involvements, sometimes with main characters, sometimes with authors themselves, and sometimes with mere hints contained in minor characterizations. I'm thinking, for instance, of that girlfriend named George. It's possible that I viewed this nonconforming name as merely an idiosyncratic choice on the part of the imagined author, Carolyn Keene, a peculiar but nonetheless insignificant act of naming a minor character. But I wonder, now, at the end of a long, personal history that might just possibly have been abetted by the hint contained in that choice, whether it didn't imply—as perhaps did Alcott's suggestion that a girl named Jo could have a boyfriend named Laurie—that gender and gender relations were themselves unstable. Perhaps this supposedly inconsequential bit of word play and characterization managed to hint to some readers that the parties to gender relations could be named and therefore categorized differently, that girlfriends might perform some of the offices and functions usually reserved for men, and that men might themselves behave as sensitively, exuberantly, and "femininely" as women were expected to. It's hard to say. What would constitute evidence for such a claim? How *is* lesbian desire, or traditional femininity, for that matter, constituted? Are we ready to assert that reading and writing have had no place in the construction of either? I, for one, am not.

Texts do not dictate their meanings to us. Stories do not control what readers remember of them or take away from them to be adapted to the particulars of their own lives. Nor do objects determine what we will do with them. Think of the simple safety pin in the hands of punk rockers in the 1970s or of the American flag that graced the backside of so many pairs of jeans in the 1960s. Neither do musical compositions fully dictate which passages will be hummed over and over again in the shower or on the way to school. Cultural materials function rather more like incitements than stamps, imprints, or molds.

In a book about the fundamental creativity of children, entitled *The Beast in the Nursery: On Curiosity and Other Appetites,* Adam Phillips (1998) argued for a kind of analysis or therapy that "aims to restore the artist in the patient, the part of the person that makes interest despite, or whatever, the early environment" (pp. 4–5). He continued, "At its most extreme, for the artist of her own life, it is not so much a question of what she has been given but of what she can make of what she has been given.... The psychoanalytic model here is the dream ... in which so-called reality functions more like a hint than an instruction, setting the dreamer and the child off on the work of transformation." Phillips' reading of Freud stressed not the automatism and the universality of the Oedipal developmental trajectory. Rather, he foregrounded the inevitable idiosyncratic creativity of dreaming in which every individual captures and reworks the detritus of the ordinary day and puts it to use in wholly disguised form in an effort to puzzle out yet again the nature of his or her own place within the family romance. Phillips suggested further that this dreamwork is not different in kind from the alchemical processes that take place in certain kinds of reading and learning, which he believes are not different from the active process of artistic creation. Indeed, Phillips is much more interested in learning than in teaching because, as he put it, "the student finds [herself] unwittingly drawn to specific bits of the subject being taught—whatever the emphasis of the teacher happens to be—which [she] will then, more or less secretly (even to [herself]) transform into something rather strange" (p. 67).

ABETTING GIRLS AT PLAY

What I am trying to suggest here is that we should not be too quick to assume that we know what girls are making of the cultural materials they are being given. Nor should we assume that we know what they will make later of what they produce now. Self-fashioning is a process of accretion and perpetual transformation, it seems to me, of making something anew every time a story is told, a tune is hummed, or a piece of clothing is selected and put on. As Phillips (1998) observed:

> The child has foisted upon her the culture's repertoire of acceptable ways of being and answers back, often in rage, but more acceptably in inventiveness and innovation.

> The child's freedom, the child's self-fashioning project depends upon her being able to treat orders and instructions as though they were also hints and suggestions, as open invitations rather than merely prescriptions. (p. 115)

Too often, it seems to me, official education teaches the child to lose interest in what matters most to her. Indeed there are reasons why so many children today insist that reading doesn't interest them, that books are "boring." In part that has to do with the fact that television and popular music as multimillion dollar industries have made it their business to figure out what interests kids and, as a result, kids' interests and appetites are constructed from the cultural materials those industries turn out. But it also has to do with the fact that official education—especially that of the English classroom—still conceives of itself as the guardian of different and inherently better materials, as the moral savior and counter to the devilish temptation of popular culture. Too often still, it teaches writing in connection with the valorized and deliberately intimidating category of literature. It demands imitation rather than queer creation, explication rather than flights of fancy.

If schools and other sites of intergenerational contact are really to assist kids in their projects of self-construction, then they must provide the space for them to engage the materials that fascinate them. They must acknowledge the significance of fashion and beauty magazines, say, to some girls, and provide them with the opportunity to explore what, quite literally, they can make of them. As Phillips (1998) suggested, "the value of the hint—(what one borrows or has spoken to you) is irrespective of its aesthetic value ... whatever it is in oneself that is struck by these things has quite a different set of criteria of value" (p. 88). The good hint, he suggested, is in the eye of the beholder; the most valuable objects are those a girl can work with. Stories are dead letters to kids when they are presented as things merely to abide by. For that reason, reading and writing need to be decoupled, at least initially, from authorized forms of criticism and allied much more closely with the ordinary and the everyday commonplaces. What we need to revive is an attentiveness to the irregular and to the odd, to the wayward, vagrant itinerary of interest, appetite, and affinity. If we do, it seems to me, we will be able to see and hear the ways in which girls are not merely at risk now but also already struggling to make something new of the deadly and deadening culture they still too often encounter in the narratives they find ready to hand.

THE INSUBORDINATE CREATIVITY OF GIRLS' ZINES

There are many forms, practices, and modes that one could point to in girl culture today to illustrate this kind of insubordinate creativity. I think particularly of the many collages girls construct to adorn their rooms, their notebooks, and their diaries. But because I have been so preoccupied here with the nexus between reading and writing, I would like to look very quickly before I close at what girls have done to explode, fragment, and recreate traditional forms of mass culture by wedding print culture in new ways to certain musical subcultures. I am thinking here of zine culture, that form of writing, composing, and publishing that kids carry out "on their own" using pens and pencils, cut-out photos and glue, Kinko's and the U. S. mail, listservs and the internet. Zines, as you may already know, are individually produced creations that combine writing and visual images and they are usually circulated through the mail, although they can be sold at concerts, at schools, at alternative bookstores, and even through websites like that designed by Factsheet Five, or F5, the zine bible. F5 can be accessed at: (http://www.wel.com/conf/f5/f5index2.html). The term zine comes from the neologism, fanzine, which was originally created to refer to mimeographed fan newsletters that were first created and circulated by fans of science fiction in the 1960s. Now, they are created by boys and girls, by young men and women, for all sorts of reasons. There are personal zines, political zines, music zines, queer zines, comix, and literary zines, to name only a few. There are also girl zines, some of which were inspired initially by Riot Grrrl culture, a subculture of girls that developed in the wake of punk around certain all-girl bands like Bikini Kill, Bratmobile, and Heavens to Betsy.

RIOT GRRRLS AND THEIR ZINES

Recently, Riot Grrrl culture has drawn a considerable amount of attention both among mainstream media and young female academics. There have been articles in the magazines *Time*, *Newsweek*, and *Sassy*, as well as in the scholarly journal *Signs* (1998), and a book entitled *Third Wave Agenda: Being Feminist, Doing Feminism* (Heywood & Drake, 1997). For the moment, I am less interested in the content of the whole, complex riot grrrl subculture than in its structure and function and the critical place of zines within it. It is important to know, however, that the defiant spelling of girl as g-r-r-r-l, intended to be spoken with a growl, the coinage of which is usually attributed to Kathleen Hanna of Bikini Kill, perfectly encapsulates both the anger at the heart of riot grrrl practice and its insistent desire to be loud. As Jessica Rosenberg (Rosenberg & Garafalo, 1998) put it in her preface to an interview with riot grrrls from around the country, "At a time in their lives when girls are taught to be silent, Riot Grrrl demands that they scream" (p. 810).

Zines have played a central role in the circulation and extension of Riot Grrrl Culture. Although most girls who associate themselves with Riot Grrrl suggest that they were first hailed by its scream when they stumbled across the music of Bikini Kill or Heavens to Betsy, their search for more music of the same kind often led them to discover zines like *Girl Germs*, *Jigsaw*, and *Chainsaw*. As Jake Greenberg explained to Rosenberg and her collaborator Gitano Garofalo, "I got involved in Riot Grrrl through hearing a Bikini Kill song and really liking it and looking for more music like that. When I got on-line, I found a B. K. [Bikini Kill] bulletin board and got sent to a R. G. [Riot Grrrl] board from there and somehow went from asking if there were going to be any conventions on the East Coast that year to helping organize one in Philly a year later. I write for the zine *Queer Fish*" (p. 814). What is contained in Greenberg's narrative here, which echoes those of many other Riot Grrrls, is a powerful contestation of the still too-persistent theories of the way mass culture functions, theories that are at the heart of girls-at-risk narratives of Pipher and Brumberg. These theories surmise that kids have forsaken active reading and writing and print culture for the lure of visual and aural culture, for the passive position of the consumer of movies, television and music. The history of Riot Grrrl suggests otherwise.

Apparently disturbed by the ways in which girls were inscribed into punk culture as traditional girly-girl fans, Kathleen Hanna and her collaborators deliberately acted to form their own bands composed entirely of girl musicians and they began to create their own, perhaps even angrier version of the punk form. Neither their desires nor their self-expression, however, could be contained within the musical forms they developed. Instead, that desire spilled out beyond the club and the privately produced CD as both band members and the girls who listened attentively to their music acted to spread the word. They aimed to connect with other like-minded girls by putting pen to paper and foot to pavement to circulate the explosive, category-defying, pasted-together products of their imaginations that had been incited by the music. Although they only produced their zines in small numbers, when they passed them out to others, sold them for a minimal fee, or simply exchanged them for someone else's zine, they acted to create a community that began to snowball in size. Indeed, as Emily White put it, Riot Grrrl is an underground culture with no Mecca, built of paper (Rosenberg & Garafalo, 1998, p. 811).

As the writers of zines then logged on to the Internet in search of other zines and other readers, the process of community-formation developed even greater reach as girls connected with girls, formed Riot Grrrl chapters at local sites, and began to plan concerts and conventions. This, it seems to me, is nothing else but the process of grass roots organizing, organizing born of playing, screaming, listening, writing, *and* reading. As another of Rosenberg and Garafalo's interviews put it, "the main thing about riot grrrl that I find so attractive is how it made me feel connected with all these girls from hundreds of miles away" (p. 815). Still another observed, "My best friend's sister was into Hole and then she got into Bikini Kill. I found out about Riot Grrrl through a zine type of thing. I heard Heavens to Betsy, Bikini Kill, and a Kill Rock Stars compilation. It just went from there. I thought, 'Oh, there's all these people out there.' I really identified with what they went through. I really wanted to be part of it, and I started my zine" (p. 817).

For the listeners who eventually became Riot Grrrls, the misogyny and exclusionary practices of punk music neither silenced them nor acted unilaterally to position them as mere sexual objects and toys. Rather, that misogyny acted as hint and incitement, it pushed them to answer back, to pick up guitars *and* pens, to scream out a girl's rage, to speak of the slights, and pains, and crimes suffered—rather than stoically endured—by girls. Instead of fitting either their interests or their many angers into the already specified form of the book with its typical, focused, unitary subject, rendered both as topic and as author, they turned to the more miscellaneous format of the collage and the magazine with their capacity for juxtaposition, contradiction, intertextuality, and multiplicity. Zines are nothing if not riotous jumbles with their mixture of handwriting and print that refuses to stay put within the lines or even confined within the margins of a single page. They sport images that overlap and bleed into one another. Girl zines are filled with an energy that refuses to be circumscribed within the decorous confines of the print form or the ordered circuits through which print usually circulates. They also defy familiar social binaries like those of public/private, personal/political, or feminist/feminine. They discuss the most quotidian slights that happen to a girl on an ordinary school day and then juxtapose that with what they defiantly call "rants" on political issues like vegetarianism, atomic power, and, sexual harassment, and rape.

This is not the moment to launch into a full-scale analysis of Riot Grrrl culture or the hundreds of zines that have been inspired by it. In fact, the complexity and multiplicity of both suggest that this will be a daunting project, yet also one that will very likely yield invaluable results. Already, as I indicated before, this vibrant culture has attracted many observers and commentators, as well as proponents who sincerely want to advertise the pleasures of zining and the strength of the girl community so that others might join in. But with its ever-watchful eye, the culture industry has acted as well to capitalize on this desire and has begun to produce guidebooks to girl culture and handbooks about how to make a zine. Although there is nothing inherently wrong with these efforts—in fact, one of the most prominent guidebooks has been produced by young women deeply involved with girl readers and zine-makers, Francesca Lia Block and Hilary Carlip (1998)—they run the risk of functioning once again as orders and instructions rather than as hints, as official guidelines and prescriptive standards rather than as open-ended invitations.

What I have been trying to suggest here in my account of the connections between reading, narrative gleaning, and self-fashioning is that girls might better be served by a pedagogy that recognizes the vigor and validity of their own, ongoing, deeply creative efforts at self-fashioning. Although it is true that girls' efforts always take place within an already ordered environment and employ materials that are themselves always already structured, those orders and structured forms sometimes fail to discipline the girls who were their intended targets. Readers can be both wayward and recalcitrant. As such, they can fail or even refuse to take up the meanings that texts were intentionally crafted to convey. If we are worried about the misogynist forms that the culture industry continues to spew out redundantly and ever more extensively, we would do well to find ways to encourage and abet girls' creative propensities to take what they can use from the cultural forms they encounter. Although we may still want to promote the notion that texts can convey and teach in an informational way, we might actually be more helpful to girls by encouraging a less subservient attitude toward texts and narratives, one that approaches both as suggestive, as insinuating, as conjectural, that is, as hints rather than directions, as incitements rather than orders. At the same time, we need to find ways to encourage girls in their efforts to make new forms of their narrative gleanings. We need to encourage them in the practice of adaptive re-use. By inserting images, thoughts, models, and ideas gleaned from earlier readings into newly crafted narratives, stories, collages, jokes, and other cultural forms, girls might just find ways to fashion a more open-ended future for themselves both as individuals and as members of a more just social community.

ENDNOTES

[1] I am referring here to the work of Alison Light (1984) and Cora Kaplan (1986). Both use psychoanalytic concepts, especially the notion of fantasy, to discuss the complexities of a reader's interaction with, and response to, a text. Where Kaplan explores the ways in which "the relation of reader to character is often deliciously blurred" (p. 120), Light suggests that, as fantasies, fictions explore and produce desires that "may be in excess of the socially possible or acceptable" (p. 9). Kaplan is particularly significant for my project here precisely because she suggested that reader identifications can be mobile, contradictory, and not necessarily developed in response to character alone. She draws particularly on Freud's essay, "A Child Is Being Beaten," and on J. Laplanche and J. B. Pontalis, "Phantasy," in *The Language of Psychoanalysis* (1973).

[2] For a discussion of the practice of interpretive reading, that is, reading for meaning or significance, which places it in a specifically modern and professional context, see Jane Tompkins, "The Reader in History," in *Reader-Response Criticism* (1980).

[3] With this reference to stepping I mean to draw a parallel between the reading and writing activities I am discussing here and other self-generated, creative, cultural activities engaged in by girls. Although the ones I am discussing here are undoubtedly engaged in more frequently by privileged girls who are both white and middle-class (because, as a function of their privilege, they are endowed with a particular relationship to literacy) I do believe that all girls engage in forms of creative cultural production that draw on their previous exposure to narrative forms, images, and sounds that they encounter through their antecedent use of all kinds of cultural media. Thus, it seems to me, it would be extremely useful to compare the ways in which African American girls, say, draw on their previous cultural experiences when they craft step routines in their church groups, sororities, and dorms with the ways the predominantly white zinesters respond to and make use of the media culture they find around them.

[4] If the kind of reading strategies I have described here as "gleaning" are always going on around us, it is important to address the question of why it would be necessary to enlarge the body of materials presented to girls through the educational apparatus. I think it is necessary to do the latter in part because different materials or archives are almost always taught along with approved strategies for engaging them. What I mean here is that children are given textbooks to read *and then examined over their contents*. Thus they are taught to read for information. Similarly, they are "exposed" to literature in highly specific ways, by which I mean, they are given certain texts precisely as *superior* examples of their cultural inheritance and taught to take up a particular relationship of homage and reverence to such texts. They subsequently construe such texts as their teachers and therefore as their superiors. I suspect that, when operating

together, these textual archives and contextualizing practices work against the possibility that children might glean them in idiosyncratic ways for material useful to them. Popular culture tends to be approached both differently and more leniently. Although popular forms are received in contexts and through frames produced by others (advertisers and publicists, for instance), the legitimating apparatus surrounding them is less elaborated. Children may feel more empowered, then, to do with them what they will. Thus, I believe that children should be given the opportunity to engage all kinds of cultural materials from the popular culture precisely so as to encourage a relationship of play both to them and to other materials.

REFERENCES

Alcott, L. M. (1926). *Little women*. New York, NY: The Saalfield Publishing Company.
Block, F. L., & Carlip, H. (1998). *Zine scene: The do it yourself guide to zines*. New York: Girl Press.
Brumberg, J. J. (1997). *The body project: An intimate history of American girls* (Vintage Edition). New York: Vintage Books, Random House.
de Certeau, M. (1984). *The practice of everyday life* (Steven F. Rendall, Trans.). Berkeley: University of California Press.
Heywood, L., & Drake, J. (1997). *Third wave agenda: Being feminist, doing feminism*. Minneapolis: University of Minnesota Press.
Kaplan, C. (1986). The Thorn Birds: Fiction, fantasy, femininity. In *Sea Changes: Essays on culture and feminism* (pp. 117–146). London: Verso.
LaPlanche, J., & Pontalis, J. B. (1973). *Phantasy. The language of psychoanalysis*. (Donald Nicholson-Smith, Trans.) New York: Norton.
Light, A. (1984). "Returning to Manderley"—Romance fiction, female sexuality and class. *Feminist Review, 6*, 7–25.
Miller, S. (1998). *Assuming the positions: Cultural pedagogy and the politics of commonplace writing*. Pittsburgh: University of Pittsburgh Press.
Phillips, A. (1998). *The beast in the nursery*. New York: Pantheon.
Pipher, M. (1994). *Reviving Ophelia: Saving the selves of adolescent girls*. (Ballantine edition). New York: Putnam.
Radway, J. (1984). *Reading the romance: Women, patriarchy, and popular literature*. Chapel Hill, NC: The University of North Carolina Press.
Radway, J. (1986). Identifying ideological seams: Mass culture, analytical method, and political practice. *Communication, 9*, 93–124.
Radway, J. (1993). Romance and the work of fantasy: Struggling with female subjectivity and sexuality at century's end. In J. Cruz and J. Lewis (Eds.), *Reading, viewing, listening: Audiences on cultural reception* (pp. 213–232). Boulder, CO: Westview.
Radway, J. (1997). *A feeling for books: The Book-of-the-Month Club, literary taste, and middle-class desire*. Chapel Hill, NC: The University of North Carolina Press.
Rosenberg, J., & Garafalo, G. (1998). Riot Grrl: Revolutions from within. *Signs*, 809–842.
Tompkins, J. (1980). *Reader-response criticism: From formalism to poststructuralism*. Baltimore, MD: Johns Hopkins.
Warner, G. C., *The boxcar children*. Chicago: Albert Whitman.

9

The Narrative Integration of Personal and Collective Identity in Social Movements

Ronald N. Jacobs
State University of New York, Albany

Debates about identity have become increasingly tendentious in recent years. Rejecting earlier arguments that assumed an integrated and transparent self, contemporary social theories are more likely to stress the multiple, hybrid, opaque, and often contradictory nature of personal and collective identity. The very possibility of an "essential," unitary identity is now viewed by many as an ideology, masking the important differences in class, gender, ethnicity, region, and sexual orientation that inevitably divide any group of people. "Given this theoretical and conceptual de-centering," asked Stuart Hall (1996, p. 343), "given the relativization of the great stable identities that have allowed us to know who we are, how can we think about the question of cultural identity?"

Rejecting arguments that give up on the notion of identity altogether, Hall (1996, p. 346) came to think about identity as a *narrative of the self*: "it's the story we tell about the self in order to know who we are." Narratives of selfhood provide templates for orienting and acting in the world: by differentiating between good and evil, by providing understandings of agency and selfhood, and by defining the nature of social bonds and relationships (Taylor, 1989, p. 105). These stories are not optional extras, used to pass the time during moments of rest and reflection; rather, they are a central component of social life, which people experience in a "storied" way (Somers,

1994, p. 614; see also MacIntyre, 1981; Ricoeur, 1984). Narratives help individuals, groups, and communities to "understand their progress through time in terms of stories, plots which have beginnings, middles, and ends, heroes and antiheroes, epiphanies and denouements, dramatic, comic, and tragic forms" (Alexander & Smith, 1993, p. 156). By arranging characters and events into stories, people are able to develop an understanding of the past, an expectation about the future, and a general understanding of how they should act.

Narratives also provide important cultural resources for linking personal and collective identities. Individuals depend on the existence of shared stories—or collective narratives—in order to express their sense of self. In defining herself, a woman might identify as a daughter, a mother, a feminist, a New Yorker, an American, an African-American, a Catholic, a lawyer, a radical, an environmentalist—the number of potential group stories in which to narrate oneself is virtually endless. Each of these stories has a different plot, a different set of characters, and a different expected ending. Individuals rely on these collective narratives in order to evaluate their own lives, even if they did not participate in the key historical events of the narrative (Steinmetz, 1992, p. 505). In many ways, then, collective narratives direct individual beliefs, identities, and actions.[1] Social movements and other groups depend on this fact to attract new members and to mobilize existing ones.

If social movements use collective narratives as a crucial strategic resource, however, they do so in a highly competitive environment. After all, individuals inhabit multiple, overlapping identities. Any one of these identities has the potential to lay claim to a person's allegiance; because there are many different stories available to people, there is no guarantee that the story of one group will come to predominate over other shared stories. The fate of any group—whether large or small, long-established or still in formation—depends on its ability to marshal and maintain a shared story that allows potential and existing members to feel at home, to say, in effect, that "these are my people, this is my history, and this is my future."

This chapter reviews how sociologists have thought about narrative and group identity in order to study social movements, nationalism, and civil society. Synthesizing the findings from these research domains, I argue that collective identities are created and transformed through the integration of personal and collective narratives. They are activated through "mobilizational narratives" (Hart, 1992), which emphasize agency and block the formation of antagonistic or competing identities. Using the structural properties of narratives as resources for creating (and resisting) social change, different groups circulate competing narrations of civil society—particularly during times of social crisis—in the attempt to gain a more powerful public voice and to influence public opinion.

NARRATIVE AND SOCIAL MOVEMENTS: BEYOND POLITICAL ECONOMY AND RESOURCE MOBILIZATION

For a long time, the sociological study of social movements was dominated by materialist approaches emphasizing organizational resources and strategic mobilization. Class-based approaches, assuming that collective protest only succeeded when working class groups were organized into working class movements, emphasized the processes by which these working class movements were able to mobilize sufficient resources to effectively challenge elite interests (Alford & Friedland, 1985, pp. 345–353). Different versions of the resource mobilization paradigm dominated the study of social movements into the 1980s, focusing on the ability of social movement organizations to generate enough money, recruit a sufficient number of participants, and mobilize enough political support to achieve their objectives of social change (e.g., Jenkins, 1983; McCarthy & Zald, 1973, 1977). Political process theory, which has become one of the dominant approaches for studying social movements today, emphasizes the importance of emergent political opportunities, and the strategic responses to these opportunities by movement leaders: mobilizing existing social networks and institutional infrastructures, employing familiar and powerful repertoires of protest, and drawing on representational frames that resonate with broadly shared cultural understandings (e.g., McAdam, 1982; Tarrow, 1994; Tilly, 1978).[2]

All of these approaches, even when they admit that group identities are crucial for building a strong membership base, tend to treat those identities in overly unitary and static ways. Rather than examining how movement identities actually form, they treat identity as an exogenous variable, which has the capacity to enable or block the recruitment of new members. The prevailing assumption is that social movement leaders as well as potential recruits enter the public arena with preformed identities; by communicating the circumstances and outcomes of collective action to a sufficiently large number of people who already share the same identity, the likelihood of mobilizing new recruits increases (e.g., Gamson, 1991; Klandermans, 1988; McAdam, 1986; Oberschall, 1989). Implicit in this simplification is the assumption that, under "normal" conditions, the material changes and structural contradictions that exist in a society should lead to the emergence of new collective groupings and new forms of collective action (Somers, 1992, p. 595). Seen from this view, group identity and collective protest become an automatic and teleological process.

Against these materialist and strategic approaches, a number of scholars have begun to criticize social movement researchers for holding to untenable, reified assumptions about collective identity.[3] Melucci (1995, p. 50) argued that collective identity is a system of relations and representations that, in its concrete form, is always in motion. There are important discursive processes that begin well before the consolidation of group formation, and there are discursive processes that bring about change in those identities (Polletta, 1998, p. 138). Important consequences result from this way of thinking about collective identities. Because of the temporal and ever-changing nature of group identity, social movement leaders are not limited to recruiting people who are "like them"; what successful social movement leaders do, instead, is to convince people that the movement narrative coincides with their own personal narratives. During the 1960s student movement, for example, student identities became linked to activist identities through a narrative of spontaneity and antipolitics in which students replaced adults as the protagonists of social progress; tales of the movement described it as a spontaneous outbreak of moral concern, contrasting its development with the gradualism and strategic concerns of adult politics (Polletta, 1998, pp. 146–147). This plot of heroic ascendance linked the student identity with a powerful moral purpose, providing the kind of "mobilizational narrative" that is such a crucial factor helping to motivate adherents to participate in the often dangerous acts of resistance (Hart, 1992).

As a process requiring continual activation by social actors (cf. Melucci, 1995, p. 62), collective identity involves the coordination of collective narratives with personal ones. Steinmetz (1992, pp. 502–505), in his reflections about working-class formation, developed a number of hypotheses about when this type of coordination is most likely to occur. First, and most obviously, individual and collective histories should be organized in a way that privileges the group identity. For class formation, this means that the events forming the plot should be class events, the characters in the story should be class heroes and class villains, and the underlying explanation giving coherence to the narrative should be a class explanation. These narratives will be maximally powerful if their plots emphasize agency and ultimate success, rather than fate and/or ultimate failure. They should be able to synchronize a multitude of diverse life histories and local narratives, by allowing a diverse set of individual life histories to "fill in the details" of the collective narrative without contradicting its main story. Finally, they should be able to do this more effectively than other "major" collective narratives (such as those of race, ethnicity, religion, nation, and liberalism), by retelling those stories as class narratives. These things do not simply happen, of course; they require the active retranslation of society and history by culturally astute social movement intellectuals. Indeed, Marx's (1977) own narrative of working-class formation was one of the most powerful tools of social retranslation, and served as the organizing feature for the autobiographies of a large number of French and German workers during the 19th century (Steinmetz, 1992, p. 504). Most of these autobiographies were written by militant members of labor organizations; not only did these social movement organizations provide the publication facilities required for producing autobiography, but they also offered the self-awareness and the narrative framework that likely motivated the decision to write (Maynes, 1992, p. 524).

Because individuals inhabit multiple identities, the creation (or mobilization) of a particular collective identity is a historically contingent accomplishment that must be explored empirically. There is no necessary reason, for example, that class formation be organized around a class narrative. If a different type of narrative can link together class events in a way that emphasizes agency and success while remaining sufficiently general so as to allow a diverse set of individual life histories to "fill in the details" of the collective narrative, then it too could be a powerful agent of class formation. Somers (1992, p. 616) argued that, for the English case, class formation occurred primarily through a legal narrative: "working families carried with them into the nineteenth century a robust narrative identity based on a long culture of practical rights—a culture honed, revised, and adjusted over many centuries, and one they were not likely to dismiss as the crossing of an 'event' dubbed by historians only years later as the industrial revolution." The theme stressed in all of the English working-class protests was that working people, as citizens of England, had inviolable rights to social participation and justice, local governmental control, and individual independence—even from capitalists (Somers, 1992, p. 612). Because they understood their rights within a legal narrative, they envisioned the setting of their protest as being the legal arena rather than the shop floor; as a result, they tended to aim their protests at legal institutions. But the outcome of these legal protests was the formation of a coherent and solidaristic working class.

Social movements' success often requires the development of collective narratives that actively mask potentially antagonistic identities that group members bring with them, and that retranslate those potential differences through the common story of the social movement. In her ethnographic study of American civic groups, for example, Eliasoph (1998, pp. 28–31) found that people often avoided talk of racial conflict and racial difference, favoring a common narrative of practical accomplishment. Similarly, in her study of the Irish Land Movement of the late-19th century, Kane (1997, pp. 259–271) found that the successful mobilization against English absentee landlords could only take place after the deep-seated and potentially explosive class differences among Irish land tenants were transformed through a common narrative, combining themes of retribution, conciliation, national separation, and constitutionalism. In both cases, the activation of putatively preformed identities would have excluded certain groups from participation, hindering mobilization efforts and weakening the power of collective action. The ability to overcome such powerful group differences was a narrative accomplishment.

"Rather than simply persuasive devices deployed by strategic actors," Polletta (1998, p. 154) argued, "narratives help to *constitute* new strategic actors." For this reason, the narrative creation of group identity is one of the most important resources for social movement leaders, and must be considered alongside the more conventionally studied resources such as financial and social capital.

CULTURAL RECOVERY, CULTURAL PROJECTION, AND COLLECTIVE IDENTITY: THE CASE OF NATIONALISM

In order to see how powerful the narrative creation of group identity can be for a social movement, one need look no further than the phenomenon of nationalism, which has been the most powerful source of collective identity, social change, and institutional power for most of the last 200 years (Calhoun, 1997). Claims about national identity have been crucial in assertions of political autonomy, attempts to integrate disparate polities, movements of separation from colonizing powers, and struggles to strengthen civil society from within nondemocratic states (Calhoun, 1993). Indeed, the power of nationalism is so strong that the nation is the only internationally recognized structure of political association (Smith, 1995, p. 104). For supranational entities such as the European Union, the ability to create a collective identity similar in power to nationalism is likely to be a major factor determining their success (Perez-Diaz, 1998).

Up until very recently, there have been two dominant ways of thinking about the likely causes of successful nationalist mobilization. Instrumentalist positions emphasized the manipulation of "the masses" by elites, typically for the purpose of state building and for the consolidation of power (e.g., Hobsbawm & Ranger, 1983; Mann, 1993; Tilly, 1990). Primordialist approaches viewed nationalism as the eruption of a deeply held, almost biologically driven form of ethnic identity. Some primordialist views held that ethnic nations were "natural" historical extensions of kin groups, which shared a common biological and cultural origin (e.g., van den Berghe, 1979). Others, which resembled more of a synthesis of the instrumentalist and primordialist positions, began with the assumption that ethnic bonds were the most powerful forms of collective identity (and therefore the best vehicles for nationalist mobilization), but argued that these identities needed to be successfully activated by nationalist entrepreneurs (e.g., Geertz, 1963; Shils, 1957).

9. NARRATIVE INTEGRATION IN SOCIAL MOVEMENTS 211

Consistent with the new thinking about collective identity, more recent scholars have criticized the primordialist and instrumentalist explanations of nationalism for treating culture and identity in an overly static way. Given the fact that individuals inhabit multiple, overlapping identities, any of which has the possibility of laying claim to their allegiance, it is problematic that neither approach provides an account for why the nationalist identity is the most powerful (Smith, 1995, p. 33). If nationalism simply involves the activation of preexistent ethnic identities, then individuals who form the same ethnic group should be part of a single nation; this is clearly not the case, as the history of England, Australia, and New Zealand demonstrates (Calhoun, 1997, p. 48).[4] Whereas kinship, ethnicity, and other forms of categorical identity have certainly been powerful sources for nationalist mobilization, what really needs to be explained are the processes by which certain categorical identities come to predominate over others (Gellner, 1983).

In the process of exploring how certain categorical identities get transformed into successful nationalist movements, research on nationalism has begun to incorporate more of a narrative sensibility. Research findings have consistently pointed to the fact that, if a nationalist movement is to succeed, its members must be furnished with a set of stories about a shared past, present, and future. Anthony Smith (1995, p. 63) called these stories of a common past *ethno-histories*, and emphasized the narrative properties that these histories share: selective appropriation of historical events, romance, heroism, and perhaps even the liberation from oppression and the establishment of a unified community. The narrative constitution of national identity has accommodated an extremely diverse set of ethno-histories: through the politicization of ancient religious traditions, as was the case with the Franciscan Spiritualist roots of Jacobin France and the Kimbalinguist roots of Congo nationalism in the 1920s (Smith, 1979, pp. 17–30); through the cultivation of sacred spaces and the commemoration of a golden age, as was the case with Zionist, Palestinian, Bohemian, and Finnish nationalisms; through the use of the Judeo-Christian narrative of exodus, as was the case with American nationalism (Greenfeld, 1992, pp. 403–411). But regardless of the specifics of its development, the ethno-history of a successful nationalist movement is built on a romantic narrative of a "national" community with a distinct and ascending destiny. And it is this destiny story that provides such a powerful mobilizing force.

NARRATIVE STRUCTURES, COLLECTIVE IDENTITIES, AND PUBLIC LIFE

Whereas the formation of a strong collective identity is only possible through the creation of a shared set of narratives, and the integration of these collective narratives within a diverse set of personal life histories, this does not mean that social movement leaders and nationalist entrepreneurs are free to create any collective identity they choose. In any given sociocultural space, there are powerful forces at work that limit the types of stories people are able to tell about themselves, their history, and their future. At the microsociological level, people live their lives in webs of interpersonal relationships, and their narratives of self tend to reflect those relationships, getting filled with tales of friends and family. At the macrosociological level, people tend to be influenced heavily by public narratives that are attached to powerful cultural and institutional formations such as class, gender, nation, race, ethnicity, family, and even modernity itself (Somers, 1992; Taylor, 1989).

The circulation of certain public narratives (rather than others) is closely linked with issues of power and hegemony. Those narratives that circulate in the dominant public spheres tend to reserve the heroic character positions for the dominant groups in a society, creating public environments that favor those dominant groups at the expense of minorities. Out of a desire to create "active consent," dominant groups establish communicative spaces in which they include the subordinate groups, but do so under discursive rules that favor the dominant group. Appeals to such seemingly "neutral" values as rationality and objectivity are situated within a narrative history of criticism against the putatively "undisciplined" and "mob-like" activity of the working class, the "natural" sexuality and desire of women, and the "natural" passivity and indolence of non-Whites.[5] In other words, as Alexander (1992, 1994) demonstrated so convincingly, virtually all public narratives developed through a contrast in which criteria of inclusion have been intertwined with criteria of exclusion, and where the ideal of civic virtue required an anti-ideal of civic vice. As a form of social closure, this binary discourse advantages dominant groups by being formally open yet informally closed; although in principle anyone can participate in creating public narratives, "insiders" and "outsiders" are defined and identified by the tacit, uncodified classificatory schemes of the binary code, the practical mastery of which is unequally distributed among the participants.[6]

Despite the complicity of culture, power, and history, social actors and social groups are still able to use narratives effectively to challenge power and create social change. The reason for this has to do with the nature of cultural structures. Because cultural structures require knowledgeable actors, they can be generalized, transposed onto new situations, and used as resources for creating social change (Giddens, 1984; Sewell, 1992). "Narrating the social" is a contingent process that never ends, where each new event is a potential resource for changing public meanings (Sherwood, 1994). In the remainder of this chapter, I discuss three struc-

9. NARRATIVE INTEGRATION IN SOCIAL MOVEMENTS

tural features of social narratives—plot, character, and genre—that I have used in my own research in order to explore how group identities are mobilized and changed through competing narrations of racial crises (Jacobs, 1996, 2000). This is by no means an exhaustive list—other structural features of narratives, summarized in Table 9.1, include evaluative systems (Linde, 1986; Polanyi, 1985), cardinal functions and catalyzers (Barthes, 1977), inferential systems (Eco, 1994), tropes (White, 1978), silences (Bhabha, 1994), and levels of narration (Barthes, 1977). Nevertheless, by limiting myself to a discussion of three narratological techniques, I hope to show how the structural features of social narratives operate as both opportunities and constraints, helping to create certain identities at the same time as they block others. This type of in-depth analysis of texts may fully realize the promise of a narrative approach to studying group identity (Sewell, 1992, p. 487).

Plot

Perhaps the most important feature of a social narrative is plot, which refers to the selection, evaluation, and attribution of differential status to events. A narrative's plot is fluid and complex in its relationship to events; as Eco (1994) showed, it can "linger" on a particular event, flash back to past events, or leap forward to imagined events in the future. Plot is the best way to study what Abbott (1988) has called the "time-horizon problem," where events can differ in their speed and duration. A focus on which events are selected for narration (and which events are not selected), as well as which events provoke a focusing and slowing down of narration, provides important clues about how a given individual, group, or collectivity understands the past, present, and future. Because of the selective appropriation involved in transforming events into episodes of a coherent story, emplotment is fundamental to processes of evaluation, causal determination, and action orientation (Somers, 1992, p. 602).

For an example of how plot shapes causal determination and evaluation, thereby becoming a resource for creating or resisting social change, we can examine media narratives of the 1965 Watts uprisings in Los Angeles.[7] This event, which lasted 5 days and resulted in 34 deaths, 1,032 injuries, over 4,000 arrests, and an estimated $40 million in property damage,[8] galvanized public attention for months, and still has the ability to provoke discussion and reflection today. In the initial weeks after the uprisings, little else was reported in the American media. But the narrative lingering caused by Watts produced very different plots, depending on what other events were included as relevant to the story. In the *Los Angeles Times*, the events surrounding Watts were initially connected to a larger Cold War narrative, inserting the crisis into the middle of a plot in

TABLE 9.1

Some of the Different Structural Features of Narratives

Plot	The sequence of events that makes up a story.
Character	The different people in a story, and their relationship to one another; usually arranged in terms of a contrast or tension (e.g., hero vs. villain, protagonist vs. antagonist, donor vs. donee, etc.).
Genre	The "type" of story that is being told (e.g., romance, comedy, tragedy, melodrama, etc.). By recognizing the genre that the story falls into, the reader is able to generate expectations about how it will end.
Evaluative system	That part of the narrative that assigns significance to some events in the story, while signaling that other events are less important.
Cardinal function	Actions or events that serve as turning points in the story.
Catalyzer	Actions or events that simply fill in the details, taking up space until the next significant event or turning point in the story. Barthes (1977, p. 95) argued that catalyzers serve a phatic function for narratives, serving to maintain contact between narrator and reader.
Inferential System	A strategy of narration whereby different parts of the story encourage the reader to let her mind wander about, and to draw comparisons between the story and one's own life. According to Umberto Eco (1994), inferential systems tend to get generated during those points where the story slows down, and where the narrator herself takes "inferential walks." Proust used this strategy extensively; Eco's own novel *The Island of the Day Before* provides another good example.
Trope	A form of representation that suggests a way of thinking about two separate things: for example, the trope of synecdoche encourages the reader to think of something as part of a larger whole, whereas the trope of metonymy encourages the reader to think about it as capable of substituting for something else.
Silence	Those voices or events that are excluded from the explicit narration, and that are noticeable for their absence.
Level of narration	The social conditions and the set of protocols through which a story is transmitted, displayed, and received.

9. NARRATIVE INTEGRATION IN SOCIAL MOVEMENTS 215

which all criticism of the American government was deemed illegitimate, and most likely the product of communist influence:

> Rioting in Los Angeles has received mixed treatment in foreign newspapers, with some handling the story in a restrained manner and others giving it full front-page display. Several Communist press agencies took the opportunity to criticize the United States. ("Reds Call," 1965)

> Charges that police brutality led to south Los Angeles' riot were branded Tuesday by Mayor Samuel W. Yorty as part of a "big lie" technique shouted by "Communists, dupes and demagogues." In a bristling statement blaming the riots on "criminal elements," Yorty said that "for some time there has existed a worldwide subversive campaign to stigmatize all police as brutal." ("Riot Area," 1965)

The *Los Angeles Times*, which was strongly anticommunist and propolice, had historically ignored African American issues, failing to cover many of the early civil rights events (Gottlieb & Wolt, 1977, pp. 343–344). By interpreting the Watts crisis through the interpretive lens of the Cold War, those writing and speaking in the *Los Angeles Times* were able to provide narrative continuity for their readers at the same time as they actively blocked critical discussion about racism, police brutality, or urban policy (see Jacobs, 2000). Indeed, by attaching the events of the Watts uprisings to a Cold War plot, the anticommunist convictions of White Angelenos became part of a mobilizational narrative against the Civil Rights movement. This understanding of Watts was reflected in the opinions of White residents of Los Angeles, 74% of whom believed that Watts hurt the Civil Rights movement, 71% that it increased the gap between the races, and 79% of whom supported Chief Parker and his inflammatory statements against African American leaders (Morris & Jeffries, 1970; Sears & McConahay, 1973). Although the acceptance of the Cold War narrative was only partly responsible for these opinions, it was nevertheless a significant part; 15% of White Angelenos believed that Communist influence was the *primary* cause of the uprising.[9]

Whereas the Cold War emplotment of the Watts uprisings blocked consideration of the historical deprivations suffered by African American urban residents, and forced African American leaders to spend their time explaining why they were not communists, efforts to engage in serious dialogue about racial crisis in American cities were more fruitfully pursued in other publics and other news media. Those writing and speaking in the *Los Angeles Sentinel*, the city's dominant African American newspaper, took active steps to renarrate the Watts crisis, and to counter the damaging plot in the *Los Angeles Times*. Although the *Sentinel* did criticize the rioters, describing them as "lawless" and "shameful," these criticisms were made in the context of a search for possible motivations behind the violence, and ultimately were used as a jumping-off point to get to a different narrative, one of police brutality and White racism (Jacobs, 2000). In this narrative environment, where the plot development was in the direction of causes and solutions, the *Sentinel*'s news stories were concerned primarily with the criticism of the Los Angeles Police Department and its chief, and explained the unrest in Watts as being caused by "resentment over the tactics of white police officers in minority communities."[10] These criticisms of the police department placed the Watts crisis in the middle of an ongoing story about community-government and community-police relations. Here, Watts did not evince evidence of the excesses of civil disobedience, but rather the lack of real concern for civil rights on the part of local government officials. African American leaders were represented as forces of order, whereas Los Angeles police and politicians were the forces of disorder. The problem was not with African American leaders, but rather with Los Angeles' politicians who refused to engage in a serious dialogue about race and urban crisis. In reversing the *Los Angeles Times*' character oppositions, the *Los Angeles Sentinel* recalled a series of past events, molding them into a coherent sequence demonstrating the racism and inaction of Los Angeles' politicians and its White constituents. Placed within this alternative plot of events, and counterposed against the more cynical anticommunist plot of White Los Angeles, the events of Watts became crucial for galvanizing African American opposition against Los Angeles Mayor Samuel Yorty, and they were central to the biracial coalition through which Thomas Bradley was eventually able to defeat Yorty and become mayor (Jacobs, 2000; Sonenshein, 1993). For Los Angeles politics, then, the battle over plot became an important cultural resource for African American groups trying to effect social change.

Character

As events become emplotted into narratives, they shape the symbolic relationships between the different characters in a story. Indeed, in Aristotle's poetics, the primary function of the characters in a narrative was to realize the "soul" of the plot (Frye, 1957, p. 52). Because plots require protagonists and antagonists, who are arranged in relations of similarity and difference to each other, the characters of a narrative serve as embodiments of a society's deep cultural codes. Bruner (1986, p. 39) suggested, in fact, that the construal of character is the most important step in dealing with another person, and the part of social interaction that is inherently dramatic.

By arranging the characters of a narrative in binary relations to one another, and doing the same thing with the descriptive terms attached to those characters, narratives help to charge social life with evaluative and dramatic intensity. In this way, the binary structure of character relations becomes a potent resource for individuals and groups trying to gain power and influence in civil society (Alexander, 1992; Alexander & Smith, 1993). Public actors engage in competitive and conflictual narrative struggles, trying to circulate stories that "purify" themselves and their allies, and "pollute" their enemies. In order to narrate themselves as powerful and heroic, they describe their enemies as dangerous, foolish, weak, irrational, deceitful, or antiheroic in some other way; by contrast, they describe themselves and their allies as rational, reasoned, and straightforward. They describe the projects and policies of their enemies as perverse, futile, and jeopardizing, whereas those of their friends are synergistic, mutually supportive, and progressive.[11] Over time, these identifications of similarity and difference, which have their origins in the character oppositions so central to all narratives (cf. Barthes, 1977; Greimas, 1982), develop into a cultural structure based on sets of homologies and antipathies, resulting in a semiotic system of civil society discourse. This "common code" allows for a degree of intersubjectivity among public speakers as well as a relatively stable system for evaluating persons. Members of a civil society know when they are being "symbolically polluted," and must spend a great deal of their time trying to repair the symbolic damage.[12] Groups and associations that find themselves continually polluted, to the extent that they wish to engage in that public sphere, must continually operate from a defensive and reactive position.

We can witness the tremendous cultural power of character structures by considering the narrative link that developed between Rodney King and O.J. Simpson. After the videotaped police beating of Rodney King in 1991, every possible negative description was mobilized in characterizing the Los Angeles Police Department. Its police officers were described as wild, out of control, lying racists; its police chief, Daryl Gates, was described as unaccountable, racist, ego-driven, and contemptuous of the American public and Constitution (Jacobs, 1996). During the 1992 uprisings that followed the return of not-guilty verdicts in the trial of the officers charged with beating Rodney King, these negative characterizations continued; the cowardly and impassive police officers, as well as the unprepared and politically motivated Gates, received much of the blame for the duration and severity of the civil disorder. As a cultural symbol, any association with the Los Angeles Police Department was taken as evidence of moral corruption. The jurors in the trial, coming from the same Simi Valley community as many of the police officers, were criticized frequently as racist police sympathizers, "people who ran away from Los Angeles to get away from Rodney King."[13]

Even 2 years after the Los Angeles uprisings, the negative characterization of the Los Angeles Police Department, sedimented in the thousands of public conversations that had taken place since the Rodney King beating, still had tremendous power to influence the evaluative structure of public narratives. The O.J. Simpson trial demonstrated this clearly. Judge Lance Ito's actions during the trial tended to be interpreted in the media through a comparison with the first Rodney King beating trial; mentions of the Los Angeles Police Department evoked memories of the 1991 videotape. As Gibbs (1996, pp. 200–201) argued, one of the most significant components of the Simpson defense team strategy was to keep the memory of Rodney King vivid and recurrent: "More than any single factor, [defense attorney] Cochran had evoked the memory of Rodney King, the innocent victim of a vicious LAPD beating, police conspiracy, and subsequent cover-up only four years previously.... For the defense during the year-long trial, Rodney King was indeed the thirteenth juror, unobserved in the jury box but clearly visible in the imaginations of the black jurors." Linked together with Rodney King in a common story of police misconduct, O.J. Simpson enjoyed the cultural rewards of the Rodney King narrative, and it became possible to see him as a victim. The prosecuting lawyers in the case, assuming that the jurors would make their decisions based on a rational determination of the facts, failed to offer any significant alternatives discrediting the narrative link between King and Simpson. Underestimating the symbolic, evaluative, and emotional power of character structures, they lost the case.

The narrative ordering of character relations is a strategic resource for social movement leaders just as much as for lawyers. All collective mobilization involves the identification of an adversary, and not merely a general sense of dissatisfaction or frustration (Melucci, 1996, p. 293). The abolitionist movement had slaveholders as its adversary, the Civil Rights movement had White racists, the feminist movement had patriarchal men, and the environmental movement had transnational corporations. The identification of friends, enemies, and how the tensions between the two groups are to be understood within a recovered past and a projected future, will in many cases determine the actions and outcomes of social movement activity.

Genre

What should be becoming clear by now is that narrative provides the dramatic dimensions of public culture, which are so necessary if individuals are to feel a sense of collective identity that overlaps in significant ways with nation and civil society. Plot encourages the public concentration of attention onto specific events, encouraging discussion about the meaning of those events. Strongly opposed characters serve to dramatize a society's deep cultural codes, increasing the likelihood of a continued emotional investment in public life. What ties these two properties of narrative together is genre:

9. NARRATIVE INTEGRATION IN SOCIAL MOVEMENTS 219

Genre seems to be a way of both organizing the structure of events and organizing the telling of them—a way that can be used for one's own storytelling or, indeed, for "placing" stories one is reading or hearing. Something in the actual text "triggers" an interpretation of genre in the reader, an interpretation that then dominates the reader's own creation of what Wolfgang Iser calls a "virtual text." (Bruner, 1986, p. 6)

We can understand how genre operates by considering Frye's (1957, pp. 158–239) discussion of the four narrative "archetypes" of Western literature. In *comedy*, the protagonists, or heroes, are viewed from the perspective of their common humanity, and the general theme is the integration of society. The movement in comedy is usually from one kind of society, where the protagonist's wishes are blocked, to another society that crystallizes around the hero. Comic heroes have average or below-average power, and typically fall into three general types: the imposter, the buffoon, and the self-deprecator. In *romance*, the hero has great powers, the enemy is clearly articulated and often has great powers as well, and the movement takes the form of an adventure with the ultimate triumph of hero over enemy. Romantic genres are viewed by the audience from a perspective of wish fulfillment, where heroes represent ideals and villains represent threats. In *tragedy*, the hero typically possesses great powers, but is isolated from society and ultimately falls to an omnipotent and external fate or to the violation of a moral law. Because the reader expects catastrophe as its inevitable end, tragedy is a particularly dangerous form of discourse if one values civic engagement because, as Frye (1957, p. 211) described it, tragedy "eludes the antithesis between moral responsibility and arbitrary fate." Finally, in *irony* the protagonist is viewed from an attitude of detachment and through the negative characterization of parody and satire. As I have argued elsewhere (Jacobs & Smith, 1997), irony encourages reflexivity, difference, tolerance, and healthy forms of critique in civil society.

These genres are not neutral carriers of preexisting interests and dispositions toward public engagement; rather, genres constitute interests and dispositions at the same time as they help to express them.[14] For example, romantic narratives organize powerful and overarching collective identities that unite people together in the pursuit of a utopian future; not surprisingly, it is the romantic genre that is found most often in the self-descriptions of activist social movements (Jacobs & Smith, 1997).[15] Virtually every nationalist movement presents to its target audience a totalistic picture of communal development that ties together the community's past, present, and future into a romantic narrative of common destiny (Smith, 1979, pp. 17–42). Wherever romantic narratives are present, the likelihood of translating debate into action is increased immeasurably.

By contrast, tragic narratives encourage a flight from the world, privileging the act of private contemplation over that of public interaction or public engagement. As Nietzsche (1956) argued, tragedy delivers us from our thirst for earthly satisfaction, reminding us of another existence and a higher delight. Tragedy encourages a mechanistic ordering of events that tends to discredit agency and contingency in favor of structural determinism. Although Hayden White (1978, pp. 128–129) maintained that the tragic structure of emplotment bears an affinity with radical historiography, Ricoeuer (1967, p. 313) reminded us that, as a dramatic form, tragedy encourages in the reader an attitude of resigned acceptance, pointing to an evil "already there and already evil." By emphasizing the inevitability of fate, the acceptance of evil in the world, and the necessity of achieving transcendence or redemption through a contemplative and mythic "flight from the world," unchecked tragic discourse discourages collective mobilization, public engagement, and motivation to work through difficult public problems.

During periods of social crisis, the dramatic power of civil society is often heightened by the tension between these two genres, romance and tragedy. Will the crisis end with unity or fragmentation? Trust or suspicion? An opening of social boundaries, or an increase in tribalism and other hyperactive forms of social closure? People who are otherwise disengaged from public life turn on their television sets and open their newspapers during a social crisis, in the process having often heated arguments about its meaning and proper resolution. During the 1965 Watts uprisings, for example, the tragic narratives of self-destruction and urban neglect were counterposed against a competing interpretation, in which the challenges of fragmentation and anomie could be romantically overcome. White indifference could be overcome through African American empowerment. Political factions could be overcome through political leadership. Mass society could be overcome through grass roots community organizing. In these instances, the tension between romance and tragedy served to heighten the sense of social drama surrounding the crises, encouraging social movement actors to participate in the interpretive struggle over public meanings.

The selection of genre also relates in important ways to the ability of different groups and movements to accommodate new narratives, new points of difference, and open-minded debate. Indeed, although the romantic narratives can be extremely effective for mobilizing people, they often suffer from an "excess of plot," in which the teleological power of mythically validated past origins and future destinations precludes reflexivity and the interrogation either of present or of possible destinations (Jacobs & Smith, 1997, p. 69). This problem is most clearly identified in the instance of fascism, but less extreme versions operate for many collective identities narrated through the romantic genre. In positing common goals and identities, romantic narratives are too often insensitive to the needs and wishes of marginal individuals within the group. Public narratives told through the comic genre tend to be similarly inflexible, although for different reasons and often for more reactionary purposes. Comic narratives tend to deflate social protest by defining agitators as buffoon or imposter characters, with the ultimate message serving to reinforce the status quo. This genre strategy was deployed by the *New York Times* in its early coverage of the American student movement, frequently describing the protesters as simply taking a holiday from exams (Gitlin, 1980, p. 46). The message was clear. Once these youthful agitators grew up, they would abandon the misguided leaders of the movement; projected into the future was a ritual of conversion, which would incorporate the misguided protagonist back into the social order (cf. Frye, 1957, p. 165).

On the other hand, whereas comic genres assume a singular source of knowledge and an archimedean point from which to criticize those who are "less enlightened," ironic genres permit the formation of multiple identities and allow for the construction of multiple and overlapping reflexive communities. This is seen clearly in African American press responses to "mainstream" media coverage of racial issues, where expressions of outrage about the latest instance of police brutality are ironically deconstructed as yet another case of false sincerity, no doubt to be overwhelmed by the recurring phenomenon of memory loss (Jacobs, 1996, 2000). When used effectively, the use of the ironic genre can be extraordinarily effective in subverting the intended and hegemonic meanings of public events. As Smith (1996) suggested, public executions fell out of vogue largely because they were so susceptible to ironic and satirical performances by the executed, which tended to shift public sentiment toward the victim and thereby deny the hegemonic interpretation of the ritual: "the melodramatic signification of execution as a destruction of evil by good is confounded by a switch in genre.... Events are no longer solemn, tragic, and exemplary, but rather evoke a differing set of aesthetic and emotional reactions by casting events in terms of a trivial, even farcical narrative." Yet, if irony has proven highly effective in subverting hegemonic meanings and messages, it contains dangers of its own. Where positive goals and destination narratives are missing there is always the possibility of a nihilistic form of irony coming to predominate in political cultures (Jacobs & Smith, 1997). Many ironic narratives reflect an elitism that can result in pain, humiliation, and, ultimately, backlash (Rorty, 1989, pp. 91–92). There is also the problem that one becomes weary of irony if confronted by it everywhere and all the time (Muecke, 1969, p. 201). For all of these reasons, ironic narratives are most effectively used by social movements when they are combined with other genre strategies.

Whereas groups are able to exercise a relatively broad range of control over plot and character, introducing changes from story to story, genre operates more at the supranarrative level than it does at the level of the individual story. This is because the power of genre resides in its ability to structure audience expectation, to make them expect a certain type of story. If nationalist narratives tend to encourage people to expect romantic stories, other groups encourage their members to expect ironic stories[16]; still others encourage a tragic expectation. Mobilizing a group's collective identity requires, in many respects, that its narrators stick to the expected genre.

CONCLUSION

Because narrative is so basic to the formation of identity, it is an essential resource for social movements. In order to mobilize actual and potential members into a committed and coherent movement, cultural entrepreneurs generate a set of collective narratives that situate the group in time and place. These collective narratives tend to be most effective when they are flexible enough to integrate a diverse set of life histories, when they tell a story of agency and ultimate success, and when they are able to effectively block or demobilize other competing (and potentially antagonistic) group identities. In order to try to create or resist social change, these groups engage in interpretive struggle to "narrate the social" (Sherwood, 1994), drawing on the structural features of narratives to try to influence public opinion. Recognizing the importance that these symbolic resources play during periods of collective action, an increasing number of scholars have begun to empirically study the narrative constitution of collective identities.

As the "narrative turn" continues to win over social scientists interested in culture and meaning, what is sorely needed is methodological refinement: that is, the attempt to delineate specific narrative processes, and relate them to other social processes, such as social formation, social conflict, and group formation. In my own work I have attempted to contribute to this methodological project, by focusing on the narrative structures of plot, character, and genre, and by exploring how these structures offer opportunities and constraints for individuals and groups trying to influence public culture and social change. The mobilization of narrative resources is not only important for group formation and social change; it is equally consequential for the maintenance of existing identities as well as mainstream conceptions of self and society. Further research is needed in order to identify the conditions under which interpretive conflicts favor stability, and when they favor change. In addition, more research is needed that would link the sociological and psychological levels of analysis. The text-based approach to group identity presented here contains certain assumptions about how individuals use and interpret collective narratives. Specifically, I make the assumption that collective identities and public narratives provide a language for the expression of personal identity; as such, they are at the same time the product and the instrument of personal identity. This assumption is of course a controversial one, particularly with regard to the recent history of reception studies emphasizing active audiences, oppositional readings, and radical contextualism in the relationship between texts and their interpretation (e.g., Ang, 1991; Fiske, 1989; Liebes & Katz, 1993; Press, 1991). In order to identify more clearly the relationship between personal and collective identity, it will be necessary to examine the relationship between group and personal narratives psychologically, from the perspective of the individual.

ENDNOTES

[1] If individuals need collective narratives in order to help them express their personal identities, this does not mean that they are passive recipients of these narratives, or that their relationship to collective narratives is a completely dependent one. Research on audiences has shown conclusively that individuals are active agents in the interpretation of any text (e.g., Dahlgren, 1988; Fiske, 1989; Hall, 1980; Liebes & Katz, 1993; Long, 1994; Press, 1991). Nevertheless, in the sense that these collective narratives provide a language for expressing the self, they are in important respects beyond an individual's control, much in the same way that any language exceeds the control of an individual's speech (cf. Barthes, 1973).

[2] For a more extended discussion and critique of political process theory, see Goodwin and Jasper (1999).

[3] Assumptions about objective and unitary identities actually get much of their justification from the naturalizing power of specific historical narratives of social-scientific inquiry and concept formation. Touraine (1977) and Melucci (1985, 1988), for example, have argued that the materialist and strategic bias of social movement theory reflected an anachronistic 19th-century culture of technological and economic determinism, which, with the rise of "new social movements," had been superseded by a more nuanced sensibility emphasizing symbolic contestation and identity politics. Along similar lines, Somers (1992, pp. 595–598) argued that research about class formation has imported the metanarrative of modernization theory, and its story about the transformation from preindusrial to capitalistic society.

[4] In Australia in particular, despite deep feelings of ethnic affiliation with England, it was the American story that served as the most important source of identity and aspiration, and it was the American Constitution that most informed constitutional debate (Bell & Bell, 1993). It was the story of freedom, prosperity, and decolonization that most captured the Australian imagination, leading to the formation of a uniquely Australian identity.

[5] On the exclusionary nature of civil society discourse, see Eley (1992), and Jacobs (1998).

[6]In arguing that the binary discourse of civil society operates as an open and informal system of social closure, I am relying on the excellent discussion of social closure by Brubaker (1992, esp. pp. 29–31).

[7]My research compares the different institutional narratives produced by African American and "mainstream" newspapers in Los Angeles, New York, and Chicago. These papers claim to act as public forums for a diversity of voices, and indeed they do act this way in many respects. Nevertheless, each paper tends to emphasize certain themes and certain voices at the expense of others; furthermore, these differences are patterned in important and nonaccidental ways. Because I am interested in the overarching similarities and differences of media coverage about racial crisis in different news publics, I tend to treat each newspaper as if its stories constituted a single (or, in many cases, two or three competing) ongoing narrative about race and civil society. This treatment is justified in more depth, both emprically and theoretically, in Jacobs (2000).

[8]More detailed descriptions of the events surrounding the Watts uprisings can be found in Fogelson (1967/1969) and McCone (1965).

[9]These results were reported in the *Los Angeles Times* ("Results of Harris," 1965).

[10]*Los Angeles Sentinel* ("Urge Parker," 1965).

[11]Hirschman (1991) argued that these oppositions regulate reactionary and progressive political rhetoric.

[12]According to Alexander and Smith (1993, pp. 164–165), "the codes have an evaluative dimension that enables them to play a key role in the determination of political outcomes. In American civil society, the democratic code has a sacred status, whereas the counter-democratic code is considered profane. The elements of the counter-democratic code are dangerous and polluting, held to threaten the sacred center of civil society, which is identified with the democratic code. To protect the center, and the sacred discourse that embodies its symbolic aspirations, the persons, institutions, and objects identified with the profane have to be isolated and marginalized at the boundaries of civil society, and sometimes even destroyed.... Strategically, this dual capacity will typically result in efforts by competing actors to tar each other with the brush of the counter-democratic code, while attempting to shield themselves behind the discourse of democracy."

[13]*Los Angeles Times*, quoted in Jacobs (2000).

[14]Brubaker (1992, p. 16) made much the same argument about cultural idioms of nationhood and citizenship.

[15]The Civil Rights Movement, for example, translated then-present circumstances through a future-oriented and romantic exodus narrative in order to mobilize its adherents to action (Omi & Winant, 1994, pp. 99–100).

[16]Many radical urban movements are characterized by this preference for irony (Debord, 1983; Soja, 1996); the same is true regarding the gay liberation movement Queer Nation (Meeks, 2001).

REFERENCES

Abbott, A. (1988). Transcending general linear reality. *Sociological Theory*, 6, 169–186.

Alexander, J. C. (1992). Citizen and enemy as symbolic classification: On the polarizing discourse of civil society. In M. Fournier & M. Lamont (Eds.), *Where culture talks: Exclusion and the making of society* (pp. 289–308). Chicago, IL: University of Chicago Press.

Alexander, J. C. (1994). Modern, anti, post, neo: How social theories have tried to understand the "New World" of "Our Time." *Zeitschrift fur Soziologie, 23*(3), 165–197.
Alexander, J. C., & Smith, P. (1993). The discourse of American civil society: A new proposal for cultural studies. *Theory and Society, 22,* 151–207.
Alford, R., & Friedland, R. (1985). *Powers of theory: Capitalism, the state, and democracy.* Cambridge, UK: Cambridge University Press.
Ang, I. (1991). *Desperately seeking the audience.* London: Routledge.
Barthes, R. (1973). *Elements of semiology.* New York: Hill and Wang.
Barthes, R. (1977). Introduction to the structural analysis of narratives. In *Image-Music-Text* (pp. 79–124). New York: Hill and Wang.
Bell, P., & Bell, R. (1993). *Implicated: The United States in Australia.* Melbourne, Australia: Oxford University Press.
Bhabha, H. (1994). *The location of culture.* London and New York: Routledge.
Brubaker, , R. (1972). *Citizenship and nationhood in France and Germany.* Cambridge, MA: Harvard University Press.
Bruner, J. (1986). *Actual minds, possible worlds.* Cambridge, MA: Harvard University Press.
Calhoun, C. (1993). Nationalism and ethnicity. *Annual Review of Sociology, 19,* 211–239.
Calhoun, C. (1997). *Nationalism.* Minneapolis: University of Minnesota Press.
Dahlgren, P. (1988). What's the meaning of this? Viewers' plural sense-making of TV news. *Media, Culture & Society, 10,* 285–307.
Debord, G. (1983). *Society of the spectacle.* Detroit, MI: Black and Reed.
Eco, U. (1994). *Six walks in the fictional woods.* Cambridge, MA: Harvard University Press.
Eley, G. (1992). Nations, publics, and political cultures: Placing Habermas in the Nineteenth Century. In C. Calhoun (Ed.), *Habermas and the public sphere* (pp. 289–339). Cambridge, MA: The MIT Press.
Eliasoph, N. (1998). *Avoiding politics: How Americans produce apathy in everyday life.* Cambridge, UK: Cambridge University Press.
Fiske, J. (1989). *Understanding popular culture.* Boston, MA: Unwin Hyman.
Fogelson, R. (1967/1969). White on black: A critique of the McCone Commission Report on the Los Angeles Riots. In R. Fogelson (Ed.), *Mass violence in America: The Los Angeles Riots* (pp. 111–145). New York: Arno Press and the New York Times.
Frye, N. (1957). *Anatomy of criticism.* Princeton, NJ: Princeton University Press.
Gamson, W. (1991). Commitment and agency in social movements. *Sociological Forum, 6,* 27–50.
Geertz, C. (1963). *Old societies and new states.* New York: Free Press.
Gellner, E. (1983). *Nations and nationalism.* Oxford: Blackwell.
Gibbs, J. T. (1996). *Race and justice: Rodney King and O.J. Simpson in a house divided.* San Francisco, CA: Jossey-Bass.
Giddens, A. (1984). *The constitution of society: Outline of the Theory of Structuration.* Berkeley: University of California Press.
Gitlin, T. (1980). *The whole world is watching: Mass media in the making and unmaking of the New Left.* Berkeley: University of California Press.
Goodwin, J., & Jasper, J. M. (1999). Caught in a winding, snarling vine: The structural bias of Political Process Theory. *Sociological Forum, 14*(1), 27–54.
Gottlieb, R., & Wolt, I. (1977). *Thinking big: The story of the Los Angeles Times.* New York: Putnam.
Greenfeld, L. (1992). *Nationalism: Five roads to modernity.* Cambridge, MA: Harvard University Press.
Greimas, A. J. (1982). *Semiotics and language: An analytical dictionary.* Bloomington, IN: Indiana University Press.
Hall, S. (1996). Ethnicity: Identity and difference. In G. Eley & G. Suny (Eds.), *Becoming National* (pp. 341–356). New York: Oxford University Press.

Hall, S. (1980). Encoding/Decoding. In S. Hall (Ed.), *Culture, media, language*, 128–138. London: Hutchinson.
Hart, J. (1992). Cracking the code: Narrative and political mobilization in the Greek Resistance. *Social Science History, 16*(4), 631–668.
Hirschman, A. O. (1991). *The rhetoric of reaction.* Cambridge, MA: Harvard University Press.
Hobsbawm, E., & Ranger, T. (Eds.). (1983). *The invention of tradition.* Cambridge, UK: Cambridge University Press.
Jacobs, R. N. (1996). Civil society and crisis: Culture, discourse, and the Rodney King beating. *American Journal of Sociology, 101*(5), 1238–1272.
Jacobs, R. N. (1998). The racial discourse of civil society: The Rodney King affair and the City of Los Angeles. In J. Alexander (Ed.), *Real civil societies: Dilemmas of institutionalization* (pp. 138–161). Thousand Oaks, CA: Sage.
Jacobs, R. N. (2000). *Race, media, and the crisis of civil society: From Watts to Rodney King.* Cambridge, UK: Cambridge University Press.
Jacobs, R., & Smith, P. (1997). Romance, irony, and solidarity. *Sociological Theory, 15*(1), 60–80.
Jenkins, J. C. (1983). Resource Mobilization Theory and the study of social problems. *Annual Review of Sociology, 9*, 527–553.
Kane, A. E. (1997). Theorizing meaning construction in social movements: Symbolic structures and interpretation during the Irish Land War, 1879–1882. *Sociological Theory, 15*(3), 249–276.
Klandermans, B. (1988). The formation and mobilization of consensus. *International social movement research, 1*, 173–197.
Liebes, T., & Katz, E. (1993). *The export of meaning: Cross-cultural readings of Dallas.* Oxford, UK: Polity Press.
Linde, C. (1986). Private stories in public discourse: Narrative analysis in the social sciences. *Poetics, 15*, 183–202.
Long, E. (1994). Textual interpretation as collective action. In J. Cruz & J. Lewis (Eds.), *Viewing, reading, listening: Audiences and cultural reception* (pp. 181–212). Boulder, CO: Westview Press.
MacIntyre, A. (1981). *After virtue: A study in Moral Theory.* Notre Dame, IN: University of Notre Dame Press.
Mann, M. (1993). *Sources of social power: Vol. 2.* Cambridge, UK: Cambridge University Press.
Marx, K. (1977). The German Ideology. In R. Tucker (Ed.), *The Marx-Engels Reader* (2nd ed.; pp. 146–200). New York: W. W. Norton & Company.
Maynes, M. J. (1992). Autobiography and class formation in Nineteenth-Century Europe: Methodological considerations. *Social Science History, 16*(3), 517–537.
McAdam, D. (1982). *Political process and the development of black insurgency.* Chicago, IL: University of Chicago Press.
McAdam, D. (1986). Recruitment to high risk activism: The case of freedom summer. *American Journal of Sociology, 92*, 64–90.
McCarthy, J. D., & Zald, M. (1973). *The trends of social movements in America: Professionalization and resource mobilization.* Morristown, NJ: General Learning Press.
McCarthy, J. D., & Zald, M. (1977). Resource mobilization and social movements: A partial theory. *American Journal of Sociology, 82*, 1212–1241.
McCone, J. (1965). *Violence in the city—An end or a beginning? A report by the Governor's Commission on the Los Angeles Riots.* Los Angeles.
Meeks, C. (2001). Civil society and the sexual politics of difference. *Sociological Theory, 19*, 325–343.
Melucci, A. (1985). The symbolic challenge of contemporary movements. *Social Research, 52*, 781–816.
Melucci, A. (1988). Getting involved: Identity and mobilization in social movement. In B. Klandermans, H. Kriesi, & S. Tarrow (Eds.), *From structure to action: Comparing social movement research across cultures* (pp. 329–348). Greenwich, CT: JAI Press.

Melucci, A. (1995). The process of collective identity. In H. Johnston & B. Klandermans (Eds.), *Social movements and culture* (pp. 41–63). Minneapolis: University of Minnesota Press.

Melucci, A. (1996). *Challenging codes: Collective action in the information age.* Cambridge, UK: Cambridge University Press.

Morris, R., & Jeffries, V. (1970). The White Reaction Study. In N. Cohen (Ed.), *The Los Angeles riots: A socio-psychological study.* New York: Praeger.

Muecke, D. C. (1969). *The compass of irony.* London: Methuen.

Nietzsche, F. (1956). The birth of tragedy. In F. Golffing (Trans.), *The birth of tragedy and the geneology of morals* (pp. 1–146). New York: Anchor Books.

Oberschall, A. (1989). The 1960 Sit-ins: Protest diffusion and movement take-off. *Research in Social Movements, Conflict and Change, 11*, 31–53.

Omi, M., & Winant, H. (1994). *Racial formation in the United States.* New York: Routledge.

Perex-Diaz, V. (1998). The public sphere and a European civil society. In J. Alexander (Ed.), *Real civil societies: Dilemmas of institutionalization* (pp. 211–238). London: Sage.

Polanyi, L. (1985). *Telling the American story.* Norwood, NJ: Ablex.

Polletta, F. (1998). 'It Was Like a Fever'. Narrative and identity in social protest. *Social Problems, 45*(2), 137–159.

Press, A. (1991). *Women watching television: Gender, class, and generation in the American television experience.* Philadelphia: University of Pennsylvania Press.

"Reds call L.A. rioting evidence of race bias: Communist reaction critical of U.S." (1965, August 15), *Los Angeles Times*, p. A2.

"Results of Harris poll." (1965, August 30). *Los Angeles Times*, p. A3.

Ricoeur, P. (1967). *The symbolism of evil.* Boston, MA: Beacon Press.

Ricoeur, P. (1984). K. McLaughlin & D. Pellauer (Eds. and Trans.), *Time and narrative.* Chicago, IL: University of Chicago Press.

"Riot area curfew ends, but city stays on guard." (1965, August 18). *Los Angeles Times*, p. A3.

Rorty, R. (1989). *Contingency, irony and solidarity.* Cambridge, UK: Cambridge University Press.

Sears, D., & McConahay, J. (1973). *The politics of violence: The new urban blacks and the Watts Riot.* Boston: Houghton Mifflin.

Sewell, W. H., Jr. (1992). Narratives and social identities. *Social Science History, 16*(3), 480–489.

Sherwood, S. (1994). Narrating the social. *Journal of Narratives and Life Histories, 4*(1–2), 69–88.

Shils, E. (1957). Primordial, personal, sacred, and civil ties. *British Journal of Sociology, 7,* 113–145.

Smith, A. (1979). *Nationalism in the Twentieth Century.* New York: New York University Press.

Smith, A. (1995). *Nations and nationalism in a global era.* Cambridge, UK: Polity Press.

Smith, P. (1996). Executing executions: Aesthetics, identity, and the problematic narratives of capital punishment ritual. *Theory and Society, 25,* 235–261.

Soja, E. W. (1996). *Thirdspace: Journeys to Los Angeles and other real-and-imagined places.* Cambridge, MA: Blackwell.

Somers, M. (1992). Narrativity, narrative identity, and social action: Rethinking English working-class formation. *Social Science History, 16*(4), 591–630.

Somers, M. (1994). The narrative constitution of identity: A relational and network approach. *Theory and Society, 23,* 605–649.

Sonenshein, R. (1993). *Politics in black and white: Race and power in Los Angeles.* Princeton, NJ: Princeton University Press.

Steinmetz, G. (1992). Reflections on the role of social narratives in working-class formation: Narrative theories in the social sciences. *Social Science History, 16*(3), 489–516.

Tarrow, S. (1994). *Power in movement: Social movements, collective action and politics.* Cambridge, UK: Cambridge University Press.

Taylor, C. (1989). *Sources of the self: The making of modern identity.* Cambridge, MA: Harvard University Press.

Tilly, C. (1978). *From mobilization to revolution.* Reading, MA: Addison-Wesley.

Tilly, C. (1990). *Coercion, capital, and European states, AD 990–1990.* Cambridge, UK: Blackwell.

Touraine, A. (1977). *The self-production of society.* Chicago, IL: University of Chicago Press.

"Urge Parker ouster: Police attack Muslims." (1965, August 19), *Los Angeles Sentinel*, p. A1.

van den Berghe, P. (1979). *The ethnic phenomenon.* New York: Elsevier.

White, H. (1978). *Tropics of discourse.* Baltimore, MD: The Johns Hopkins University Press.

III

Theoretical Perspectives

10

How Does the Mind Construct and Represent Stories?

Arthur C. Graesser
Brent Olde
Bianca Klettke
University of Memphis

Narrative discourse has received a large amount of attention in discourse psychology during the last 25 years (Bruner, 1986; Gerrig, 1993; Goldman, Graesser, & van den Broek, 1999; Graesser, Golding, & Long, 1991; Mandler, 1984; Rumelhart, 1977; Schank & Abelson, 1977, 1996). For several reasons, narrative has a privileged status among the various types of discourse. The situations and episodes in narrative have a close correspondence to everyday experiences, so the comprehension mechanisms are much more natural than those recruited during the comprehension of other discourse genres (such as argumentation, expository text, and logical reasoning). Narrative is the primary genre of oral discourse and it may be the easiest genre to remember (Graesser & Ottati, 1996; Rubin, 1995). Not surprisingly, therefore, the wisdom of cultures was passed from generation to generation through stories for several millennia (Rubin, 1995). The plots and themes in these stories reflect the conflicts, solutions to problems, humor, and values of the culture. Perhaps the easiest way to understand the mind of a culture is to understand its stories.

Discourse psychologists have systematically dissected the representations and processing components of narrative discourse. A good theory in discourse psychology is sufficiently detailed in that it specifies (a) how the meaning of a story is represented in the mind of the comprehender, (b) how these meaning representations are constructed during the process of comprehension, and (c) how the meaning representations are subsequently used in different tasks (such as retrieving the story from long-term memory, judging whether a statement is true or false, and answering questions about the story). A good theory generates distinctive predictions that differ from everyday intuitions and from other theories. A good theory also has straightforward practical applications. For example, the theory would inform us how to write stories that are coherent, informative, persuasive, memorable, emotionally salient, and/or interesting. The purpose of this chapter is to introduce the reader to some theories and models of narrative comprehension that have recently been developed in the field of discourse psychology.

It is widely acknowledged in the discourse psychology community that the explicit text does not adequately capture the meaning representation of a narrative. The meaning representation taps background world knowledge and includes information that goes beyond the explicit information. The inferences are inherited from a large inventory of world knowledge that is known to members of the culture. There undoubtedly is some fluctuation in the representations and inferences that get constructed among adults. After all, people do differ in cognitive abilities, social backgrounds, and personal histories. However, this chapter focuses on the similarities more than the differences among comprehenders. The working assumption is that comprehension mechanisms are quite stable across individuals within and between cultures. There allegedly is some consistency in the mechanisms that are utilized when different narratives are comprehended, even narratives that radically differ in complexity, modality, and medium. For example, the process of comprehending the plots and points of narratives are quite similar in narratives that range in complexity from simple folktales to literary short stories; the process is similar when comprehending oral narrative, written narrative, comic strips, and film (Gernsbacher, 1997; Graesser & Wiemer-Hastings, 1999).

Inference mechanisms have had a controversial status in psychological studies of narrative comprehension. Most research efforts concentrated on the representation of explicit text and the process of linking anaphoric expressions (e.g., noun-phrases, pronouns) to previous explicit text constituents. Recently, there have been serious efforts by discourse psychologists to dig deeper and understand how readers construct "situation models" i.e., mental models of what the text is about. The situation model for a story is a microworld with characters who perform actions in pursuit of goals, events that present obstacles to goals, conflicts between characters, emotional reactions of characters, spatial settings, the style and procedure of actions, objects, properties of objects, traits of characters, and mental states of characters. Much of this content is filled in by background world knowledge that is relevant to the explicit text. The situation model is coherently organized by constructing themes and messages that convey interesting points to comprehenders.

Recent research on inferences has produced a wealth of theoretical positions, each of which makes distinctive claims about situation model construction and inference generation. This chapter focuses primarily on our theory, the *constructionist theory* (Graesser, Singer, & Trabasso, 1994; Graesser & Wiemer-Hastings, 1999). However, our discussion of comprehension and of the constructionist theory will set the stage for identifying highlights of other theories, models, or hypotheses in discourse psychology. These theoretical frameworks include the minimalist hypothesis (McKoon & Ratcliff, 1992), the resonance model (Myers, O'Brien, Albrecht, & Mason, 1994; O'Brien, Raney, Albrecht, & Rayner, 1997), the structure building framework (Gernsbacher, 1997), the event indexing model (Zwaan, Langston, & Graesser, 1995; Zwaan & Radvansky, 1998), the landscape model (van den Broek, Young, Tzeng, & Linderholm, 1999), the construction-integration model (Kintsch, 1998), the schema copy plus tag model (Graesser, Kassler, Kreuz, & McLain-Allen, 1998), and structural-affect theory (Brewer & Ohtsuka, 1988). Although we focus on the constructionist theory, we point out how other theoretical positions fit into the landscape of comprehension research.

AN EXAMPLE STORY AND LEVELS OF REPRESENTATION

An interesting folktale has percolated throughout the city of Memphis during the last decade. The story is paraphrased below.

> A young start-up company in Memphis was doing quite well and growing at a very fast pace, thanks to a brilliant idea of its founder and president. However, the president of the company was seriously worried about covering the payroll during one of the months. So the president flew to Las Vegas and placed a $40,000 bet on one hand of blackjack. He won. So the lucky president flew back to Memphis and paid the monthly salary of his employees. Today, the company is a multibillion dollar enterprise.

Those of us in Memphis know that this story is about Fred Smith in the early days of Federal Express Corporation. For several years, the first author of this chapter believed the story was true. Eventually, folktale was exposed as fiction. But the factuality of the story was somewhat irrelevant to the significance of the story in the city of Memphis. Fred Smith was a hero in the eyes of the citizens of the city, and the story is a touchstone of the risks taken by this financial wizard. Fred Smith helped lift the city from poverty to a modern distribution center. The truth of this story does not lie in the matter of placing a large bet on a blackjack table. The story is fiction, but there is a truth in the story that meshes with the history and culture of Memphis.

There are many levels of discourse in this story of a risky gamble. Each of these levels is allegedly constructed in the mind of the reader during the course of comprehension. There are linguistic and discourse features affiliated with each level of representation. These features impose constraints and prevent unbridled hallucinations when the meaning representations are constructed. The composition of each level of representation has a theoretical format or code that is declared by the discourse analyst. The precise nature of these theoretical formats and codes is sometimes hotly debated, but most researchers agree that six levels are needed.

Surface Code

This level of cognitive representation preserves most, if not all, of the exact wording and syntax of the explicit text. In the case of oral discourse, the intonation patterns are preserved as well. In the example story about Fred Smith, the winning hand is articulated as "He won," but alternative expressions capture approximately the same meaning, such as "The president won" or "His hand beat the dealer's." The surface code would contain the explicit wording in the text, hopefully in sufficient detail to distinguish it from alternative wordings. Some of the alternative surface forms would be vague and underspecified ("He did it"), whereas others would be stilted and overspecified ("The total points in the hand of the president exceeded the total points in the hand of the blackjack dealer"). These alternative surface forms are awkward when they are substituted in the example story. A text is "inconsiderate" and difficult to comprehend to the extent that its surface code is not in harmony with the other levels of representation and also to the extent that the other levels are not in harmony with each other.

A small change in wording can have dramatic repercussions on other levels of representation. Experimental psychologists sometimes overlook this important fact about discourse. In an effort to create texts that satisfy various controls and counterbalancing constraints, experimental psychologists have an unfortunate tendency to create bizarre texts that are inconsiderate at some level (e.g., they are pointless, lack coherence, are uninteresting, or violate linguistic and communication norms). Discourse psychologists are more sensitive to the implications of working with texts that are inconsiderate (if not pathological).

Textbase

This level preserves the meaning of the explicit propositions in the text, but in a stripped down form that glosses over the details of the surface form. The textbase is cognitively represented as a structured set of propositions (Britton & Black, 1985; Graesser & Clark, 1985; Kintsch, 1974). A proposition contains a predicate (e.g., main verb, adjective, connective) that interrelates noun-like arguments (referring to people, objects, locations, etc.). A proposition refers to a state, event, or action that may or may not be true about the storyworld. The following propositions would capture the sentence "The lucky president flew back to Memphis and paid the monthly salary of his employees."

P1 (predicate: *fly*, agent: *president*, goal-location: *Memphis*)

P2 (predicate: *lucky*, person: *president*)

P3 (predicate: *pay*, agent: *president*, recipient: *employees*, object: *salaries*)

P4 (predicate: *possess*, person: *president*, person: *employees*)

P5 (predicate: *monthly*, object: *salaries*)

P6 (predicate: *and*, event: P1, event: P3)

Propositions P1 and P3 are actions in the plot, whereas propositions P2, P4, and P5 are static propositions. Proposition P6 links together other propositions in the text (P1 and P3). There is some evidence that these proposition units are natural cognitive units because they are encoded holistically and retrieved from memory in an all-or-none fashion (Graesser & Clark, 1985; Kintsch, 1974).

The surface code decays from memory rather quickly, lasting less than a minute, whereas the textbase hangs around for an hour or so (Kintsch, 1998; Graesser & Nakamura, 1982). In contrast, the deeper levels of text representation, as discussed below, are preserved in memory for several days, months, or years. Reading times increase as a function of the number of propositions in text excerpts, after statistically controlling for auxiliary variables, such as number of content words, syntax, topic familiarity, and discourse genre (Graesser, Hoffman, & Clark, 1980; Haberlandt & Graesser, 1985; Kintsch, 1974). When a new argument is introduced in the textbase for the first time, such as a new character or location, it takes extra time to insert and ground the referent in the storyworld (Gernsbacher, 1997; Haberlandt & Graesser, 1985; Kintsch, 1998). It also takes extra time to link a pronoun (e.g., he, it) to previous text constituents (e.g., Fred Smith, company), particularly when there is some ambiguity about which referent is an appropriate match to the pronoun (Gernsbacher, 1997). Gernsbacher's structure building framework (Gernsbacher, 1997) and

Kintsch's construction–integration model (Kintsch, 1998) have adequately modeled the process of constructing the textbase and subsequently retrieving it from memory.

Situation Model

The situation model is a deeper level of representation than the surface code and textbase. As mentioned earlier, the situation model is the mental microworld of what the story is about. The situation model includes the spatial setting and the chronological sequence of episodes in the plot. In most plots, there are characters who perform actions in pursuit of goals, events that present obstacles to goals, conflicts between characters, clever methods of resolving conflicts, and consequences of these resolutions. The following plot structure could be assigned to the gambling story.

Conflict: President was worried about covering the payroll of his employees

Goal: President wanted to cover the payroll

Action: President placed a large bet in blackjack

Outcome: President won the bet

Consequence: The company is now a multi-billion dollar enterprise

In addition to the core plot, the situation model includes explicit and inferred information that fleshes out the plot and adds color. Such ornamentation includes the spatial setting (Memphis), the style and procedure of actions (flying to Las Vegas as opposed to driving), props (blackjack table), objects (chips), properties of objects ($40,000 bet), and traits of agents (the president being lucky). Discourse psychologists have reported evidence that the main causal chain that chronologically unfolds in the plot is retained in memory much longer than the ornamental details (Graesser & Clark, 1985; Kintsch, 1998; Trabasso & van den Broek, 1985). So the citizens of Memphis may forget whether Fred Smith was playing craps or blackjack, and whether the bet was $40,000 or $32,000. But they will remember that he placed a large bet and he won.

The situation model in narrative includes the chronological order of episodes that causally unfolds. In most narrative discourse, the order of mentioning the propositions in the textbase is in synchrony with the chronological order of episodes in the situation model. Most readers routinely assume that an incoming episode occurs after the preceding episode (Givon, 1993; Graesser, Kassler, Kreuz, & McLain-Allen, 1998; Ohtsuka & Brewer, 1992), unless there are explicit cues in the text that signal asynchronies. When asynchronies occur, as in the case of flashbacks ands flashforwards, there are temporal discourse markers that signal deviations from the implicit chronological synchrony between the textbase and situation model (e.g., many years earlier; later on in her life, just before she died...). Such asynchronies often occur when a story is told from the point of view of a particular character, when there is a stylistic focus on a pivotal episode, and when the narrative is crafted to elicit a particular emotion from the comprehender (Brewer, 1980, 1996).

Thematic Point

This is the moral, adage, or main message that emerges from the plot configuration. For example, the thematic point of the gambling story might be an ironic or paradoxical message: The fate of a large, invincible, corporate giant once rested on the outcome of a split-second risky bet. A computational challenge has been to determine how the thematic point is derived from the plot structure (Dyer, 1983; Lehnert, 1981). That is, how does the point of a story systematically emerge from the configuration of important goals, actions, obstacles, conflicts, and resolutions expressed in the plot? The relationship between these two levels appears to be as mysterious and complicated as the relationship between word meanings and sentence meanings.

Discourse psychologists have occasionally studied the processing of thematic points but there are significant gaps in the literature. Schank and Abelson (1996) suggested that one of the primary goals in everyday conversations is to tell a story that is thematically similar to the previous story. That is, one way of having coherent and entertaining conversations is to take turns telling similar stories. Story N in the conversation has a thematic structure that reminds a person about a structurally similar story N'; story N' is told if it is a bit more interesting than story N (Schank, 1982). There may be a "one-upsmanship game" in the delivery of stories, with the stories having progressively more interesting structural analogues. The ability to do this rests on several premises: that a person is capable of interpreting thematic points during comprehension, that analogical remindings occur, and that the person is capable of generating the structurally similar stories.

One or more of the above premises may fail, however. One central question is the process of constructing the thematic points during comprehension (Seifert, McKoon, Abelson, & Ratcliff, 1986). Is the thematic point routinely constructed during the process of text comprehension (i.e., "on-line" processing)? Or is it constructed only when the comprehender has the opportunity to reflect on the narrative experience after comprehension is completed (i.e., "off-line" processing)? Another research challenge is to assess whether comprehenders are capable of constructing a particular theme, even when they have had time for reflection. Available empirical evidence indicates that it is very difficult for many children and adults to construct a theme spontaneously during comprehension (Seifert et al., 1986).

It is also difficult for some people to construct a theme after comprehension is completed (Goldman, 1985; Williams, 1993). When adults are asked to sort a large set of short stories (i.e., 100–250 words) on similarity of theme, the adults show high agreement on the patterns of classification; these categories tap the deep plot structure rather than the surface features of the stories (Seifert et al., 1986). However, these same themes are rarely generated on-line. It appears that comprehenders can judge whether a theme is appropriate for a story, but most children and adults have difficulty generating a theme during comprehension, and many have difficulties generating themes after narrative comprehension is completed. Nevertheless, when an appropriate theme is identified, it does have a major influence on the comprehension and memory of story events (Narvaes, 1998; Williams, 1993).

Agent Perspective

This level of narrative representation is considerably less salient in the minds of most comprehenders. Because of the low salience, many researchers unfortunately miss some important distinctions and mechanisms. Comprehenders potentially construct multiple *agents* in their cognitive representations when they read narrative (Clark, 1996; Graesser, Bowers, Olde, & Pomeroy, 1999; Keysar, 1994). (For the present purposes, we will assume the narrative is being read, rather than being embedded in oral conversation.) Each agent has human qualities, such as speaking, perceiving, believing, knowing, wanting, liking, acting, and experiencing emotions. One set of agents consists of the society of characters in the storyworld. Each character views the storyworld from his or her point of view, or what is sometimes called character perspective (Duchan, Bruder, & Hewitt, 1995; van Peer & Chatman, 1999). When participants are asked to recall a story that has different characters, such as a burglar versus a home buyer, the content that is recalled depends on whether it is told from the perspective of the burglar or the home buyer (Anderson & Pichert, 1978; Owens, Bower, & Black, 1979). A different set of agents, called *pragmatic agents*, participate in acts of communication during the telling (reading) of the story. The story is told from the narrator to narratee (and arguably from the author to the reader). The narrator is an imaginary agent who communicates the story to an imaginary recipient or addressee (called the narratee). The author and reader agents are pretty much self-explanatory. It should be acknowledged, however, that the narrator is conceptually separate from the author and the narratee is conceptually separate from the reader (van Peer & Chatman, 1999).

The character agents are fused with the pragmatic agents in some narrative forms, but not in others. This becomes apparent when we contrast first-person, second-person, and third-person narration.

First-person narration. I flew back to Memphis and paid the monthly salaries of my employees.

Second-person narration. You fly back to Memphis and pay the monthly salaries of your employees.

Third-person narration. The lucky president flew back to Memphis and paid the monthly salaries of his employees.

In first-person narration, the narrator is fused with one of the character agents. The narrator takes the point of view of one character (e.g., Fred Smith) and speaks to the narratee through the character's eyes. The comprehender ends up viewing the world and experiencing consciousness from the perspective of the one character. In contrast, third-person narration keeps the various agents functionally separate. The narrator sits perched above the microworld and omnisciently reports the actions, events, and states of the situation model to an imaginary narratee. In the case of second-person narration, there is a fusion of four agents: narrator, narratee, character, and reader. That is, the referent of "you" is not one single agent, but rather corresponds to all four agentive roles. The narrator is in the process of talking to himself (narrator to narratee) and links "you" to both a character in the plot (who also is the narrator) and to the reader. Second-person narrative is rarely used as a perspective in western culture, but has some intriguing potential consequences on comprehension and memory. The author uses this fusion of agents to sweep up the reader as a participant in the microworld and thereby increase reader involvement. Because there is a fusion of multiple agentive roles, the agent should be more salient and accessible in memory.

Graesser, Bowers, Olde, and Pomeroy (1999) reported that a narrator is indeed more salient in memory when it is fused with more agentive roles. They used a source memory test (i.e., memory for "who said what") to assess the salience of agents in memory. College students read published literary short stories and later completed a test on who said what. That is, statements in the story (e.g., Glenda is pregnant, David often has a cigarette after sex) were either expressed by a narrator or by particular characters. The source memory test listed a set of alternative agents (i.e., narrator, character A, character B, neither) and the participant decided who expressed the statement. Source memory should be more accurate for those agents that are more salient in memory. According to a fusion facilitation hypothesis, the predicted gradient in memory is: second-person > first-person > third-person. This prediction was supported when comparing first-person and third-person narration; second-person narration has not yet been tested because of the difficulty of finding second-person short stories.

Another agent, which is perhaps least visible to the reader, will be articulated by a metaphor to a camera operator in a film crew. There is an imaginary camera operator who positions the camera at some location in the microworld and views each focal action, event, or setting from that perspective (Black, Turner, & Bower, 1979; Duchan et al., 1995). The systematic positioning of the mental camera appears to be more common when professional authors write short stories and novels, probably because of the lucrative potential for film adaptations. The mental camera operator is frequently fused with a particular character or the narrator. When the gambling story states that "the president flew to Las Vegas," the camera is positioned somewhere in Memphis and views the exit of the president from the Memphis scene. The camera would also be positioned in Memphis if the action were articulated as "the president went to Las Vegas". However, if the action was articulated as "the president came to Las Vegas", the camera is positioned in Las Vegas, rather than Memphis, and it views the arrival of the president's flight. Thus, the selection of the main verb "went" versus "came" signals the deictic location of the mental camera. There is some empirical support for the existence of this mental camera operator (or something analogous to it). Reading time studies have shown that it takes additional processing time to shift the mental camera from one location to another location in the storyworld, to shift the "mind's eye perspective" from one character to another, and to shift the perspective from a character stance to a narrator stance (Black, Turner, & Bower, 1979; Millis, 1995; Morrow, Greenspan, & Bower, 1987). Narrative text is awkward or confusing when there is not a coordinated positioning of the mental camera (e.g., After Fred arrived in Las Vegas, he drove to the Golden Nugget casino, and came to the blackjack table).

The reader is obviously a critical agent for the author to consider while composing narratives. The author needs to know what a typical reader knows. Communication will not succeed if the writer fails to keep track of the *common ground* (shared knowledge) between reader and writer, and when a speaker fails to keep track of the common ground between speaker and listener (Clark, 1996; Schober, 1998). The *emotions* of the reader are monitored by a good author in addition to keeping track of the knowledge of the reader. The author of narrative crafts the story in a fashion that has a particular emotional impact on the reader. According to Brewer's structural affect theory, for example, the emotions of the reader are determined by the configuration of the plot and the knowledge states of the various characters (Brewer, 1996; Brewer & Ohtsuka, 1988). Consider the emotion of suspense. There is an initiating event that has the potential to lead to a significant outcome; the outcome is either very good or bad for a central character. In the gambling story, the initiating event would be the president placing a $40,000 bet on one hand of blackjack. The comprehender might be held on a precipice of suspense before the actual outcome is expressed (he won); that is, the suspense could be drawn out by a number of intervening episodes between the precipitating event and the outcome (e.g., the dealer might need to reshuffle or a drink may be served). In the case of suspense, as well as other reader emotions, the author controls the tension and arousal level of the reader by manipulating the plot and character knowledge (Vorderer, Wulff, & Friedrichsen, 1996). The suspense can even be recreated (i.e., re-enacted, re-experienced) when the story is comprehended on multiple occasions and the comprehender already knows the outcome (Gerrig, 1993).

Genre

The term *genre* simply means the category of text under consideration. Narrative is frequently contrasted with persuasion (argumentation), expository, and description, but scholars in rhetoric have developed rich taxonomies of genre that attempt to handle large corpora of texts. Within the category of narrative, there are many hierarchical levels of nested subcategories. A particular genre G, at whatever level of specificity, has conventional features that members of a community learn. These linguistic/discourse features guide the comprehenders' attention, comprehension, and memory. For example, we would expect a writer of a mystery to withhold telling who the culprit is until late in the story, and to honor the implicit agreement that statements that are mentioned out of the blue are likely to be important clues.

It is possible to classify narratives and other discourse genres according to their different pragmatic functions (Biber, 1988; Brewer, 1980). The use of stories for persuasion is well documented. For example, we later review studies on jury decision making that have shown that stories help the juror make sense of the evidence and to formulate a verdict of guilt or innocence (Pennington & Hastie, 1992, 1993; Voss, Wiley, & Sandak, 1999). In fact, a coherent story sometimes has a greater impact on the jury than the quality of the evidence (Kuhn, Weinstock, & Flaton, 1994). Adults frequently confuse the quality of the evidence with a narrative explanation that coherently binds the various facts about a case (Brem & Rips, 1996).

A different pragmatic function of narrative is simply to inform the listener. As mentioned earlier, the wisdom of a culture is often passed down in the form of stories (Rubin, 1995). Prior to the invention of print, stories were the primary form of dissemination of knowledge. Narrative still reigns supreme in civilized literate cultures because stories are easy to comprehend and remember (Graesser & Ottati, 1996; Rubin, 1995; Schank & Abelson, 1996). There are some powerful demonstrations of the special status of the narrative genre. In one study by Graesser,

Hauft-Smith, Cohen, & Pyles (1980), college students read 12 texts that were selected from published collections of stories and from encyclopedias. The texts were approximately 275 words in length. The texts varied in narrativity, with half being in the narrative genre and half in the expository genre. Orthogonal to this genre split was a dimension of familiarity; half had familiar content and half had unfamiliar content. Within 5 minutes of reading each text, the participants recalled the text in writing. Recall proportions were computed by observing the proportions of propositions in the explicit text that were in the recall protocols. The recall proportions correlated .92 with the narrativity ratings, whereas the correlation with the familiarity ratings was low and nonsignificant. Sentence reading times were collected on the same passages in a study by Graesser, Hoffman, and Clark (1980). The sentence reading times had a robust negative correlation with narrativity ratings ($r = -.87$), but were not correlated with familiarity ratings. The results of these studies are compatible with the claim that narrative text is recalled approximately twice as well as expository text and is read approximately twice as fast.

It remains somewhat of a mystery why narrative text is so easy to comprehend and remember. Perhaps it is because the content of narrative text has such a close correspondence with everyday experiences. Perhaps it is because the language of oral conversation has a closer similarity to narrative text than other discourse genres. Perhaps it is because there are more vivid mental images, or a more elegant composition of the conceptual structures. Narratives are more interesting, so perhaps they are more motivating to read. This latter explanation is a bit suspect, however, because interestingness ratings failed to have much of an impact on recall and reading times in the above studies by Graesser, Hauft-Smith, et al. (1980) and by Graesser, Hoffman, and Clark (1980). Researchers have not yet provided a satisfying answer to the question of why narrative has such a privileged status in the cognitive system.

It is somewhat of a paradox that narrative is so easy to comprehend and remember because there are so many levels of representation. In this section we have identified the surface code, the textbase, the situation model, the thematic point, a society of character agents and pragmatic agents, the manipulation of reader response, and genre. Somehow the constraints from these different levels need to mesh in harmony as the cognitive representations get constructed during comprehension. Comprehension breaks down and the quality of the text suffers when there are asynchronies among levels. We believe that the conventions of a genre play an important role in facilitating synchrony among levels. The conventions guide both the creation of narrative text and the comprehension of the narrative text, so the same constraints operate at both ends of the communication process.

Pragmatic Context

This level of representation is absolutely critical, but lies outside of the scope of the narrative per se. The pragmatic context frames the telling of the narrative. When a story is told in oral conversation, there is a particular speaker who tells the story to a particular listener or audience. The story is told for a purpose, whether it be to entertain, to gripe, to inform, or to persuade the listener. Stories in print have similar functions, although the stories are "decontextualized" in the sense that the authors and readers are not experiencing the story at a shared time and place (Clark, 1996).

An analysis of the pragmatic functions of a story is needed to explain why the surface code is articulated in a particular fashion and why some episodes in the narrative are emphasized. The Federal Express story would be told quite differently if the speaker were trying to shock the listener versus amuse the listener. The Federal Express story no doubt fluctuates in content and form each time that a given speaker tells it to different audiences, or even the same audience (Norrick, 1998; Schiffrin, 1984).

The remarkable achievement of narrative comprehension is undeniable. However, we will also argue that there are limitations on what the human mind can accomplish in the arena of narrative comprehension. Several facts about the human mind are widely acknowledged in the field of cognitive science and discourse psychology. Table 10.1 lists and describes a number of components and assumptions that have been adopted in most of the contemporary models of discourse psychology (as will be discussed later). These place constraints on a plausible cognitive theory of narrative comprehension. For example, the human mind has a working memory with a limited capacity. It can focus on only one or two ideas at a time. These bottlenecks force the comprehender to retain in working memory only the recent episodes and the important episodes in the plot. As another example, it takes a nontrivial amount of time (a handful of seconds) to construct a rich mental image of a setting in the mind's eye. Therefore, a detailed spatial mental model cannot be constructed on-line when a reader reads at a rate of 250 to 400 words per minute. Consequently, the mental representation of the situation is not the fine-grained depiction of reality that could be produced by a high-resolution video.

The remainder of this chapter concentrates on the construction of situation models during the comprehension of narrative discourse.

THE CONSTRUCTIONIST THEORY OF BUILDING SITUATION MODELS AND KNOWLEDGE-BASED INFERENCES

Graesser et al.'s (1994) constructionist theory attempts to account for the process of building situation models when narrative text is comprehended.

TABLE 10.1
Components and Assumptions of Models in Discourse Psychology
(see Graesser, Singer, & Trabasso, 1994)

1.	Information sources	Three important information sources are the explicit text, relevant background knowledge structure (both generic and episodic), and the pragmatic context of the message.
2.	Levels of representation	The three levels of code are constructed as a result of comprehension: the surface code, the textbase, and the situation model.
3.	Memory stores	The three memory stores are short-term memory (which holds the current clause being processed), working memory (which has both dynamic processing operations and passive storage), and long-term memory.
4.	Discourse focus	The concept or proposition that is directly in consciousness (i.e., the mind's eye or focus of the mental camera).
5.	Convergence and constraint satisfaction	Both explicit information and inferences are encoded more strongly in the meaning representation to the extent that they are activated by several information sources and satisfy the constraints imposed by various information sources.
6.	Repetition and automaticity	Repeated activation of an idea, proposition, or structure increases the speed of accessing it and the elements within it. Automatized packages of knowledge (such as a schema, script, stereotype, or other generic knowledge structure) are holistically accessed and utilized at very little cost to the processing resources in working memory and the discourse focus.

7.	Satisfaction of comprehender goals	Readers are motivated by one or more comprehension goals when reading a text. The goals either are dictated by the discourse genre, are default comprehension goals, or are idiosyncratic goals of the reader. Readers allocate more resources to explicit information and the generation of inferences that address the reader's comprehension goals.
8.	Local and global coherence	The comprehender tries to construct a meaning representation that establishes local and global coherence among the actions, events, and states expressed in the text. Local text coherence is established when contiguous clauses can be connected conceptually, whereas global coherence spans larger chunks of text. Global coherence can be successfully achieved to the extent that (a) the linguistic and discourse features of the explicit text support a coherent representation, (b) the reader has relevant world knowledge, and (c) the reader has the goal of comprehending the meaning of the text.
9.	Explanation	The comprehender attempts to explain why episodes in the text occur and why the author explicitly mentions particular information in the text. Such explanations include motives of characters' actions, causes of events, and pragmatic justifications of the explicit mention of information. Stated differently, why-questions guide comprehension to a greater extent than other types of questions (e.g., where, when, how, and what happens next).

A central goal lies is in specifying the set of knowledge-based inferences that are routinely activated and encoded during this process. Knowledge-based inferences are those inferences that are inherited from generic knowledge structures (e.g., scripts, stereotypes) and from specific episodic structures created in the past (i.e., from prior texts, discourse, and experiences). For example, the Fred Smith story activates a "gambling" script and a "company president" stereotype. The generic script on gambling would include typical actions that are performed while gambling (placing chips on a board, giving the dealer money), the typical setting (casino), prompts (tables, chairs), goals (make more money). A generic script has typical information about an activity that a person frequently enacts or witnesses. Similarly, a generic stereotype contains typical information about a class of people. In contrast to generic packages of knowledge, episodic structures are associated with episodes that a person experiences at a particular time and place. The knowledge-based inferences in the situation model are inherited from both generic and episodic knowledge structures.

Knowledge-based inferences are not the same sort of inferences as the products of syllogistic reasoning, statistical reasoning, and other challenging computational systems. These latter inferences are not routinely made on-line during comprehension because they are difficult and require effortful reflection. Sometimes they are only made with the assistance of a physical artifact (e.g., paper and pencil, Venn diagrams, a computer). In contrast, knowledge-based inferences are constructed more quickly and with much less effort. Examples of knowledge-based inferences will be presented shortly.

Some of the components and assumptions of the constructionist theory are not controversial because they are also adopted by alternative theoretical frameworks in discourse psychology. The components and assumptions in Table 10.1 that are uncontroversial are 1–7. That is, models in discourse psychology normally assume that there are multiple information sources, multiple levels of representation, multiple memory stores, a discourse focus, convergence, constraint satisfaction, and automaticity through repetition. As with other positions in discourse psychology, the constructionist theory assumes that the inferences and content of the situation model are systematically influenced by variations in reader goals. Assumptions 1–7 are adopted in the resonance model (Myers, O'Brien, Albrecht, & Mason, 1994; O'Brien, Raney, Albrecht, & Rayner, 1997), the structure building framework (Gernsbacher 1997), the event indexing model (Zwaan, Langston, & Graesser, 1995; Zwaan & Radvansky, 1998), the landscape model (van den Broek, Young, Tzeng, & Linderholm, 1999), and the construction–integration model (Kintsch, 1998), for example.

The constructionist theory has two distinctive assumptions that substantially narrow down the set of inferences that are routinely generated on-line during narrative comprehension. These are the *coherence* assumption (number 8 in Table 10.1) and the *explanation* assumption (number 9). Inferences have a high likelihood of being generated in the situation models if they participate in building coherent meaning representations or in building explanations.

Coherence

According to the coherence assumption, the comprehender attempts to build a situation model that establishes both local and global coherence among the actions, events, and states that are explicitly mentioned in the text. Local coherence is established if an incoming explicit statement (S) can be linked conceptually to a recent proposition (P) that resides in working memory (WM). Comprehenders monitor several conceptual dimensions simultaneously during the attempts to achieve local coherence (i.e., linking S to a P in working memory). Studies by Zwaan (Zwaan, Magliano, & Graesser, 1995; Zwaan & Radvansky, 1998) reported that reading time increases for an explicit sentence in a narrative text if it involves a break in coherence (or continuity) on any one of the following five dimensions:

1. *Protagonist.* The protagonists in explicit statement S are not among the protagonists (main character agents) in WM.
2. *Temporality.* The action or event expressed in S involves a gap or shift in the chronological timeline.
3. *Causality.* The action or event expressed in S does not causally flow from the content in WM.
4. *Motivation.* The action expressed in S is not part of an agent's plan in WM.
5. *Spatiality.* The action or event expressed in S is in a different spatial region from the content in WM.

Experiments have revealed that a break on any one dimension is sufficient to increase reading time (Zwaan, Magliano, & Graesser, 1995). Reading time also increases to the extent that there are continuity breaks on an increasing number of dimensions. Zwaan's event indexing model specifies both (1) the process of monitoring these 5 dimensions during comprehension and (2) the extent to which the multidimensional representation can explain the strength of association between pairs of events in the narrative.

Global coherence is established when local segments of discourse can be organized into higher order chunks. In the simplest case, there is a hierarchical organization of episodes, chunks, super-chunks, and thematic points. For example, flying to Las Vegas, placing a $40,000 bet on a hand of blackjack, winning the hand, and returning to Memphis could funnel into a single chunk expressed as "obtaining the needed money from a risky casino gamble." At a higher level, the chunks would funnel into super-chunks. The chunks of encountering a financial deficit for making payroll, obtaining the needed money from a risky gamble, and paying the employees could funnel into a super-chunk of "the president solving a financial problem for his company." At the highest level, the super-chunks would support the thematic point: "A large corporation was saved by a risky gamble of its president." Of course, there could be other thematic points that take slightly different slants: "The fate of a large, invincible, corporate giant once rested on the outcome of a split-second risky bet", "a small shift in fate can be enough to stop a large enterprise from growing", or "the powerful were once fragile." A thematic point has a high coverage to the extent that its subordinate "nodes" (i.e., super-chunks) and its descendents at lower levels in the tree structure (i.e., chunks, episodes) cover a high proportion of the explicit episodes in the text (Lehnert, 1981; Schank, 1982). It should be noted, however, that the structure need not be a strict hierarchy. There can be more complex, scruffy networks that deviate from strict hierarchies (see Lehnert, 1981). Regardless of the exact structural composition, a good thematic point has tentacles that cover a large proportion of the episodes, whereas a poor theme covers a small subset of the episodes (Graesser & Clark, 1985; Lehnert, 1981).

In order to establish global coherence, the incoming explicit statement S sometimes needs to be linked to content several sentences or pages earlier in the discourse context, content that is no longer in WM (Singer, Graesser, & Trabasso, 1994). To what extent can an adult reader successfully link the current sentence with earlier, far-reaching discourse constituents? If a reader is comprehending statement S on page 72 in a novel, can the reader reinstate relevant content from page 13? Available research has not completely resolved this question. The constructionist theory assumes that such global linkages can be achieved if the story is well written in the sense that there is harmony among the levels of representation, but not if the narrative is pointless, choppy, and difficult to relate to general world knowledge. The reader settles for local coherence under these adverse conditions. According to the resonance model (Myers et al., 1994; O'Brien et al., 1997), an incoming statement S can reinstate a statement (P) several pages earlier if (1) there are a rich set of features in statement S, (2) there is a high overlap between the features of S and the features of P, and (3) the features of P are readily discriminable from other episodes in the prior discourse context. Stated differently, statement S will reinstate statement P if S has a high resonance (i.e., similarity) with P and if P has few, if any, competitors.

Explanation

The second distinctive assumption of the constructionist theory is the explanation assumption. Comprehenders attempt to explain *why* the explicit actions, events, and states occur in the narrative. Comprehenders also attempt to explain *why* the author bothers to mention explicit information and *why* any unusual surface features are expressed in the text. Thus, comprehension is driven by why-questions to a much greater extent than other types of questions (when, where, how, what-happens-next). The causal explanation of an intentional action includes the motives (superordinate goals) for performing the action and the events/states that initiate these motives. In the language of attribution theory, these are the motives, dispositions, traits, and situational events that explain why agents perform actions (Alicke, 1992; Burger, 1981; Hilton, Smith, & Kim, 1995; Read & Marcus-Newhall, 1993). It is important to distinguish the intentional actions of agents from unintentional events that occur in the material world. The causal explanation of an unintentional event includes the causal antecedents that lead up to the event. Inferences are more likely to be made if they are more recent events on a causal chain (i.e., they more directly lead to event being explained) and if the inferences are connected to many other events on the chain (Graesser & Clark, 1985; Trabasso & van den Broek, 1985; van den Broek et al., 1999).

According to the explanation assumption, why-questions are fundamental questions that drive comprehension. The strong version of this assumption is that why-questions drive the comprehension of all genres of text, not just narratives. Stated differently, explanation-based reasoning is an invariant feature of all comprehension, whether the input be narrative text, expository text, film, or physical and social activities in everyday life. The weaker version of the explanation assumption is that why-questions drive comprehension whenever the input involves episodes that causally unfold over time. Why-questions may be important for narrative text, but other question categories (such as where or what-happens-next) might be more natural for other discourse genres. It is beyond the scope of this chapter to identify the precise conditions in which the explanation holds up. However, we do claim that its scope is much broader and invariant than many psychologists would predict. For example, Graesser and Bertus (1998) reported that why-questions drive the comprehension of expository texts that describe scientific or technological mechanisms.

The Status of Example Inferences: Are They Constructed in the Situation Model During Comprehension?

In order to illustrate various explanation-based inferences, as well as some other classes of inference, consider once again the gambling story presented earlier. Listed below is a set of potential inferences at the point in the story when the president placed the $40,000 bet on one hand of blackjack. Each inference is evaluated from the standpoint of being constructed in the situation model. Once again, these predictions are based on the constructionist theory (Graesser et al., 1994). The predictions would be different for other theoretical positions.

1. *Fred Smith wanted to pay his employees.* This is a *superordinate goal* of the act of placing the $40,000 bet. It is part of the following explanation: Fred Smith placed the bet in order to win $40,000, which would then be used to pay his employees the monthly salaries that he owed them on the payroll. Superordinate goals explain *why* intentional actions are performed by human agents, so this inference would have a high likelihood of being constructed on-line in the situation model.

2. *Fred moved his chips into the circle.* This action elaborates the *subplan* (i.e., subgoal, procedure, method, style) of the act of placing the $40,000 bet. A more complete subplan would involve lifting $1000 chips, moving them to the circle, counting the chips, signaling to the dealer, and so on. This information specifies *how* the bet was made, but does not explain *why* it was made. Therefore, it would have a low likelihood of being constructed in the situation model according to the constructionist theory. It is mere ornamentation, not part of the explanatory guts of the plot. Such inferences are only made if the reader has a comprehension goal that encourages the construction of such procedural details.

3. *Fred needed a large amount of cash.* This is an important *causal antecedent* that leads to Fred's placing the $40,000 bet. It is on the causal chain that helps explain *why* the bet was made, so it should be constructed on-line according to the constructionist theory.

4. *Fred lost his business.* This is a plausible *causal consequence* (expectation) of placing the $40,000 bet. It answers a what-happens-next question, but not a why-question, so it is theoretically not generated on-line in the situation model. The expectation ends up being incorrect when we comprehend the next event. Sometimes expectations are confirmed and sometimes they end up being disconfirmed. Graesser and Clark (1985) collected expectations during story comprehension by having students answer "what-happened next" questions after each sentence in the story. Most of these expectations were disconfirmed when the full story was known. If these expectations had been actually generated on-line during normal comprehension, the comprehender would have ended up doing cognitive work to no avail. There would have been a large

amount of cognitive wheel spinning with very little payoff because there is an extensive degree of uncertainty in most narrative texts, particularly the interesting ones. Instead of viewing the comprehension of narrative as a "situation model guessing game," where the comprehender attempts to predict the future, it is more appropriate to view the comprehender as a "Monday morning quarterback," attempting to explain what has happened.

The distinctive, and perhaps counterintuitive, claim of the constructionist theory is that expectation-based causal consequences are not routinely drawn on-line during comprehension. Humans are not very good at forecasting the future; this not a prominent activity during comprehension.

5. *Fred was in front of the table.* This is a plausible *spatial* location for Fred Smith as he made his $40,000 bet. But it fails to explain why the bet occurred, so theoretically it will not be constructed in the situation model.

6. *The bet was extremely risky.* The risk is conveyed by the large $40,000 bet and the fact that it was placed on only one hand of blackjack. A low risk bet would not explain *why* the author bothered mentioning the large amount and *why* the author mentioned there was only one hand. The storyteller might have simply mentioned that Fred went to Las Vegas, gambled, and won a large amount. But that would not convey the dramatic risk. The risk is conveyed by the author's *explicit mention* of particular details that are explained by the inference of risk.

These six examples show how the constructionist theory provides a principled and decisive foundation for predicting what knowledge-based inferences are encoded in the situation model during narrative comprehension. When viewed probabilistically or quantitatively, the constructionist theory has a principled way of predicting the gradient of encoding strengths for different classes of inferences; however, we will stick with the more discrete and simpler framework for the present purposes. The explanation-based inferences and coherence-based inferences are products of an overlearned, automatized comprehension strategy that attempts to explain the text and to integrate the content of the text coherently. The comprehension strategy may either be conscious or unconscious, depending on the degree to which the skill has been automatized. For most adults, the strategy is entrenched in the cognitive system, overlearned, automatized, and unconscious.

There may be other inferences that are products of passive activations of knowledge, such as an inference that is activated by multiple information sources (Kintsch, 1998) or an inference that is very typical of a package of relevant world knowledge (Bower, Black, & Turner, 1979; Graesser & Nakamura, 1982; Schank & Abelson, 1996). The constructionist theory has a separate set of assumptions to handle the inferences that are products of these passive activations (see assumptions 5 and 6 in Table 10.1). Such inferences can be isolated methodologically and distinguished from explanation-based or coherence-based inferences.

Empirical Tests of the Constructionist Theory

The distinctive claim of the constructionist theory is that readers routinely attempt to achieve explanation and coherence, and that particular classes of inference are products of these efforts. These comprehension strategies are automatized in the comprehension mechanism, so they tend to be invariant among readers, text genres, and reading situations.

There is empirical evidence for the distinctive predictions of the constructionist theory. The predictions have been supported in narrative text (Graesser et al., 1994; Long, Golding, & Graesser, 1992; Magliano, Baggett, Johnson, & Graesser, 1993), expository text (Graesser & Bertus, 1998; Millis & Graesser, 1994), and short vignettes composed by experimental psychologists (Singer et al., 1994; Singer & Halldorson, 1996). Two types of evidence are briefly described. One form of evidence taps conscious reflections of readers while they read text. The other type of evidence taps unconscious processes that occur within a second after a sentence is comprehended.

The first type of empirical test collects "think-aloud" protocols from readers as they comprehend stories, sentence by sentence. The think-aloud protocols provide a snapshot of the conscious content of the reader at different points in the story. The content in the think aloud protocols for stories includes a higher incidence of knowledge-based inferences than of the explicit text statements (Trabasso & Magliano, 1996; Zwaan & Brown, 1996). But more to the point, Trabasso and Zwaan have reported that *explanation*-based inferences account for the lion's share of the content of think aloud protocols. Such inferences include superordinate goals and causal antecedents. There is a much lower incidence of *expectations* about future plot (i.e., causal consequences) and nonexplanatory *associations* (such as spatial inferences). Therefore, most of the content that pops into consciousness during reflective comprehension consists of explanations, not expectations or nonexplanatory associations.

Think-aloud protocols do not tap the unconscious processes that are quickly executed during comprehension. The second type of empirical evidence examines the time-course of inferences being activated when an explicit statement is being comprehended. An unconscious inference would be activated quickly (i.e., within 600 milliseconds), before there is time for conscious reflection. Studies have collected reaction time data on test items that are presented during the process of narrative comprehension. The test item is a word or letter string that appears immediately after a sentence in the text when the story is read. In a *word naming* task, a test word is presented and then the reader quickly names the word out loud. The word naming latency is the time between the onset of the test word and the onset of the voice. In a *lexical decision* task, the test item is either a word (WORD) or nonword (WROD) and participants quickly decide whether the test item is a word or nonword; they register their decisions by pushing one of two response keys. The test items of interest to the researcher are the words that match distinctive words in the inferences. For example, consider the six examples of gambling story inferences presented above. The distinctive test words might be "employee" (superordinate goal), "chips" (subplan), "cash" (causal antecedent), "lost" (causal consequent, expectation), "table" (spatial), and "risky" (wording-based). We would expect the word naming latencies and the lexical decision latencies to be comparatively fast for those inferences that are predicted to be constructed on-line. All things being equal, the constructionist theory would predict faster latencies for words from superordinate goals, causal antecedents, and wording-based inferences than from subplans, causal consequences, and spatial inferences. Available evidence supports such predictions. For example, inference words that refer to superordinate goals have comparatively short latencies, whereas subplans do not (Long et al., 1992). Inference words that refer to causal antecedents show a facilitation in latencies whereas there is no such facilitation for most categories of causal consequent inferences (Magliano et al., 1993).

Researchers can trace the time-course of inference activation and encoding by presenting test words at specific durations after the end of the sentence (e.g., 150, 500, 1000 vs. 2000 milliseconds). The extent to which an inference is encoded can be measured by subtracting the latency for a word in an inference condition from the latency for the same word in an unrelated text condition; this difference score is called the *inference encoding score*.

Discourse psychologists have also provided control over the information sources that produce the inferences. Word-triggered inferences are derived from the lexical knowledge and scripts associated with individual words. For example, the inference about "moving chips into the circle" may be derived from the blackjack script. *Word-triggered inferences* emerge in normative tasks that involve word associations (i.e., what words come to mind when you hear the word blackjack?) or free generation of attributes (e.g., please list the properties, actions, and ideas associated with the game of blackjack). These normative data are collected on all of the explicit content words (nouns, adjectives, main verbs) in the text, but not in the context of the story. *Novel situational inferences* occur in the think aloud protocols when stories are comprehended, sentence by sentence, but the inferences are not triggered by any of the words. It is important to keep track of and control whether the knowledge-based inferences are word-triggered inferences versus novel situational inferences (Graesser & Clark, 1985; Long et al., 1992; Magliano et al., 1993; Millis & Graesser, 1994). Such control is necessary to segregate inferences that are products of passive activations (see assumptions 5 and 6 in Table 10.1) from inferences that are products of the coherence and explanation assumptions (assumptions 8 and 9 in Table 10.1). The most rigorous test of the constructionist theory would include the latter inferences. Of course, an inference may be a product of both of these mechanisms, but such cases do not help us in testing the constructionist theory.

Spatial inferences have traditionally received a large amount of attention in the literature on situation models (Glenberg, Meyer, & Lindem, 1987; Morrow et al., 1987; Zwaan & Radvansky, 1998). What does the constructionist theory claim about this class of inference? According to the constructionist theory, the comprehender does construct a *spatial setting* for the story episodes, but the representation is stark and fuzzy unless there is substantial support from explicit information and auxiliary information sources. The mental representation of the spatial setting can be quite elaborate if (a) it is described explicitly in the text, (b) the reader has prior experience with the setting (e.g., a story about Memphis for the co-authors of this chapter), (c) the reader has memorized a map of the setting, or (d) the reader has a special goal of tracking spatiality at a fine-grained level. Otherwise, the setting is a barebones, stark, and fuzzy frame rather than a rich sensuous image (that would be easy to capture on film). The spatial setting for the $40,000 bet in the Federal Express setting would be a casino, but there would be no details about the floor plan, location of characters, location of objects, and visual properties of entities. The constructionist theory assumes there is a rudimentary topological organization of global spatial regions, but no details about layout of entities and visual features are strongly activated by passive constraint satisfaction mechanisms, or are intentionally tracked by the reader unless they are explicitly mentioned in the text.

It should be quite apparent that the constructionist theory does make discriminating claims about the content that gets constructed in the situation model during story comprehension. Adult readers have a comprehension strategy that constructs those inferences that provide explanations and coherence. These are the signature inferences of the constructionist theory. It should be emphasized, once again, that additional inferences are constructed by virtue of particular reader goals and passive activations of knowledge from multiple information sources; such inferences would be predicted by most models in discourse psy-

10. CONSTRUCTION AND REPRESENTATION OF STORIES 253

chology, so they are not unique to the constructionist theory. However, for the sake of completion, it is important to briefly point out these other classes of inferences. We refer to these inferences as *reader goal-driven* inferences (see assumption 7 in Table 10.1) and *passive activation* inferences (see assumptions 5 and 6 in Table 10.1).

Inferences via Reader Goals

The fact that there are reader goal-based inferences is widely accepted and not particularly controversial. For example, there is a phenomenon known as identification, where a reader identifies with a particular character. The reader might identify with a particular character for several different reasons, such as the reader being similar to the character, the reader worshipping what the character represents, or the reader's having faced a very similar situation to the character in the past. Readers presumably would have little difficulty reporting whether they have a strong identification with a particular character in a story. When identification occurs, there should be an increased focus on the explicit information and inferences that have a direct bearing on that character. The reader is predicted to paint a very detailed portrait of the physical features, traits, motives, emotions, and episodes associated with the character and to construct a large number of inferences about the character that are not constructed about other characters.

Inferences via Passive Activation of Knowledge

Discourse psychologists have extensively investigated the inferences that are products of assumptions 5 and 6 in Table 10.1. These inferences are quite predictable from standard theories of memory and cognition. Consider an inference that is activated by several content words in the text. For example, the inference "person X gambled" would be activated by the following content words in the Fred Smith story: Las Vegas, bet, and blackjack. This inference is not merely activated by a single content word, but is re-activated by several additional content words. Virtually any theory of cognition would predict that such a word would end up being encoded in the meaning representation, assuming that it does not conflict with other information in the text. The strength of encoding would also be expected to increase as a function of the number of information sources that trigger the inference (presumably following a logarithmic function). Next consider an inference that is activated by a single information source, but fits the constraints imposed by other information and levels of representation. That is, it survives a process of constraint satisfaction (Graesser & Clark, 1985; Kintsch, 1998; Rumelhart & McClelland, 1986), a process that is routinely incorporated in models of cognition. Such an inference would have a higher likelihood of being encoded as an inference than would a comparable inference that clashes with the constraints of other information and levels of representation.

Psychologists have extensively investigated inferences that are inherited from generic packages of world knowledge, such as scripts, stereotypes, and other types of schemata (Bower, Black, & Turner, 1979; Davidson, 1994; Graesser & Nakamura, 1982; Hastie & Kumar, 1979; Schank & Abelson, 1977; Strangor & McMillan, 1992; Wyer & Gordon, 1984). Consider a script for "gambling in a casino," which is very likely to be activated while reading the Fred Smith story. This script is automatized by most adults because they have either directly participated in gambling or have experienced gambling vicariously through film or other people's stories. When this script is activated, a wealth of additional information is also activated very quickly because it is very typical of the gambling script. There are typical goals (X wants to win money), actions (X buys chips), action sequences, props (tables, chips), settings (casino layout), expectations (X loses money), and so forth. Information that is *very* typical of the gambling script is encoded as an inference routinely. That is, it is included in the meaning representation with a high encoding strength even when it is never expressed explicitly.

Graesser and Nakamura (1982) reported recall and recognition data that strongly support the claim that very typical script actions are routinely encoded as an inference. College students listened to stories that contained a series of scripted activities. There were two different versions of each story so that a test action was presented in one version but not the other. After the story, the participants were given test actions and asked to judge whether or not each test action had been presented in the stories. As virtually any theory would predict, hit rates and false alarm rates increased as a function of an action's increasing typicality. A hit rate is the likelihood that participants claimed that an action was presented and the action was in fact presented; a false alarm rate is the likelihood that participants incorrectly decided that a nonpresented action had been presented. The more interesting finding, however, involved the very typical script actions. Hit rates were found to be equivalent to the false alarm rates for these very typical test actions. This finding indicated that the participants were entirely unable to discriminate whether a very typical action was explicitly presented versus merely inferred. That is, the recall likelihood was nearly the same as the intrusion likelihood. In contrast, memory discrimination (i.e., the difference between hit and false alarm rates) was higher for moderately typical script actions and very high for atypical actions (i.e., actions that are irrelevant to or that clash with the script).

Whereas very typical script actions are routinely encoded as an inference, moderately typical actions require some confirmation from additional information sources. Suppose that a "gambling in a casino" script is activated during the comprehension of the Fred Smith story. There initially would be an activation of the various typical items (e.g., X wins money, X buys chips, tables, chips, X loses money). However, the activation levels of these inferences would eventually die out unless there is additional input that supports their encoding. The story explicitly stated that "the president placed a $40,000 bet on one hand of blackjack." This explicit input confirms the activation of "X buys chips" so this inference would be more likely to be encoded in the meaning representation (rather than having its activation die out). The story explicitly states that "He won", which ends up disconfirming (i.e., deactivating) the inference "X loses money." Most of the typical script nodes that are initially activated will only be encoded as an inference in the meaning representation if they are reinforced by convergence from multiple information sources and by constraint satisfaction. If these confirmatory mechanisms were not recruited, then the comprehender's meaning representation would inherit a large amount of inappropriate information from the generic packages of world knowledge (Kintsch, 1998).

The Relevance of the Constructionist Theory to Jury Decision Making

Pennington and Hastie (1992, 1993) proposed a *story model* of jury decision making that is compatible with the major claims of the constructionist theory. According to the story model, stories play a critical role in persuading members of a jury to arrive at a decision. A good story explains the evidence put before the jury and coherently integrates the various pieces of evidence. A coherent explanatory story has a more robust impact on the decisions of a jury than any other variable, model, or mechanism that was tested by Pennington and Hastie. The fact that coherence and explanation are central to their story model has a direct parallel to the distinctive assumptions of the constructionist theory (see assumptions 8 and 9 in Table 10.1). Moreover, world knowledge is accessed and inferences are generated during the construction of the coherent explanatory story.

Pennington and Hastie's story model of jury decision making has three sequential phases. In phase 1, evidence is evaluated by constructing a story that attempts to capture the various pieces of evidence. Participants viewed a filmed murder trial on a particular case in some studies, and read statements from the prosecution and defense in others. This information (i.e., evidence) was categorized into Initiating Events (J and Ca are in a bar, Ca threatens J, J has no weapon, J leaves), Goals (J intends to find Ca, J intends to kill Ca), Actions (J goes home, J gets a knife, J goes back to the bar, Ca hits J, J stabs Ca), and Consequences

(Ca is wounded, Ca dies). The participants had variable interpretations of the stories they constructed. Think-aloud protocols revealed the sort of story structures that each participant constructed. The story structure determined what pieces of evidence were extracted from the text, the importance of each piece of evidence, and the relationships between pieces of evidence.

In phase 2, the participants receive the different verdict categories and the attributes of each category. Example categories are first-degree murder, second-degree murder, manslaughter, and not guilty. Example attributes are killing in pursuance of a resolution, intent to kill, interval between resolution and killing, and person identity.

In phase 3, the participants mentally compute a match between the story features from phase 1 and the verdict attributed from phase 2. The verdict that has the highest match to the story features is the verdict that the vast majority of the participants ended up selecting. The stories ended up predicting the verdicts much more robustly than alternative quantitative models of decision making (such as linear updating models).

Given that the composition of the story has such a robust influence on jury decisions, Pennington and Hastie dissected the content and structure of the story representations in great detail. They mapped out the causal structures and goal structures that *explain* the evidence. Their concern with causal and intentional structures parallels the explanation assumption of the constructionist theory. Pennington and Hastie also suggested some metrics that measure the *coverage* and *coherence* of a story. These are analogous to the assumptions about local and global coherence in the constructionist theory. A story's coverage of the evidence refers to the extent to which the story can account for a higher proportion of the pieces of evidence. Pennington and Hastie's analysis of coherence has three dimensions: Consistency, plausibility, and completeness. Consistency is the extent to which the story does not have internal contradictions. Plausibility is the extent to which the story is consistent with events in the real world (i.e., world knowledge structures outside of the scope of the murder trial). Completeness is the extent to which a story has all of its parts. In summary, the central components of Pennington and Hastie's story model are directly analogous to the distinctive assumptions of the constructionist theory.

Jury decisions should be sensitive to the weighting of coverage, consistency, plausibility, completeness, and other dimensions (such as the status of the lawyer). However, additional research is needed to explore these dimensions. Kuhn et al. (1994) reported that some individuals quickly construct a story that handles most of the evidence, and subsequently are resistant to conflicting evidence that comes in; consistency is not an important parameter for these individuals. Other individuals are more flexible in coordinating stories with evidence, and are open to story revisions and multiple stories. These individuals ended up being less confident in their decisions.

The plausibility parameter is relevant to the intriguing paradox of the difference between truth and fiction. Consider an individual who assigns a high weight to the plausibility parameter. This person would be carefully scrutinizing each piece of evidence and determining how well it meshes with what the person already knows (i.e., the person's background world knowledge). Adults presumably do this when they read a newspaper. At the other extreme is the individual who assigns a low weight to plausibility and evaluates the internal consistency of a story on its own terms. One of the hallmarks of narrative fiction is that the reader should have a "willing suspension of disbelief" (Coleridge, 1967). That is, instead of the reader constantly evaluating the truth or falsity of information in relation to the reader's general world knowledge, the reader should suspend such evaluations and become absorbed in the hypothetical world. Whether adults can do this is currently being investigated empirically (Prentice, Gerrig, & Bailis, 1997; Wheeler, Green, & Brock, 1999). On the flip side, there is the question of whether fiction can influence our beliefs about reality. For example, Prentice et al. (1997) reported that blatantly false statements (e.g., A college education will reduce your chances of getting a good job) received higher agreement ratings from college students if they were embedded in conversations in a fictional narrative. This result is remarkable because the material is classified as fiction, yet it changed beliefs about the real world. The fine line between truth and fiction was also a complex matter in the story of Fred Smith at the beginning of this chapter. There is something that rings true about the Fred Smith story although he never did make that $40,000 gamble in Las Vegas. Instead of asking *whether* there is truth in fiction, the alternative question to ask is: *Where* is the truth in fiction?

SUMMARY

During the past 25 years, discourse psychologists have investigated the processing of narrative text at different levels of representation. These levels of cognitive representation include the surface code, textbase, situation model, thematic point, agent perspective, and discourse genre. In addition, acts of communication are embedded in a pragmatic context that includes speakers and listeners in oral discourse, authors and readers in printed text, and directors and viewers of film. Comprehension is successful when there is synchrony among these different levels of representation. Comprehension breaks down to the extent that there are incongruities within and between levels.

The process of constructing the situation models of stories is not as mysterious as it was 25 years ago. The situation model is a microworld that includes a spatial setting, agents in pursuit of goals, and causal chains of events that unfold chronologically. These microworlds are systematically constructed through mechanisms that are widely accepted in contemporary theories in cognitive science (see Table 10.1). When it comes to delineating the inferences in situation models for stories, the constructionist theory of Graesser et al. (1994) provides one account of the systematicity. Readers reliably generate inferences that provide local and global coherence, that explain why episodes in the text occur, and that explain why the author uses particular linguistic and discourse forms. Readers also construct inferences that are relevant to their comprehension goals. Some inferences are products of passive activations of knowledge, as has been modeled by Kintsch's construction–integration model (Kintsch, 1998). The distinctive components of the constructionist theory, namely the coherence and explanation assumptions, are also incorporated in some contemporary theories in social psychology that attempt to account for causal attribution and jury decision making.

AUTHOR NOTE

Correspondence concerning this article should be addressed to Arthur C. Graesser, Department of Psychology, Campus Box 526400, The University of Memphis, Memphis, TN 38152–6400, a-graesser@memphis.edu. This research was partially funded by grants to the first author by the Office of Naval Research (N00014-95-11113 and N00014-98-0331) and the National Science Foundation (SBR 9720314).

REFERENCES

Alicke, M. D. (1992). Culpable causation. *Journal of Personality and Social Psychology, 63,* 368–378.

Anderson, R. C., & Pichert, J. W. (1978). Recall of previously unrecallable information following a shift in perspective. *Journal of Verbal Learning and Verbal Behavior, 17,* 1–12.

Biber, D. (1988). *Variations across speech and writing.* Cambridge, MA: Cambridge University Press.

Black, J. B., Turner, T. J., & Bower, G. H. (1979). Point of view in narrative comprehension, memory, and production. *Journal of Verbal Learning and Verbal Behavior, 18,* 187–198.

Bower, G. H., Black, J. B., & Turner, T. J. (1979). Scripts in memory for text. *Cognitive Psychology, 11,* 177–220.

Brem, S., & Rips, L. (1996). Explanation and evidence in formal reasoning. In W. G. Cotrell (Ed.), *Proceedings of the Eighteenth Annual Conference of the Cognitive Science Society* (pp. 271–276). Mahwah, NJ: Lawrence Erlbaum Associates.

Brewer, W. F. (1980). Literacy theory, rhetoric, and stylistics: Implications for psychology. In R. J. Spiro, B. C. Bruce, & W. F. Brewer (Eds.), *Theoretical issues in reading comprehension* (pp. 221–239). Hillsdale, NJ: Lawrence Erlbaum Associates.

Brewer, W. F. (1996). The nature of narrative suspense and the problem of rereading. In P. Vorderer, H. J. Wulff, & M. Friedrichsen (Eds.), *Suspense: Conceptualizations, theoretical analyses, and empirical explorations* (pp. 107–127). Mahwah, NJ: Lawrence Erlbaum Associates.
Brewer, W. F., & Ohtsuka, K. (1988). Story structure, characterization, just world organization, and reader affect in American and Hungarian short stories. *Poetics, 17,* 395–415.
Britton, B., & Black, J. B. (Eds.). (1985). *Understanding expository text.* Hillsdale, NJ: Lawrence Erlbaum Associates.
Bruner, J. (1986). *Actual minds, possible worlds.* Cambridge, MA: Harvard University Press.
Burger, J. M. (1981). Motivational biases in the attribution of responsibility for an accident: A meta-analysis of the defensive attribution hypothesis. *Psychological Bulletin, 90,* 496–512.
Clark, H. H. (1996). *Using language.* Cambridge, UK: Cambridge University Press.
Coleridge, S. T. (1967). Biographia literaria. In D. Perkins (Ed.), *English romantic writers.* New York: Harcourt, Brace, & World.
Davidson, D. (1994). Recognition and recall of irrelevant and interruptive atypical actions in script-based stories. *Journal of Memory and Language, 33,* 757–775.
Duchan, J. F., Bruder, G. A., & Hewitt, L. E. (Eds.). (1995). *Deixis in narrative: A cognitive science perspective.* Mahwah, NJ: Lawrence Erlbaum Associates.
Dyer, M. G. (1983). *In-depth understanding: A computer model of integrated processing for narrative comprehension.* Cambridge, MA: MIT Press.
Gernsbacher, M. A. (1997). Two decades of structure building. *Discourse Processes, 23,* 265–304.
Gerrig, R. J. (1993). *Experiencing narrative worlds: On the psychological activities of reading.* New Haven, CT: Yale University Press.
Givon, T. (1993). Coherence in text, coherence in mind. *Pragmatics and Cognition, 1,* 171–227.
Glenberg, A. M., Meyer, M., & Lindem, K. (1987). Mental models contribute to foregrounding during text comprehension. *Journal of Memory and Language, 26,* 69–83.
Goldman, S. R. (1985). Inferential reasoning in and about narrative texts. In A. C. Graesser & J. B. Black (Eds.), *The psychology of questions* (pp. 247–276). Hillsdale, NJ: Lawrence Erlbaum Associates.
Goldman, S., Graesser, A. C., & van den Broek, P. (Eds). (1999). *Narrative comprehension, causality, and coherence.* Mahwah, NJ: Lawrence Erlbaum Associates.
Graesser, A. C., & Bertus, E. (1998). The construction of causal inferences while reading expository texts on science and technology. *Journal of the Scientific Studies of Reading, 2,* 247–269.
Graesser, A. C., Bowers, C. A., Olde, B., & Pomeroy, V. (1999). Who said what? Source memory for narrator and character agents in literary stories. *Journal of Educational Psychology, 91,* 284–300.
Graesser, A. C., & Clark, L. C. (1985). *Structures and procedures of implicit knowledge.* Norwood, NJ: Ablex.
Graesser, A. C., Golding, J. M., & Long, D. L. (1991). Narrative representation and comprehension. In R. Barr, M. L. Kamil, P. Mosenthal, & P. D. Pearson (Eds.), *Handbook of reading research* (Vol. 2, pp. 171–204). London, UK: Longman.
Graesser, A. C., Hauft-Smith, K., Cohen, A. D., & Pyles, L. D. (1980). Advanced outlines, familiarity, text genre, and retention of prose. *Journal of Experimental Education, 48,* 209–220.
Graesser, A. C., Hoffman, N. L., & Clark, L. F. (1980). Structural components of reading time. *Journal of Verbal Learning and Verbal Behavior, 19,* 131–151.

Graesser, A. C., Kassler, M. A., Kreuz, R. J., & McLain-Allen, B. (1998). Verification of statements about story worlds that deviate from normal conceptions of time: What is true about Einstein's Dreams? *Cognitive Psychology, 35*, 246–301.

Graesser, A. C., & Nakamura, G. V. (1982). The impact of schemas on comprehension and memory. In G. H. Bower (Ed.), *The psychology of learning and motivation*, Vol. 16 (pp. 59–109). New York: Academic Press.

Graesser, A. C., & Ottati, V. (1996). Why stories? Some evidence, questions, and challenges. In R. S. Wyer (Ed.), *Knowledge and memory: The real story* (pp. 121–132). Mahwah, NJ: Lawrence Erlbaum Associates.

Graesser, A. C., Singer, M., & Trabasso, T. (1994). Constructing inferences during narrative text comprehension. *Psychological Review, 101*, 371–395.

Graesser, A. C., & Wiemer-Hastings, K. (1999). Situation models and concepts in story comprehension. In S. R. Goldman, A. C. Graesser, & P. van den Broek (Eds.). *Narrative comprehension, causality, and coherence* (pp. 77–92). Mahwah, NJ: Lawrence Erlbaum Associates.

Haberlandt, K., & Graesser, A. C. (1985). Component processes in text comprehension and some of their interactions. *Journal of Experimental Psychology: General, 114*, 357–374.

Hastie, R., & Kumar, P. A. (1979). Person memory: Personality traits as organizing principles in memory for behavior. *Journal of Personality and Social Psychology, 37*, 25–38.

Hilton, D. J., Smith, R. H., & Kim, S. H. (1995). Processes of causal explanation and dispositional attribution. *Journal of Personality and Social Psychology, 68*, 377–387.

Keysar, B. (1994). The illusory transparency of intention: Linguistic perspective taking in text. *Cognitive Psychology, 26*, 165–208.

Kintsch, W. (1974). *The representation of meaning in memory*. Hillsdale, NJ: Lawrence Erlbaum Associates.

Kintsch, W. (1998). *Comprehension: A paradigm for cognition*. Cambridge, UK: Cambridge University Press.

Kuhn, D., Weinstock, M., & Flaton, R. (1994). How well do jurors reason? Competence dimensions of individual variation in a juror reasoning task. *Psychological Science, 5*, 289–296.

Lehnert, W. G. (1981). Plot units and narrative summarization. *Cognitive Science, 5*, 293–331.

Long, D. L., Golding, J. M., & Graesser, A. C. (1992). Test of the on-line status of goal-related inferences. *Journal of Memory and Language, 31*, 634–647.

Magliano, J. P., Baggett, W. B., Johnson, B. K., & Graesser, A. C. (1993). The time course of generating causal antecedent and causal consequence inferences. *Discourse Processes, 16*, 35–53.

Mandler, J. M. (1984). *Stories, scripts, and scenes: Aspects of schema theory*. Hillsdale, NJ: Lawrence Erlbaum Associates.

McKoon, G., & Ratcliff, R. (1992). Inference during reading. *Psychological Review, 99*, 440–466.

Millis, K. K. (1995). Encoding discourse perspective during the reading of a literary text. *Poetics, 23*, 235–253.

Millis, K., & Graesser, A. C. (1994). The time-course of constructing knowledge-based inferences for scientific texts. *Journal of Memory and Language, 33*, 583–599.

Morrow, D. G., Greenspan, S. L., & Bower, G. H. (1987). Accessibility and situation models in narrative comprehension. *Journal of Memory and Language, 26*, 165–187.

Myers, J. L., O'Brien, E. J., Albrecht, J. E., & Mason, R. A. (1994). Maintaining global coherence during reading. *Journal of Experimental Psychology: Learning, Memory, and Cognition, 20*, 876–886.

Narvaes, D. (1998). The influence of moral schemas on the reconstruction of moral narratives in eighth graders and college students. *Journal of Educational Psychology, 90*, 13–24.

Norrick, N. R. (1998). Retelling stories in spontaneous conversation. *Discourse Processes, 25*, 75–98.

O'Brien, E. J., Raney, G. E., Albrecht, J. E., & Rayner, K. (1997). Processes involved in the resolution of explicit anaphors. *Discourse Processes, 23*, 1–24.

Ohtsuka, K., & Brewer, W. F. (1992). Discourse organization in the comprehension of temporal order. *Discourse Processes, 15*, 317–336.

Owens, J., Bower, G. H., & Black, J. B. (1979). The "soap opera" effect in story recall. *Memory & Cognition, 7*, 185–191.

Pennington, N., & Hastie, R. (1992). Explaining the evidence: Tests of the story model for juror decision making. *Journal of Personality and Social Psychology, 62*, 189–206.

Pennington, N., & Hastie, R. (1993). Reasoning in explanation-based decision-making. *Cognition, 9*, 123–163.

Prentice, D. A., Gerrig, R. J., & Bailis, D. S. (1997). What readers bring to the processing of fictional texts. *Psychonomic Bulletin & Review, 4*, 416–420.

Read, S. J., & Marcus-Newhall, A. (1993). Explanatory coherence in social explanations: A parallel distributed processing account. *Journal of Personality and Social Psychology, 65*, 429–447.

Rubin, D. C. (1995). *Memory in oral traditions: The cognitive psychology of epic, ballads, and counting-out-rhymes*. New York: Oxford University Press.

Rumelhart, D. E. (1977). Understanding and summarizing brief stories. In D. LaBerge & S. J. Samuels (Eds.), *Basic processes in reading: Perception and comprehension* (pp. 265–303). Hillsdale, NJ: Lawrence Erlbaum Associates.

Rumelhart, D. E., & McClelland, J. L. (1986). *Parallel distributed processing:Explorations in the microstructure of cognition*, Volume 1. Cambridge, MA: MIT Press.

Schank, R. C. (1982). Reminding and memory organization: An introduction to MOPS. In W. G. Lehnert & M. H. Ringle (Eds.), *Strategies of natural language comprehension* (pp. 455–493). Hillsdale, NJ: Lawrence Erlbaum Associates.

Schank, R. C., & Abelson, R. P. (1977). *Scripts, plans, goals, and understanding: An inquiry into human knowledge structures*. Hillsdale, NJ: Lawrence Erlbaum Associates.

Schank, R. C., & Abelson, R. P. (1996). Knowledge and memory: The real story. In R. S. Wyer (Ed.), *Advances in Social Cognition*. Mahwah, NJ: Lawrence Erlbaum Associates.

Schiffrin, D. (1984). How a story says what it means and does. *Text, 4*, 313–346.

Schober, M. F. (1998). Different kinds of conversational perspective taking. In S. R. Fussel & R. J. Kreuz (Eds.), *Social and cognitive psychological approaches to interpersonal communication* (pp. 145–174). Mahwah, NJ: Lawrence Erlbaum Associates.

Seifert, C. M., McKoon, G., Abelson, R. P., & Ratcliff, R. (1986). Memory connections between thematically similar episodes. *Journal of Experimental Psychology: Learning, Memory, and Cognition, 12*, 220–231.

Singer, M., Graesser, A. C., & Trabasso, T. (1994). Minimal or global inference during reading. *Journal of Memory and Language, 33*, 421–441.

Singer, M., & Halldorson, M. (1996). Constructing and validating motive bridging inferences. *Cognitive Psychology, 30*, 1–38.

Stangor, C., & McMillan, D. (1992). Memory for expectancy-congruent and expectancy-incongruent information: A review of the social and social developmental literatures. *Psychological Bulletin, 111*, 42–61.

Trabasso, T., & Magliano, J. P. (1996). Conscious understanding during comprehension. *Discourse Processes, 21*, 255–287.

Trabasso, T., & van den Broek, P. (1985). Causal thinking and the representation of narrative events. *Journal of Memory and Language, 24*, 612–630.

van den Broek, P., Young, M., Tzeng, Y., & Linderholm, T. (1999). The landscape model of reading inferences and the on-line construction of memory representations. In H. van Oostendorp & S. R. Goldman (Eds.), *The construction of mental representations during reading* (pp.71–98). Mahwah, NJ: Lawrence Erlbaum Associates.

van Peer, W., & Chatman, S. (Eds.). (1999). *Narrative perspective: Cognition and emotion.* Albany: SUNY University Press.

Vorderer, P., Wulff, H. J., & Friedrichsen, M. (Eds.). (1996). *Suspense: Conceptualizations, theoretical analyses, and empirical explorations.* Mahwah, NJ: Lawrence Erlbaum Associates.

Voss, J. F., Wiley, J., & Sandak, R. (1999). On the use of argument. In S. R. Goldman, A. C. Graesser, & P. van den Broek (Eds.), *Narrative comprehension, causality, and coherence: Essays in honor of Tom Trabasso* (pp. 235–252). Mahwah, NJ: Lawrence Erlbaum Associates.

Wheeler, S. C., Green, M. C., & Brock, T. C. (1999). Fictional narratives change beliefs: Replications of Prentice, Gerrig, and Bailis (1997) with mixed corroboration. *Psychonomic Bulletin & Review, 6*, 136–141.

Williams, J. P. (1993). Comprehension of students with and without learning disabilities: Identification of narrative themes and idiosyncratic text representations. *Journal of Educational Psychology, 85*, 631–641.

Wyer, R., & Gordon, S. E. (1984). The cognitive representation of social information. In R. S. Wyer & T. K. Srull (Eds.), *Handbook of social cognition, Vol. 1* (pp. 73–150). Hillsdale, NJ: Lawrence Erlbaum Associates.

Zwaan, R. A., & Brown, C. M. (1996). The influence of language proficiency and comprehension skill on situation model construction. *Discourse Processes, 21*, 289–327.

Zwaan, R. A., Langston, M. C., & Graesser, A. C. (1995). The construction of situation models in narrative comprehension: An event-indexing model. *Psychological Science, 6*, 292–297.

Zwaan, R. A., Magliano, J. P., & Graesser, A. C. (1995). Dimensions of situation model construction in narrative comprehension. *Journal of Experimental Psychology: Learning, Memory, and Cognition, 21*, 386–397.

Zwaan, R. A., & Radvansky, G. A. (1998). Situation models in language comprehension and memory. *Psychological Bulletin, 123*, 162–185.

11

How Fictional Tales Wag Real-World Beliefs

Models and Mechanisms of Narrative Influence

Jeffrey J. Strange
Public Insight

The publication of Harriet Beecher Stowe's *Uncle Tom's Cabin (UTC)* (1852/1994) produced an effect that Frederick Douglas described as "amazing, instantaneous, and universal" (as cited in Levine, 1994, p. 539). Indeed the novel is widely accepted to have played a pivotal role in galvanizing public opinion against slavery. Nineteenth-century writers were convinced that *something* about Stowe's book had led it to succeed where previous modes of discourse had failed. Some located its power in the dissemination of "real knowledge of the facts and workings of American Slavery" (anonymous, cited in Bailey, 1852, p. 62). A contrasting view was advanced by Charles Dudley Warner (1896), for whom the myriad abolition tracts, pamphlets, newspapers, and books of the preceding decades "had left little to be revealed" about the nature of slavery. For Warner, the distinguishing mark of *UTC* resided not in its diffusion of facts, but rather in its ability to "go to the heart," to strike "the public conscience," and, ultimately, "to carry the sort of conviction that results in action" (p. 312). Many were left with the question that Warner left hanging at the end of the century: "What was this book and how did it happen to produce such an effect?" (p. 312).

The aim of this chapter is to suggest and, where possible, to document mechanisms through which stories, particularly "fictional" ones, influence the judgments and beliefs of readers.[1] Although *UTC* and its reception are in many ways unique, the issues they raise are as pertinent today as they were then. How might a story about invented characters in imaginary situations influence readers' judgments about people, problems, and institutions in the everyday world? How might fictional discourse be used to convey an author's real-world beliefs? Is fiction particularly prone to the communication of misinformation? Finally, what characteristics of readers, reading, and texts tend to facilitate and constrain the impact of stories?

VARIETIES OF FICTIONAL DISCOURSE

On one view, the assertions made within fictional discourse refer exclusively to an imaginary world, and, as such, have no direct bearing on extratextual referents. What might be called the "mere pretense" position was voiced by psychologist Richard Gerrig (1988) who, commenting on assertions about Beethoven and Rossini in Thomas Pynchon's *Gravity's Rainbow*, argued that "we should discount them entirely because they are spoken by fictional characters" (p. 258). "Logically," he concluded, "we ought to enjoy the prose but ignore the opinions" expressed by fictional characters.[2] According to Schmidt (1976), this normative view has been adopted as a pragmatic convention, one that describes how modern readers learn to approach literature. Whether or not readers do consistently adopt this approach, its reality as a pedagogical principle is confirmed by Adler & van Doren's popular treatise *How to Read a Book* (1940/1972), where they remind us of "the obvious fact that we do not agree or disagree with fiction." Therefore, they instruct us, "Don't read fiction by the standards of truth and consistency that properly apply to the communication of knowledge" (p. 213). Historian Paul Hutton (1991) extended these views of the logic, pragmatics, and pedagogy of fiction to an ethical prescription for writing and evaluating historical fiction. "It is simply ridiculous to expect films to be true to the facts of history," he contended. "They are works of fiction" (p. 42). Underlying Hutton's assertion is the commonly held assumption that the label *fiction* gives viewers and readers fair warning that the ensuing discourse should not be taken seriously with respect to the extratextual world.

It is certainly the case that, much of the time, fiction writers do not intend the assertions and states-of-affairs present in their novels to be taken as claims about the extratextual world. They do not, of course, expect us to believe that dogs can fly, that men can transform into werewolves, or that time travel is possible. Robert Coover could not believe, or intend his readers to believe, that Julius and Ethel Rosenberg were executed at Times Square, or that Richard Nixon carried on with Ethel, as he does in *The Public Burning* (1977). Harriet Beecher Stowe did not expect her readers to believe that a man named Simon Legree existed in the American South.

In cases such as these, the standard definition of fiction as "something invented by the imagination or feigned" is appropriate, and it would surely constitute an error of judgment if readers were to integrate such assertions into their beliefs about the world. The questions remain, however, whether the designation of a work as "fictional" conveys the message that all assertions and depictions within it are intended as acts of mere pretense and whether they are evaluated as such by readers.

Although *UTC* was a novel populated with fictional characters, the grounds on which it was criticized and defended make it clear that it was intended and received as a set of serious assertions about the nature of slavery in America. In scores of attacks printed in newspapers across the country, the book was deemed to be replete with "miserable misrepresentations"; its incidents were declared "too shocking for belief"; and its author was labeled "a deliberate liar," set to "libel and vilify" southerners (e.g., Holmes, 1852/1994, pp. 468–469). Now it could be that these critics were either naïve or disingenuous in applying "standards of truth and consistency" to a work of mere pretense. Had this been the case, however, Stowe would have felt no compulsion to defend her novel on these terms. She could simply have responded, like Hutton, that this was merely fiction, a genre of discourse that makes no claims about extratextual reality.[3] Instead, Stowe answered with a full length book, *A Key to Uncle Tom's Cabin* (1853/1998), where she sought to counter doubts about "whether the representations of *Uncle Tom's Cabin* are a fair representation of slavery ..." (p. 5). To do so, she meticulously documented historical cases that paralleled those presented in *UTC*. In summarizing the reality claims of her book, Stowe wrote that, "This work ... has been a collection and arrangement of real incidents—of actions really performed, of words and expressions really uttered—grouped together with reference to a general result ..." (p. 5). Moreover, she continued, "it is *treated* as a reality—sifted, tried, and tested, as a reality; and therefore as a reality it may be proper that it should be defended" (p. 5).

This example shows that the "mere pretense" view of fiction is surely wrong when taken as a general statement of the logic and pragmatics of fictional discourse. But *UTC* is, indeed, a work of fiction. To say that something is a work of fiction does imply that it in some way diverges from the conventions of true-to-facts description that govern nonfiction writing. It does imply that *something* is consciously and openly "feigned." But the nature and extent of this feigning is genre- and work-specific. The mode of pretense present in *UTC* is one in which the author creates a world populated by what she deems to be analogues of real-world persons, events, and relationships. She invites her readers to enter this world, to empathize with and adopt the perspectives of its inhabitants, and, having done so, to pass judgment on the extratextual institution of slavery. Unlike pure fantasy, the illocutionary force of assertions about real-world institutions and relationships is left intact, albeit through an indirect mode of reference. In other words, Stowe uses the vehicle of a fictional world to seriously refer to the historical world.

UTC comments on the real world through a succession of dramatized pictures (Warner, 1896, p. 319) that the author deems to reflect real-world institutions and relations. Fictional discourse is also filled with direct assertions of accepted historical and scientific fact. For instance, Tolstoy's novel *War and Peace* [1869/1967] accurately informs readers that Napoleon left Dresden on May 29, 1812. Most obvious in this respect are fictional programs designed to teach children. For example, *Sesame Street*'s Big Bird and The Count communicate accurate knowledge of the alphabet and math.

Rather than clearly announcing the intended referential status of its assertions, fiction often leaves us hanging. For example, historian Alvin Josephy, Jr. (1995) called the popular Errol Flynn movie, *They Died With Their Boots On*, "a hodgepodge of truth and ... fairy tale" (p.146). The Custer of *Boots On* dies at the Little Big Horn as he did in life. At the same time, however, he is falsely depicted as a champion of Indian rights and a foe of the evil developers who spur the Black Hills gold rush.[4] What are readers to think about the assertion, made in Michael Crichton's *Congo* (1993), that "There was no longer any doubt that chimpanzees occasionally kidnapped —and ate—human babies"? (p. 227). Does the author believe this to be true? Does he intend readers to accept it as a serious assertion about animal behavior?[5] Similar questions can be raised about Pynchon's Rossini: Was he a womanizer who retired at 36?

In rejecting the "mere pretense" view of fictionality, then, we allow that authors may legitimately intend and be interpreted to make serious statements about the actual world from within the context of fictional discourse. At the same time, of course, much of what comprises fictional discourse is designed to entertain, enrich, or inspire without aiming to increase our knowledge or to alter our views of the world around us. Or, as Bruner (1991) suggested, fictional narratives may provide models of *how* to think about life's situations (e.g., with humor, or irony, or epistemic doubt) without aiming to change *what* we think about life's particulars. Whatever the aims of a specific work of fiction, we are left with a mode of discourse that allows authors to liberally intermix plausible statements and portraits that they believe to be true of the world with those that are knowingly false. Without the benefit of the explicit local marking of referential intent that characterizes everyday speech (e.g., Sanders & Redeker, 1996), readers are often left guessing as to whether or not real-world truth claims are being made.

CONTEXT MANAGEMENT IN MULTIMODAL WORLDS

A signature characteristic of fictional discourse is that it allows authors, through their literary personas, to utter knowingly untrue assertions without these statements being deemed to be lies. This is the poetic license that Oscar Wilde celebrated, in *The Decay of Lying* (1889/1920), as the source of art's "distinction, charm, beauty, and imaginative power" (p. 13). Art, he argued via the personas of Cyril and Vivian, "is absolutely indifferent to fact, invents, imagines, dreams, and keeps between herself and reality the impenetrable barrier of beautiful style, of decorative or ideal treatment"(p.21). An adamant critic of realism, Wilde represents an ideal in which life mimics art, not the reverse: "A great artist invents a type, and Life tries to copy it, to reproduce it in a popular form, like an enterprising publisher" (p. 32).

Of course, popular literature has seen fit to embrace both realism and aestheticism, to treat life both as an object to be reflected and as the raw material from which to shape new visions, experiences, and forms. Stories both mirror and invent, and to the extent that their inventions are construed as reflections of the world, the license that fiction is granted can lead to misconceptions about the way things work, what and how things happened, and who individuals and communities are.

The tension between the poles of reflection and invention is present in all coherent stories at different levels of abstraction. In the character of Uncle Tom, for instance, Stowe has been criticized for inventing a type that has been received as a reflection (Levine, 1994). This tension is nowhere more apparent than in historical fiction and docudrama, where specific historical events and the lives of named historical individuals become the raw material from which authors fashion their fictional tales. How readers process historical fabrications can offer insights into how they treat similar information in other genres, but it is no less important to historical reasoning per se. Historian Herbert Aptheker (as cited in Current, 1986) argued this point when he criticized William Styron's novel, *The Confessions of Nat Turner*: "History's potency is mighty," he wrote. "The oppressed need it for identity and inspiration; oppressors for justification, rationalization and legitimacy" (p. 86). On a specific count, historian Alvin Josephy, Jr. (1995) lamented the effects of the "twisted and distorted" portrait presented in *Boots On*: "If the producers gave any thought to what Indians in the audiences might have known or felt about how they or their history were portrayed, there is no evidence of it" in this movie (p. 148).

Opinions are mixed on the empirical question of whether and when readers integrate fictional fallacies into their real-world beliefs. Historian Paul Hutton was convinced that "For eight decades film has been the leading factor in determining the popular perception of [Custer]" (1991, p. 56). Conversely, Japanese author, Yoshiaki Aramaki (Pollack, 1995, p. 5), who writes "simulation novels" that promiscuously rewrite WWII history claims that "The readers understand that this has nothing to do with reality." In the remainder of this section, I first identify a set of processes through which readers might mistakenly incorporate fabrications of historical fiction into their beliefs about history. I then present an empirical study in which I examine how a sub-set of these processes characterize actual reading practices.

Referential Contexts

Following James (1889/1981), we can conceive of knowledge as being assigned to one or another world, to the actual one or to one of its alternatives (e.g., dreams, wishes, fantasy, the opinions of others). In acts of communication, language is used to signal the world, or context, to which reference is intended. In the unmarked, indicative mode that characterizes direct assertions, utterances are assumed to carry the speaker's conviction that assertions are true of the actual world (Ryan, 1991). To the extent that listeners accept a speaker's description, they will include it in their own set of beliefs about the actual world.

Through the use of *context specifications*—variously called *space builders*, *world-creating predicates*, and *nonfactive predicates*—language is used to signal a shift in reference from the speaker's actual world to another mental or symbolic representation of a world—to dreams, paintings, beliefs, wishes, stories, and the like. Examples of such context specifications include "In my dream," "I wish that," "In John's mind," "In the story," or "Once upon a time." From a representational perspective, such context specifications are assumed to initiate the construction of a *referential context*—variously called *belief contexts*, *mental spaces*, or *nested representations*—within which information is categorized as referring to a world of dreams, wishes, stories, and the like (Dinsmore, 1991; Rapaport, 1986; Rapaport & Shapiro, 1995). Given this framework, we can approach the question of how people might come to believe false or nonevidentiary information presented in fictional discourse as a question of how such contexts might fail.

Modes of Context Failure

The status of truth claims in fictional discourse is underdetermined and governed by unstable pragmatic conventions. As suggested earlier, the fact that Crichton's *Congo* is presented as a novel, a work of fiction, does not clearly inform us of the writer's referential intent. Notice the difference when statements like "Chimps eat human babies" are read in *Science*, where the type of truth claim is specified through fairly stable institutional conventions. *Context specification failure* is an intrinsic propensity of fiction as a mode of discourse that permits the liberal mingling of unmarked assertions of fact, hypothesis, and fancy. It denotes the case in which readers come to believe an assertion because they wrongly interpret it to be a claim about the real world.

Context encoding failure and *context comprehension failure* are related to context specification failure in that the reader is not successfully informed of the referential intentions of the author. The lead-in to *War of the Worlds* clearly specified the make-believe status of this radio drama (Cantril, 1940/1986). However, many did not hear or comprehend these specifications and, as a result, found themselves fleeing to the countryside to avoid the alien invasion.

A reader might also encode and comprehend, but reject the specification that "any resemblance to actual persons or events is purely coincidental." The characters in novels sometimes bear a striking resemblance to, or share a name with, people in the real world. Libel and "false light" invasion of privacy cases have been brought under these circumstances (Silver, 1978). Readers may sometimes be correct in rejecting such disclaimers, which have become standard practice even when the portrayal is about or based on a real person. But when the resemblance is, in fact, coincidental, *context rejection* may lead readers to mistakenly incorporate beliefs about the story-world character into their models of a real-world person.

Some historical fiction writers have provided specifications of the intended reality status of story-world assertions. For example, James Michener prefaced his novel *The Source* (1965) as follows: "Characters and scenes are imaginary except as noted. The hero, Rabbi Akiba, was a real man who died as described in 137 C.E. All quotations ascribed to him can be verified. King David ... and Dr. Maimonides were also real persons and quotations ascribed to the last are also verifiable." *Context specification forgetting* occurs when we encode, comprehend, and accept such specifications, but later forget which characters are historical or imaginary, or which dialogue is intended to convey a character's actual words or beliefs.

The final three forms of context failure were the focus of the study (Strange, 1993) I describe later. First, one might fail to discriminate the contexts in which propositions are embedded. To modify an earlier example, suppose that we read Crichton's well-specified statement that "In my imaginary world, chimpanzees eat human babies." We should be more apt to believe that chimpanzees eat babies if we misremember having read it in *Science*. *Context discrimination failure*, as evidenced in this example, describes the case in which we actually forget what we read where. The possibility of context discrimination failure across alternative *fictional* worlds is found in William James' (1889/1981) observations concerning the distinctive Ivanhoes sketched by Scott and Thackeray. "Ivanhoe did not *really* marry Rebecca, as Thackeray falsely makes him do," wrote James. "The real Ivanhoe-world is the one which Scott wrote down for us. *In that world* Ivanhoe does *not* marry Rebecca" (p. 922). In this instance, context discrimination failure would entail misremembering aspects of Thackeray's Ivanhoe as those of Scott's portrayal.[6]

It is also possible that the context (e.g., Crichton's imagination vs. *Science*) remains available in memory, but that we fail to associate context and content when an opportunity arises to utilize this knowledge (e.g., that chimps eat babies). As a result, we may act on the "belief" that chimps eat babies even if we simultaneously "know" that it was the product of a writer's imagination. In *context activation failure*, then, context is ignored when content is brought to mind. A personal example helps provide an intuitive understanding of this process:

As a teen-ager, I was in a serious car wreck. The typical prime-time car wreck concludes in a massive explosion and, as I bolted from the car, this story-world image captured my mind. I ran and dove, and as I hit the ground, my immediate reaction was a strong sense of incredulity that no explosion had accompanied my landing. My next emotion was a sense of embarrassment: If you asked me what the chances were of an explosion, I would have said they were very low. But in that moment, there was no doubt in my mind that "car wrecks result in explosions." Once in memory, story-world assertions may migrate to a reasoner's real-world belief space when they are *temporarily* dissociated from the nonfactive context in which they are embedded.

Finally, suppose that at the time we judge the truth of an assertion, we actively consider that it was fabricated and evidentially ungrounded. Might we still believe this statement more than if we had not read the fictive account? *Context engulfment* denotes the possibility that beliefs are influenced by reading nonevidentiary statements even when the context is specified, encoded, comprehended, believed, remembered, and activated during judgment. This is the least intuitive of the modes of context failure proposed here, and I discuss possible cognitive processes underlying it further on in this chapter.

The "facts of fiction" study (Strange, 1993) was designed to examine whether readers would incorporate fictive statements into their historical beliefs and to determine whether they do so because of context failure, context suspension, or context engulfment. The study was designed to ensure that the context of statements was adequately specified and that readers encoded, comprehended, believed, and remembered the specifications themselves.[7]

11. FICTIONAL TALES AND REAL-WORLD BELIEFS 271

Participants (students at Columbia University) were divided into 5 groups, all of which first read an historical narrative ostensibly written by an historian about the political history of the Panama Canal ("Where the Seas Meet"). The 4000-word "Seas Meet" was intended to provide readers with a relatively uniform base of historical knowledge. After reading "Seas Meet," a control group read an unrelated filler text, whereas the other 4 groups read a second 4000-word story about the canal, "Continental Divide." The history group was informed that this text was also written by an historian, whereas the 3 fiction groups were informed that it was highly fictionalized. To alert readers to which parts of "Continental Divide" were fabricated, the story was preceded by a writer's preface. The gist of this preface is captured by the writer's statements that "My only knowledge of the events covered here comes from what I read in 'Where the Seas Meet,'" and "any new information is the product of my imagination."[8] Two versions of "Continental Divide" were written such that they conflicted on a series of 13 key points that were not covered in "Seas Meet." For example, whereas one version shows the Panamanian revolution to be a popular revolt, the other shows it to be the revolt of a rich elite, and whereas one version shows that the Panamanian Senate eagerly ratified the Canal treaty with the United States, the other shows that the Senate was coerced by gunboat diplomacy.

The dependent measures were designed to determine whether readers incorporated the fictive assertions into their beliefs about history, and if so, through which cognitive routes. About 30 minutes after reading "Continental Divide," readers were presented a list of 68 statements that included ones presented in both stories, ones presented only in "Seas Meet," and, critically, ones that appeared only in "Continental Divide." The list also included statements contrary to the ones they read. For each statement, participants stipulated whether they believed it to be true of actual Panamanian history (truth ratings); whether they had read it in either of the texts (recognition); and, if so, in which text ("Seas Meet," "Continental Divide," or both) it had appeared (context attribution). By manipulating the time at which the latter task was completed, one of the fiction groups (the context-cued group) was implicitly prompted to bring the context of statements to mind as they rated their truth.

A series of checks and a debriefing held at the end of the study showed that all valid participants encoded, understood, believed, and remembered the context specifications contained in the writer's preface. Recognition results showed that readers remembered the statements somewhat better when they were told they were based on historical research. Truth rating results, more relevant to the current discussion, were adjusted for recognition differences.

First, readers in the three fiction groups reported much stronger beliefs in the set of fictive assertions than did control-group readers. In other words, the fiction groups were much more likely to believe that the Panamanian revolt was either a popular one or an elite one, depending on the version they read, although they believed that the author had spun these data from his imagination.

Second, context discrimination failure did function as a source of belief in the groundless assertions. Averaged across the three fiction groups, readers misattributed about 50% of the correctly recognized fictive items to the historian. In other words, they falsely remembered having read 50% of the groundless assertions as emanating from the research of the historian. As expected, readers were somewhat more likely to believe the fictive statements if they attributed them to the historian.

More surprising was the degree of confidence readers continued to hold in the truth of those fictive statements that they correctly attributed to the imagination of the fiction writer. On a 6-point truth rating scale (6 = definitely true), the history group rated these items at 5.16, whereas a matched fiction group rated them at 4.77. Although statistically reliable, this difference is small compared with the distance between the fiction groups and the control group. Averaging 3.4, readers in the control group showed decided ambivalence over the truth of these items, which is what one would expect, as they had no evidence one way or the other.

Of the processes I have proposed, this leaves context activation failure and context engulfment as explanations for why the fiction groups so confidently believed those statements that they correctly attributed to the writer's imagination. The results showed evidence of both processes. First, analyses indicated that readers sometimes believed an assertion that they knew to be fictive *because* they failed to query its context when judging its truth (context activation failure). Second, readers sometimes believed an assertion that they knew to be fictive *although* they queried its context when judging its truth (context engulfment). This is perhaps the most intriguing of these findings and I consider it in the following paragraphs.

Some insight into readers' strategic processes can be gained from their own explanations of what they thought they were doing. These explanations typically included a claim of context monitoring. For a representative example, one reader wrote that "I assumed that most of the information contained in the first essay was factual and tried to ignore 'facts' in the "Continental Divide" story. I suppose at times I did base my [judgments] on my own opinions though." On correctly attributed statements, this reader averaged 4.85 on the truth rating scale, more than a standard deviation above the *highest* control group reader. As a member of the context-cued group, this reader was also prompted to query the source of his knowledge each time he rendered a truth judgment. Strikingly, his beliefs about what happened were changed by reading statements that he both believed to have been mere fictions *and* that he attempted to judge as if he had not read them at all.

11. FICTIONAL TALES AND REAL-WORLD BELIEFS

These findings are in line with the results of a wide range of studies that have found that once an outcome, a hypothetical explanation, or a decision rule is considered and deemed plausible, people are biased toward seeking evidence that supports it, tend to view ambiguous information as supporting it, and overestimate their ability to ignore information once they have considered it (for a review, see Strange, 1993). In their study of reasoning, Wason & Johnson-Laird (1972) found that people attempt to combine the premises of a syllogism in a way that renders the conclusion true. "Of course," they comment, "this merely shows that conclusions and premises are consistent, not that the conclusion follows from the premises" (p. 157).

Participants in this study were faced with the similar task of combining known fabrications from "Continental Divide" with the relatively reliable information they read in "Seas Meet." If the verification strategy they use is to determine whether a fit exists between the fictive information and the "known facts," their conclusion will be affirmative. As put by one reader, "If it was in the second text and not the first, it wouldn't have any real basis, unless it made sense to me." This strategy ignores, dismisses, or discounts the fact that many conflicting motivations, causes, and descriptions will "make sense," as they fit equally well with prior knowledge.

Although a true-if-it-fits strategy was apparently at work, it does not explain why the matched fiction group discounted statements relative to the history group or why readers were not equally certain of statements contrary to those they read, as these statements fit equally well with information in "Seas Meet." It also does not conform to many readers' reports that they attempted to "ignore" the fictive facts, or to "judge them with more skepticism."

A model of how fictive information is represented in memory can help account for these findings (Strange, 1993). When reading "Continental Divide," readers partially isolate this information in memory. This allows them to tell the story without completely conflating it with prior knowledge. At the same time, however, links are formed between prior knowledge and the fictive facts. For example, an event that occurred in "Seas Meet" (the Senate approved the treaty) is directly linked to a cause provided in "Continental Divide" (they were coerced). When verifying the truth of correctly-identified fabrications, readers first use a true-if-it-fits verification strategy, assessing its degree of coherence within this explanatory network (Thagard, 1989). When they identify assertions as fictive, readers try "to judge them with more skepticism." This downward adjustment is, however, insufficient (Tversky & Kahneman, 1982). Owing to the direct links between prior knowledge and the fictive facts, it is extremely difficult for readers to determine *what they would have believed* had they not read the story. In other words, even when fictive information is independently retrievable in memory, it is not partitioned in a manner that fully isolates it from knowledge that is deemed to be reliable (Dinsmore, 1991).[9]

When faced with an equally coherent fact that is contrary to one they read (e.g., The Senate was elated with the terms of the Canal Treaty), readers also engage a true-if-it-fits verification strategy. The question, however, is "true-if-it-fits-what?" Contrary assertions tend to be judged against an explanatory network that includes the fictive story elements, and, as such, are deemed not to fit at all.

This is but a sketch of one of several models that can explain what I have called context engulfment. It highlights the functional requirements of models needed to explain the seeming paradox that we can, at the same time, (a) know that an assertion is nonevidentiary, (b) treat it with a measure of skepticism, and yet (c) incorporate it into our beliefs about the world.

These results may seem to support an "automatic update" model of belief. Following the lead of Spinoza, Gilbert (1991) found experimental support for the idea that we believe a proposition in the very act of considering it, and that once considered, it is only through conscious scrutiny that we "unbelieve" it. A number of researchers have adopted Gilbert's account to explain how people come to believe fiction. In concert with Gilbert's views, Gerrig (1993) proposed a model that "strongly supposes that special effort is required to prevent [fictional] information from affecting real-world beliefs" (p. 227).

Although conscious effort was required for facts-of-fiction readers to reject the fictive propositions of "Continental Divide," it is unlikely that such effort is required for all forms of fiction. The salient prototype here is dreams. Although we believe our dreams while we are in them, it generally requires no special effort to disbelieve them once we awaken. Similarly, after putting down *Alice in Wonderland*, closing *Cinderella*, or turning off *Sesame Street*, it generally takes no special effort to relegate the existence of Cheshire cats to Wonderland, to disbelieve that coaches can turn into pumpkins, or to stop ourselves from searching for Sesame Street on a map of New York.

Gilbert's model is a two-state system, in which propositions are considered either true or false in relation to a single, undifferentiated referential space. As such, it is not sensitive to differences between the processing of direct assertions (uttered in an indicative mode) and assertions embedded under referential contexts such as dreams, wishes, and stories. The limitations of this system can be seen in its inability to deal with questions of the form, "Does Big Bird live in New York"? Well, yes, he lives there—on *Sesame Street*. On the other hand, no, he does not live in the real New York. The crux of the problem is that belief is world- or context-sensitive. In other words, propositions are not simply considered true or false; rather, their truth is evaluated with respect to some referential context. To accept the truth of the proposition that "In the story, it is true that coaches can turn into pumpkins," does not necessarily entail an automatic belief in the object of this assertion (i.e., that coaches can turn into pumpkins) with respect to the actual world.

As shown in the facts-of-fiction study, there are conditions under which conscious effort will be required to reverse the acceptance of fictive facts. In launching alternative referential contexts, however, we often construct worlds that differ radically from our own. It would be a very inefficient and error-prone system that demanded conscious attention to prevent the propagation of all we encountered in the worlds of dreams, wishes, and pretense to our real-world beliefs (cf., Leslie, 1987). On this view, consideration of a proposition does entail an initial acceptance of its truth. Often, however, these beliefs will not be *about* the real world at all, but only about the worlds of dreams, wishes, stories, and the like. A task of future research is to explicate the conditions under which some contents of stories remain effortlessly sequestered in memory while others migrate to our models of practical reality unless they are effortfully constrained (Rapaport & Shapiro, 1995).

GENERALIZING FROM PARTICULAR CASES

The facts-of-fiction study examined how we might incorporate statements known to be fictive into our beliefs about the extratextual world. Although it focused on assertions about history, its findings are applicable to other plausible assertions that cohere with existing knowledge. Of course the acceptance of direct assertions about historical events, social groups, scientific relationships, and the like are but one way that fiction can influence beliefs. Many of the assertions made in fictional stories are neither narrowly focused statements about historical events, nor broadly focused statements about the "truths" of life (e.g., Chimpanzees eat human babies; Poverty is caused by indolence). Fiction animates the lives of specific individuals in pursuit of concrete goals; its penchant is to show, not tell. It is this characteristic that sets narratives apart from analytic treatments of issues. Accordingly, the bulk of sentences in fictional discourse consist of narrowly focused statements about the lives of fictional characters. Narratives hold the potential to provide readers with in-depth understandings of specific cases. However, their wider influence on socially relevant beliefs lies in the propensity to generalize from particular cases to society at large.

In another line of research, I focused on the influence of narrative accounts on more general beliefs about current social problems (Strange & Leung, 1999). Which of the many problems that confront our communities should we attend to and which should we ignore? What causes these problems and how should they be solved? Through voting behavior, polls, and civic involvement, judgments of this sort affect how society is run. However, our understanding of how our experience in narrative worlds, particularly fictional ones, influence such judgments is limited.

Research indicates that in making judgments of problem urgency (Should the budget be spent to combat drugs or to bolster education?) we tend to favor those issues that we have recently encountered in the media (e.g., Gibson & Zillmann, 1994; Iyengar & Kinder, 1987). If the day's news deals with defense preparedness (vs. health care, education, drugs, crime, etc.), we are more apt to think that *this* is an important issue. In short, *agenda setting* research has supported Walter Lippmann's (1922/1965) early pronouncement that the press acts like "the beam of a searchlight" that focuses our attention on some issues at the expense of others.

But what about fiction? When we tune in the latest crime drama, few of us do so with the expectation that it might influence our judgments about the urgency with which we should fund the "war on drugs," etc. The choice of which issues make it to prime time has more to do with vagaries of popular appeal than with the current severity of the problem. Like news, which also favors the dramatic over the mundane and the unique over the commonplace, fiction may promote perceptions of problem importance that are out of synch with fluctuations in problem severity.

How might narratives influence judgments of problem causes and solutions? One suggestion (Iyengar, 1991) is that accounts that focus on individual actors lead readers and viewers to attribute responsibility for social problems to individuals (crime is caused by criminal tendencies) rather than to broader social conditions (crime is caused by economic disparity). On this view, narrative treatments of problems also bias readers toward solutions that target individuals (lock up the criminals) rather than conditions (combat poverty).

Even where there is a propensity to frame social problems in terms of individualistic causes, it is unlikely that this focus is an intrinsic characteristic of narrative form. Stowe's (1852/1994) aim, for instance, was to demonstrate that cruelty to slaves was an inevitable consequence of a legalized institutional practice, not an intrinsic tendency of individual slave owners. Other novelists, from Dickens to Zola to Dreiser, have sought to illuminate the societal roots of social problems by drawing readers into the experience of story-world individuals and viewing out, as it were, at the problems they face. These examples suggest that in following the vicissitudes of individual actors, stories may be particularly well equipped to channel attention toward the situational determinants of individual action. In designing a study to examine this issue, my intuition was that narratives could promote either situational or dispositional attributions of responsibility depending on the causal focus present in the narrative case.

In the "anecdotal accounts" study (Strange & Leung, 1999), I worked with Cynthia Leung to examine the influence of narratives on readers' judgments of problem urgency and responsibility. Are readers' judgments of problem urgency influenced by reading fictional as well as news narratives (agenda setting)? Do the circumstances implied to cause a problem in a particular narrative case influence readers' judgments of the problem's causes and cures in society at large (causal generalization)? If so, is this influence moderated by the mode of discourse (news vs. fiction)? Finally, can we identify processes of reader engagement that promote the generalization from a singular narrative case?

Participants (students at Columbia University) read one of two versions of a 900-word story, "Downward Bound." Both versions focus on the plight of a single student, Michael, who decides to drop out of high school. In the *situational* version, focus is placed on an underfunded urban school as the cause of Michael's decision to quit. In the *dispositional* version, focus is placed on Michael, who suffers from teen indecision and angst. Readers were alternately told that the story was excerpted from a feature news article or from a fictional short story. A control group read an unrelated story.

Agenda Setting. To assess judgments of problem urgency, participants ranked the order in which they believed policy makers should address six issues, including K–12 education, and health care, which topped the national agenda at the time of the study. Analyses showed that the perceived urgency of dealing with education rose for the groups who read about a failing student, whereas the urgency of dealing with healthcare declined. This occurred whether the story was read as news or as fiction. These results showed that fiction, like news, can influence judgments of the relative urgency with which social problems should be addressed.

Causal Generalization. Causal generalization was assessed with two free-response items in which participants listed the most common causes of high school failure and dropout and prescribed actions they believed would most effectively address the problem. Those who read the situational account were about as twice as likely as those who read the dispositional account to generate causes and solutions implicating resource deficiencies in the school and its surrounding community. For instance, they were more apt to say that school failure is caused by large classes and poorly trained teachers and that the problem could be solved by reducing class size, increasing funding, and so forth. These differences did not depend on whether the account was read as news or fiction.

These data strongly supported the expectation that readers generalize from the causes of a problem instantiated in a specific case to their judgments of the problem's causes and cures in society at large. Both fictional and nonfictional narratives can focus attention on the situational determinants of social problems.

Narrative Engagement. Whereas we might isolate aspects of the story or of the reader for practical and heuristic purposes, it is clear that the qualities of narrative experience that result in lasting impact are to be found in a dynamic interaction between the two. To describe the cognitive-emotional states that readers experience when they successfully shut out their immediate environment and enter into the world of a story, researchers have proposed the related constructs of entrancement (Nell, 1988) and transportation (Gerrig, 1993; Green & Brock, 2000). In the present study, we were interested in how components of "losing oneself" in a story might moderate the extent to which readers generalized from case to category. We hypothesized that those who became more engaged in a story would be more likely to generalize the causes of Michael's failure to the causes of school failure in the United States.

To measure engagement, we used a series of 7-point Likert-scale items that assessed story-focused attention (e.g., "While reading, I was completely immersed in the text"), story-cued elaborations ("How much were you thinking about the problems of education in the United States?"), remindings (e.g., "While reading the text, how much were you thinking about someone you've known?"), and imagery ("Rate the strength of visual imagery you experienced").

The results confirmed our expectations. Readers of the situational version who reported higher levels of engagement were more apt to attribute responsibility for school failure to resource-related causes and solutions. Readers who experienced higher levels of engagement in the dispositional group were less likely to attribute responsibility to resource-related causes and solutions.

As can be seen in the items with which we measured engagement, we conceptualized this process somewhat differently than other researchers. Particularly, when we become "lost in a book" (Nell, 1988), we may shut out our immediate surroundings, but we do not close out our previous lives. In fact, a story's success in drawing us in might be gauged by the extent to which it resonates with our prior experience. Thus, we were particularly interested in the remindings experienced during reading. Researchers have identified remindings as a pillar of narrative understanding (Schank & Abelson, 1995) and enjoyment (Larsen & Seilman, 1988), and as a condition of empathy and affect in the story-world (Zillmann, 1991).

In the current study, we hypothesized that higher levels of remindings during reading would facilitate generalization. Our *episodic recruitment* processing model for this facilitation effect was built on the assumption that our judgments of causal responsibility are rarely stored in memory as rigid, predetermined propositions (e.g., "School failure is caused by overcrowding"). They are based, rather, on incidents that come to mind during judgment. When judging the causes of school failure, for instance, our conclusions will be influenced by whether images of run-down schools or, alternatively, of undisciplined students, rush first to mind. By resonating with past experience, a story recruits memories that spring to the fore during judgment. Our second assumption, confirmed in a companion study, was that stories tend to recruit remindings of people, places, and events that are similar to those present in the story.

Analyses of the reminding data confirmed our expectations in a pattern that paralleled our findings on the overall engagement index. Reminding effects were independent of attention, recall, imagery, liking and sympathy for the main character, and of judgments of how representative the student, teachers, and school were of their counterparts in the United States.

In summary, this study showed that our encounters with invented characters in imagined situations can influence our decisions about real-world policy concerns. They can influence what we think causes these problems, how we think such problems should be solved, and which of the myriad problems we face warrant our attention. The reminding data show how story-world particulars resonate with the idiosyncratic memories of diverse individuals to augment a story's impact.

THE PERILS AND POWER OF THE PARTICULAR

A particular peril of stories is that they are equally good at communicating prototypical and atypical cases, and rarely announce how representative they are. As shown previously, the tendency to generalize may be independent of judgments of the typicality of a case. Even when typicality information is provided, people often ignore it (Hamill, Wilson, & Nisbett, 1980). As seen in the title of Hyman's (1998) article, *Lies, Damned Lies, and Narrative*, the suspicion that particular cases prey on the human bias to overgeneralize sometimes leads to a blanket condemnation of narrative cases as a source of human judgment. In closing this section, I first consider when narrative cases may be particularly adaptive and then offer some further speculations on how they achieve their potency.

In many instances narrative accounts can be seen as redressing human biases rather than catering to them. First, particular cases respond to a human tendency to ignore abstract information. Stowe put it this way in *A Key to UTC* (1853/1998):

> The atrocious and sacrilegious system of breeding human beings for sale ... fails to produce the impression on the mind that it ought to produce, because it is lost in generalities. It is like the account of a great battle, in which we learn, in round numbers, that ten thousand were killed and wounded, and throw the paper by without a thought. (pp. 151–152)

Second, whether the depicted person or event is actual or fictional, cases are often selected *because* they represent a type. Third, typicality is not always pertinent to the decisions at hand. In *UTC*, for example, Stowe's argument did not rest on whether few or most slave families were torn apart, or whether some or all slaveholders were as savage as Simon Legree. What mattered was that the institution of slavery engendered such barbarism, a lesson her story conveyed with visceral impact. Finally, atypicality is often a virtue, not a vice. Atypical cases are often used in teleological fashion, to exemplify what can be aspired to, or avoided, rather than to reflect what tends to be. Fictional narratives hold particular advantages in this respect. As Wilde (1889/1920) noted, fiction provides the means to construct, consider, and potentially emulate possible future worlds, ones that are not only atypical, but hitherto nonexistent.

How else might narratives achieve their potency? First, humans are particularly proficient at selectively ignoring information that either conflicts with or fails to advance personal interests. Stories may partially circumvent defense mechanisms exercised through selective exposure and attention. Well-crafted stories hold an intrinsic appeal that draws readers' interest and attention to topics they would tend to avoid in other genres. For instance, readers of David Guterson's *Snow Falling on Cedars* (1995) are more likely to be attracted to this novel as a romantic whodunit than as a lesson about the selective perception and treatment of Japanese-Americans during WWII. Stories may thwart social as well psychological defense mechanisms. In the guise of entertainment, they allow readers and viewers to openly consider viewpoints and themes that are proscribed in the social and public spheres they frequent.

Second, and relatedly, stories offer a means through which we can partially escape the conceptual constraints imposed by entrenched ways of seeing. The central gesture of narrative fiction may ve viewed as a process of *subjective recentering* (Ryan 1991, cf. Rapaport, 1986, Zubin & Hewitt, 1995). On this view, the author of a fictional story constructs an imaginary world from within which she speaks through the multiple personas she creates. The act of relocation establishes a new deictic center, a new here and now, that becomes temporarily ensconced as the actual world of cooperative readers. In reference to Walter Scott's novel, *Ivanhoe* (1819/1977), William James (1889/1981) put it this way: "Whilst absorbed in the novel, we turn our backs on all other worlds, and, for the time, the Ivanhoe-world remains our absolute reality" (p. 922). The difference between the outside view we take on a story when we describe it and the inside view we take when centered within it is akin to the difference between describing a dream and experiencing it. From the outside view, we maintain a critical distance from which the dream world can be constantly contrasted with the real one (e.g., "In the dream, dad appears as a lion"). From the inside view, the frame that sets off the dream from reality disappears, and even improbable events are unquestioningly accepted as true (i.e., Dad *is* a lion). In temporarily acting *as if* an alternative world is the actual one, we suspend assumptions and evaluative criteria that are operative when our frame of reference is grounded in the actual world.

Of course, fiction differs from dreams in that we can pop out of fictional worlds at will. Fiction also differs from dreams in that the situation models we construct tend to be based on the distinction and integration of several, often-divergent perspectives of multiple characters. Once we are in the fictional world, our viewpoint may be further recentered on the perspectives of the characters within it. Through the use of various stylistic devices (Chatman, 1978), readers are invited to adopt particular visual perspectives (Bower, 1978; Strange, Black, & Ottaviani, 1990) and to privilege particular conceptual (Pritchert & Anderson, 1977), and affective perspectives (Sanders & Redeker, 1996) over others. As put by Dennis Diderot (1762/1966) in reference to a fictional character, "we put ourselves in his place or by his side, we passionately support or oppose him, we identify with his role if he is virtuous and we draw indignantly away if he is unjust and vicious" (p. 30).

In fictional worlds, authors decide who to characterize as virtuous or vicious, and which perspectives they would like us adopt or reject. Wolfgang Petersen's film *Das Boot* (1981) can be seen as an invitation to view WWII from the perspective of a German submarine captain, something Americans are unlikely to have previously even contemplated. Similarly, the Costa-Gavras film *Missing* (1982) invites viewers to track the perspective of a conservative businessman as his conception of U.S. policy in Central America changes over the course of the film. *Snow Falling on Cedars* and *UTC* also invite the adoption of conceptual and emotive perspectives that many readers are unlikely to have previously considered.

In summary, through a process of subjective recentering, fiction invites readers to adopt perspectives and commitments they would not entertain in their actual worlds. Issues to be addressed within this framework include the conditions under which readers accept or reject these invitations, the extent to which perspectives adopted in narrative experience are internalized and recruited as guides to future action (for provocative examples, see Caughey 1984), and the degree to which story-world commitments carry over to real-world convictions. When is it the case, as Diderot (1762/1966) surmised, that "the sacrifice one makes of oneself in the imagination is a predilection to do the same in reality" (p. 31)?

Finally, the reminding data (Strange & Leung, 1999) suggested allied processes through which stories may influence judgments. We also found the influence of remindings on responsibility judgments to be independent of readers' generic beliefs about teachers, schools, and failing students, and of the priming of those beliefs by the respective versions. In other words, stories recruited memories that were sometimes at odds with readers' stereotypes (cf. Smith, 1992). As argued by Schank & Abelson (1995), we understand new situations by recognizing in them ones we have experienced before, and we understand others by seeing in them something of ourselves, or of others we have known. In conclusion, I suggest that the impact of particular cases lies, in part, in their ability to recruit prior memories that are at odds with what we, ourselves, "believe." These memories, in turn, enable us to empathize with story-world characters (Zillmann, 1991) and to adopt perspectives that, though different from our own, find resonance in aspects of our prior experience.

VARIETIES OF FICTIONAL IMPACT

Stories can both reconstruct life experiences and invent new experiential forms. Given their thematic breadth and stylistic diversity, no single model can possibly capture either the processes through which stories spill over into life, or the kinds of judgment and behavior they influence. The models advanced above treated misconceptions communicated through direct assertions in fiction, the power of particular instances to influence judgments about social issues, and the potential for perspectives adopted while reading to be activated in subsequent reasoning. Other processes that have received scholarly attention include priming (Murphy, 1998), modeling (Bandura, 1986), social comparison (Mares & Cantor, 1992), and availability effects (Shrum & O'Guinn, 1993). Fictional stories may influence our perceptions of social groups, our proclivity toward violent or prosocial behavior, and our perceptions of the frequencies of real world events (Bryant & Zillmann, 1994). Important directions for future research include the manner in which fictional portrayals influence perceptions of group norms, and how popular stories anchor and structure group identity.

In conclusion, our story-world encounters vastly extend the life space that constitutes our everyday worlds. Through the vehicle of fiction, we are invited to reconceptualize present, past, and future, and to consider alternatives to our entrenched points of view. The inventory of the narrative world both expands our own mental inventories and, by resonating with items already in stock, brings some to the fore and allows others to recede. In this process of dynamic interaction between readers and the extended environment, new visions, decisions, and commitments emerge.

As individuals and as members of groups that favor one public sphere over another, we have the freedom to choose which parts of the symbolic environment we will visit. Once there, we may opt to experience this environment from the vantage of the different characters who live there (Strange, 1996), or to reject these perspectives entirely. Similarly, we may opt to assign some of its inventory to the shelf of imagination, and allow others entry to our models of practical reality (James,1889/1981). Through these choices we exercise agentic control over the environmental inputs to our decisions and beliefs. At the same time, however, the symbolic environment has dynamics of its own, which constrain the choices before us. Although narrative experience may, in the end, involve a relationship between an author and a reader, cultural norms and institutional structures intercede to select the kinds of content and viewpoints that will be offered or withheld and how readers will learn to approach them. The visions that emerge from the interaction between reader and text can thus be seen as a point of inflection in a larger process that brings the two into contact. The task of research is to help inform the decisions we make, in our roles as producers who fashion narrative worlds, and as readers who traverse them.

ENDNOTES

[1] Here and throughout this chapter I use the term readers both in the standard sense and to refer simultaneously to readers, viewers, and listeners.

[2] Gerrig modifies this view in *Experiencing Narrative Worlds* (1993).

[3] As put by Producer Dawn Steel, when fielding criticism of Oliver Stone's film *JFK*: "Filmmakers are artists.... We're making fiction here, we're not making a documentary" (quoted in Weintraub, 1991, p. 12).

[4] Although many, like Hutton (1991, above), are willing to accept such distortions in the name of entertainment or myth making, few would support the equivalent proposition that it is "simply ridiculous to expect" the Count's arithmetic (above) to be true to the facts of math. This disjuncture indicates that societies are willing to sacrifice some, but not other, facts to the often-competing goals of story-telling. The question of which facts are permissibly modified is likely to rest on lay theories about the psychological consequences of considering fictive facts, and the value ascribed to entertainment and art, on the one hand, and accuracy in different domains, on the other (Johnson, 1998).

[5] Those who find this assertion patently implausible might consider what follows: "When Jane Goodall studied Gombe chimpanzees, she locked away her own infant to prevent his being taken and killed by chimps" (Crichton,1993, p. 227).

[6] Context discrimination differs from source discrimination (Mitchell & Johnson, 2000) when a single source includes multiple referential contexts, for instance, when Peter tells us about Susan's dreams, desires, and actions.

[7] This characteristic differentiates this study from other research in which readers have been found to incorporate direct assertions made in fictional discourse into their beliefs (Gerrig, 1993; Green & Brock, 2000; Slater, 1990; Wheeler, Green, & Brock, 1999). Given the referential ambiguity of fictional discourse, it is likely that readers in these studies believed the "fictional" statements, at least in part, because they interpreted them to be sincere authorial assertions that the propositions were true. These studies do tell us that fictional discourse influences beliefs; however, they do not tell us whether or how readers might come to accept assertions that they know to be mere fabrications.

[8] The latter point is hammered in before readers begin the story.

[9] This model is similar to one advanced by Gerrig (1993). Both accounts are independently based on research by George Potts and his colleagues (e.g., Potts, St. John, & Kirson, 1989).

REFERENCES

Adler, M. J., & van Doren, C. (1940/1972). *How to read a book*. New York: Simon & Schuster.
Bailey, G. (1852, April 15). Uncle Tom's Cabin. [Publication notice]. *The National Era, 6*, 62.
Bandura, A. (1986). *Social foundations of thought and action*. Englewood Cliffs, NJ: Prentice-Hall.
Bower, G. H. (1978). Experiments on story comprehension and recall. *Discourse Processes, 1*, 211–231.
Bruner, J. (1991). The narrative construction of reality. *Critical Inquiry, 18*, 1–21.
Bryant, J., & Zillmann, D. (Eds.). (1994). *Media effects: Advances in theory and research*. Hillsdale, NJ: Lawrence Erlbaum Associates.
Cantril, H. (1940/1986). *The invasion from Mars: A study in the psychology of panic*. Princeton, NJ: Princeton University Press.
Caughey, J. L. (1984). *Imaginary social worlds*. Lincoln, NE: University of Nebraska Press.
Chatman, S. (1978). *Story and discourse: Narrative structure in fiction and film*. Ithaca, NY: Cornell University Press.
Coover, R. (1977). *The public burning*. New York: Viking Press.
Costa-Gavras, C. (Director). *Missing*. [Film].
Crichton, M. (1993). *Congo*. New York: Ballantine.
Current, R. N. (1986). Fiction as history: A review essay. *The Journal of Southern History, LII*, 77–90.
Diderot, D. (1762). Eloge de Richardson. In P. Verniere (Ed.), *Oeuvres esthetiques* (pp. 29–48). Paris: Garnier.
Dinsmore, J. (1991). *Partitioned representations*. Dordrecht, Netherlands: Kluwer.
Gerrig, R .J. (1988). Text comprehension. In R. J. Sternberg and E. E. Smith (Eds.), *The psychology of human thought*, pp. 242–266. Cambridge, MA: Cambridge University Press.
Gerrig, R. J. (1993). *Experiencing narrative worlds*. New Haven, CT: Yale University Press.
Gibson, R., & Zillmann, D. (1994). Exaggerated versus representative exemplification in news reports: Perception of issues and personal consequences. *Communication Research, 21*, 603–624.
Gilbert, D. T. (1991). How mental systems believe. *American Psychologist, 46*(2), 107–119.
Green, M. C., & Brock, T. C. (2000). The role of transportation in the persuasiveness of public narratives. *Journal of Personality and Social Psychology, 79*, 701–721.
Guterson, D. (1995) *Snow falling on cedars*. New York: Vintage Books.
Hamill, R., Wilson, T. D., & Nisbett, R. E. (1980). Insensitivity to sample bias: Generalizing from atypical cases. *Journal of Personality and Social Psychology, 39*, 578–589.
Holmes, G. F. (1852/1994). Review of Uncle Tom's Cabin. In E. Amons (Ed.), *Uncle Tom's Cabin: A Norton critical edition*, 467–477. New York: Norton.
Hutton, P. A. (1991). Correct in every detail: General Custer in Hollywood. *Montana: The magazine of western history, 41*(1), 28–57.
Hyman, D. A. (1998). Lies, Damned Lies and Narrative. *Indiana Law Journal, 73* (3). Available: http://www.law.indiana.edu/ilj/v73/no3/hyman.html
Iyengar, S., & Kinder, D. (1987). *News that matters*. Chicago, IL: University of Chicago Press.
Iyengar, S. (1991). *Is anyone responsible? How television frames political issues*. Chicago, IL: University of Chicago Press.
James, W. (1889/1981). *The principles of psychology*. Cambridge, MA: Harvard University Press.

Johnson, M. K. (1998). Individual and cultural reality monitoring. In *Annals of the American Academy of Political and Social Sciences, 560*, 179–193.
Josephy, Jr., A. (1995). They died with their boots on. In T. Mico, J. Miller-Monzon, & D. Rubel (Eds.), *Past imperfect: History according to the movies* (pp. 146–49). New York: Henry Holt and Company.
Larsen, S., & Seilman, U. (1988). Personal remindings while reading literature. *Text, 8*, 411–429.
Leslie, A. M. (1987). Pretense and representation: The origins of "Theory of mind." *Psychological Review, 94*, 412–426.
Levine, R. S. (1994). UncleTom's Cabin in Frederick Douglas' paper: An analysis of reception. In E. Amons (Ed.), *Uncle Tom's Cabin: A Norton critical edition*, pp. 523–42. New York: Norton.
Lippmann, W. (1922/1965). *Public opinion*. New York: Macmillan.
Mares, M-L., & Cantor, J. (1992). Elderly viewers' responses to televised portrayals of old age: Empathy and mood management versus social comparison. *Communication Research, 19*, 459–478.
Michener, J. (1965). *The source*. New York: Random House.
Mitchell, K. J., & Johnson, M. K. (2000). Source monitoring: Attributing mental experiences. In E. Tulving, & F. I. M. Craik (Eds.), *Oxford handbook of memory*, pp. 179–195. New York: Oxford University Press.
Murphy, S. T. (1998). The impact of factual versus fictional media portrayals on cultural stereotypes. In *Annals of the American Academy of Political and Social Sciences, 560*, 165–178.
Nell, V. (1988). *Lost in a book: The psychology of reading for pleasure*. New Haven, CT: Yale University Press.
Petersen, W. (Director and Scriptwriter). (1981). *Das boot*. [Film].
Pollack, A. (1995, March 4). Japanese refight the war, and win, in pulp fiction. *New York Times*, pp. 1,5.
Potts, G. R., St. John, M. F., & Kirson, D. (1989). Incorporating new information into existing world knowledge. *Cognitive Psychology, 21*, 303–333.
Pritchert, J. W., & Anderson, R. C. (1977). Taking different perspectives on a story. *Journal of Educational Psychology, 69*, 309–315.
Rapaport, W. J. (1986). Logical foundations for belief representation. *Cognitive Science, 10*, 371–422.
Rapaport, W. J., & Shapiro, S. C. (1995). Cognition and fiction. In J. F. Duchan, G. A. Bruder, & L. E. Hewitt (Eds.), *Deixis in narrative: A cognitive science perspective* (pp. 107–128). Hillsdale, NJ: Lawrence Erlbaum Associates.
Ryan, M-L. (1991). *Possible worlds, artificial intelligence, and narrative theory*. Bloomington, IN: Indiana University Press.
Sanders, J., & Redecker, G. (1996). Perspective and focalization in nonfiction narrative texts. In E. Sweetser & G. Fauconnier (Eds), *Spaces, grammar and discourse* (pp. 290–317). Chicago, IL: University of Chicago Press.
Sanders, J., & Redeker, G., (1993). Linguistic perspective in short news articles. *Poetics, 22*, 69–87.
Schank, R. C., & Abelson, R. P. (1995). Knowledge and memory: The real story. In R. S. Wyer (Ed.), *Advances in Social Cognition, Volume VIII* (pp. 1–86). Hillsdale, NJ: Lawrence Erlbaum Associates.
Schmidt, S. (1976). Toward a pragmatic interpretation of 'fictionality.' In T. van Dijk (Ed.), *Pragmatics of language and literature* (pp. 161–178). New York: North-Holland Publishing.
Scott, Sir W. (1819/1977). *Ivanhoe*. New York: Modern Library.
Shrum, L. J., & O'Guinn, T. C. (1993). Processes and effects in the construction of social reality. *Communication Research, 20*, 436–471.
Silver, I. (1978). Libel, the "higher truths" of art, and the first amendment. *University of Pennsylvania Law Review, 126*, 1065–1098.
Slater, M. (1990). Processing social information in messages. *Communication Research, 17*, 327–343.

Smith, E. R. (1992). The role of exemplars in social judgment. In L. L. Martin & A. Tesser (Eds.), *The construction of social judgments* (pp. 107–132). Hillsdale, NJ: Lawrence Erlbaum Associates.

Stowe, H. B. (1852/1994). *Uncle Tom's Cabin*. New York: Norton.

Stowe, H. B. (1853/1998). *A key to Uncle Tom's Cabin: Presenting the original facts and documents upon which the story is founded, together with corroborative statements verifying the truth of the work*. Bedford, MA: Applewood Books.

Strange, J. J. (1993). The facts of fiction: The accommodation of real-world beliefs to fabricated accounts. (Doctoral dissertation, Columbia University, 1993). *Dissertation Abstracts International, 54*(2-A), 358.

Strange, J. J. (1996). Leben in Bildschirmwelten — Formen der narrativen Involviertheit [Varieties of narrative engagement]. In P. Vorderer (Ed.), *Fernsehen als 'Beziehungskiste': Parasoziale Beziehungen und Interaktionen mit TV–Personen* (pp. 173–180). Wiesbaden, Germany: Westdeutscher Verlag.

Strange, J. J., Black, J. B., & Ottaviani, B. (1990, April). *Readers as vicarious actors: Imagined point of view and causal inference in narrative understanding*. Paper presented at the meeting of the American Educational Research Association, Boston, MA.

Strange, J. J., & Leung, C. C. (1999). How anecdotal accounts in news and in fiction can influence judgments of a social problem's urgency, causes, and cures. *Personality and Social Psychology Bulletin, 25*, 436–449.

Thagard, P. (1989). Explanatory coherence. *Behavioral and Brain Sciences, 12*, 435–502.

Tolstoy, L. (1869/1967). *War and Peace*. Harmondsworth, UK: Penguin Books.

Tversky, A., & Kahneman, D. (1982). Judgment under uncertainty: Heuristics and biases. In D. Kahneman, P. Slovic, & A. Tversky (Eds.), *Judgment under uncertainty: Heuristics and biases* (pp. 3–20). New York: Cambridge University Press.

Warner, C.D. (1896, September). The story of Uncle Tom's Cabin. *Atlantic Monthly, 78* (Issue number 467), 311–322.

Wason, P. C., & & Johnson-Laird, P. N. (1972). *Psychology of reasoning: Structure and content*. Cambridge, MA: Harvard University Press.

Weintraub, B. (1991, December 24). Hollywood wonders if Warner Brothers let *JFK* go too far. *New York Times*, Section C, pp. 9, 12.

Wheeler, S. C., Green, M. C., & Brock, T. C. (1999). Fictional narratives change beliefs: Replications of Prentice, Gerrig, & Bailis (1997) with mixed corroboration. *Psychonomic Bulletin and Review, 6*, 136–141.

Wilde, O. The decay of lying (1889/1920). In O. Wilde (Ed.), *Intentions* (pp. 3–54). New York: Boni and Liveright Publishers.

Zillmann, D. (1991). Empathy: Affect from bearing witness to the emotions of others. In J. Bryant & D. Zillmann (Eds.), *Responding to the screen: Reception and reaction processes* (pp. 135–167). Hillsdale, NJ: Lawrence Erlbaum Associates.

Zubin, D., & Hewitt, L. E. (1995). The deictic center: A theory of deixis in narrative. In J. F. Duchan, G. A. Bruder, & L. E. Hewitt (Eds.), *Deixis in narrative: A cognitive science perspective* (pp. 129–155). Hillsdale, NJ: Lawrence Erlbaum Associates.

12

The Pervasive Role of Stories in Knowledge and Action

Roger C. Schank
Tamara R. Berman
Northwestern University

People love to tell and hear stories. We devour movies, books, and television shows filled with people telling us their stories. We have endless conversations with friends as we work through the iterative process of building our knowledge base of stories. In this chapter we propose that most of the knowledge we use in our day-to-day lives is stored in our memory structures as stories. Some of the stories are our own past experiences that we mentally structure as stories, relay to ourselves and others, and restore in our memories in the new story format. Others are stories that we hear from outside sources. Either way, we use stories to help us make sense of events in the world, and to help us achieve our goals (Schank & Abelson, 1995).

We discuss the "what, how, why, and when" of stories. Specifically, we examine what a story is, how we learn from stories, why stories have stronger impact than abstract principles (Schank, 1990; Schank & Abelson, 1995), and when is the optimal time to tell or hear a story. In the process, we will reveal how most of the knowledge we use in our day-to-day communication and reasoning is comprised of stories.

We cite relevant empirical research whenever possible, as well as other literature in which some ideas were initially published. However, the tenor of our discussion is closer to that of a cognitive science approach, stemming from a computational model of memory (Hammond, 1989; Kolodner & Jona, 1991; Riesbeck & Schank, 1989; Schank, 1982; Schank & Abelson, 1977), rather than an empirically oriented, cognitive psychology approach. Therefore, in some cases we make strong claims that may be unsupported, as of yet, by empirical research. In such cases, readers should perceive the claims as ideas, open for future experimentation.

Background

The core of the theory of story-based memory and the backbone of the discussion to follow is anchored in the notion that the experiences we have in life and those we hear from others as stories (real or fictitious) each constitutes a "case" of encountering that particular experience (Schank & Abelson, 1995). Our view is that cases are stories of sorts, in that stories are essentially well-constructed cases, each with a point. When we have an experience, such as going to a movie, we store it as one case of a movie-going experience in our memories. Similarly, if someone tells us a story about his relationship with his father, we can store this story as one case of a father–son relationship. Eventually, as we hear stories and construct stories from our experiences for many years, our minds become repositories for thousands of stories. Fortunately, we are able to organize our story repositories by cleverly and complexly labeling and filing our memories for efficient future retrieval. This process is known as *indexing* (Schank, 1982).

Our theory of how we use stories once we have stored them in our memories is closely aligned with and supported by the theory of "case-based reasoning," or CBR (Hammond, 1989; Kolodner & Jona, 1991; Riesbeck & Schank, 1989; Schank & Abelson, 1977). In our discussion of creating, storing, and retrieving stories we draw from the CBR paradigm, and we allude to some of the key concepts from that theory throughout this chapter. Primarily, however, for the purposes of this book, we discuss cases as they take the form of stories.

What Do We Mean By "Stories?"

A story is a structured, coherent retelling of an experience or a fictional account of an experience. A satisfying story will include the following elements: themes, goals, plans, expectations, expectation failures (or obstacles), and perhaps, explanations or solutions. We discuss each of these story elements later in the chapter. In some sense, all stories can be considered to be didactic in nature, in that they are intended to teach, or convey something to the listener (who is sometimes ourselves). This is true even when our stories are intended to entertain. To understand this perspective, we have to ask why we are telling the story. We can assume we are motivated to do so to achieve a goal of some sort. If we tell the story for entertainment purposes, we are also telling our listeners something about ourselves as persons and our current purposes.

Every story has at least one point and has at least one reason for being told. The point and the reason suggest what is intended to be taught. Sometimes the point is not direct, like a moral of a story, but is instead indirect, as in when we mean to convey to our listener that we are funny, worldly, or interested in similar topics. We may simply mean to convey that we enjoy what we are conversing about with our listener, so we tell stories to continue the conversation. Whether or not the listeners understand or receive the lesson we mean to teach, the utterance is meant to inform. So we consider stories to be didactic when we choose to relay them.

Types of Stories

We can identify five types of cases that we have stored in our memories as stories: official, invented, firsthand experiential, secondhand, and culturally common (Schank, 1990). We hear official stories from organized groups who have general messages to relay. Often they will relay these stories in simplified forms to make the message widely understood. For instance, Nancy Reagan's "Just Say No" campaign references a story most of us can imagine, but may not address all of the real, complex issues that could be involved in deciding whether to use drugs or cigarettes. Official stories are those that people in authority instruct us to tell. We can even tell our own such stories. For example, President Clinton claimed to the American public, "I did not have sexual relations with that woman ... Monica Lewinsky." This official story hides details to create a more favorable image of the president during a potentially harmful scandal. Schank (1990) explained:

> Official stories are ones that have been carefully constructed by one or more people to tell a version of events that is sanitized and presumed to be less likely to get anyone in trouble. Alternatively, official stories are often the position of a group that has a message to sell and treats that message independently of the facts. (p. 32)

These stories are not necessarily negative. Religious groups have many positive official stories, such as ones illustrating how "God makes everything happen for a purpose." This may or may not be true, but it is helpful to believe, especially in difficult times.

Invented stories are those we "make up" from scratch. The interesting thing about invented stories is that they contain elements of stories we know well from our own past experiences or stories we have heard before. In *Scripts, Plans, Goals, and Understanding* (Schank & Abelson, 1977), and in *Tell Me a Story* (Schank, 1990), Schank recalled two stories that his daughter told at early ages. Roger asked his daughter to tell him a story, and at approximately 3 years of age she responded by recalling the events of the day in sequence. At age 4, Roger's daughter responded to the same question with a more imaginative story, in that the events she described in the story did not happen in real life exactly as she described them. However, the separate events did happen at various times and she remembered them. She reconstructed the order of events to string together a new story. Similarly, when adults construct stories, we borrow from what we know to create new forms of existing concepts.

Firsthand stories are retellings of experiences we personally had. However, they do involve some imagination, and they are not told the same way each time we tell them. We shape our experiences into stories that will satisfy our listeners. Listeners are likely to have different reasons for being interested in one of our stories. We make our stories interesting by highlighting certain facts more than others, embellishing some elements, and leaving out some information altogether. The ways in which we play with our stories may change many times. However, each time we tell the story, that telling becomes our most recent memory of the event. The more times we tell it a particular way the more it becomes our memory of the event.

Therefore, if we repeatedly leave out certain elements of the actual experience in our telling of a story, we are likely to forget those elements and we will not be able to retrieve them very easily, if at all, in the future. Similarly, if we embellish some element in a believable way, and it goes over well with our listeners, we may repeat that embellishment enough that we forget it did not actually happen that way. In other words, our story formation becomes our memory formation as well. We remember stories by telling them, and when we tell stories, we shape what we remember.

Secondhand stories are the stories of others that we remember and retell. The retelling of others' stories, which we often do, is a less imaginative and less complex process than creating coherent stories out of our own experiences. When we retell others' stories, we simply try to recall the details that we heard before, filling in elements that we cannot exactly remember with something that will work to keep the story coherent. We are not always aware that we are fabricating parts of the story. We may add a detail that seems logical, and therefore we may assume that it happened that way in the actual story. Because we did not have these experiences ourselves, our indexes for such stories will be less rich, more precise, and will often have one specific point associated with them.

Culturally common stories are highly generalized so that they can be applied in a variety of contexts, often with interchangeable details. No one in particular told them to us or constructed them in the first place, we just know them because they are pervasive in our particular environment. Not everyone will understand a culturally common story, because not everyone lives in the same cultures. We can live in the same neighborhood or city, but be parts of (or be excluded from) numerous subcultures. Our subcultures are defined by our work, our age, our religious background, and so on. Many Jewish people will use Yiddish phrases to characterize people or situations, but only those who are Jewish or who are around them enough to be a part of the culture will understand the references. Teenagers, through their language, music, films, and so on, have a culture of their own as well.

"Culturally common stories are usually referred to rather than told" (Schank, 1990, p. 38). The referent is a familiar scene, which is the culturally common story. For example, in *Tell Me a Story*, Roger recalled a joke from the Woody Allen movie, *Love and Death*:

> There are worse things in life than death—if you have ever spent an evening with an insurance salesman, you know what I mean.

We have a culturally common understanding of what it would be like to spend an evening with an insurance salesman. We imagine, if we have not had the experience ourselves, that it would be very long, very boring, and the sales technique would be overly pushy. Because many people share essentially the same mental representation[1] of the insurance salesman story, it can be referred to without explanation and many of us will understand the point.

What Do We Do With Stories?

There are three general categories of things we do with stories. First, we tell stories, both to ourselves and to other people. We tell people stories for three potential purposes. First, we tell stories to convey something that satisfies our own goals, including: achieving catharsis, getting attention, winning approval, seeking advice, and describing ourselves (Schank, 1990, p. 41). We may also tell stories to have an effect on our listener(s), including: "... illustrat(ing) a point, ... mak(ing) the listener feel some way or another, ... tell(ing) a story that transports the listener, ... transfer(ing) some piece of information in our head into the head of the listener, (and) ... summariz(ing) significant events" (Schank, 1990, p. 48). Finally, we tell stories to satisfy the goals of the overall conversation, such as opening a topic, changing a topic, continuing a topic, or being responsive (Schank, 1990, p. 51).

The second thing we do with stories is listen to the stories of others. When we do so, we seek to *match* what is being told to us to ideas we have already stored in our memories. We are essentially attempting to confirm the beliefs we constructed earlier. If we have difficulty doing so, we may learn something new, or we may revise a belief.

The third thing we do involving stories is turn our own experiences into stories and then file them into our memories. We also file the stories of others into our memories. In this way, we continuously construct and reconstruct our story repository for future uses, including more storytelling and story understanding. A primary purpose of constructing and communicating stories is to help us make sense of new situations and derive sensible solutions to novel problems. Without our cases and stories, we could not perceive and act in the world as efficiently as we do.

Using Stories to Assist Understanding

Everything we experience or listen to we understand through what we have understood before, by constantly referring to our vast knowledge base of cases and stories. Our ability to do so involves storing and retrieving indexes. Each time we have an experience we label it in various ways, with many indexes, so that it can be sorted and grouped with other similar memories. The indexes correlate to a variety of the features contained within the experience. Indexes may be "surface features," such as tastes and smells, people, activities, and so forth, as well as "thematic features," (Gentner & Landers, 1985; Gentner & Stevens, 1983; Gick & Holyoak, 1980; Schank, 1982) such as goals, plans, types of surprises (the surprises are also known as *expectation failures*; Schank, 1982), and so on. Our memories are complex groupings of similar features that serve as story indexes. As we receive new information we seek similarities to indexes we have already stored in memory. The indexes serve as triggers for remindings (Schank, 1982). Remindings are the recollection of past events or stories, when such memories are evoked. When an index is triggered, we may be reminded of a story or scene from our past.

We group together similar experiences to make generalizations of our conceptions. So, for instance, our first movie-going experience merges together with dozens of other similar experiences. Eventually, our concept of going to a movie becomes an amalgam of many prior memories. Schank and Abelson, in their book, *Scripts, Plans, Goals, and Understanding* (1977), called these generalized conceptions *scripts*, and Schank reconceived them in his 1982 book, *Dynamic Memory*, as more personally unique *scenes*. Scripts and scenes are, essentially, representations. So, after many movie-going experiences, we construct a general representation of movie-going activities, a script or scene.

There are times, however, when we confront an element of a case for which we can find no index in our memories. When we experience or hear of such cases, those in which something strange or special occurs (in other words, something anomalous from our generalized representation of a particular scene), we create a special index according to the anomalous feature. We will not be able to create a generalized conception of such anomalies until we have more cases that match the oddity. For this reason, we hold our memories of the parts of cases that were particularly surprising separate from our clustered memories until we encounter more similar anomalies. As we compile additional examples, we may begin to see patterns that suggest satisfactory explanations, at which point we may create a new generalization (Schank & Abelson, 1995). The anomalous story features to which we are referring constitute the *expectation failures* mentioned previously.

The purpose of creating these representations, or scripts and scenes, out of the many cases we encounter, is to lessen the burden of understanding new events. Scripts help us to use our minds efficiently (Schank & Abelson, 1977). For example, scripts provide that "You don't have to figure out every time you enter a restaurant how to convince someone to feed you. All you really have to know is the restaurant script and your part in that script" (Schank & Abelson, 1995, p. 5).

We use scripts, scenes, and other generalizations (such as personality types) to enable us to make plans, predictions, and have expectations (Hammond, 1989; Kolodner & Jona, 1991; Riesbeck & Schank, 1989; Schank & Abelson, 1977), to make judgments (Ross, 1977; Lalljee, Lamb & Abelson, 1992), to make sense of novel cases and to solve new problems (Gick & Holyoak, 1980; Kolodner & Jona, 1991; Ross, 1989). We do this by comparing each new case with other cases and generalized concepts we are reminded of (that we previously stored). We attempt to prove to ourselves that the new case is like ones we have already understood; we make analogies between cases (Gentner, 1983; Gick & Holyoak, 1980; Ortony, 1979). We may be reminded of prior experiences due to similarities in either surface or structural features (Gentner & Landers, 1985; Rattermann & Gentner, 1987; Seifert, McKoon, Abelson, & Ratcliff, 1986).

Whether stories are firsthand or relayed to us in another form, it becomes important to turn them into the more formal story-form to help us remember particular events and to communicate effectively with others. For communication, memory, and learning purposes, stories are likely to be richer, more compelling, and more memorable (Schank & Abelson, 1995, p. 7) than the abstracted points we ultimately intend to convey or learn when we converse with others. We contend that this is because they have more indexes than abstract points. The more indexes, the more likely we will be reminded of something through which we will understand the new example (Schank & Abelson, 1995). This is why we contend that stories have greater impact than abstract principles.

As we experience life, we make mistakes, we experience failures of our expectations, make adjustments to our mental representations of relevant tasks, and these processes are central to how we learn new information (Schank & Abelson, 1977). These experiences become our stories. Similarly, oftentimes we hear stories that teach us about the mistakes and expectation failures of others and we can adjust our mental models using information gleaned from those stories too.

How Do We Turn Our Experiences Into Stories?

Often we think about our cases following our experiences and construct story-like memories out of them. We do this by reconstructing what happened in the experience so that it sounds good as a story to tell someone, or to tell ourselves. As we mentioned in our discussion of first-hand stories, when we prepare the story version of the experience, or the case, we include some details, embellish some with potentially fictional details, and leave much of the experience out of the story altogether. This process is called *leveling and sharpening* (Allport & Postman, 1945). We do this so that the story does not take as long to tell as the experience took to live, and so that we can make a coherent, interesting point for our listeners' benefit. Each time we find a reason to tell the story, we level and sharpen in different ways to meet our current need, or the need of our listener. As the story changes, so does our memory of the story.

Ultimately, our memories are constructed of the stories we have created from our experiences. We are less likely to remember experiences that we do not talk about. Certainly there is no need to remember everything that we experience, and there is no need to relay to someone else all of our experiences.

> The experiences we do remember form the set of stories that constitute our view of the world and characterize our beliefs. In some sense, we may not even know what our view of the world is until we are reminded of and tell stories that illustrate our opinion on some aspect of the world. (Schank, 1990, p. 29)

So, we construct and tell stories, in part, to teach ourselves what we know and what we think.

We also create stories to teach others about us, what we know and what we think. When we consider the stories of others, or when we have new experiences, our existing thoughts and beliefs are sometimes challenged. These expectation failures lead us to examine our beliefs and sometimes build on them or change them. This is how we learn, and this is why we believe that knowledge is largely constructed of stories.

DETAILED EXAMPLE

To illustrate the story telling process and how we learn from stories, we will review a brief storytelling interchange that we, the authors of this chapter, had with each other. Notice that in our conversation, each one of us tells a story to the other, and that by telling these stories, each one of us gains new knowledge.

An American Jew Drinks Wine in France

To provide some context for this story, it might be helpful for readers to know that Roger C. Schank and Tammy Berman are both Jewish, and often discuss issues of Jewish culture and tradition. The day this story was told, they had just been discussing a trip that Tammy and her family took with her brother's non-Jewish and non-English speaking in-laws. They discussed the ways in which communication between the families was difficult because they were from both different cultures and different countries. This reminded Roger of a story regarding his own recent experience with a clashing of cultures.[2]

Roger began his story by explaining to Tammy that he had recently returned from a trip to France. While he was there, he was seated in a bar with three women to his left and three men to his right. There were two bottles of wine in front of him, and he wanted a glass of one of them.

Roger explained that he has spent enough time in France to know that the French culture has a particular social custom regarding the drinking of wine. The custom, as Roger understood it, is that if you would like a drink of wine, you must pour for everyone else at the table before pouring for yourself.

Roger decided to pour for the men, who he could reach, from the bottle near him, and figured he would leave the women who were engaged in heavy discussions and who had their own bottle in front of them, to their own devices. He proceeded to pour wine for the men sitting to his left and then poured for himself. When the women saw what Roger had done, they began to laugh and poke fun at his American boorishness.

Roger was annoyed. He pointed out to the women that the French culture is not the only culture on the planet. He noted that in Japan, for instance, these women would have been considered rude and offensive because they did not follow the Japanese custom of drinking wine. It dictates that people wanting wine should lift their glass to notify the pourer that they accept the drink, and to appear to be assisting in the pouring process.

The women did not know this custom. "What's your culture's custom for drinking wine, then?" the women asked Roger. He began to think. "Wait, are you going to tell us the American or the Jewish custom?" "The

Jewish custom," he replied. But Roger had a problem. Although he grew up exposed to a rich Jewish culture, as he was raised in a traditional Jewish home in Brooklyn, he quickly realized he had no idea what this custom was. Therefore, he quickly fabricated a custom off the top of his head to save himself.

He shared his new "theory" with the women. "Well, in Jewish culture wine pouring is a patriarchal activity. Fathers pour wine for the children. So, if I poured wine for you, it would be as if I were treating you as a child!" It worked. The women became relieved that Roger had not poured wine for them.

Roger was not satisfied however. He knew that his theory of the Jewish wine pouring custom was complete nonsense. So, although he got himself out of trouble with the French women, he raised an unanswered question in his own mind. What was the Jewish custom? There must be one, he thought. After some consideration, he decided that a typical Jewish dinner table is fraught with commotion: people discussing, laughing, shouting, that no one has time to notice how anyone gets their wine.

Roger thought that this was a fun story that Tammy would enjoy, and he thought he had made an important point. However, when he finished the story, Tammy was not quite sure what that point was. When she asked him, he decided that there were actually lots of points to be made with this story. The first one he intended to make was the following: Just because you follow a particular custom with its own set of rules, someone who does not follow it is not necessarily being rude. He may just be following a different set of rules belonging to a different custom.

Similar points, or themes, of his story might be:

1. No one culture has the right set of customs.
2. Annoyance at someone for not following a particular custom shows ignorance regarding others' cultural customs.
3. When in Rome act like the Romans so as not to offend.
4. Jews are so socially demonstrative during mealtimes that other customs are overshadowed.
5. Do not judge people from other cultures who misbehave in yours. You might find yourself in their position someday.

Because it has so many possible themes, this story could be told for the purpose of illustrating various lessons or beliefs depending on the context in which it is told. It is likely that when a story is told the point will be determined by the listener, especially if the teller does not make the intended point explicit. Even if the point is explicitly stated, the listener may learn something else, depending on the stories and scripts she has in her memory. So, what did Tammy do when she heard the story? She dwelt on the parts in which she was most interested (which were the parts that related most closely to her personal goals and prior experiences) and then she came up with a modification to Roger's theory.

"I think that Jews don't believe in such formalities—period. To impose them on others would be uncomfortable for the guest and rude of the host. Such rules in and of themselves go against Jewish culture." Once she explained the belief, she went on to "prove it" with a story.

"When my parents have guests stay at their house, they make people feel very comfortable and at home. They do not do this by closely adhering to a set of rules. They make it understood that their kitchen should be considered the guests' kitchen, and visitors should feel free to help themselves. Guests quickly come to behave as if the house resources are theirs to use as they wish and my parents do not pay much attention to what their guests do."

Although this ended Tammy's story, she reiterated her point by bridging the end of the story to the original point of the discussion. "In this sense, Jewish hospitality is letting your guests know that there are no formalities to be followed. The wine custom is the same. If it is on the table, whether in someone's home or at a restaurant, there are no formalities. If you want the wine, take it!" Roger agreed with Tammy's thoughts.

Story Analysis

Goals. Stories have several elements that make them worth telling or hearing. Experiences become stories as people attempt to achieve their goals (Schank & Abelson, 1977). Events occur that affect the pursuit of the goals, often obstructing them in some way, and the resolution or lesson learned concludes the story. In this way, stories are all about goals and how they are or are not achieved.

In the story above, Roger had several competing goals. On the one hand, he wanted to enjoy a glass of wine, but on the other, he wanted to behave in accordance with French culture, so as not to offend anyone. His challenge was to figure out how to achieve both goals simultaneously. He had to devise a plan.

Plans. When we pursue a goal, we use whatever we know about the domain to assist us in forming the most effective "plan" (Schank & Abelson, 1977) of action to get us to goal achievement. A plan is the set of actions a person chooses to take in order to get from his existing state to his goal state. Each action leads to "chains of results and enablements" (p. 70). Either we do what we have done in the past, or we reason from what has worked in other situations and build on those methods, taking into consideration any new issues that require a modification of our old methods.

For example, if we live in Chicago and regularly take the "El" (city train) to get around, we are used to paying for our ride with a pass that we purchase from a machine. Our goal is to get somewhere, and our plan is to purchase a ticket from the machine. In this case, we will always do what we have done before. However, if we go to another city, we might find that the ticket machines do not exist. We will have to modify the old plan to create a new one. To do so, we will use cues from the scene to help us reason about what to do. Cues trigger similar scenes from our memory structures that we then bring to bear on the new situation.

In our subway example, because we cannot pay by using our usual strategy, we look for cues that will trigger memories of other "pay scenes." We have frequented other businesses, like movie theaters, in which we pay a person behind a ticket window for our tickets. In this new city, if we see a ticket window with a worker sitting inside, this will serve as a visual trigger to retrieve past pay scenes of ticket windows, such as movie theaters, for example. Comparing our past memories with the current cues will inform our construction of a new plan of action to pay for our subway ticket. We will now assume that we should purchase a ticket from the person at the ticket window.

In Roger's story, to form a plan he drew on his knowledge of the French custom regarding the drinking of wine. Roger has lived in France and he formed his theory of their customs by creating a generalized belief from a number of experiences, or cases. According to his constructed mental representation of appropriate behavior in his circumstance, he could pour himself wine if he first poured it for others. This became his plan. He would open one of the bottles of wine, pour it for the men seated beside him, and then pour for himself.

Expectations. When we develop plans, we usually expect that execution of the plans will successfully lead to goal achievement. Certainly, there are times when we make a plan but we are unsure whether or not it will work. This happens when we do not have a clear model (representation) of the domain, so we are not sure what to expect. If we have an adequate script constructed, if we have had many similar experiences before, we will trust our plans more than if the experience is fairly new.

Roger's model of the wine situation informed his belief that by executing his plan he would be acting in accordance with the custom he learned. Therefore, he expected that the action would go somewhat unnoticed, or perhaps he would receive a subtle "thank you," from the gentlemen. He did wonder if the men would upbraid him for not pouring for the women, but he decided, given the machismo of the French culture, that this would not happen and indeed it did not. Instead, however, he was surprised by what happened following his action.

Expectation Failures. As we discussed earlier, when something happens that is contrary to what we expected, we experience an expectation failure. When the train traveler goes to the new city and does not see the ticket machine he expected to see, that is an expectation failure. So, when the women to Roger's right began to laugh and poke fun at him, it was an expectation failure for him. His plan did not work, which meant that something was wrong with his reasoning when he created the plan.

Expectation failures are the opportunities that lead to learning in most situations. It is true that we can learn in other ways, such as memorization, but this sort of information is not as efficiently retrievable (Ross & Kilbane, 1997). If we cannot readily find the information when we need it, it is not well learned. Expectation failures resulting from experiences and stories are highly indexable, which is why they are so effective for learning. We begin with perceptions of how the world works. We make plans to achieve our goals based on those perceptions, and if our plans fail, we realize that something is wrong with our initial perceptions. When we are told abstract principles, we do not necessarily change our initial beliefs; but when our beliefs are proven faulty, we understand that we need to change them, and we do so (Schank, 1982).

Explanations. As soon as we experience an expectation failure, we attempt to find reasons why our expectations failed. In order to achieve our goals in the future we need to set our expectations straight so we can form and execute effective plans. We do this by generating possible explanations for the expectation failure. Sometimes failed expectations are a result of our own faulty representations of something about a domain, and sometimes something about the domain actually changes, so our old understanding is no longer correct.

But how do we construct sensible explanations? We rely on the stories we have stored in memory. As we have discussed, when we encounter a new case that is anomalous to the cases we understood previously, we use the old cases to make sense of the new ones. In other words, we look for ways to make the new case seem similar to cases we have already encountered and indexed (Ayerhoff & Abelson, 1976; Lamb, Lalljee, & Abelson, 1992; Langer, 1975; Schank, 1986; Tversky, 1977). Expectation failures serve as triggers for remindings of past experiences in which we encountered similar expectation failures. Once we find stories that suggest reasonable explanations for our new expectation failure, we choose one that we believe is appropriate.

In Roger's story, he decided his representation of French culture was faulty. This was his explanation for the expectation failure he encountered.

His explanation may or may not have been correct. For instance, maybe the women were intentionally trying to make him uncomfortable, or maybe they were looking for an excuse to talk to him, but he was satisfied with his initial explanation, so he stopped trying to find more possibilities.

Once we decide on an explanation, whether it is right or wrong, we modify our memory structures by grouping both the expectation failure and the explanation together in our indexing scheme. In this way, if the expectation failure index is triggered so that we recall the story, we will also recall the explanation. This is how we use our old experiences and the stories we hear to devise new solutions. We are reminded of a similar expectation failure, and we are also reminded of the explanation or solution, which we use in the new problem (Schank, 1986).

As a story, the explanation is typically the lesson the story is intended to teach, and it establishes the theme. Interestingly, in Roger's telling of his story, he did not make explicit a new understanding of French customs, although he may have constructed one. The listener awaits the explanation constructed from the expectation failure, and perceives it as the point of the story, but Roger skipped this part and continued to tell about a different part of the experience. So, from Tammy's perspective, the story recipient, there was no acceptable explanation for Roger's expectation failure that she could consider to be the point of his story. This was her clue that the story was not over, and also that it was probably not about what Roger learned from his own expectation failure.

Roger ended his story by telling Tammy how he made the women reconsider their own actions. So, in some sense, Roger's explanation for his expectation failure was that the women seated beside him were out of line in their behavior toward him. Therefore, the story was more about his defense, and what he taught the women, than what he learned himself. The story was about Roger's beliefs—a self-defining story. Because Tammy recognized Roger's expectation failure when he told the story, and thus she expected an explanation of it that would teach her something about French custom, she was surprised when the point of the story was about something else entirely. This is, perhaps, why she became confused and asked Roger what the point was when he finished the whole story.

Roger pointed to many possible "themes" (Schank, 1990) in his retelling of his own experience as a story. Although his raw experience could have been formed as a story with a theme about what he learned, he chose to express details relevant to a different theme, which was what he taught to the women. He added another theme: what he learned about Jewish culture. The themes the listener understands result, in part, from those expectation failures and explanations.

Theme. A theme is an organizing structure of an event that implies all of the fundamental elements of a story we have discussed, including the overall lesson to be learned. Usually themes are about "general life topics" (Schank, 1990, p. 86), which is why there are so many stories with universally understood themes. In Roger's story, many of us can relate to the theme of fitting in with another culture. As we have seen, a story may have a number of themes depending on which details a storyteller decides to focus, and the lessons he implies the listener should learn. Likewise, one theme can be told through a variety of stories. Culturally common themes are sometimes conveyed through proverbs or fables. They are often so well known that just the title of the fable serves as an index to the full mental representation (understanding) of the theme. For instance, if we talk about "The Boy who Cried Wolf, " or "The Tortoise and the Hare," many people will understand the lesson, or the theme, without telling the story, because many people have heard these fables numerous times.

One theme from Roger's story was that one should not be fast to criticize those of other cultures for how they behave in one's own culture. His explanation for the belief was that anyone could have an experience in which she is the foreigner and does not understand the right way to behave. We understand Roger's initial goal when he devised his wine pouring plan: "When in Rome, act like the Romans."

As we mentioned, however, a story can have a number of themes that the listener gleans from it, even when the storyteller did not intend to relay them. Each listener brings to the story his or her own unique perspective and agenda, which is why different listeners can learn different things from the same story.

HOW WE LEARN FROM STORIES

What is Learning?

As we experience life, we form increasingly complex memory structures that explain how the world works. These memory structures are what we are also calling "mental representations," "scripts" and "scenes" in this chapter (Schank & Abelson, 1977). They gain complexity as we have new experiences (and hear new stories). This new input shows us the exceptions, additions, and replacements for what we understood previously, and thereby broadens our knowledge base.

Our memory structures are experience-based, or "case-based" which means, in essence, that they are story-based. We may modify the structures because of our own new experiences or because of stories we are told. In either case, we make modifications to our memory structures when we have expectation failures, and the modifications are related to our accepted explanations for the failures. It is the modification of our memory structures, our mental representations, that constitutes learning.

Learning From Stories

Expectation failures and explanations are elements of both firsthand experiences (which we often construct into stories) and secondhand stories. It follows that we can just as easily and effectively find opportunities to adjust our memory structures from our own stories or someone else's well-told stories. Therefore, once grouped together, or "indexed," under a theme, our own stories and others' stories become functionally similar structures in our minds.

We learn from both internal stories (those created from our firsthand experiences) and external stories (those conveyed to us by an outside source); we tell both to others to depict understanding or to convey a point, and we get reminded of both to understand and problem solve in new contexts. The major difference between internal and external stories, as we mentioned earlier, is that external stories are typically not as richly indexable as are firsthand experiences. Therefore, we may not be reminded of external stories by as many potential inputs as internal stories. For example, a scent may remind us of an internal story, because it is similar to a scent we smelled during another experience we once had. Scent is difficult to convey through external stories, so such sensory input during a new experience or when listening to a new story is less likely to trigger a reminding of a prior experience or story.

Factual and fictional stories are also functionally the same, once indexed into memory. Strange and Leung conducted research on this topic (1999). They gave their research subjects one of two versions of a narrative about a student planning to drop out of high school. One version was presented as a news article, the other was presented as a fictional account. Each narrative aimed to implicate different causes of the student's decision to drop out (either situational or dispositional). The researchers found that the causal generalizations (explanations) that readers constructed for the problem were unaffected by whether they thought the narrative was fiction or news. So, in other words, just as internal and external stories can have similar impact, so can either fact or fiction.

In the end, these researchers also found that readers were influenced to agree with the causes the stories implicated when the stories "evoked memories of similar characters and causal circumstances in the minds of the readers" (Strange & Leung, 1999, p. 444). This evidence supports our claim that when we hear stories we seek to confirm our existing beliefs by comparing the new input to familiar/similar indexes in our memories. When we find similar stories (when we are reminded) to compare to the new stories, we say we understand the new story. The subjects in the experiment used the reasoning that matched their existing beliefs.

Because we need to evoke existing representations for modification when we learn, reminding is essential in the learning process. In order to be reminded, we must have our memories sorted and labeled such that they can be easily triggered, or retrieved. Therefore, as we mentioned earlier, the key to learning is, in essence, the process of indexing. Efficient storage of new information in our memory structures requires that we index such that we can easily retrieve the information when we need to use it. Intelligent people are reminded of the right stories at the right times, which enables them to understand new input and to tell appropriate stories during conversations (Schank, 1990).

When we have new experiences that touch on the same themes as stories we have heard or experiences we have had, we should be able to easily trigger and retrieve the lessons we learned from them. We should use these lessons to form better expectations and plans in our new experiences. To do this, we need to store the lessons we learn with the appropriate themes in our memory structures.

So, in many ways the listener of a story goes through a similar process as the characters in the story. The listener seeks to understand the goals, plans, expectations, and all salient parts of the story for each character. Major characters' goals and the tales of their goal pursuits will be made explicit in the story, while minor characters' often will not. Listeners identify these story elements and match them to familiar (similar) goals, plans, and so on, from their memory structures.

Like the characters in the story, the listener forms expectations based on the goals and plans of the characters in the story. The listener will either agree with the plan based on his representation of the domain, or disagree. Therefore, he will also have expectations for the outcome of the actions taken. If the outcome is as expected, the listener will not make any modifications to his memory structures. If the outcome is a surprise, then it will constitute an expectation failure, and the listener will need to find an adequate explanation for the failure, as does the character in the story.

Once a satisfactory explanation is either provided in the story, or constructed by the listener, the listener will modify his mental representation of the domain accordingly. The listener's memory structure will contain, indexed together, the essential story details, the theme, topic, goal, action, result of the action (expectation failure), and the lesson learned (Schank, 1990). Later, when the listener encounters a new experience or story that touches on the same theme, the memory of this story is likely to be triggered, along with the expectation failure that occurred and the lesson learned, or the explanation. Because of this, when the listener is forming his own plan for the goal pursuit in the new story, his expectations will have changed, and his plan is likely to be different than it would have been prior to the modification of his representation of the domain.

DETERMINANTS OF NARRATIVE IMPACT

Interest

The problem with learning from stories, as opposed to learning from experiences, is that the storyteller cannot guarantee that the listener will care enough about the theme to modify his memory structures. Caring, or interest, insures that listeners will pay attention to the expectation failures that relate to their personal goal pursuits and that they will actively seek explanations within the story. If listeners are not motivated by an expectation failure to find an explanation, then they will not be likely to either find or remember the explanation, and they are also not likely to store it effectively in their memory structures. Strange and Leung (1999) found evidence for this theory in the research we cited earlier, regarding subjects generating causes for why the boy was dropping out of high school. They found that the more engaged the readers were as they read the story, the more likely they were to suggest causes and solutions to the problem that were consistent with what they read in the story presented to them. This is true of the details within a story and with the story itself. Listeners search for the parts of a story, and for stories in general, that interest them, those to which they can relate.

Listeners will relate most to the parts of the story that speak to their personal experience. For instance, someone who is going to visit Israel in the near future is likely to care much more about the news reports of political tension than someone who has never been there and never cares to go. Each listener hears the parts of the story that relate to him, personally. Schank and Abelson discussed this issue in their lead article in the book, *Knowledge and Memory: The Real Story* (1995):

> We cannot think about all of the possible ramifications of something we are being told, so we pay attention to what interests us. We settle on a story we have been reminded of, and, in effect, we hear no more. On the basis of what interests us, we select the mental paths to take. We express our interests by focusing on certain indexes, those that we can say we have been looking for, ignoring the potential indexes we are not prepared to deal with. Because we can only understand things that relate to our own experiences, it is actually very difficult for us to hear things that people say that are not interpretable through those experiences. In other words, we attend to what we are capable of understanding. (pp. 16–17)

This is true of stories as a whole and of details within the story. Just as the person who never cares to visit the Middle East may not attend to the news story about Israel at all, various people who are interested enough to attend to the story may find different points of interest within the story. The person who is planning a trip has the personal goals of being safe, having a fun vacation, and avoiding violence. When this person listens to news reports about Israel, she will take away a lesson about whether or not her trip is in jeopardy. On the other hand, a Palestinian American may have very different goals, such as the long-term goal of receiving a homeland for his people. He will be listening to the news report to learn whether there are any developments bringing Israel closer to accommodating such a homeland.

When Tammy heard Roger's story, she knew that she was supposed to be attending to the issue of how people deal with foreigners who do not exhibit appropriate cultural customs, but she has a personal, continuous goal of better understanding her own Jewish culture and identity. Therefore, she heard the part of the story she cared about, the part to which she could personally relate. As she listened to Roger speak, the part she thought through most carefully was identifying the Jewish custom for drinking wine, and for that matter, identifying Jewish customs in general. Tammy responded to this aspect of Roger's story. However, had Tammy been planning a business trip to France, for example, she would have cared much more about Roger's comments regarding French customs. The stories and parts of stories that have the most impact are those that relate most closely to the listeners' goals.

Frame of Reference

If we know absolutely nothing about the story's domain, if we have no similar stories in our memories, this means we have no frame of reference. We simply will not understand the theme or any point of the story. We may not even know that we heard it. For example, Tammy mentioned Roger's story to a friend of hers. While Tammy was heavily focused on whether or not Roger's assessment of Jewish cultural customs was correct, due to her personal frame of reference, Tammy's friend had a totally different frame of reference. First, he is not Jewish. Second, he grew up in Europe and spent time in France and other European countries with similar customs to the French. On hearing the story, his immediate thought (based on his own remindings of similar circumstances) was that Roger's understanding of the custom was incorrect. He told Tammy that the actual custom is that one never drinks wine alone, and that a man should always first pour wine for the women he is with before he pours for other men or himself.

Tammy's friend listened for Roger's goals, beliefs (regarding the French custom), related plan, and expectations, and then he was not surprised by the event that caused Roger's expectation failure. During the telling of the story he had searched his own memory structures to compare Roger's beliefs with his own (which are presumably based on his prior experiences), and he found that they were different. Therefore, he knew that Roger's mental representation was faulty, and this friend did not learn anything from the story—other than, perhaps, forming a new opinion that Roger does not have a clear understanding of French cultural customs.

At the end of Roger and Tammy's discussion, through their interchange of stories, Tammy formed a belief that she did not necessarily know prior to the conversation. She learned that Jewish custom is to avoid too much formality in order to be hospitable. She learned it by going through the process of listening to Roger's stories and beliefs, and comparing them with her own memory structures, or frame of reference. As a result of the conversation, Tammy and Roger provided each other with new stories and reasons to modify their beliefs. Later, it happened that Tammy had more discussions with others about the stories she and Roger shared, and she changed her beliefs again, realizing that stereotypical Jewish mothers do plenty of doting on their children and guests. This made her realize that her parents may be atypical, causing her to construct a faulty model of Jewish custom.

When To Tell a Story

Sometimes we hear a story and it causes no change whatsoever in our beliefs or our behavior. Nevertheless, the issue here is the timing of the storytelling with regard to the goals of the learner.

As we mentioned earlier, listeners of stories must have goals to direct what they look for in a story, and they come to stories with their own frames of reference. Both of these factors work together; stories must convince listeners that their current mental representations are inaccurate, or are lacking information, and that the information or theories proposed in the stories have the potential to enable them to fill in gaps or correct inaccuracies in their mental representations.

In essence, to maximize impact, listeners should want or need the information embedded in stories because they recognize the flaws in their existing representations. When that occurs, the listener's mental representations will be susceptible to comparisons and analyses. The listener will be intentionally seeking to test her representations against the details in the story. So, the information she hears in the story will likely be indexed appropriately. Therefore, the right time for a story is, "just in time," when listeners want to receive the lessons that the story will relay, so that they can use the lessons to help them achieve their goals.

Poor timing is one of the most common mistakes in educational environments, whether in the home, school, or work. For example, brides and grooms receive endless advice from their friends and family about how to make a marriage work. A student of Roger and colleague of Tammy received much advice from her mother about keeping her relationship with her new husband alive and healthy through the years. Her mother told her stories about women who, over time, ceased to attend to their appearances. They let their hair grow out of style, gained weight, stopped wearing make-up, and stopped buying attractive clothing, because they began to take their relationships for granted.

When her mother first began sharing these stories and this advice, this woman was in her early twenties. She and her husband were very much in love, and they both were quite attractive without much effort. The information in her mother's stories was useless to her, because it did not take work to keep up her appearance, and she was not concerned about losing her husband's love.

Her mother continues to remind her of the stories to this day, some years later. Now that she is a graduate student and a mother, busy with life, the stories carry more meaning. Now, she focuses more on the goal of keeping her marriage fresh. She thinks about the lessons in the stories and relates them to her own mental representation of marriage. When she thinks about the stories, she makes appointments with her hairdresser and she works harder to select her outfits. Meaning came from the stories as they related to her more appropriate frame of reference, and more relevant goals.

Researchers at the Institute for the Learning Sciences (ILS) at Northwestern University have been creating computer-based educational simulations that help students find a goal so they have a reason to listen and learn information. For example, in learning about the French Revolution, history students using the simulation might play the role of a time-traveling consultant to the French president. They must solve problems by finding out about the issues that arose during the Revolution. The goals created by the computer program allow students to effectively index the knowledge they have gained.

Therefore, the most effective time to tell a story is when the learner has a goal that makes the information in the story relevant to the learner's achievement of the goal. The information has to satisfy a need that the listener perceives he has. If he does not know he needs the information, he will not index it in a usable way.

What Makes the Best Stories?

In accordance with this theory of the right time to hear a story, the stories with the most impact are those that apply to listeners' goals and that are relevant to their personal frames of reference. Any story can be good or bad depending on who is hearing it, and what they are thinking about or caring about at the time. Well-told stories tend to have lots of details that make the stories seem relevant to the listeners.

The most powerful storytellers and speakers address the topics and questions about which the audience is most curious. This is why, as pointed out in *Tell Me a Story*, (Schank, 1990, pp. 212–218) people like Jimmy Swaggart, who tell stories intended to impact a broad public, are such powerful storytellers. The same is true of strong political candidates as they run for office. They all tell stories that have indexes that are similar to the indexes people already have in their memory structures, so they are within listeners' frames of reference, and the goals discussed in the stories are goals that listeners "understand," which essentially means they possess the goals themselves.

Storytellers can make their stories more appealing to listeners, more interesting to them, if they add appropriate details to bring the story within listeners' frames of reference. The strongest stories are those in which listeners can see themselves in the role of the hero. The closer we can come to relating to the hero, the more personally relevant the story becomes, and the more likely we are to learn from it. That means that if the storyteller can get us to really sympathize with the hero, it also implies that we can imagine being in the same circumstances, and we begin to think about what we might do, or how we might feel if we were in the hero's shoes. Adding to a story rich details that touch on references the broader public understands assists this effect.

President Clinton used this strategy in his final State of the Union Address. He mentioned as abstract principles, issues on which he wanted the government and the nation to focus attention. For instance, he talked about the government helping a father having difficulty paying child support. Then he introduced this father on national television. He treated the dad as a hero who did his duty to support his child. Viewers, having indexed many stories of poor children being neglected, could imagine an innocent little boy needing financial assistance to have a healthy future. We were relieved to "meet" this proud father who was able to help the child because of our government's support.

Clinton used the same strategy with the father of a student at Columbine High School who was shot and killed during the 1999 student massacre. This father was fighting for gun safety laws, and his plight was made more urgent when people saw his face, saw a photo of his innocent and intelligent-looking son pinned to his jacket. The visual details allowed the listeners to the story to easily imagine the father's pain. In so doing, when we, the voters, are asked to take a stand on gun safety and control issues, we will be reminded of the sad and desperate look on the father's face. We will remember his story, and we will, Clinton hopes, vote in favor of gun safety.

However, an NRA member who listened to Clinton's speech and saw the father he introduced may not have been interested in changing his view. Instead, this listener may have been reminded of 10 counter-stories that referenced the importance of having quick and easy access to guns without it taking too long to get them ready for firing: stories of freedom, empowerment, safety. When we listen to stories we attempt to find evidence that confirms what we already believe. Changing our beliefs requires expectation failures powerful enough to convince us there is actually something wrong with our existing beliefs, our representations of the domain.

Why Stories Have Strong Impact

Why is it that the best speakers tell stories? Why do they not simply tell us the point of their stories, the lessons we are supposed to learn from them? Storytellers may not know why, but they know that stories have far greater impact than abstract principles alone. A strategy Jimmy Swaggart uses to give more impact to his stories is to include rich detail that relates to many listeners' frames of reference. Another great presenter of stories, Oprah Winfrey, will often include a montage video with music to add more detail and impact to the words in a viewer's letter. It is exactly because they tell stories with rich detail, rich context, and do not simply explain the principle, that they have such impact.

Details that show more context trigger remindings, so more details mean greater potential for more people to get reminded of something from their remembered stories. In this way, details can help people perceive stories to be personally relevant, and details heighten indexability, so they are more easily remembered. That is why we have difficulty remembering abstractions, or decontextualized principles (Schank, 1990; Schank & Abelson, 1995). As Schank noted in *Tell Me a Story* (1990),

> Memory, in order to be effective, must contain both specific experiences (memories) and labels (memory traces). The more information we are provided with about a situation, the more places we can attach it to in memory, and the more ways it can be compared with other cases in memory. (p. 11)

Again, as we hear stories we search our memory structures for similar content to use for comparison purposes. This is how we decide whether or not we are missing information in our current representations of a domain, and how we decide whether we agree or disagree with the message in the new story. It is also how we find more stories to tell back to the person with whom we are conversing, if we are in a conversational context. Details in stories provide features, themes, expectation failures, and so on, to match to what we already know. Abstract principles do not give us enough fodder for examination. So when people do try to tell us abstract principles, we will often say we do not fully understand, and we will request an example. The example we are given is a story of sorts, whether hypothetical or real.

Once we have listened to a story rich with detail, we are provided with more information, or indexes, to file story elements into our memory structures. The story provides us with much more information to index than abstract principles would provide. That information will fit into a greater variety of categories and contexts in our memory structures. More complex and diverse indexes make it more likely that an element of a new story will trigger the old story as a reminding. The reminding allows us to understand the new story.

Stories are comprised of details that give context and meaning to abstract principles. They allow listeners to match the story elements against their current frames of reference to see the relevance of the lessons. The best stories are those that have rich detail, because they broaden the context to allow more listeners to find themselves in the stories. Stories, therefore, enable listeners to learn from their lessons in deeper ways than lessons alone allow. Stories also provide more indexes to help listeners remember the lessons so they may use them to solve novel problems. For these reasons, stories have stronger impact than abstract principles alone.

A LOOK TOWARD THE FUTURE OF STORIES

Computers offer incredible potential for stories to impact our lives in ways never before possible. The information age is here, and new technological developments will increasingly bring us the exact stories we want to hear when and where we want to hear them. Older technologies have constrained how we receive information.

Television only provides us with information that programmers and news editors want us to know. We are expected to become interested in stories just because network staffs choose to broadcast them. Often, however, even when there are stories of actual interest to us, we miss them because no one is available to let us know those topics will be covered.

Another limitation of television is that even when we are there to watch stories that address topics of personal interest, the stories may or may not address the issues we really care about within those topics. Television, because it is not an interactive medium, does not allow us to ask questions to focus material on those areas about which we are most curious.

There has been an interactive technology available to us for many years however, which makes up for some of television's shortcomings: the telephone. The telephone allows those who know us well to inform us of information when they know it, and they know we want to know it.

However, if we have an interest that our acquaintances do not know about, how can we find information that exists on the subject, especially new developments that have not yet been published in books? Computers offer us the solution. The Internet, for instance, already contains endless web sites about every topic under the sun. The problem with the Internet is that we have to work hard to find the information within it. There are search engines that only do a fair job of finding sites relevant to our requests. The good news is that these engines will continue to improve so that we may initiate searches for information whenever we desire it.

Someday the Internet and intelligently constructed databases will continuously grow warehouses for an infinite number of stories from which we will be able to learn about any topic, from any perspective, from the best experts in the world. These limitless libraries will be the most accessible tools for gathering stories, experiences, and information the world has ever known.

CONCLUSION

Stories will always be an integral part of our lives, for entertainment, communication, teaching, and learning. Our minds are structured so that we cannot help but construct stories out of our own experiences, and we listen to stories with an innate ability to pull apart the details and fill out our memory structures where they are lacking. In essence, our knowledge is constructed of stories in various forms. The more stories we hear and tell, the more expert we become in those subjects. The key to narrative impact, then, is to find ways to provide the right stories in the most rich and accessible forms, so people may find them as they need them.

ENDNOTES

[1] A "mental representation," also referred to as a "mental model" (Gentner & Stevens, 1983; Johnson-Laird, 1983) is a person's conception of something. A classic example is when someone mentions the word *chair*, three different people are likely to imagine three different looking chairs in their minds. Although they have somewhat different representations of what a generic chair looks like, their representations of the chair are functionally the same, in that they will all know that it is something created for the purpose of supporting one sitting person. Mental representations or mental models correspond with the world but are not exact copies of it.

[2] Remindings often result from the "availability" of the experience in memory (Tversky & Kahneman, 1973). Availability is the ease with which thoughts

come to mind. Availability results, in part, from a combination of similarity of story details as well as recency of an experience or recall of the experience. In this case, Roger and Tammy touched on a topic that was similar to one of Roger's recent experiences.

REFERENCES

Allport, G. W., & Postman, L. J. (1945). The basic psychology of rumor. *Transactions of the New York Academy of Sciences, Series II, Vol. 8*, 61–81.

Ayeroff, F., & Abelson, R. P. (1976). ESP and ESB: Belief in personal success at mental telepathy. *Journal of Personality and Social Psychology, 34*, 240–247.

Gentner, D. (1983). Structure-Mapping: A theoretical framework for analogy. *Cognitive Science, 7*, 155–170.

Gentner, D., & Landers, R. (1985). Analogical reminding: A good match is hard to find. *Proceedings of the International Conference on Cybernetics and Society* (pp. 607–613). Tucson, AZ/New York: The Institute of Electrical and Electronic Engineers.

Gentner, D., & Stevens, A. L. (1983). *Mental models*. Hillsdale, NJ: Lawrence Erlbaum Associates.

Gick, M. L., & Holyoak, K. J. (1980). Analogical problem solving. *Cognitive Psychology, 12*, 306–355.

Hammond, K. (1989). *Case-based planning: Viewing planning as a memory task*. San Diego, CA: Academic Press.

Johnson-Laird, P. N. (1983). *Mental models*. Cambridge, MA: Harvard University Press.

Kolodner, J., & Jona, M. Y. (1991). *Case-based reasoning: An overview* (Tech. Rep. No. 15). Evanston, IL: Northwestern University.

Lalljee, M., Lamb, R., & Abelson, R. P. (1992). The role of event prototypes in categorization and explanation. In W. Stroebe & M. Hewstone (Eds.), *European review of social psychology* (Vol. 3, pp. 153–182). Chichester, UK: Wiley.

Langer, E. J. (1975). The illusion of control. *Journal of Personality and Social Psychology, 32*, 311–328.

Ortony, A. (1979). Beyond literal conformity. *Psychological Review, 86*, 161–180.

Ratterman, J. J., & Gentner, D. (1987). Analogy and similarity: Determinants of accessibility and inferential soundness. In J. Anderson (Ed.), *Proceedings of the Ninth Annual Meeting of the Cognitive Science Society* (pp. 23–25). Hillsdale, NJ: Lawrence Erlbaum Associates.

Riesbeck, C. K., & Schank, R. C. (1989). *Inside case-based reasoning*. Hillsdale, NJ: Lawrence Erlbaum Associates.

Ross, B. H., (1989). Distinguishing types of superficial similarities: Different effects on the access and use of earlier problems. *Journal of Experimental Psychology: Learning, Memory, and Cognition, 15*, 456–468.

Ross, B. H., & Kilbane, M. C. (1997). Effects of principle explanation and superficial similarity on analogical mapping in problem solving. *Journal of Experimental Psychology: Learning, Memory, and Cognition, 23/2*, 427–440.

Ross, L. D. (1977). The intuitive psychologist and his shortcomings: Distortions in the attribution process. In L. Berkowitz (Ed.), *Advances in Experimental Social Psychology* (Vol. 10, pp. 174–220). New York: Academic Press.

Schank, R. C. (1999). *Dynamic memory revisited*. New York: Cambridge University Press.

Schank, R. C. (1982). *Dynamic memory: A theory of reminding and learning in computers and people.* New York: Cambridge University Press.
Schank, R. C. (1986). *Explanation patterns: Understanding mechanically and creatively.* Hillsdale, NJ: Lawrence Erlbaum Associates.
Schank, R. C. (1990). *Tell me a story.* Evanston, IL: Northwestern University Press.
Schank, R. C., & Abelson, R. P. (1977). *Scripts, plans, goals, and understanding.* Hillsdale, NJ: Lawrence Erlbaum Associates.
Schank, R. C., & Abelson, R. P. (1995). Knowledge and memory: The real story. In R. S. Wyer, Jr. (Ed.), *Advances in Social Cognition* (Vol. 8, pp. 1–85). Hillsdale, NJ: Lawrence Erlbaum Associates.
Seifert, C. M., McKoon, G., Abelson, R. P., & Ratcliff, R. (1986). Memory connections between thematically similar episodes. *Journal of Experimental Psychology: Learning, Memory, and Cognition, 12,* 220–231.
Strange, J. J., & Leung, C. C. (1999). How anecdotal accounts in news and in fiction can influence judgments of a social problem's urgency, causes, and cures. *Personality and Social Psychology Bulletin, 25*(4), 436–449.
Tversky, A. (1977). Features of similarity. *Psychological Review, 84,* 327–352.
Tversky, A., & Kahneman, D. (1973). Availability: A heuristic for judging frequency and probability. *Cognitive Psychology, 5,* 207–222.

13

In the Mind's Eye

Transportation-Imagery Model of Narrative Persuasion

Melanie C. Green
University of Pennsylvania

Timothy C. Brock
The Ohio State University

The power of narratives has often appeared to be limitless, yet scientific understanding of how such power is exerted on individuals is in its infancy. This chapter offers a testable theory derived from recent research on the mechanisms of narrative influence.

Totalitarian governments have long recognized the power of narratives to bring about social change and have therefore engaged in widespread suppression of even fictional narratives (e.g., censorship of Nobel laureates Pasternak and Solzhenitsyn in the former Soviet Union). On the positive side, the abolition movement leading to the Civil War has been attributed in part to exposure to *Uncle Tom's Cabin*, a novel of the 19th century that enkindled antislavery sentiment. At Harvard Medical School, physician training has included a course in which students read selected stories and novels: The course is recommended in order to produce physicians whose treatment of patients will be caring and humane (Coles, 1987). The range of putative perils and benefits from exposure to narratives has always been virtually unlimited.

Why are narratives—from Jesus' parables to modern-day soap operas and romance novels—thought to have such an enormous impact? There is no simple answer in terms of any single psychological mechanism. Nevertheless, some argue (e.g., Schank & Abelson, 1995) that people are "wired" to be especially sensitive to information in narrative format. Indeed, according to the strong claim of these authors,

> stories about one's experiences and the experiences of others are the fundamental constituents of human memory, knowledge, and social communication...when it comes to interaction in language, all of our knowledge is contained in stories and mechanisms to construct them and retrieve them. (pp. 1–2)

As if to capitalize on this natural susceptibility to stories, there now appears to be increasing blurring of factual and fictional narratives in the media. For example, reading Christian fiction has been claimed to enhance religious experiences (e.g., Niebuhr, 1995) and, on the other side of the coin, former Vice-President Dan Quayle used the unwed motherhood of a fictional television character, Murphy Brown, as an example of the nation's moral decay. Even commercials use minidramas to persuade consumers to purchase products (Deighton, Romer, & McQueen, 1989).

Although narratives may cause change on a cultural or national scale, these effects begin with individual recipients. Although the study of attitude and belief change has been a central concern of social psychologists for decades, surprisingly little attention has been paid to the specific processes by which narrative or fictional communications might have persuasive effects. The bulk of persuasion research has dealt with communications comprised of advocacies, arguments, and other forms of rhetoric (e.g., Eagly & Chaiken, 1993; but see Gerbner, Gross, Morgan, & Signorielli, 1994; Shrum, Wyer, & O'Guinn, 1998; Slater, chap. 7, this volume, for exceptions). We return later to the question of whether theories developed for rhetorical persuasion can be extrapolated to narrative persuasion.

In summary, the study of narrative persuasion is important yet neglected. A major problem is lack of testable theory: theory may help to organize experimental approaches to increase scientific understanding.

Our theory, the Transportation-Imagery Model[1], consists of the following five postulates.

> Postulate I. Narrative persuasion is limited to story texts (scripts) (a) which are in fact narratives, (b) in which images are evoked, and (c) in which readers' (viewers) beliefs are implicated.

Postulate II. Narrative persuasion (belief change) occurs, *other things equal*, to the extent that the evoked images are activated by psychological *transportation*, defined (below) as a state in which a reader becomes absorbed in the narrative world, leaving the real world, at least momentarily, behind.

Postulate III. Propensity for transportation by exposure to a given narrative account is affected by attributes of the recipient (for example, imagery skill).

Postulate IV. Propensity for transportation by exposure to a given narrative account is affected by attributes of the text (script). Among these moderating attributes are the level of artistic craftsmanship and the extent of adherence to narrative format. Another conceivable moderator, whether the text is labeled as fact or fiction (as true or not necessarily true), does not limit transportation.

Postulate V. Propensity for transportation by exposure to a given narrative account is affected by attributes of the context (medium). Among these moderating attributes may be aspects of the context or medium that limit opportunity for imaginative investment and participatory responses.

We first provide an intuitive introduction to key elements of the theory, and then present the postulates and their implications. The next section compares the Transportation-Imagery approach to persuasion with dual-process models of rhetorical persuasion; specifically, we contrast our theory with the Elaboration-Likelihood Model (ELM). We then discuss selected research implications, and conclude with a discussion of possible areas in which the ideas of narrative persuasion can be applied.

INTUITIVE APPROACH TO TRANSPORTATION-IMAGERY MODEL OF NARRATIVE PERSUASION

Most people have had the sensation of being "lost in a book" (Nell, 1988), swept up into the world of a story so completely that they forget the world around them. These readers are transported into the realm of the narrative. Instead of seeing activity in their physical surroundings, transported readers see the action of the story unfolding before them. These readers react emotionally to events that are simply words on a page.

Although this experience may be common in everyday life, it has been granted little empirical attention. Our research program begins with this phenomenological experience of being transported to a narrative world, and explores the causes and the consequences of this type of narrative-based mental processing. One of the specific questions we ask is how transporting narratives—even fictional ones—can have an impact on individuals' real-world beliefs.

Paramount Role for Imagery

The central role of imagery in our model stems in part from the requirement that a seriously-intended theory of narrative impact must not set aside the most obvious and important exemplar. In our view of narrative impact, *Uncle Tom's Cabin* (Stowe, 1852; see also chap. 1, this volume) must be addressed by seriously intended theories because, although it spawned the notorious "Uncle Tom" epithet (fawning servility), overall it has had the greatest impact of any public narrative.

For almost a century, *Uncle Tom's Cabin* and its pullulating theatrical derivatives and other industries suffused Western culture (e.g., black-faced Judy Garland and black-faced Betty Grable played Topsy in 1936 and 1945, respectively).[2] Henry James wrote: "There was for that triumphant work no classified condition; it had all the extraordinary fortune of finding itself, for an immense number of people, much less a book than a state of vision" (James, 1913, pp. 167–168). Indeed, visual imagery, startling and absorbing, comprised the engine of the *Uncle Tom* panphenomenon (Birdoff, 1947; Wood, 2000). A theory of narrative impact must foreground the role of imagery to readily account for the impact of *Uncle Tom* on the behavior of hundreds of millions of people for many decades; without such emphasis the theory would fail to address its chiefest exemplar.

Experimental Investigation

To create the transportation experience in the laboratory (Green & Brock, 2000), we selected highly involving, imagery-rich narratives. We used a narrative called "Murder at the Mall," a story about a college student, Joan, whose little sister Katie is brutally stabbed to death by a psychiatric patient while they are at the mall. The story is a slightly adapted version of a true story published by Yale surgeon Sherwin Nuland in his best-selling book, *How We Die* (1994). "Murder at the Mall" (*Murder*) is a graphic account of the attack and of Joan's reaction to it. The author describes the attack in vivid detail, focusing on images such as the killer's knife repeatedly stabbing Katie, and the child's glassy stare as she lays dying after the stabbing: Readers report being shocked and saddened.

In addition to being involving, this narrative met other important research criteria. First, it was plausible as either fiction or nonfiction, allowing us to investigate the effects of fiction/nonfiction labeling on both transportation and belief change. Events are presented realistically; however, *Murder* has a rich descriptive style that would not be typical of a straight wire-service journalistic account. Although our studies thus far have focused primarily on realistic narratives, we believe that the same processes would apply to stories that have all the trappings of pure fiction—science fiction or fantasy stories set on different planets or in distant times, for example.

Because we hypothesize that transportation is at least partially due to the craftsmanship of an author, we wanted a well-written text. The quality of the narratives can be attested to by their external successes, and Nuland's book sold thousands of copies around the country. Finally, we were able to derive testable belief items from the content of the story. *Murder* implicates beliefs about public safety and the desirability of freedoms for psychiatric patients, as well as more general beliefs about justice (Lerner & Miller, 1978).

Results using *Murder* and other stories showed that individuals who were more highly transported into a narrative showed greater belief change, more positive evaluations of sympathetic major characters, and less rejection of story content (Green & Brock, 2000). These findings were replicated with both measured and manipulated transportation, indicating that transportation may be a key mechanism of narrative-based belief change.

Transportation-imagery theory emphasizes the role of imagery in belief change. The images in this story buttress certain conclusions related to the derived beliefs. For example, the vision of a knife-wielding, disheveled psychopath grabbing a young girl in a shopping mall suggests that individuals with violent mental disorders should not be allowed in the community without supervision (if at all!).

This story and others are not simply collections of provocative descriptions, however. Narratives must have, in fact, a real story line: Questions are raised which are only answered in subsequent portions of the narrative. In Bruner's words, "[Narrative] deals in human or human-like intention and action and the vicissitudes and consequences that mark their course" (1986, p. 13). The order is logical, and in this case, generally chronological, although we expect similar effects would occur even if flashbacks and other nonchronological literary techniques were employed. Narrative structure affects the potency of the imagery used in the story. (For an alternative perspective, see Rubin, 1995, p. 53, where imagery compensates for lack of structure.) The image of a maniac with a hunting knife is always disturbing, but without the framework of the story, does not necessarily implicate beliefs about mall safety, supervision of psychiatric patients, or belief in a just world.

These intuitive descriptions are intended to provide a framework for the more formal presentation of the theory in the following sections. We realize that we are introducing the transportation/imagery concepts using a somewhat grisly tale; *Murder* was negatively arousing for most participants. However, we have replicated the effects of transportation on beliefs with more cheerful narratives (Green & Brock, 2000). There is no a priori reason why the arousal of negative affect should be necessary for belief change to occur.

POSTULATES OF TRANSPORTATION-IMAGERY MODEL OF NARRATIVE PERSUASION

Postulate I. Narrative persuasion is limited to story texts (scripts) (a) which are in fact narratives, (b) in which images are evoked, and (c) in which readers' (viewers) beliefs are implicated.

Narrative Versus Rhetoric

In essence, a "narrative account" requires a story that raises unanswered questions, unresolved conflicts, and/or depicts not yet completed activity. A story line, with a beginning, middle, and end, is identifiable.[3] In an advertising context,

> A story is a fictional or true account of how the expectations or wishes of (a person) or the inclinations or tendencies (of a person or product) are first opposed, frustrated, or are otherwise in doubt, then in some way prevail, succeed, or are redressed. (Deighton et al., 1989, p. 338)

Bruner suggested that one critical difference between stories and nonstories might be the standards of truth to which people hold narratives versus other types of communications:

> A good story and a well-formed argument are different natural kinds...The one [argument] verifies by eventual appeal to procedures for establishing formal and empirical proof. The other [story] establishes not truth but verisimilitude. (1986, p. 11)

The difference in standards for these information formats is consonant with our proposal that different mental processes may be involved when one encounters a narrative versus an argument.

Following Bruner, we distinguish narrative persuasion from rhetorical persuasion. Rhetorical persuasion refers to the vast variety of messages such as editorials, many advertisements, public education campaigns, and political speeches, in which arguments are adduced on behalf of an advocated opinion or position (e.g., Petty & Cacioppo, 1986). Rhetorical persuaders sometimes include stories (e.g., State of the Union addresses of Presidents Reagan and Clinton; TV advertising using vignettes) but the bulk of rhetorical persuasion consists of arguments, reasoning, claims, evidence, and so forth.

Is it theoretically warranted to distinguish narrative from rhetorical presentations? Are the principles of narrative persuasion in fact different from those that govern editorial and rhetorical persuasion? How effective is narrative persuasion in comparison to nonnarrative versions? These are important questions in light of the massive social and cultural commitment to narratives. Theory-guided experiments can provide informative answers.

Imagery

The Transportation-Imagery Model is limited to texts in which measurable images are evoked; images that can be recalled, recognized, and responded to. Readers could encode powerful images from their reading of *Murder*. For example, readers of *Murder* could imagine Katie's "peaceful glassy" stare immediately after her lethal stabbing. More generally,

> Images are considered mental contents that possess sensory qualities in the absence of external stimuli that provoke the relevant senses or in the absence of appropriate immediate sensory input. Images can resemble any of the sensory modalities, however, visual imagery appears the most common type of imagery experienced by people and the most well studied. A mental image is a representation of a particular stimulus that is formed by activation of a sensory system and, thus, is experienced by the organism as having similar qualities to the actual perception of the stimulus. (Dadds, Bovbjerg, Reed, & Cutmore, 1997, p. 90)

Although we believe that evocation of imagery is vital to narrative persuasion, the generation of images can occur during or after exposure to the focal text. Narrative that never or hardly elicits imagery—for example, an account of a bridge game—is excluded from the domain of the present model.

The role of imagery in narrative absorption and persuasion has been debated. Gerrig's (1993) conceptualization of transportation does not explicitly include a role for imagery. Nell's (1988) investigations of ludic or pleasure reading summarized evidence for both sides. At first, he suggested that the creation of mental images is too difficult and time-consuming for most readers, who might prefer to simply process the text propositionally rather than imaginally. He discounted the role of imagery in the experience of narratives, relying on Gass (1972) and Kosslyn (e.g., 1981) to state (p. 220): "we can conclude that image generation will seldom form part of ludic reading."

Although theories of imagery that are not specifically linked to narratives appeared to support his above conclusion, later, in light of his own empirical evidence, Nell (1988) reversed himself and concluded that: "imagery is an essential aspect of the reading experience for all of them [participants in his reading groups], good and poor imagers alike" (p. 246). Nell's studies, conducted with individuals for whom pleasure reading was an important and frequent leisure activity, revealed a positive correlation between imagery during reading and reading involvement (a concept similar to transportation). According to Nell, "the reader, using a ready-made store of images, at once sees the whole picture—mistily, perhaps, but well enough" (p. 246). He further stated that "vivid imagery is indeed frequently associated with reading involvement."

Nell did not provide a reconciliation between the theoretical positions he summarized earlier in the book and his later empirical evidence; one purpose of the current chapter is to fill in those gaps with a theory explicitly designed to link the subjective experience of transportation with the formation of mental images.

Imagery Versus Vividness

Perhaps the closest parallel in the persuasion literature to our focus on imagery has been the debate on the vividness effect. Studies in this tradition compare vivid information—defined by Nisbett and Ross (1980) as information that is "(a) emotionally interesting, (b) concrete and imagery-provoking, and (c) proximal in a sensory, temporal, or spatial way" (p. 45)—to pallid information. Of course, this definition, and many of the subsequent operationalizations, mix imagery with other components of vividness. Theoretically, vivid information should have a greater effect on judgments, and some early studies showed that individuals were more likely to use vivid testimonials than pallid base-rates in making decisions. However, later reviews of the literature (e.g., Taylor & Thompson, 1982) showed little evidence of vividness effects. In fact, some kinds of vividness can distract from the persuasive impact of rhetorical messages (e.g., Frey & Eagly, 1993). Our paradigm may avoid some of the ambiguities of the vividness literature by focusing on imagery in the course of transportation. Another advantage is that, as discussed below, the model integrates imagery into a narrative context, where the images take on meaning from the story, rather than simply serving as "window dressing" for a rhetorical communication.

Images and Beliefs

Narrative persuasion requires measurable correspondence between the constituent images and story line, on the one hand, and recipients' beliefs and opinions, on the other. In *Murder*, there is a clear relationship between the representation of a dangerous psychiatric patient strolling off the grounds of a mental hospital and the belief that security at institutions for the criminally insane should be increased. The image therefore supports beliefs about protecting society from harm.

Some narratives include protagonists who advocate for certain positions and policies; in other narratives there is no explicit advocacy. Explicit advocacy is not a requirement of narratives that may be persuasive. However, in order to test the persuasive effectiveness of any narrative it must be possible to identify beliefs that are implicated for most recipients. These beliefs may be particular (e.g., "Psychiatric patients should not be given furloughs") or general (e.g., "The world is unjust"). Empirically, the relevance of particular beliefs to a narrative may be verified by asking a subset of participants to evaluate the relevance of each belief to the narrative.

> Postulate II. Narrative persuasion (belief change) occurs, *other things equal*, to the extent that the evoked images are activated by psychological *transportation*.

Images may be activated by a person's powerful experience with a narrative account, that person's "transportation."[4] In the Transportation-Imagery Model, a narrative account induces in *some recipients* a powerful experience of "transportation." Constituents of the narrative, chiefly its evoked scenes, then take on new meaning as a result of their links with the experience of entering the narrative world. A prior belief can be changed by an imagery-driven juxtaposition with new information. Thus, the beliefs of the recipients may be affected to the extent that there has been a powerful transportation experience.

This perspective makes clear that separate, isolated presentation of images—apart from their role in a focal story—would be unlikely to endow those images with sufficient power to affect corresponding beliefs. The belief-affecting power of images stems from their association with the experience of "transportation" into a specific narrative. No picture "is worth a thousand words" if it fails to prompt a poignant narrative account.

Transportation

To this point we have not formally defined *transportation*, but we have repeatedly suggested that it is a process that is differentially influenced by reader, text, and context attributes (discussed in Postulates III, IV, and V). Here, we define the construct *transportation* in terms of its conceptual antecedents and its role in recent empirical research as a measured and manipulated variable. In our usage, transportation is not confined to the reading of written material. The term "reader" may be broadly construed to include listeners or viewers or *any recipient* of narrative information.

Transportation into a narrative world is conceptualized as a distinct mental process, which may mediate the impact of narratives on beliefs. In the words of Kenneth Burke (1950, p. 58), "A yielding to the form prepares for assent to the matter identified with it." Individuals are swept away by a story, and thus come to believe in ideas suggested by the narrative.

Our conceptualization of transportation is based on a metaphor used by Gerrig (1993). He described transportation as follows:

> Someone ("the traveler") is transported, by some means of transportation, as a result of performing certain actions. The traveler goes some distance from his or her world of origin, which makes some aspects of the world of origin inaccessible. The traveler returns to the world of origin, somewhat changed by the journey. (pp. 10–11)

Gerrig uses the literal experience of traveling to explain the processes that occur when a reader encounters a text. The feeling of being "lost" in a story is familiar to many people; one of the challenges of our research was to specify the components and consequences of this experience.

Following Gerrig, we conceived of transportation as a convergent process, where all of the person's mental systems and capacities become focused on the events occurring in the narrative. As the above quotation suggests, the reader must perform some action in order to be transported. At a minimum, the reader must pay attention to the text (the "means of transportation"). The extent to which the transportation experience is under conscious and/or strategic control, however, remains to be investigated.

Empirical Assessment of Transportation

We have created a conceptually-grounded paper and pencil scale (Green, 1996; Green & Brock, 2000) to assess the extent of individuals' experience of being transported into narratives. This scale has a cognitive component (example item: "While I was reading the narrative, activity going on in the room around me was on my mind" [reverse-scored]), an emotional component ("The story affected me emotionally"), and an imagery component ("While reading, I had a vivid mental image of [character]").[5] The transportation scale has shown good internal reliability, as well as convergent and divergent validity (see Green, 1996; Green & Brock, 2000 for details). Use of the scale allows us to distinguish between individuals who were more or less transported into a particular story, and mean levels of transportation can also be used to rate the quality of stories: some tales instigate more immersion than others.

Consequences of Transportation. According to Gerrig, there are several important consequences of transportation. The first, as mentioned in the quotation earlier, is that parts of the world of origin become inaccessible. In other words, the reader loses access to some real world facts in favor of accepting the narrative world that the author has created. This loss of access may occur on a physical level—a person transported by a story may not notice others entering or leaving the room, for example. More important, however, is the psychological distance from reality. While the person is immersed in the story, she may not be thinking of real-world facts that contradict the assertions made in the narrative.

Although not included in Gerrig's description of transportation, we also believe that a loss of public self-awareness (e.g., Duval & Wicklund, 1972) may accompany a transportation experience. In leaving the real world behind, individuals leave their worries and public self-consciousness behind as well. (The uses and gratifications literature in communication provides further discussion of readers' and viewers' motivations; see, for example, Rubin, 1986.) This aspect of transportation may prove critical in explaining individuals' motivation to seek transporting experiences; entering a narrative world may be a release from the stress of personal concerns, problems, and contexts that elicit social anxiety.

An important additional outcome is that, on returning from being transported, people are somewhat changed by the experience. At a minimum, individuals are changed by having a memory of what they read; evidence suggests, however, that the changes may be more profound, including belief change. Further consequences of being transported may include a feeling of suspense or other emotional responses. Gerrig referred to one aspect of this emotional reactivity as the "paradox of fiction" (p. 185); people may exhibit strong affective responses, but generally will not show the types of behavioral changes that would occur if those emotions had corresponded to actual events. In other words, a person reading *Murder* might become agitated when reading about the killer attacking Katie, but would not rush to the phone to call the police (see Walton, 1978).

Related Concepts. Other concepts in the literature appear phenomenologically related to the experience of a transported reader. In particular, flow, trait absorption, and Epstein's experiential mode of processing share qualities with transportation.

Flow. Csikszentmihalyi has examined optimal experience, or "flow" (e.g., 1990). Optimal experiences are considered to be ends in themselves; they may involve the loss of a sense of time as well as the disappearance of self-consciousness. "The person's attention is completely absorbed by the activity ... [individuals] stop being aware of themselves as separate from the actions they are performing" (p. 53). The phenomenological experience of flow seems highly similar to that of transportation. In fact, reading is a common means of achieving flow (Csikszentmihalyi, 1982). We propose that transportation, because of the specific interaction between person and text, may have effects that cannot be predicted from the general flow theory (e.g., belief change).

One important component of flow is the match between challenges and skills. Extended to transportation, this suggests that if a text is too simple or too difficult, transportation will not occur. Explorations of the effect of text difficulty or simplicity may eventually become important in the exploration of the qualities of transportation.

The concept of flow also suggests that the experience of transportation is one that would be rewarding and pleasurable to individuals. Just as people may arrange their lives to experience flow, individuals may seek out narratives that transport them to other worlds. People plan for and protect experiences in which they expect to be transported. For example, romance readers buy books that will allow them to escape to another place and/or time and they protect settings in which they can enjoy these books (Radway, 1984).

Absorption. A second concept related to both transportation and flow is absorption, particularly as formalized by Tellegen (1982). Tellegen's Absorption Scale has been influential in predicting hypnotic susceptibility. Absorption is defined as a dispositional characteristic, a tendency to "enter under conducive circumstances psychological states that are characterized by marked restructuring of the self and the phenomenal world" (1982, p. 1). Empirically, transportation shows a moderate positive correlation with absorption (p. 20; see Green, 1996). Transportation specifies a particular circumstance (a state) under which some people might, to use Tellegen's terminology, experience changes in the phenomenal field and the boundaries of the experienced self. Specifically, during a transportation experience, the phenomenal field may become the story-world rather than the physical reality surrounding the individual. The person may lose awareness of the self as a distinct entity. Instead of focusing on one's own identity, the reader may "become" the story characters, or feel as if she is experiencing narrative events.

Experiential Mode. Finally, transportation bears some similarity to the experiential mode of Epstein's cognitive-experiential self theory (CEST; 1990). The experiential system relies on emotions and encodes reality in terms of concrete images, both of which are characteristic of a transported reader. The experiential system also emphasizes a holistic approach to information processing, rather than an analytical one; this distinction echoes the differences between transportation and elaboration. However, there are also conceptual differences between transportation and the experiential mode. The experiential system is designed to "assess events rapidly and promote immediate decisive action" (p. 168); in contrast, a transported reader may linger over the experience, and is not necessarily moved to any particular action. Furthermore, the experiential system is proposed to operate in the background of mental experience, whereas transportation is consciously experienced and absorbs much of one's mental capacity.

Although the phenomenological characteristics of transportation resemble flow, experiential processing, and absorption, the specificity of transportation, particularly its link with imagery, makes it particularly useful for predicting impact of narratives.

> Postulate III. Propensity for transportation by exposure to a given narrative account is affected by attributes of the recipient. Among these moderating attributes is imagery skill.

Imagery and Absorption Aptitudes

Ability to create vivid images and to experience absorption are two conceptually distinct capabilities that may function multiplicatively to facilitate transportation. In the rare instance where either of these capabilities is set to zero, felt transportation may not occur. Thus, transportation, although a measure of state, not ability, may derive its force from most recipients' general ability to create vivid images (e.g., Betts Questionnaire Upon Mental Imagery, QUMI, Sheehan, 1967; Sheehan & McConkey, 1982). Although imagery ability differences may produce some variance in transportation, the above research suggests that even persons with generally low imagery propensity may experience images in response to an especially vivid description in a narrative. A correlated skill or tendency may be the ability to immerse oneself and become fully involved in various experiences (Tellegen, 1982; Tellegen & Atkinson, 1974). Our transportation scale includes items assessing immediate experiences of imagery and absorption.

> Postulate IV. Propensity for transportation by exposure to a given narrative account is affected by attributes of the text (script). Among these moderating attributes are the level of artistic craftsmanship and the extent of adherence to narrative format. Another conceivable moderator, whether the text is labeled as fact or fiction (as true or not necessarily true), does not limit transportation.

Artistry

Every reader, every movie-goer, knows from direct experience that fictional narratives can vary in quality. We stop reading bad books; we walk out of boring movies. On the other hand, some books and movies are so enjoyable that we look forward to returning to them—to finish reading a book, to seeing a film a second time. There is no doubt that the artistic craftsmanship of the book or film has some responsibility for enormous differences in reader (viewer) appreciation. Accordingly, we expect that craftsmanship should directly affect amount of transportation and, hence, persuasive impact. Unfortunately, we know of no direct empirical evidence. There are no studies in which craftsmanship has been empirically varied or in which highly regarded narrative persuasion is directly compared with strong rhetorical persuasion. However, we have observed striking differences in self-ratings of transportation in response to texts that differed widely in how well their artistic merit had been acclaimed (Green & Brock, 2000). For example, readers regularly reported greater transportation into *Murder*, a powerful narrative taken from a bestseller, than into "The Kidnapping," a less-vivid story created by researchers (Gerrig & Prentice, 1991) for experimental, rather than literary, purposes. Of course, neglect of the study of the impact of high versus low quality *narratives* on beliefs stands in contrast to the wide use of strong versus weak messages in the study of *rhetorical* persuasion (e.g., Petty & Cacioppo, 1986).

Adherence to Narrative Format

A minimum requirement of high craftsmanship involves structuring the narrative appropriately. For instance, suspense of some kind is the engine of narration: We wonder how a story will turn out and/or how the events lead to a particular story ending. We may experience tension due to our concern over the fate of a well-liked protagonist. Without this suspenseful adherence to story format, opportunity for transportation may be diminished (Radway, 1991). People appear to protect the enjoyment of narrative formats by not wanting to know the "ending" of a movie or how a book "turns out." Reviewers of books and movies comply to protect the story format: They routinely omit describing the sometimes surprising endgames.

Although it is certainly true that books and movies are revisited, we believe high levels of artistry are necessary to assure that the original magnitudes of transportation will be re-elicited (see footnote 3). Books (e.g., *Uncle Tom's Cabin*) have enduring effects on beliefs because their powerful images continued to function as persistent "arguments" in favor of a particular policy (e.g., abolish slavery).

Fiction Versus Nonfiction

Narratives can be actually true or not true, or simply labeled as fiction or nonfiction. To what extent the power of a narrative is affected by being considered (labeled) true or not true is an important empirical issue. Although it is clear that rhetorical-persuasion suffers from being labeled beforehand as false or untrue (Eagly & Chaiken, 1993), narrative persuasion often is not discounted even when it is explicitly labeled as fiction. We found that labeling *Murder* as fiction versus nonfiction did not affect transportation, critical scrutiny, or attitude change; perceived verisimilitude appeared to override the fiction label (Green & Brock, 2000).

One possible hypothesis is that narrative persuasion, but not rhetorical persuasion, survives being labeled as potentially false because it is responded to with the expectation of entertainment: Critical scrutiny may be reduced or completely precluded by an ensuing transportation experience. Even in the case of rhetorical persuasion, however, "fiction" appears not to be equated with "false." Investigations of the fiction/nonfiction label in a nonnarrative context (Garst, Green, & Brock, 2001) showed that individuals were equally persuaded by a speech that was alleged to be fictional as one that was alleged to be factual (see also Strange & Leung, 1999). It appears that individuals are accustomed to gaining useful information from fiction, and that a fiction label alone—in contrast to "false" label—is insufficient to inspire discounting of the communication. Authors may base their made-up characters on real situations; fiction is often a mix of truth and imagination. Individuals seem to approach fiction with a plausibility criterion in mind—if the information seems reasonable, it appears to have an impact equal to information labeled as fact.

Clearly, there may be limiting conditions to fiction's power. For example, Gerrig & Prentice (1991) differentiated between context-free assertions and context details, and provide evidence that people are more affected by the context-free assertions. Individuals might change their belief about politicians after reading about a fictional government (which might include a context-free assertion or implication that legislators are trustworthy, for example), but they rarely become confused about the identity of the current President (a context detail that might be changed in a fictional world). Additionally, when the fiction label explicitly included statements that the author did not have accurate knowledge about the events he narrated, individuals did not show equivalent belief change in response to fact versus fiction (Strange, 1993; Strange, chap. 11, this volume).

> Postulate V. Propensity for transportation by exposure to a given narrative account is affected by attributes of the context (medium). Among these moderating attributes may be aspects of the medium that limit opportunity for imaginative investment and participatory responses.

Investment in imagery is the extent to which a recipient deploys cognitive and perceptual resources in order to contribute to imagery. Sometimes such investment is externally limited. For example, filmed narratives, because they are typically concrete, complete, and fast-flowing, appear to constrain imaginative investment in comparison with print narratives. In the latter modality, imagination is encouraged, if not required, because imagery is suggested rather than rendered in complete detail. Furthermore, as we note later, film does not ordinarily allow time for the formation and relishing of images, at least, not to the same extent as does text.

On the other hand, Gerrig and Prentice (1996) suggested that some forms of *participatory responses*, or p-responses (see Polichak & Gerrig, chap. 4, this volume), are more often evoked by film. Allbritton and Gerrig defined p-responses as activities such as "thoughts about characters, expressions of preferences about events, or reflections on the broader implications of the story" (1991, p. 604). In one type of p-response, viewers may respond as if the events in the narrative were actually taking place. Gerrig and Prentice (1996) stated that "formal properties of film—and particularly, the ability of film to fix the focus of attention—make it especially likely that such *as if* responses will occur...even more than in the experience of texts—individuals are likely to lose track of the fact that they can't really participate" (p. 2, p. 9). To the extent that p-responses and role-playing responses are psychologically equivalent commitments, p-responses may contribute to attitude change. Both types of responses may involve active behavioral commitment with corresponding impact on beliefs (Kiesler, 1971).

Pacing is defined here as the ability of the recipient to control the duration of her tracking of story elements. In the case of reading, pacing is maximized: both text exposure and response to the text are normally under the reader's temporal control. A reader can slow down and savor particular scenes, or race ahead in the text. In the case of film, it is sometimes possible but unusual for a recipient to "pause" at particular scenes (e.g., when using a home VCR or DVD player).

Self-pacing would appear to encourage transportation because the recipient can contribute to the development of powerful images and there is unlimited opportunity for participatory response. Thus, overall, reading is more likely to instigate transportation than film-viewing. Consequently, to the extent that transportation causes narrative persuasion, books, more than films, are likely to have enduring impact on beliefs.

COMPARISON OF NARRATIVE PERSUASION (TRANSPORTATION-IMAGERY MODEL) WITH RHETORICAL PERSUASION (ELABORATION LIKELIHOOD MODEL)

It may be informative to compare the Transportation-Imagery Model of narrative persuasion with a well-known model for rhetorical persuasion

(Elaboration Likelihood Model, ELM, Petty & Cacioppo, 1986). If we take ELM as a proxy for current well-developed persuasion theories, and if ELM cannot encompass narrative persuasion, then there is additional justification for proffering a new theory, the present Transportation-Imagery Model.

Domain Differences

Inspection of the standard graduate-level textbook (Eagly & Chaiken, 1993) on the psychology of attitudes revealed negligible attention to narrative-based persuasion: there were no studies of participants who read or heard a fictional story in which no conclusion or policy was advocated (but see Slater, chap. 7, this volume). The ELM, like earlier well-known attitude change models (Hovland, Janis, & Kelley, 1953), addresses the processing of argument-containing messages. Nevertheless, although the ELM and our model pertain to different domains—argument-containing messages versus image-bearing stories—it is still possible that, with minor and reasonable conceptual translations of key constructs, the ELM could encompass the latter domain as well as the former.

Theoretical Divergences

Personal Relevance of the Communication. According to the Elaboration Likelihood Model, the most important variable affecting the motivation to process a persuasive message is the personal relevance of the advocacy (Petty & Cacioppo, 1986, p. 81). We use personal relevance to mean that the advocacy is about the recipient's outcomes (her own taxes, say) or important opinion-issues (abortion choice). Research in the ELM tradition has consistently shown that as personal relevance of a message increases people become more likely to appreciate the strength of cogent arguments and the flaws in specious ones (Petty & Cacioppo, 1986, p. 87). In line with this reasoning, Prentice, Gerrig, and Bailis (1997) proposed an analogous prediction for fictional narratives in which protagonists make weakly supported assertions (e.g., "Eating chocolate helps you lose weight"). They proposed that narratives occurring in a familiar setting would be considered more personally relevant and therefore would receive more cognitive scrutiny than narratives occurring in an unfamiliar setting. Consequently, the weakly supported assertions would have less impact in the personally more relevant condition (familiar setting). Although Prentice et al. obtained support for this prediction in one of their two experiments, three exact replications failed to reproduce their proposed personal relevance effect (Wheeler, Green, & Brock,

1999). In Wheeler, Green, & Brock (1999), weakly supported assertions affected beliefs just as strongly regardless of the familiarity (personal relevance) of the narrative setting.

In a general consideration of fictional narratives that have been considered powerful (e.g., the parables of Jesus) we found no dearth of narratives that achieved verisimilitude by exploiting familiar settings, familiar personages, and familiar events. Where image-bearing stories are concerned, transportation, and consequent belief change, appeared no less likely for personally relevant than for personally irrelevant story contexts. Indeed, the capable writer (e.g., John Steinbeck) takes the reader just as compellingly into another world (e.g., *The Pearl*) as he does into a back alley of his hometown (e.g., *Tortilla Flat*).

We further note that the traditional persuasion literature has espoused a relatively narrow definition of personal relevance (for example, the outcome relevance typically used in experimental manipulations). It is possible that the skill of the writer may make a story seem relevant to the transported reader, although the topic itself has no objective personal relevance to the real life of the reader.

In summary, the ELM and our model make different predictions with respect to a key determinant of the effect of a communication on belief change. The ELM, in contrast to our model, limits intensive processing to personally relevant communications (all else being equal).

Inherent Value of Critical Elements and Their Order of Presentation in the Communication: Arguments Compared to Images. In rhetoric-based persuasion, messages consist of arguments; in narrative-based persuasion, stories feature images. Of course, arguments are not the same as images, but we can ask if "argument" and "image" may be interchangeable in their functional impact on beliefs. If so, then an extension of ELM might suffice to encompass narrative-based persuasion.

Unfortunately, the status of image and argument appear to be too disparate to allow such an extension. Arguments can stand alone and can be assessed for their inherent strength or weakness, whereas images derive their strength and power from their evocation of story events. Consider two arguments on behalf of implementing senior comprehensive exams, a commonly used advocacy (Petty & Cacioppo, 1986, p. 54 ff): (a) "The results of a study by the National Scholarship Achievement Board showed that since the comprehensive exam has been introduced at Duke, the grade point average of undergraduates has been increased by 31%"; and (b) "Graduate students have always had to take a comprehensive exam in their major area before receiving their degrees, and it is only fair that undergraduates should have to take them also." The first argument was empirically established as strong, and the second as weak, by measuring students' reactions. Just as important, these arguments lose or gain no power by standing alone, and their order of presentation is immaterial to the effectiveness of any otherwise-equivalent messages in which they appear as constituents.

Next, consider two images from *Murder*, two representations that support limiting the furloughs of psychiatric patients: "People were scattering in all directions, trying to get away from a large, disheveled man who stood over a fallen little girl, his outstretched right arm pummeling furiously away at her"; and "The child's head and neck were covered with blood and her face was soaked in it, but her eyes were clear. She was gazing at me and beyond me." Both images are quite moving in the context of the story, but they have reduced strength as isolated representations. More important, their order of presentation cannot be altered without detracting from the story's impact: the pummeling image must precede the image of the bloody head and neck. The images acquired particular intensity because of their role in the *Murder* story; whether they caused corresponding belief changes in readers is hypothesized to be a function of the extent of transportation experienced by those readers.

In summary, although attitude change is driven by message arguments in rhetorical persuasion and by imagery in narrative persuasion, we consider the psychological statuses of "argument" and "image" to be too disparate to accommodate functional interchangeability.

Individual-Difference Determinants of Belief Change: Need for Cognition Versus Imagery/Absorption Propensity and Transportedness. We now compare the roles of Need for Cognition (Cacioppo & Petty, 1982; Cacioppo, Petty, Feinstein, & Jarvis, 1996) in rhetoric-based persuasion with the roles of imagery ability and transportedness in narrative-based persuasion. In rhetorical persuasion, individuals low in need cognition (LNC) think less about persuasive communications than individuals high in need for cognition (HNC); in addition, people who tend to enjoy thinking (HNC) show greater differentiation of strong and weak arguments than people who do not characteristically enjoy thinking (LNC). In this fashion, individual differences in need for cognition have been found to affect message processing and susceptibility to rhetorical persuasion (Cacioppo, Petty, Feinstein, & Jarvis, 1996).

The Transportation-Imagery Model of narrative persuasion identified two individual-difference variables (Postulate III) that may moderate extent of transportation: imagery ability (Sheehan, 1967) and absorption propensity (Tellegen & Atkinson, 1974). As the previous section made clear, it is not helpful to conceive of evoked images as independently strong or weak; rather, their intensity and enduring force is theorized to stem from the extent of experienced transportation. Thus, instead of marking stories as "strong" or "weak," our model scores stories on a continuum of transportingness. The transportation scale (described previously) is a reader's overall evaluation of the magnitude of her transportation experience with a particular story.

In the current model, stories can vary from high to low in transportingness; an *a priori* classification is feasible. Imagery ability and absorption propensity should have straightforward moderating effects such that narrative-based persuasion may be a joint function of text transportingness (high vs. low) and individual differences in the propensity to engage in imagery and experience absorption.

Empirical work is needed to verify the above derivations and to show what role, if any, is played by other individual difference factors such as Need for Cognition (Cacioppo & Petty, 1982) and intelligence. To the extent that narrative-based persuasion is found to be moderated by imagery/absorption rather than Need for Cognition (and/or intelligence), further justification is adduced for a separate model.[6] In fact, our studies have indicated that Need for Cognition does not moderate attitude change in response to narratives (Green & Brock, 2000).

Selected Research Implications

A number of interesting research questions arise from the Transportation-Imagery Model (in addition to those already mentioned in the previous sections).

Transportation Effects Upon Cognitive Processing of Narratives (Pinocchio Circling). Transportation appears to have an effect on the willingness of the reader to accept the story as authentic. The traditional means of assessing acceptance of a rhetorical passage is through the use of cognitive responses (Petty, Ostrom, & Brock, 1981). In our studies (Green & Brock, 2000), however, thought listings did not seem to provide a sensitive measure of unfavorable responses to narratives. To address this concern, we created a new measure of story acceptance/rejection called "Pinocchio circling." After reading a narrative and filling out dependent measures, participants were instructed to go back over the story and circle any "false notes," or parts of the story that did not ring true to them. False notes were described as something in the story that contradicts a fact or does not make sense. The instructions explained that sometimes authors leave clues when they are being untruthful, just as Pinocchio's nose grew after he told a lie. For narrative communication, "false-noting" may be roughly analogous to counterarguing for rhetorical communication.

We hypothesized that participants who were more transported into the story would be less likely to find false notes in the story; they would be less critical of the story. If highly-transported participants showed less false-noting, this finding would be supportive of the idea that transportation is correlated with reduced critical thinking and counterarguing.

Results using this measure supported our theorizing; for example, in a study using *Murder*, highly transported participants circled significantly fewer false notes than their less-transported counterparts. In summary, Pinocchio scoring has proved to be a meaningful and sensitive measure of cognitive processing of narrative texts.

Story Quality (Strength). To study rhetorical persuasion it has been found useful to design experiments in which recipients process messages that contain strong as compared to weak arguments (Petty & Cacioppo, 1986). The strong/weak manipulation allowed investigators to infer how much cognitive effort was applied to processing the messages. Strong messages became more persuasive with effortful processing and weak messages became less persuasive.

Previously, we proposed that narratives be scored, not for argument merit, but for transportingness. We earlier described several narratives in which we found wide differences in average self-reported transportedness. However, to date, there has been no research in which readers were exposed to narratives that differed solely in text quality (analogously to the strong vs. weak message designs in rhetorical persuasion). The transportation-imagery model proposes that, other things equal, high transporting narratives should be more influential than low transporting narratives.

Interesting research issues concern the extent to which acclaimed stories (from the canon, say) can be altered (image order changed and/or images omitted; plot altered) before decrement in transportation is observed. From an individual-differences perspective, do people high in imagery/absorption propensity overlook intruded flaws, gaps, and gibberish, or, conversely, are they, analogously to high need cognition people, especially sensitive to story irregularities? In summary, to what extent can fictional narrative be "lousy" and still effective? Do readers (viewers) appear to cut more (or less) slack to narrative than to rhetorical communications? These questions require research designs in which readers process high and low transporting versions of the same story and in which it is possible to directly compare narrative and rhetorical versions of the same advocacy. The work to develop such story materials has just begun.

Impact of Attributes of Story Images: Intensity and Load. Intense images have the following attributes in response to a verbal prompt: speed of formation, physiological reactivity, and interference with other tasks. Thus, for example, readers of *Murder* who formed intense images would be less able to visually process neutral photos of a mall ("count the number of pedestrians," say) than readers who had formed less intense images. Conceptually, intense imagery functions as a cognitive "load" that can interfere with cognate tasks. See Dadds et al. (1997).

Intense images should be slower to extinguish than less intense images. Thus, readers of *Murder* who formed intense images would be less likely to return to pre-*Murder* beliefs (e.g., "Malls are generally safe") as a result of reading further counterpropaganda, an essay on "Malls are Basically Safe."

Intense images affect mood when the image-bearing story must be processed again. If readers of *Murder* were asked to read it again, we predict that previously high transported readers, in comparison to low transported readers, would show measurable mood alteration (negative change) at the prospect of rereading *Murder*.

In summary, our theory suggests that high transported recipients, in comparison to less transported recipients, should show, in addition to heightened attitude change, an inability to process a cognate problem (count the number of persons in this photo of a mall, for *Murder* readers), slower reversion to prenarrative beliefs after reading counterpropaganda ("Malls are Basically Safe" for *Murder* readers), and measurable mood change when asked to anticipate reading the focal narrative a second time.

Attitude Change Persistence. It is an open empirical question whether narrative persuasion is more effective than rhetorical persuasion. Unconfounded tests to answer this question are not yet available in the literature. We claim that when pure tests are conducted, narrative persuasion, in comparison to rhetorical persuasion, will lead to belief changes that resist counterinfluence and that persist longer over time. This claim stems from consideration of the psychological intensity and invulnerability to decay that images attain in comparison to the limited power and susceptibility to counterargument of verbal arguments.

Consider the following strong argument on behalf of implementing senior comprehensive exams (Petty & Cacioppo, 1986, p. 54):

> The National Scholarship Achievement Board recently revealed the results of a five-year study conducted on the effectiveness of comprehensive exams at Duke University. The results of the study showed that since the comprehensive exam has been introduced at Duke, the grade point average of undergraduates has been increased by 31%. At comparable schools without the exams, grades increased by only 8% over the same period. The prospect of a comprehensive exam clearly seems to be effective.

Readers of the above strong argument listed mostly favorable thoughts and to the extent that they did so they lowered their initial opposition to comprehensive exams for graduating seniors.

13. TRANSPORTATION-IMAGERY MODEL 337

Next consider the following representation on behalf of limiting the furloughs of psychiatric patients (from *Murder*):

People were scattering in all directions, trying to get away from a large, disheveled man who stood over a fallen little girl, his outstretched right arm pummeling furiously away at her. Even through the haze of her frozen incomprehension, Joan knew instantly that the child lying on her side at the crazed man's feet was Katie. At first, she saw only the arm, then realized all at once that in its hand was clutched a long bloody object. It was a hunting knife, about seven inches long.

Using all his strength, up and down, up and down, in rapid pistonlike motions, the assailant was hacking away at Katie's face and neck.

Transported readers of *Murder* found the above image of Katie quite moving and clearly supportive of limiting the furloughs of psychiatric patients.

Our claim that narrative persuasion leads to more attitude change persistence than rhetorical persuasion is based in part on differential susceptibility to countervailing influence. It is relatively easy to imagine evidence, counterargumentation, that could weaken and/or discredit the comprehensive exam argument above. For example, other studies might fail to show the GPA increase attributable to comprehensive exams. It is relatively more difficult to imagine material, images or arguments, that could weaken the above Katie image for readers of *Murder*. The Katie death image appears largely invulnerable to discounting and diminution. The intensity of the image is conferred by its role in a well-written narrative that is highly transporting for many readers.

The narrative/rhetorical superiority claim is further based on our speculation that a story image, more than a rhetorical argument, can re-invoke the original communication for a recipient. Because the story image occurred in a natural concatenation of events, the other events and their representations become salient when a particular integral image is prompted. Thus, prompted by the above Katie death image, readers readily bring to mind the preceding and following mall events involving first a happy outing of a girl, then a crazed patient's knife attack and finally the patient's capture and identification. However, prompted by restatement of the Duke University argument, it appears less likely that readers can summon other arguments that were initially associated with it: Professional schools prefer exam takers; Ivy League colleges use such exams to sustain their excellence; etc. (Petty & Cacioppo, 1986, pp. 54–56). In summary, in narrative persuasion a part (a central image) can restore the whole, much like a bar or two from familiar music; in rhetorical persuasion, such part/whole implication is less likely.

In summary, the functional autonomy of images and their ability to serve as prompts for the entire message in which they occurred would appear to provide narrative persuasion with superior effectiveness in comparison with persuasion that relies on arguments (rhetorical persuasion). An important advantage may be to confer greater persistence on induced belief changes.

CONCLUSION

Although our research has begun to investigate key issues in narrative persuasion, there is still a long road ahead.[7] For example, here are a number of interesting questions that can be better addressed to the extent that the mechanisms underlying narrative persuasion are better understood. What is the role of "seeking entertainment" in the normal experience of narrative fiction? Is the extreme addiction-like devotion of some romance readers understandable in terms of "normal experience of narrative fiction?" When and how are narratives really dangerous; what are the justified targets of censorship? How does media fiction contribute to antisocial lifestyles? If rational judgment and objective understanding are jeopardized by exposure to narratives, how can the "intelligent layperson" nonetheless cope with the pervasiveness of stories and their impact?

The transportation-imagery model organizes our thinking about these questions. It highlights the importance of the phenomenological experience of entering into a narrative world, and the key role of images in fostering belief change.

ENDNOTES

[1]The present theory assumes primacy of visual imagery; we therefore exploit the reader's immediate, intuitive understanding of what is meant by visual imagery. Other modalities of imaging (e.g., olfactory, kinesthetic), are not considered here. Although our model underscores the role of visual imagery in driving persuasion, it does not claim that imagery is always necessary nor does it assign to imagery sovereignty over memories, cognitive associations, or other mental representations. Certain story understanding models (van Dijk & Kintsch, 1983; Zwann, Langston & Graesser, 1995) do not exclude imagery, but in these other models, imagery is not assigned the same central role. Indeed, some scholars (e.g., Zwann & van Oostendorp, 1993) have concluded that visual representation plays a negligible role in naturalistic reading situations. Whether imagery is both central and necessary to narrative persuasion are important issues whose empirical investigation is fostered by our theory.

[2]Birdoff (1947, p. 406). Because of the scale and rapidity of *Uncle Tom*'s success, and the variety of forms in which it was produced, the narrative proliferated throughout the United States, Europe and South America; it became the principal tract of abolition in Brazil (Wood, 2000, p. 146). The industries that capitalized on *Uncle Tom* imagery included stationery, clothing, food, puzzles, wallpaper, figurines, and board games (Wood, 2000, pp.146–147). The theater impact was universal.

Every inhabitant of the United States was offered a performance of *Uncle Tom* for 90 years. *Tom* troupes "traveled along every tank-water line and gave it at every whistlestop ... setting up improvised stages in prairie way-stations, in the fraternal halls, in livery stables, in dining-rooms, in courthouses....Not a year passed that elaborate revivals weren't usurping the boards in the large cities, while a score of *Tom* companies carried the folk play to the provinces. Abroad it was produced from Czechoslovakia to Polynesia" (Birdoff, 1947, p. 6, p. 8).

Uncle Tom changed the format of American theater (Birdoff, 1947, p. 9, p. 53). Among the imagery-based innovations were post-performance tableaux. "As the curtain descended the characters held their positions for a minute *frozen*—congealing them in the memory. When Legree raised his whip to strike Tom, he stood over him for a full sixty seconds" (pp. 80–81). Tableaux were among the many innovations whereby *Uncle Tom* audiences were supplied with rich "take-home" imagery.

[3]Narrative format is variously implemented (Surmelian, 1969). For example, in a crime story, a good detective writer might reveal the perpetrator at the end of the story, whereas a journalistic (less narrative) account of the crime might identify the perpetrator in the very first paragraph.

[4]Empirical research has not addressed repeated exposures to the same narratives. Our hunch is that transportation recurs and, indeed, that the re-experience of transportation is a particularly strong incentive to revisit certain narratives.

[5]Our research (Green & Brock, 2000) shows that when imagery, one of the three components of the transportation scale, is statistically excluded, the ability of transportation to predict narrative persuasion is thereby reduced.

[6]While the well-known ELM focuses on a small set of independent variables (strong vs. weak messages), classic persuasion models also deal with stylistic features of rhetoric that are thought to influence persuasion; parallel construction, climax, ellipsis, etc. In this chapter, we have used the ELM as the principal comparison foil because it specifies well-known psychological mechanisms.

[7]Although this chapter drew heavily on our empirical research, it has omitted technical considerations that should be heeded by future investigators of narrative persuasion. For example, the experimental narrative must be transporting enough to engender a range of felt transportation; the narrative must influence beliefs more than in a no-message baseline condition; and interventions aimed at affecting magnitude of transportation must sustain comprehension of the narrative text. For further technical requirements see Green and Brock (2000).

REFERENCES

Allbritton, D. W., & Gerrig, R. J. (1991). Participatory responses in text understanding. *Journal of Memory and Language, 30*, 603–626.
Birdoff, H. (1947). *The world's greatest hit.* New York: S.F.Vanni.
Bruner, J. (1986). *Actual minds, possible worlds.* Cambridge, MA: Harvard University Press.
Burke, K. (1950). *A rhetoric of motives.* New York: Prentice-Hall.
Cacioppo, J. T., & Petty, R. E. (1982). The need for cognition. *Journal of Personality and Social Psychology, 42*, 116–131.
Cacioppo, J. T., Petty, R. E., Feinstein, J. A., & Jarvis, B. W. G. (1996). Dispositional differences in cognitive motivation: The life and times of individuals varying in need for cognition. *Psychological Bulletin, 119*(2), 197–253.

Coles, R. (1987). The humanities in postgraduate training. *Journal of the American Medical Association, 257,* 1644.
Csikszentmihalyi, M. (1982). Toward a psychology of optimal experience. In L. Wheeler (Ed.), *Review of Personality and Social Psychology, 3* (pp. 13–36). Beverly Hills, CA: Sage.
Csikszentmihalyi, M. (1990). *Flow: The psychology of optimal experience.* New York: Harper & Row.
Dadds, M. R., Bovbjerg, D. H., Redd, W. H, & Cutmore, T. R. H. (1997). Imagery in human classical conditioning. *Psychological Bulletin, 127,* 89–103.
Deighton, J., Romer, D., & McQueen, J. (1989). Using drama to persuade. *Journal of Consumer Research, 16,* 335–343.
Duval, S., & Wicklund, R. (1972). *A theory of objective self-awareness.* New York: Academic Press.
Eagly, A., & Chaiken, S. (1993). *The psychology of attitudes.* Fort Worth, TX: Harcourt Brace.
Epstein, S. (1990). Cognitive-experiential self-theory. In L. A. Pervin (Ed.), *Handbook of personality: Theory and research* (pp. 165–192). New York: Guilford Press.
Frey, K. P., & Eagly, A. H. (1993). Vividness can undermine the persuasiveness of messages. *Journal of Personality and Social Psychology, 65,* 32–44.
Garst, J., Green, M. C., & Brock, T. C. (2001). Fact and fiction in persuasion: Outcome parity despite fact's processing advantages. Unpublished manuscript, University of Maryland, College Park, MD.
Gass, W. H. (1972). *Fiction and the figures of life.* New York: Vintage.
Gerbner, G., Gross, L., Morgan, M., & Signorelli, S. (1994). Growing up with television: The cultivation perspective. In J. Bryant & D. Zillmann (Eds.), *Media effects: Advances in theory and research* (pp. 17–41). Hillsdale, NJ: Lawrence Erlbaum Associates.
Gerrig, R. J. (1993). *Experiencing narrative worlds.* New Haven, CT: Yale University Press.
Gerrig, R. J., & Prentice, D. A. (1991). The representation of fictional information. *Psychological Science, 2,* 336–340.
Gerrig, R. J., & Prentice, D. A. (1996). Notes on audience response. In D. Bordwell & N. Carroll (Eds.), *Post-theory: Reconstructing film studies* (pp. 388–403). Madison, WI: The University of Wisconsin Press.
Green, M. C. (1996). Mechanisms of narrative-based belief change. Unpublished masters thesis, The Ohio State University, Columbus, OH.
Green, M. C., & Brock, T. C. (2000). The role of transportation in the persuasiveness of public narratives. *Journal of Personality and Social Psychology, 79,* 701–721..
Hovland, C. I., Janis, I. L., & Kelly, H. H. (1953). *Communication and persuasion: Psychological studies of opinion change.* New Haven, CT: Yale University Press.
James, H. (1913). *A small boy and others.* London: MacMillan.
Kiesler, C. A. (1971). *The psychology of commitment: Experiments linking behavior to belief.* San Diego, CA: Academic Press.
Kosslyn, S. M. (1981). The medium and the message in mental imagery: A theory. *Psychological Review, 88,* 46–66.
Lerner, M. J., & Miller, D. T. (1978). Just world research and the attribution process: Looking back and ahead. *Psychological Bulletin, 85*(5), 1030–1051.
Nell, V. (1988). *Lost in a book: The psychology of reading for pleasure.* New Haven, CT: Yale University Press.
Niebuhr, G. (1995, October 30). The newest Christian fiction injects a thrill into theology. *New York Times,* pp. A1, A11.
Nisbett, R. E., & Ross, L. (1980). *Human inference: Strategies and shortcomings of social judgments.* Englewood Cliffs, NJ: Prentice-Hall.

Nuland, S. (1994). *How we die: Murder and serenity* (pp. 118–139). New York: Knopf.
Petty, R. E., & Cacioppo, J. T. (1986). *Communication and persuasion: Classic and contemporary approaches.* Dubuque, IA: Brown.
Petty, R. E., Ostrom, T. M., & Brock, T. C. (Eds.). (1981). *Cognitive responses in persuasion.* Hillsdale, NJ: Lawrence Erlbaum Associates.
Prentice, D. A., Gerrig, R. J., & Bailis, D. S. (1997). What readers bring to the processing of fictional texts. *Psychonomic Bulletin and Review, 4,* 416–420.
Radway, J. A. (1984). *Reading the romance: Women, patriarchy, and popular literature.* Chapel Hill: University of North Carolina Press.
Rubin, A. M. (1986). Uses, gratifications, and media effects research. In J. Bryant & D. Zillman (Eds.), *Perspectives on media effects,* pp. 281–302. Hillsdale, NJ: Lawrence Erlbaum Associates.
Rubin, D. C. (1995). *Memory in oral traditions.* New York: Oxford University Press.
Schank, R. C., & Abelson, R. P. (1995). Knowledge and memory: The real story. In R. S. Wyer (Ed.), *Advances in Social Cognition, (Vol. VIII,* pp. 1–86) Hillsdale, NJ: Lawrence Erlbaum Associates.
Sheehan, P. W. (1967). A shortened form of the Betts' Questionnaire Upon Mental Imagery. *Journal of Clinical Psychology, 23,* 386–389.
Sheehan, P. W., & McConkey, K. M. (1982). *Hypnosis and experience: The exploration of phenomena and process.* Hillsdale, NJ: Lawrence Erlbaum Associates.
Shrum, L. J., Wyer, R. S., & O'Guinn, T. C. (1998). The effects of television consumption on social perceptions: The use of priming procedures to investigate psychological processes. *Journal of Consumer Research, 24*(4), 447–458.
Stowe, H. B. (1852). *Uncle Tom's cabin.* New York: New Era.
Strange. J. J. (1993). The facts of fiction: The accommodation of real-world beliefs to fabricated accounts. (Doctoral dissertation, Columbia University, 1993). *Dissertation Abstracts International,* 54(2-A), 358.
Strange, J. J, & Leung, C. C. (1999). How anecdotal accounts in news and fiction can influence judgments of a social problem's urgency, causes, and cures. *Personality and Social Psychology Bulletin, 25*(4), 436–449.
Surmelian, L. (1969). *Techniques of fiction writing.* Garden City, NY: Anchor Books.
Taylor, S. E., & Thompson, S. C. (1982). Stalking the "elusive" vividness effect. *Psychological Review, 89,* 155–181.
Tellegen, A. (1982). *Brief manual for the Differential Personality Questionnaire.* Unpublished manuscript. University of Minnesota, Minneapolis, MN.
Tellegen, A., & Atkinson, G. (1974). Openness to absorbing and self-altering experiences ("absorption"): A trait related to hypnotic susceptibility. *Journal of Abnormal Psychology, 83,* 268–277.
Van Dijk, T. A., & Kintsch, W. (1983). *Strategies of discourse comprehension.* New York: Academic Press.
Walton, K. L. (1978). Fearing fictions. *Journal of Philosophy, 75*(1), 5–27.
Wheeler, S. C., Green, M. C., & Brock, T. C. (1999). Fictional narratives change beliefs: Replications of Prentice, Gerrig, & Bailis (1997) with mixed corroboration. *Psychonomic Bulletin and Review, 6*(1), 136–141.
Wood, M. (2000). *Blind memory.* New York: Routledge.
Zwaan, R. A., Langston, M. C., & Graesser, A. C. (1995). The construction of situation models in narrative comprehension: An event-indexing model. *Psychological Science, 6,* 292–297.
Zwaan, R. A., & van Oostendorp, H. (1993). Do readers construct spatial representations in naturalistic story comprehension? *Discourse Processes, 16*(1–2), 125–143.

14

Insights and Research Implications

Epilogue to *Narrative Impact*

Timothy C. Brock
The Ohio State University

Melanie C. Green
University of Pennsylvania

Jeffrey J. Strange
Public Insight

The chapters of this volume have provided detailed answers to the 11 questions posed in chapter 1. In this concluding chapter, we delineate some common ground among our contributors to summarize their shared insights and to articulate research implications and continuing problems. We have already underscored the historical impact of public narratives (chap. 1, this volume); here we review what has been learned from our contributors about the underlying mechanisms and factors that foster and that constrain narrative influence.

NARRATIVE IMPACTS AND PROCESSES WITHIN INDIVIDUALS

The broadest outcome claimed for exposure to narratives is to tame the dread that stems from the salience of mortality (Nell, chap. 2, this volume). Nell's taming, or "domestication of immortality," appears to depend on the empirically demonstrable processes of entrancement and immersion (Nell, 1988), processes that are akin to transportation (chap. 13, this volume). These processes, if elicited by narratives that have a universal mythic structure (suffering, death, and rebirth), confer a sense of renewal, of relative safety, and of hope.

Nell's "hope" is not substantively different from the notion that was introduced in the myth of Pandora. Recall that Zeus was angry with Prometheus for stealing fire from the gods. With revenge in mind, Zeus sent Pandora to earth with a box full of evil creatures. Zeus told Pandora not to open the box, yet he knew that her curiosity would soon overwhelm her. As predicted, Pandora eventually opened the lid to look inside. When she did, a swarm of creatures flew out to forever plague humankind: gout, rheumatism, and colic for the body; envy, spite, and revenge for the mind. Only one creature remained in the box when Pandora finally managed to close the lid. That creature was hope, which supposedly makes human cares and troubles seem bearable (Snyder, Sympson, Ybasco, Borders, Babyak, & Higgins, 1996, p. 321).

Without attempting here to demarcate "hopefulness" from kindred concepts such as "positive illusion" (Taylor, Kemeny, Reed, Bower, & Gruenewald, 2000) we may posit that narrative, more than nonnarrative, exposition is likely to foster hopefulness. Furthermore, narrative that embodies mythic structures is likely to engender hopefulness to a greater extent than narratives that do not exploit such structures.[1] Nell's "hopefulness" and his "tranquil death" are universal impacts of narrative that deserve further empirical clarification and consideration for application in therapeutic realms.

Nell (chap. 2, this volume) emphasizes that public narrative's denial of death is an *emotional* mechanism, an emphasis that would be agreed to by Oatley (chap. 3, this volume). Indeed, for Oatley, emotion is the engine of narrative impact. In further agreement with Nell's entrancement (chap. 2, this volume) and with Green & Brock's transportation (chap. 13, this volume), the emotional transformation of the story recipient occurs *elsewhere*, "in the story world." It is noteworthy that in *Hamlet*, Oatley's chief illustrative text, there are multiple "elsewheres," the play and within the play, another play. Like Nell (chap. 2, this volume), Oatley (chap. 3, this volume) emphasized the importance of structure in causing emotional responsiveness in the viewer (reader). The purpose of overlaying structures (event, discourse, and suggestion) is to enable the readers to construct their own accounts and, in so doing, experience their own emotions, rather than those of the protagonists. In essence, structure, once realized in the mind of the reader, fosters own emotion; and own emotion leads to change or reinforcement of identity and be-

14. INSIGHTS AND RESEARCH IMPLICATIONS

liefs. In either case, cognitive transformation has occurred: We cannot be emotionally "moved" by a narrative, and, at the same time, unchanged from our prenarrative self. Thus, in experiencing a range of emotions in response to *Hamlet* we also reconfigure our stands on "great issues of the human predicament" (Oatley, chap. 3, this volume).

Although Oatley's argument utilizes the pinnacle of fictional drama, *Hamlet*, the texts used in his experiments and demonstrations were not part of the literary canon. Indeed, strong emotions can be instigated by lesser texts—by middlebrow and romance reading (DelFattore, chap. 6, this volume; Radway, chap. 8, this volume) and by potboilers like *Uncle Tom* and *Old New Land* (chap. 1, this volume). Oatley's structural configurations can be readily found in nonliterary fiction and so the conditions for eliciting transformational emotional investments are widely encountered, in fiction as well as in nonfiction.

Oatley writes about experiencing sadness, anger, joy, etc., and having these emotions color one's concomitant beliefs and perspectives; he weeps at reading "angels sing thee to thy rest" (*Hamlet*, 5, 2, 367). More generally, he emphasizes that the construction of one's own account from a narrative simulation requires emotional reactivity; but his conceptualization leaves open exactly how this might happen.

Perhaps clarification can come from examining a more *agentic* responsivity to narratives. Polichak & Gerrig (chap. 4, this volume) used the short stories "Sonny Liston Was a Friend of Mine," and "The Pugilist at Rest" to show the important role of side-participation, of participatory responses. The critical connection to narrative impact is in the cause–effect relationship between participatory responses (problem-solving, replotting), on the one hand, and evaluatory responses on the other. "After reading Kid Dynamite's story, with its vivid depictions of the Kid's injuries, the reader might come away less sure that boxing is a reasonable form of entertainment and an appropriate activity for high school students. These insights may influence the reader's later decisions to view the sport" (Polichak & Gerrig, chap. 4, p. 79, this volume). The participatory responses were posited to become part of the recollection of the narrative and, hence, responsible for subsequent evaluation and relevant behavior. The next research step, to further manipulate and measure participatory responses, and, in general, other agentic responses by the recipient, is likely to provide important new insights into the mechanisms of narrative impact. For example, at the movies, loud conversation by other audience members is usually a source of annoyance. However, rudeness notwithstanding, Polichak & Gerrig (chap. 4, this volume) have made the case that such conversation (loud or not loud!)—if it is focused on the film—is normal, natural, and, most importantly, predictive of the focal film's enduring impact. Days later, when film elements are recalled, or when they instigate "remindings" (Schank & Berman, chap. 12, this volume; Strange, chap. 11, this volume), concomitant recollection of participatory responses may affect beliefs and behavior.

The concomitant participatory responses highlighted by Polichak and Gerrig (chap. 4, this volume) occur as a series of behaviors (verbal and non-verbal) that is affected by the focal text or film but that runs its course without affecting the stimulus. If you now imagine that such participation could actually determine what happened next in text or film, you enter the world of interactive media (Biocca, chap. 5, this volume): You become an "interactant." Like preceding contributors in Part I of this volume, Biocca demonstrated the important role of strong emotional responses. However, for Biocca, emotional responses stem from "presence," the metafeeling of actually being in a different environment that one can influence and in which there may be other agents with whom to interact. One of the most important findings (Biocca, chap. 5, this volume, p. 122) is that not a great deal of technical wizardry is needed to construct an environment in which presence is felt and in which there is also a sense of interaction with other agents: "strong emotional responses can be easily achieved in interactive settings ... the interactant is likely to use and ascribe highly complex mental models of intentionality, personality, and person perception to interactive agents, even in cases in which the cues of intentionality and personality are minimal, and when there is clearly no personality or intelligence present other than in the most primitive programming use of the terms." A widely observable predilection for ersatz (or mediated) social encounters (Green, 2000; Green & Brock, 1998; Green, Wheeler, Hermann, & Brock, 1998) may stem from the ease with which individuals become engaged with interactive agents, combined with a propensity to apply human models to all manner of nonhuman or machine interactions (Reeves & Nass, 1996).

Part I's focus on the individual's response to narrative has taken us from preliterate recipients of orally transmitted myths (Nell) to wily cyberspace interactants (Biocca) who play a directional role in the unfolding narrative. Because self-awareness of bodily response and of bodily posture can affect attitudes and beliefs (e.g., Cacioppo, Priester, & Berntson, 1993), bodily "presence" (Biocca, chap. 5, this volume) provides a new, potentially powerful, determinant of attitude change.

A particularly exciting next step will be to examine the enduring impacts of different levels of participation: concomitant (Polichak & Gerrig, chap. 4, this volume) versus interactant (Biocca, chap. 5, this volume).

NARRATIVE IMPACTS WITHIN SOCIAL CONTEXTS

As we have seen in chapter 1 the importance of narrative impact lies in its social consequences. An issue at the heart of such social impact is text hegemony: Does the matter itself of books and films—when that matter is adequately comprehended by an interested recipient—outweigh attributes of the recipient and/or of the context/situation in which the matter is received? Is the text proof against attempts to increase or decrease its impact by framing, by warnings, by teaching?

Consider teaching: May our children read any book, see any film, if such exposure occurs within the context of thoughtful framing by an informed and sensitive teacher?

Posing the question casts doubt on the text hegemony position. It implies that narrative impact differs across recipients and that contexts (such as a classroom) can moderate the magnitude, or even the direction, of narrative impact.

Yet it turns out (as seen in DelFattore's chap. 6, this volume) that the absolute, unmoderated power of narratives to directly and uniformly influence beliefs is not only rarely doubted, it is widely feared. Indeed, with respect to their affirmation of text hegemony, the school censors and the film censors are bedfellows with certain influential literary critics (e.g., Bloom, 1994, p. 191).

DelFattore's painstaking review of book-banning litigation disclosed a militant agnosticism toward the key question: Does the narrative have an enduring impact on readers in the direction proposed by its critics? Recall that throughout Part I of this volume contributors specified constraints on impact: extent of mythic resonance (Nell, chap. 2, this volume), of emotion-facilitating structure (Oatley, chap. 3, this volume), of recipient participation (Polichak & Gerrig, chap. 4, this volume), and of degree of "presence" (Biocca, chap. 5, this volume).

The text hegemony hypothesis can surely be subjected to challenges in addition to the ones mounted in Part I. Despite this volume's theoretical and empirical questioning of text hegemony, the unrelenting school-based banning of public narratives (DelFattore, chap. 6, this volume) vehemently underscores both lay and legal agreement with text hegemony. "Censorship programs have not typically exempted large categories of recipients; few such programs have specified contexts in which the focal texts may be safely encountered; the devil has always been thought to be in the text, rather than in the recipient or the recipient's situation" (Green & Brock, 2000, p. 720; see also Strange, Green, & Brock, 2000).

The censor's prohibition implicitly claims that public narratives can be extremely effective. The claim leads directly to a central question for this volume, namely, the comparative efficacy of narrative versus nonnarrative (rhetorical) exposition. As noted in chapter 1, this volume, the scientific study of persuasion has neglected narrative impact. In an attempt to redress the rhetoric/poetics imbalance, Slater (chap. 7, this volume) explores the persuasive impact of entertainment and, in particular, of entertainment education. The media effects literature is reviewed in order to answer our comparative question in favor of narrative, rather than nonnarrative, exposition.[2] Slater's convincing argument is that there is no other communication genre "that can communicate beliefs, model behavior, teach skills, provide behavioral cues, and simulate consequences of behavior over time in a compelling and involving fashion"(Slater, chap. 7, p. 170, this volume). To Slater's list we may add the creation of enduring imagery (chap. 13, this volume). Indeed, Slater's example, the Peruvian telenovela, *Simplemente Maria*, deserves to be included in our pantheon of public narratives whose impact is potentially enormous (chap. 1, this volume).

Today, in the alleged "age of entertainment," it is important to consider the deployment of entertainment education. As demonstrated throughout most chapters of this volume, exposure to public narrative entails change in the recipient. Accordingly, Slater asks whether entertainment should be used to promote AIDS prevention, family health, substance abuse prevention, gender equity, and the like. We agree with Slater's answer: "stories inevitably exert some form of influence upon attitudes, beliefs, and/or behavior. In the absence of deliberate attempts to utilize the power of such communication for what can reasonably be argued to be public goods, the content of such programming is in most cases driven instead by either inertia or ratings" (Slater, chap. 7, p. 177, this volume).

The Peruvian women of *Simplemente Maria* (Slater, chap 7, this volume), who transformed themselves by using an ongoing public narrative, somewhat prefigured the young women who are on stage in Radway's chapter 8. The latter, like the former, use public narratives to refashion themselves. However, Radway's proposals for contemporary young women go beyond the unidirectional, logical, predictable impacts posited (Slater, chap. 7, this volume) for "edu-tainment." Radway's attic-foragers are using narrative gleanings in highly creative and unpredictable ways. The selves that emerge are not the clones of narrative protagonists, whether from books, magazines, TV, or MTV; there is negligible patterned identification with narrative characters. The only constraint on Radwayvian self-fashioning is the universe of narratives that is routinely available to a given young woman. Radway proposes that the readers of narratives may be quite promiscuous in their identifications and inventive in their self-reconfigurations. In the key process, renarration, they "make and remake themselves with the materials ready to hand." (Radway, chap. 8, p. 190, this volume).

Radway first observed this proactive use of narrative in romance readers (Radway, 1984) and, later (1997), in the sentiment building of middlebrow readers. Readers, such as Radway's Grrls, are reading selectively, nonlinearly, and with a self-serving pragmatic renarrative agenda. It is consequently not possible to go directly from narrative content to infer

14. INSIGHTS AND RESEARCH IMPLICATIONS   349

narrative effect; another nail seems to have been pounded into the coffin of text hegemony. However, clear and overwhelming as is Radway's evidence (chap. 8, this volume) for the polymorphous responding of vast blocks (romance, middlebrow) of tens of millions of readers, we can not be sanguine that the weight of this evidence will be generally heeded.

While Radway (chap. 8, this volume) has emphasized how narratives provide a plethora of grists that can be gleaned, "from the bottom up," for the development of personal identities, Jacobs (chap. 9, this volume) considers the overarching requirements of group, and national, membership on collective identities. He shows that a mobilizing narrative can motivate adherents of the collective "to participate in often dangerous acts" (chap. 9, p. 208, this volume).

Because social movements are posited to create social identities by integrating personal and collective narratives, there is an enormous challenge to the framers of the collective narratives. Jacobs (chap. 9, this volume) emphasized the importance of narrative structure in meeting this challenge. The mobilizing narrative must offer plot and character modules that can encompass the conflicting and/or inconsistent personal identities of targeted adherents; these conflicts and inconsistencies must be suppressed and replaced with a we–they feeling against nonadherents. Moreover, a common past must be constructed as well as a set of heroes from the dominant group within the movement. Finally, Jacobs' (chap. 9, this volume) most interesting structural proposal is that, in building collective identities, it is the genre of the mobilizing narrative that makes the most difference. In particular, Jacobs compellingly argues that of the four types of genre (comedy, tragedy, irony, and romance) it is the latter, romance, which may best serve the formation of collective identity. A primacy-of-romance hypothesis could be tested across numerous cases; such testing will inevitably advance understanding of how public narratives instigate civil participation.

In Part II we considered very broad realms of social life: schools and their stake-holders (children, teachers, parents, governments); multinational and multicultural audiences for edu-tainment as well as the implicit effects of multiple modes of entertainment; the legions of romance, middlebrow, and zine readers; and participants in the large-scale labor and social movements of today and yesteryear. Taken together, the realms portray the ubiquity of narrative impact and the corresponding importance of understanding underlying mechanisms (Part I, this volume).

NARRATIVE IMPACT:
SELECTED THEORETICAL PERSPECTIVES

In our reprise of narrative impacts, we have considered processing (Part I, this volume) within broad contexts of influence (Part II, this volume). To bring processing and context into a common focus, theory can be very helpful. Graesser and colleagues' constructionist theory (Graesser, Olde, & Kletke, chap. 10, this volume) succeeds in meeting the criteria for a good theory of narrative discourse: It specifies how story meaning is represented in the mind of the receiver, and how the representation is constructed and subsequently used. Furthermore, the theory affords distinctive predictions and generates numerous practical applications. For example, Graesser, Olde, & Kletke have shown how constructionist theory (chap. 10, this volume) can illuminate the courtroom impacts of narratives. According to the *story model* (Pennington & Hastie, 1992; 1993) of jury decision making, stories play the critical role in determining jurors' decision making. In accordance with constructionist theory (Graesser et al., chap. 10, this volume), "a coherent explanatory story has a more robust impact on the decisions of a jury than any other variable." Pennington & Hastie's analysis of coherence has three dimensions: consistency (few internal contradictions), plausibility (consistency with real-world events)[3], and completeness. These central components of the *story-model* are direct analogues to core assumptions of constructionist theory (chap. 10, this volume). In summary, constructionist theory, while emphasizing different structural features than previous contributors (Oatley, chap. 3, this volume; Jacobs, chap. 9, this volume) can predict important narrative impacts such as on jury decision making.

An unresolved issue for Graesser et al. (chap. 10, this volume) pertained to the plausibility criterion. Do individuals differ in the extent to which they evaluate every piece of evidence for how well it meshes with what a person knows already? Or, perhaps instead, recipients become involved in the focal story and suspend critical examination. Under such circumstances, fiction could have the same weight as fact (Prentice, Gerrig, & Bailis, 1997; Wheeler, Green, & Brock, 1999). In chapter 11, this volume, the impact of stories, labeled explicitly as fiction or as news, is addressed.

Chapter 11 modeled ways in which readers come to accept assertions encountered in the context of fictional stories as descriptions of the extratextual world, and how they generalize from story-world situations to real-world social problems. Strange probed the nature of pretense employed in fictional discourse and concluded that it is sometimes playful, sometimes serious, sometimes aimed toward imagining possible futures, sometimes directed toward revising consensually agreed on pasts. Some authors, like Stowe, used imaginary situations as extended analogies to real world situations, whereas others, like Wilde and the producers of Sesame Street voiced actual beliefs through the guise of imaginary characters. The trouble, Strange pointed out, is that serious and playful, reflective and inventive modes of pretense are often not clearly delineated within fictional worlds. The inability of readers to consistently di-

14. INSIGHTS AND RESEARCH IMPLICATIONS 351

vine the referential intentions of authors leads to one of the several paths through which readers might come to sketch in "imaginary coastlines" on their maps of the actual world.

In delineating different forms of fictional discourse and different routes and modes of impact, chapter 11 demonstrated how the answers we get when probing narrative impact are highly contingent on the questions we ask. Strange draws on empirical data (e.g., Strange, 1993) to show that heavy reliance on the "plausibility" criterion that characterizes jury decision making (chap. 10, this volume) will often yield maladaptive results when considering fictional worlds. When writers of historical fiction construct plausible but imaginary pasts, readers can update their beliefs in full knowledge of the nonevidentiary nature of the story-world assertions.

Chapter 11 also extends Schank's (chap. 12, this volume) theory of remindings by showing that readers' tendency to generalize from the causes and cures of story-world predicaments to real-world problems depends on the story's success in recruiting story-congruent memories. Given the research by Oatley (chap. 3, this volume), it is likely that the remindings experienced by Strange's readers (Strange & Leung, 1999) had basked in the warmth of previously experienced emotions. Taken together, the work on remindings presented in these three chapters adds an important addendum to models of narrative entrancement (chap. 1, this volume) or transportation (chaps. 3 & 13, this volume). Particularly, as posited by Strange, "when we become 'lost in a book' (Nell, 1988), we may shut out our immediate surroundings, but we do not close out our previous lives."

Finally, Strange suggested processes through which narratives may achieve the power attributed to them by those who are convinced that concrete cases hold particular potency when measured against abstract formulations. In this respect, the mechanisms he proposes to underlie "deictic recentering" implicate processes found in Graesser, Olde, & Kletke's description of narrative perspective (chap. 10, this volume), Polichak & Gerrig's account of participatory response (chap. 4, this volume), and Oately's construal of mimesis as cognitive simulation (chap. 3, this volume).

Chapter 12 (Schank & Berman) constitutes the most far-reaching claim for narrative impact. Our minds are mainly repositories of cases (stories) and learning consists largely in assimilating new stories and revising and expanding indices for our repertoires of previously received stories. Knowledge is constructed of stories in various forms. Key to the Schank/Berman theory—and to its importance to narrative impact—is the claim that all stories, whether or not initiated for the purpose of entertainment, are didactic (chap.12, p. 292, this volume). Therefore, to tell a story to oneself, or to hear a story from another, is to be changed, however imperceptibly. Other contributors, particularly Oatley (chap. 3, this volume), Slater (chap. 7, this volume) and Radway (chap. 8, this volume) would agree. Indeed, Schank's thinking (e.g., Schank, 1990; Schank & Abelson, 1995) has been so seminal that his positions on a number of other issues would likely elicit agreement from many contributors: fact no more effective than fiction (chap. 11, Strange; chap. 13, Green & Brock; chap. 4, Polichak & Gerrig); narrative is more effective than nonnarrative for changing attitudes (chap. 8, Slater; chap. 3, Oatley; chap. 13, Green & Brock).

It is in the area of narrative structure that contributors appear to espouse different requirements and different story taxonomies: compare chapter 10 (Graesser et al) to chapter 3 (Oatley) to chapter 9 (Jacobs) to chapter 2 (Nell). Future research must determine which structural elements actually foster differential narrative impact.

The final theory (transportation-imagery model, chap. 13, this volume) is largely devoid of structural requirements. Instead, emphasis is placed on imagery as the engine of enduring narrative impact. Visual imagery is thought to be augmented by psychological transportation, defined as absorption into a story that entails emotional and attentional focus (Green & Brock, 2000). Transportation, in turn, is expected to be increased by artistic craftsmanship and by adherence to narrative format; transportation may be limited by aspects of the recipient's context that limit imaginative investment (Green & Brock, 2000, Experiment 4). A principal contribution of chapter 13 has been to compare the transportation-imagery model with mainstream dual process theories (Chaiken & Trope, 1999) such as the Elaboration Likelihood Model (ELM: Petty & Cacioppo, 1986). Many novel predictions from the transportation-imagery model distinguish it from ELM. For example, highly transported recipients, in comparison to less transported recipients, should show, in addition to heightened attitude change, relative inability to process a cognate problem, slower reversion to prenarrative beliefs, and measurable mood changes on re-exposure to the focal narrative. Narrative persuasion, in comparison to rhetorical persuasion, will be more persistent. The latter claim stems from the psychological intensity and invulnerability to decay that images attain in comparison to the limited power and susceptibility to counterargument of verbal arguments.

SUMMARY OF ISSUES FOR *NARRATIVE IMPACT*

The theoretical perspectives provided testable contrasts and predictions in order to answer to what extent structure, on the one hand, and imagery, on the other, are necessary and sufficient for persisting narrative persuasion. In tests of narrative versus nonnarrative effectiveness, we now know which moderators and mediators are worth instantiating. In tests of the effectiveness of fact versus fiction (e.g., chap. 11, this volume) we now know that the burden of proof is on those investigators who claim that fact is superior; fact and fiction appeared to be blurred and intertwined in our "remindings" (chaps. 11 & 12, this volume). Finally, we repeatedly hit the stonewall of the text hegemony doctrine. It appears that text hegemony, like the creationism with which it is often associated, is a position to which undermining empirical evidence can be addressed but without much hope of changing the minds of adherents.

All of these research issues momentarily aside, public narratives must be seen as among the most formidable influences on behavior and beliefs (chapts. 1, 7, 8, 9, this volume). The incidental effects of all entertainment and the incentives for repeated self-exposure to public narratives were compellingly delineated by Radway (chap. 8, this volume) and Oatley (chap. 3, this volume). In the end—indeed, truly at the end—the tranquility of each person's final episode may stem in part from immersion in public narratives that effectively integrate personal and collective identities (chaps. 2 & 9, this volume).

ENDNOTES

[1] Of course, a substantial portion of narratives do not fit mythic structures (rebirth, restoration, and so forth) and, indeed, have dark outcomes (Conrad, Ibsen). However, Nell claims that across the eras, certain tales survive because, in describing "heroic" overcoming, they bespeak the aims of evolutionary fitness.

[2] In research practice, demonstration of narrative superiority is dependent on other factors such as the ability of the focal narrative to influence attitudes when it is compared to no message at all. Another requirement is that the focal narrative must be as informative as a nonnarrative "control" message. The most important requirement, and the one that is least often achieved, is that a version of the studied narrative be exemplary or, at least, prototypical. In research with rhetorical (advocacy) messages (e.g., Petty & Cacioppo, 1986) exquisite procedural care is taken to differentiate strong from weak messages. To date, except in rare instances (chap. 13, this volume; Green & Brock, 2000), little analogous research attention has been paid to the likely differential effect of level of narrative craftsmanship.

[3] If "real-world events" is expanded to include a person's repertory of prior stories, then plausibility is similar to Schank & Berman's index-matching (chap. 12, this volume).

REFERENCES

Bloom, H. (1994). *The Western canon: The books and school of the ages.* New York: Riverhead Books.

Cacioppo, J. T., Priester, J. R., & Berntson, G. G. (1993). Rudimentary determinants of attitudes II: Arm flexion and extension have differential effects on attitudes. *Journal of Personality and Social Psychology, 65,* 5–17.

Chaiken, S., & Trope, Y. (Eds.). (1999). *Dual-process theories in social psychology.* New York: Guilford Press.

Green, M. C. (2000). Choice of real versus ersatz social interactions in the formation of social capital: Laboratory and longitudinal approaches. Unpublished doctoral dissertation, The Ohio State University, Columbus, OH.

Green, M. C., & Brock, T. C. (2000). The role of transportation in the persuasiveness of public narratives. *Journal of Personality and Social Psychology, 79*, 701–721.
Green, M. C., & Brock, T. C. (1998). Trust, mood, and outcomes of friendship predict preferences for real versus ersatz social capital. *Political Psychology, 19*, 527–544.
Green, M. C., Wheeler, S. C., Hermann, A. D., & Brock, T. C. (1998). Social psychology and changing technologies: Reality versus caricature. *American Psychologist, 53*. 1078–1079).
Nell, V. (1988). *Lost in a book: The psychology of reading for pleasure*. New Haven, CT: Yale University Press.
Pennington, N., & Hastie, R. (1992). Explaining the evidence: Tests of the story model for juror decision making. *Journal of Personality and Social Psychology, 62*, 189–206.
Pennington, N., & Hastie, R. (1993). Reasoning in explanation-based decision-making. *Cognition, 9*, 123–163.
Petty, R. E., & Cacioppo, J. T. (1986). *Communication and persuasion: Central and peripheral routes to attitude change*. New York: Springer.
Prentice, D. A., & Gerrig, R. J. (1999). Exploring the boundary between fiction and reality. In S. Chaiken & Y. Trope (Eds.), *Dual-process theories in social psychology* (pp. 529–546). New York: Guilford Press.
Prentice, D. A., Gerrig, R. J., & Bailis, D. S. (1997). What readers bring to the processing of fictional texts. *Psychonomic Bulletin and Review, 4*(3), 416–420.
Radway, J. (1984). *Reading the romance: Women, patriarchy and popular culture*. Chapel Hill, NC: University of North Carolina Press.
Radway, J. (1997). *A feeling for books: The Book-of-the-Month Club, literary taste, and middle-class desire*. Chapel Hill, NC: University of North Carolina Press.
Reeves, B., & Nass, C. (1996). *The media equation: How people treat computers, television, and new media like real people and places*. Cambridge, UK: Cambridge University Press.
Schank, R. C. (1990). *Tell me a story*. Evanston: Northwestern University Press.
Schank, R. C., & Abelson, R. P. (1995). Knowledge and memory: The real story. In R. S. Wyer (Ed.), *Advances in social cognition*, Vol.VIII, (pp. 1–85). Hillsdale, NJ: Lawrence Erlbaum Associates.
Snyder, C. R., Sympson, S. C., Ybasco, F. C., Borders, T. F., Babyak, M. A., & Higgins, R. S. (1996). Development and validation of the State Hope Scale. *Journal of Personality & Social Psychology, 70*(2), 321–335.
Strange, J. J. (1993). The facts of fiction: The accommodation of real-world beliefs to fabricated accounts. *Dissertation Abstracts International,54*(2-a), 358.
Strange, J. J., Green, M. C., & Brock, T. C. (2000). Censorship and the regulation of expression. In E. F. Borgatta & R. J. V. Montgomery (Eds.), *Encyclopedia of Sociology* (2nd ed., pp. 267–281). New York: Macmillan.
Strange, J. J., & Leung, C. C. (1999). How anecdotal accounts in news and in fiction can influence judgments of a social problem's urgency, causes, and cures. *Personality and Social Psychology Bulletin, 25*(4), 436–449.
Taylor, S. E., Kemeny, M. E., Reed, G. M., Bower, J. E., & Gruenewald, T. L. (2000). Psychological resources, positive illusions, and health. *American Psychologist, 55*(1), 99–109.
Wheeler, S. C., Green, M. C., & Brock, T. C. (1999). Fictional narratives change beliefs: Replications of Prentice, Gerrig, & Bailis (1997) with mixed corroboration. *Psychonomic Bulletin and Review, 6*, 136–141.

Author Index

A

Aarne, A., 19, 34
Abbott, A., 213, 224
Abelson, R. P., 12, 15, 229, 235, 236, 239, 250, 254, 261, 278, 282, 285, 287, 288, 290, 293, 294, 297, 299, 301, 304, 309, 312, 313, 316, 341, 352, 354
Abend, T., 31, 36
Adelstein, B. D., 106, 126
Adler, M. J., 264, 284
Ajzen, I., 166, 177, 178
Akiyama, K., 113, 125
Albrecht, J. E., 231, 244, 246, 260, 261
Alcott, L. M., 192, 196, 197, 204
Alessi, S. M., 113, 125
Alexander, J. C., 206, 212, 217, 224
Alford, R., 207, 225
Alicke, M. D., 247, 258
Allbritton, D. W., 9, 14, 72, 86, 87, 88, 91, 93, 330, 339
Allen, W., 291
Allgood, G. O., 127
Allport, G. W., 105, 125, 294, 312
Amsel, J., xiv
Anderson, N. H., xiii, xv
Anderson, R. C., 236, 257, 258, 281, 285
Andrews, D. H., 102, 129
Ang, I., 223, 225
Antola, L., 159, 180
Applewhite, H., 117, 128
Appleyard, J. A., 61, 66
Aptheker, H., 267
Apuleius, 42, 66
Aramaki, Y., 268
Arendt, H., 30, 35
Ariès, P., 34, 35
Aristotle, 48, 49, 50, 66

Arndt, J., 30, 31, 32, 35, 36
Arthur, K., 113, 125
Atkinson, G., 327, 333, 341
Auden, W. H., 20, 37
Auerbach, E., 3, 14
Averill, J. R., 40, 66
Axelrad, E., 52, 60, 66
Ayeroff, F., 299, 312

B

Babyak, M. A., 344, 354
Baggett, W. B., 250, 251, 252, 260
Bailey, G., 263, 284
Bailis, D. S., 89, 90, 94, 174, 179, 257, 261, 331, 341, 350, 354
Ball-Rokeach, S. J., 164, 178
Baltzley, D. R., 117, 125
Bandura, A., 119, 125, 159, 165, 166, 168, 178, 282, 284
Banks, R., 53
Banks, W. C., 30, 36
Barfield, W., 102, 103, 113, 117, 121, 124, 125, 127
Bargh, J. A., 76, 93
Barkow, L., 24, 33, 35
Barnard, P. J., 73, 93
Barret, G.V., 117, 125
Barthes, R., 64, 66, 213, 214, 217, 220, 223, 225
Bartlett, F. C., 47, 48, 52, 66
Bates, S., 153, 154
Beardsley, M. C., 58, 69
Beattie, G. W., 73, 93
Becker, E., 27, 31, 35
Behe, M. J., 154, 155
Bell, P., 223, 225
Bell, R., 223, 225
Berbaum, K. S., 114, 117, 125, 127
Berman, T. R., 12, 287, 295, 307, 346, 351, 353

355

AUTHOR INDEX

Bernardo, A. B., I. 83, 84, 94
Berntson, G. G., 346, 353
Berrueta, M., 159, 178
Bertus, E., 247, 250, 259
Bhabha, H., 213, 225, 228
Biason, A., 61, 66
Biber, D., 239, 257, 258
Bickmore, T., 121, 126
Billinghurst, M., 121, 126
Biocca, F., 9, 14, 97, 98, 102, 104, 108, 109, 113, 116, 117, 118, 120, 123, 125, 127, 128, 129, 346, 347
Birdoff, H., 318, 338, 339
Black, J. B., 233, 236, 238, 250, 254, 258, 259, 261, 281, 286
Blackmon, T. T., 113, 130
Block, F. L., 202, 204
Bloom, H., 49, 55, 62, 66, 347, 353
Bocker, 104, 128
Boggs, D., 137
Booth, W. C., 2, 14, 42, 66
Boothe, R. G., 114, 125
Borders, T. F., 344, 354
Bordwell, D., 122, 125
Bostwick, S., xv
Boulay, M., 163, 180
Bouwhuis, D., 113, 127
Bovbjerg, D. H., 321, 336, 340
Bower, G. H., 58, 67, 171, 178, 236, 238, 250, 252, 254, 258, 259, 260, 261, 281, 284
Bower, J. E., 344, 354
Bowers, C. A., 236, 237, 259
Brem, S., 239, 258
Brewer, W. F., 44, 67, 82, 83, 93, 231, 234, 235, 238, 239, 258, 259, 261
Britton, B. K., 73, 85, 93, 233, 257, 259
Brnich, M. J., 165, 178
Brock, T. C., xiii, xiv, xv, 1, 2, 8, 13, 14, 15, 90, 93, 95, 171, 173, 174, 178, 181, 257, 262, 278, 283, 284, 286, 315, 318, 319, 320, 324, 328, 329, 331, 332, 334, 339, 340, 341, 343, 344, 346, 347, 350, 352, 353, 354
Brontë, C., 58, 67
Brooke, P., 161, 178
Brown, C. M., 250, 262
Browning, C. R., 30, 35
Brubaker, 224, 225
Bruder, G. A., 236, 238, 259
Brumberg, J. J., 184, 185, 200, 204
Bruner, J., 39, 40, 67, 216, 219, 225, 229, 259, 266, 284, 319, 320, 339
Bryant, J., 2, 14, 115, 130, 171, 172, 181, 282, 284
Bryson, S., 102, 125

Burch, C. W., 151
Burger, J. M., 247, 259
Burke, K., 324, 339
Burton, P. L., 129
Buss, D. M., 24, 35

C

Cacioppo, J. T., 90, 93, 173, 174, 179, 320, 328, 331, 332, 333, 334, 335, 336, 337, 339, 341, 346, 352, 353, 354
Calhoun, C., 210, 211, 225
Campbell, E. H., xiii, xv
Campbell, J., 19, 20, 24, 33, 35, 125
Campbell, L., 121, 126
Cantor, J., 115, 126, 128, 282, 285
Cantor, N., 105, 126
Cantril, J., 269, 284
Carlip, H., 202, 204
Carlson, T. B., 74, 94
Casali, J. G., 114, 117, 126
Cassell, J., 98, 121, 122, 126
Caudell, T., 124, 125
Caughey, J. L., 281, 284
Cawelti, J. G., 22, 35
Chaffee, S. H., 168, 178
Chaiken, S., 2, 13, 14, 76, 93, 316, 329, 331, 340, 352, 353
Chang, K., 121, 126
Chatman, S., 236, 262, 281, 284
Chirwa, B., 163, 181
Chorafas, D. N., 121, 126
Christel, M. G., 113, 126
Christie, B., 102, 104, 129
Churchill, E., 98, 126
Clark, H. H., 73, 74, 93, 94, 95, 236, 238, 241, 259
Clark, L. C., 12, 14, 233, 234, 246, 247, 248, 252, 253, 259
Clark, L. F., 233, 240, 259
Clinton, W. J., 289, 308, 320
Coetzee, J. M., 22, 30, 34, 35
Cohen, A. D., 240, 259
Cohen, A. R., xiii, xv
Cole, H. P., 165, 178
Coleridge, S. T., 57, 257, 259
Coles, R., 315, 340
Columbus, C., 4, 5, 6
Combs, A. W., 105, 129
Conner, R. F., 163, 179
Conrad, J., 22, 30, 35
Cook, M., 119, 126
Cooley, C., 105, 126
Coover, R., 264, 284
Cosmides, L., 24, 33, 35
Costa-Gavras, C., 281, 284
Cotton, D., 167, 179

AUTHOR INDEX

Crane, P., 120, 126
Crew, R., 143
Crichton, M., 266, 268, 269, 270, 283, 284
Cronin, H., 26, 35
Cross, J. K., 136
Csikszentmihalyi, M., 105, 114, 126, 128, 325, 326, 340
Current, R. N., 267, 284
Cutmore, T. R. H., 321, 336, 340

D

Dacunto, L. J., 120, 126
Dadds, M. R., 321, 336, 340
Dahlgren, P., 223, 225
Dam, A. V., 98, 121, 126
Damasio, A. R., 18, 35
Daneman, M., 91, 94
Dark, V. J., 100, 123, 127
Davidson, D., 254, 259
Davis, J., 5, 10, 14
de Certeau, M., 197, 204
de Ridder, H., 113, 127
Debord, G., 224, 225
Deighton, J., 316, 320, 340
Delaney, B., 102, 108, 125
DelFattore, J., 10, 14, 131, 152, 153, 155, 345, 347
Dembski, W. A., 154, 155
DeVine, A., 141, 155
Diamond, J., 25, 35
Dickens, C., 34, 192, 276
DiClemente, C. C., 167, 179
Diderot, D., 281, 284
Dill, K., 115, 126
Dillon, S., 154, 155
Dinsmore, J., 268, 274, 284
Ditton, T. B., 103, 113, 128
Donohue, G. A., 168, 180
Doody, M. A., 43, 67
Dorighi, N. S., 106, 126
Drake, J., 200, 204
Draper, N., 140, 155
Dreiser, T., 276
Duchan, J. F., 236, 238, 259
Duncker, K., 84, 94
Dunlap, W. P., 114, 117, 127
Durlach, N., 98, 102, 103, 108, 113, 116, 121, 126, 127
Duval, S., 325, 340
Dyer, M. G., 235, 259

E

Eagly, A. H., 2, 14, 90, 94, 171, 174, 179, 316, 322, 329, 331, 340
Ebenholtz, S. M., 117, 126
Eco, U., 213, 214, 225

Edwards, K., 86, 94
Eldredge, N., 154, 155
Eley, G., 223, 225
Eliasoph, N., 209, 225
Eliot, G., 65, 66, 67
Eliot, T. S., 17, 21, 35, 63, 67
Ellis, S. R., 106, 117, 126
Epstein, S., 27, 35, 326, 340
Erasmus, 57, 67
Escher, M., 98, 121, 128

F

Fagels, R., 27
Farr, R., 167, 178
Fazio, R. H., 170, 178
Feierabend, R. L., xiii, xv
Feiner, S. K., 98, 121, 126
Feinstein, J. A., 333, 339
Fernandez, J., 145, 147
Ferren, B., 98, 126
Fishbein, M., 166, 168, 178
Fiske, J., 223, 225
Flaton, R., 239, 256, 260
Fleming, I., 83, 94
Fogelson, R., 224, 225
Foley, J. D., 98, 121, 126
Forbes, D., 164, 178
Fowlkes, J. E., 117, 127
Frazer, J. G., 19, 34, 35
Freeman, J., 113, 127
Freud, S., 18, 19, 27, 31, 34, 35, 198, 203
Frey, K. P., 322, 340
Friedland, R., 207, 225
Friedland, S., 151
Friedrichsen, M., 69, 239, 262
Frijda, N. H., 63, 69
Frost, V., 133, 135, 136, 142, 153
Frye, N., 216, 219, 221, 225
Funcke, E. W., 28, 35
Furness, T. A., 113, 121, 125, 129

G

Gamson, W., 2, 14, 207, 225
Gara, M. A., 105, 129
Garafalo, G., 200, 201, 204
Garst, J., xiv, 329, 340
Gass, W. H., 321, 340
Gavras, C., 281, 284
Geertz, C., 210, 225
Gellner, E., 211, 225
Gentner, D., 292, 293, 311, 312
Gerbner, G., 2, 14, 167, 177, 178, 316, 340
Gergen, K. J., 105, 126
Gernsbacher, M. A., 230, 231, 233, 244, 259

Gerrig, R. J., 9, 14, 18, 21, 35, 40, 50, 67, 71, 72, 75, 81, 83, 84, 86, 87, 88, 89, 90, 91, 93, 94, 101, 102, 104, 126, 163, 174, 179, 181, 229, 239, 257, 259, 261, 264, 274, 278, 283, 284, 321, 324, 325, 328, 329, 330, 331, 339, 340, 341, 345, 346, 347, 350, 351, 352, 354
Gholamain, M., 60, 61, 66, 67
Gibbs, J. T., 218, 225
Gibbs, N., 30, 35
Gibson, J. J., 108, 126
Gibson, R., 276, 284
Gick, M. L., 292, 293, 312
Giddens, A., 212, 225
Giffen, W. C., 165, 178
Gilbert, D. T., 17, 35, 173, 175, 178, 274, 284
Gilkey, R. H., 113, 127
Gitlin, T., 221, 225
Givon, T., 234, 259
Glenberg, A. M., 252, 259
Goffman, E., 42, 51, 67, 104, 127
Golding, J. M., 229, 250, 251, 252, 259, 260
Goldman, S. R., 229, 236, 259
Goodwin, J., 223, 225
Gordon, R. K., 24, 28, 35
Gordon, S. E., 254, 262
Gottlieb, R., 215, 225
Gower, D. W., 117, 125
Grabe, M. E., 113, 128
Graesser, A. C., 11, 12, 14, 59, 67, 72, 73, 85, 93, 94, 171, 178, 229, 230, 231, 233, 234, 236, 237, 239, 240, 241, 242, 244, 245, 246, 247, 248, 250, 251, 252, 253, 254, 258, 259, 260, 261, 262, 341, 349, 350, 351, 352
Graves, R., 23, 35
Grazzani-Gavazzi, I., 54, 66, 67
Green, M. C., xiii, xiv, xv, 1, 8, 13, 14, 90, 93, 95, 171, 174, 178, 181, 257, 262, 278, 283, 284, 286, 315, 318, 319, 320, 324, 326, 328, 329, 331, 332, 334, 338, 339, 340, 341, 343, 344, 346, 347, 350, 352, 353, 354
Greenberg, J., 8, 14, 30, 31, 32, 35, 36, 200
Greene, S. B., 91, 94
Greenfeld, L., 211, 225
Greenspan, S. L., 238, 252, 260
Greenwald, A. G., xiii, xv
Greimas, A. J., 217, 225
Griffiths, M., 115, 127

Grisham, J., 21
Gross, L., 2, 14, 167, 177, 178, 316, 340
Grube, J., 164, 178
Gruenewald, T. L., 344, 354
Gunter, B., 115, 127, 176, 178
Guterson, D., 280, 284

H

Haberlandt, K., 233, 259, 260
Hakemulder, F., 66, 67
Haley, V. J., 165, 178
Hall, S., 205, 223, 225
Halldorson, M., 250, 261
Ham, K., 154, 155
Hamberg, R., 113, 127
Hamill, R., 279, 284
Hamilton, M. A., 166, 178
Hammond, K., 288, 293, 312
Hancock, P. A., 123, 127
Haney, C., 30, 36
Harmon-Jones, E., 30, 31, 36
Hart, J., 206, 208, 226
Hastie, R., 12, 15, 239, 254, 255, 256, 260, 261, 350, 354
Hatada, T., 113, 127
Hauft-Smith, K., 240, 259, 261
Hawkins, D. G., 102, 127
Hays, R. T., 102, 113, 127
Hazlitt, 62
Heckert, K., 163, 180
Heeter, C., 104, 127
Heilig, M., 113, 127
Heim, M., 113, 127
Held, R. M., 113, 127
Hendrix, C., 113, 127
Hermann, A. D., 346, 354
Herron, C., 142, 143, 155
Herzl, T., 3, 4
Hetrick, P., 141
Hettinger, L. J., 114, 117, 127
Hewitt, L. E., 236, 238, 257, 259, 280, 286
Heywood, L., 200, 204
Higgins, R. S., 344, 354
Hilgard, E. R., 41, 42, 67
Hilton, D. J., 247, 260
Hiorshi, Y., 113, 125
Hirschman, A. O., 224, 226
Ho, C. B. C., 104, 127
Hobsbawm, E., 210, 226
Hochberg, J., 101, 116, 127
Hoffman, H. G., 113, 129
Hoffman, N. L., 233, 240, 259
Hogan, P. C., 52, 57, 59, 66, 67
Holland, N., 60, 67
Holloway, L., 142, 155

AUTHOR INDEX 359

Holmes, G. F., 265, 284
Holyoak, K. J., 292, 293, 312
Homer, 27, 36
Homstad, W., 153, 155
Hornik, R., 163, 181
Hovland, C. I., xiii, xv, 2, 14, 331, 340
Hughes, J., 98, 121, 126
Hull, T., 137
Hullfish, K., 114, 127
Hutchinson, B., 140, 155
Hutton, P. A., 264, 265, 267, 283, 284
Hyman, D. A., 279, 284
Hymes, C., 76, 93

I

Ichinose, S., 113, 125
Ijsselseijn, W., 113, 127
Ingalls, D. H. H., 52, 67
Inhelder, B., 48, 68
Iser, W., 47, 50, 59, 67
Ishibashi, M., 113, 125
Iyengar, S., 2, 14, 276, 284

J

Jacobs, R. N., 11, 14, 205, 213, 215, 216, 217, 219, 220, 221, 223, 224, 226, 349, 350, 352
Jacobson, R., 54, 59, 61, 67
James, H., 318, 340
James, W., 43, 67, 99, 268, 269, 280, 283, 284
Janis, I. L., xiii, xv, 15, 331, 340
Jarvis, B. W. G., 333, 339
Jasper, J. M., 223, 225
Jefferson, G., 73, 94
Jeffries, V., 215, 227
Jenkins, J. C., 207, 226
Jenkins, J. M., 42, 68
Joacoby, R. H., 106, 126
Johnson, B. K., 250, 251, 252, 260
Johnson, B. T., 90, 94, 171, 174, 179
Johnson, C., 153, 155
Johnson, M. K., ix, 283, 284, 285
Johnson, N. S., 171, 179
Johnson, P., 3, 14
Johnson-Laird, P. N., 46, 67, 273, 286, 311, 312
Johnston, W. A., 100, 123, 127
Jona, M. Y., 288, 293, 312
Jones, J., 50, 67
Jones, T., 71, 78, 80, 81, 87, 94
Josephy, A., Jr., 266, 267, 285
Joyce, J., 21, 52
Jung, C. G., 19, 33, 36

K

Kafka, F., 42
Kahneman, D., 78, 87, 94, 176, 179, 273, 286, 311, 313
Kalra, P., 98, 121, 128
Kane, A. E., 209, 226
Kao, C. F., 90, 93
Kaplan, C., 203, 204
Karki, Y., 163, 180
Karmacharya, D. M., 163, 180
Kassler, M. A., 231, 234, 260
Katz, E., 12, 15, 168, 179, 223, 226
Keats, J., 55, 67
Keene, C., 192, 194, 196, 197
Kelley, H. H., 331, 340
Kemeny, M. E., 344, 354
Kennedy, C., 137
Kennedy, R. S., 114, 117, 127
Kent, D., 30, 36
Keysar, B., 236, 260
Kiesler, C. A., 330, 340
Kihlstrom, J. K., 105, 126, 128
Kilbane, 299, 312
Kill, J., 115, 126
Kim, S. H., 247, 260
Kim, T., 104, 123, 128
Kincaid, D. L., 160, 166, 179
Kinder, D. R., 2, 14, 276, 284
Kintsch, W., 85, 94, 231, 233, 234, 244, 249, 253, 255, 258, 260, 338, 341
Kirson, D., 283, 285
Klandermans, B., 207, 226
Klein, S. B., 105, 128
Kletke, B., 11, 12, 229, 350, 351
Kolasinski, E. M., 117, 128
Kolodner, J., 288, 293, 312
Kosslyn, S. M., 321, 340
Kovner, E. S., 129
Kreuz, R. J., 231, 234, 260
Krosnick, J. A., xiv, xv, xix
Kubey, R., 114, 128
Kuhn, D., 239, 256, 260
Kuiken, D., 50, 55, 57, 59, 68
Kumar, A., 254, 260
Kurtz, H., 141, 155
Kusaka, H., 113, 127

L

Lalljee, M., 293, 299, 312
Lamb, R., 293, 299, 312
Landers, R., 292, 293, 312
Lang, A., 116
Lang, P. J., 18, 36
Langer, E. J., 299, 312

Langston, M. C., 231, 238, 244, 262, 338, 341
Lanier, J., 113, 120, 128
Lankard, B. A., 151
LaPlanche, J., 203, 204
Larocque, L., 53, 60, 66
Larsen, S. F., 60, 67, 278, 285
Larson, E. J., 154, 155
Lasch, C., 32, 36
Laurel, B., 97, 98, 114, 121, 128
Lauria, R., 113, 128
Lazarsfeld, P. F., 168, 179
Lazarus, R. S., 8, 14, 80, 94
Lears, M. E., 129
Ledoux, J., 18, 26, 34, 36
Lehnert, W. G., 235, 246, 260
Lepper, M. R., 86, 94
Lerner, M. J., 319, 340
Leslie, A. M., 275, 285
Leung, C. C., xiv, xv, 15, 168, 180, 275, 276, 281, 286, 302, 304, 313, 329, 341, 351, 354
Levine, R. S., 263, 267, 285
Levy, M., 9, 14, 98, 125, 127, 129
Lewis, M., 163, 179
Lichtenstein, E. H., 44, 67, 82, 93
Lieberman, D. A., 165, 179
Liebes, T., 223, 226
Light, A., 203, 204
Lilienthal, M. G., 117, 125, 127
Linde, C., 213, 226
Lindem, K., 252, 259
Linderholm, T., 231, 244, 247, 262
Lippmann, W., 276, 285
Liu, A., 113, 130
Lively, P., 137
Livingston, S.D., xiv
Loewen, J. W., 4, 5, 6, 14
Loftus, J., 105, 128
Logan, J., 151
Lombard, M., 103, 113, 128
London, J., 134
Long, E., 223, 226
Long, D. L., 229, 250, 251, 252, 259, 260
Longinus, 56, 67
Loomis, J. M., 103, 106, 113, 128
Lord, C. G., 86, 94
Luchins, A. S., xiii, xv
Lumsdaine, A. A., 2, 14

M

Maccoby, N., 173, 180
MacIntyre, A., 206, 226
MacLean, P. D., 18, 36
MacLeish, A., 135
Magliano, J. P., 224, 245, 250, 251, 252, 260, 262

Magnenat-Thalmann, M., 98, 121, 128
Magnusson, M., 34, 36
Maibach, E. W., 167, 179
Mandell, W., xiii, xv
Mandler, J. M., 171, 179, 229, 260
Mann, M., 210, 226
Marcus-Newhall, A., 247, 261
Mares, M. L., 282, 285
Markus, H., 105, 128
Marx, K., 208, 226
Marvis, B. J., 151
Mason, R. A., 231, 244, 246, 260
Masson, J. M., 52, 67
Mavor, A., 98, 102, 103, 108, 113, 116, 121, 126
Maynes, M. J., 209, 226
Mazzocco, P., xiv
McAdam, D., 207, 226
McCarthy, J. D., 207, 226
McCauley, M. E., 114, 128
McClelland, J. L., 253, 261
McCombs, M. E., 168, 180
McConahay, J., 215, 227
McCone, J., 224, 226
McConkey, K. M., 327, 341
McConnaughy, E. A., 167, 179
McCullers, C., 62
McDonald, D., 114, 129
McGuire, W. J., xiii, xv, 2, 14, 166, 167, 179
McIntosh, P., 151
McKoon, G., 72, 91, 94, 231, 235, 236, 260, 261, 293, 313
McLain-Allen, B., 231, 234, 260
McMillan, D., 254, 261
McQueen, J., 316, 320, 340
Mead, G. H., 105, 128
Meeks, C., 224, 226
Mellers, B., 113, 130
Melucci, A., 208, 218, 223, 226, 227
Menges, R. M., 106, 126
Merikle, P. M., 91, 94
Meshkayi, N., 123, 127
Meyer, K., 117, 128
Meyer, M., 252, 259
Meyers, P., 116, 128
Miall, D. S., 50, 55, 57, 59, 68
Michener, J., 269, 285
Middlestat, S. E., 168, 178
Milgram, S., 30, 36
Miller, D. T., 78, 87, 94, 176, 179, 319, 340
Miller, S., 194, 195, 204
Millis, K. K., 238, 250, 252, 260
Minsky, M., 102, 104, 128
Mishra, S. L., 163, 179
Mitchell, K. J., 283, 285
Mitchell, L., 151

AUTHOR INDEX 361

Moffett, J., 153, 155
Montgomery, K. C., 164, 179
Moore, T. L., 152
Morgan, M., 2, 14, 167, 177, 178, 316, 340
Morris, R., 215, 227
Morrow, D. G., 58, 67, 238, 252, 260
Moscovici, S., 167, 178
Moyers, B., 33, 35, 176, 179
Mozert, A., 135, 155
Mozert, S., 133, 135, 137
Muecke, D. C., 221, 227
Muhlbach, 104, 128
Munro, A., 60, 62
Munsterberg, H., 99, 100, 128
Murphy, S. T., 76, 94, 282, 285
Murray, J., 98, 106, 113, 114, 116, 119, 124, 128
Mutz, D. C., 168, 178
Myers, J. L., 116, 128, 231, 244, 246, 260

N

Nakamura, G. V., 233, 250, 254, 260
Narvaes, D., 236, 261
Nass, C., 113, 121, 122, 129, 346, 354
Nell, V., 8, 15, 17, 18, 23, 24, 25, 26, 29, 30, 33, 34, 36, 41, 68, 171, 179, 278, 285, 317, 321, 322, 340, 343, 344, 346, 347, 351, 352, 353, 354
Newman, L., 146, 155
Neyland, D. L., 102, 120, 128
Niebuhr, G., 316, 340
Nietzsche, F., 220, 227
Nisbett, R. E., 279, 284, 322, 340
Nolan, M. D., 114, 117, 127
Norcross, J. C., 167, 179
Norman, D., 97
Norrick, N. R., 241, 261
Nowak, K., 113, 120, 125, 128
Nuland, S., 318, 319, 341
Nundy, S., 53, 60, 66, 68
Nunley, E. P., 40, 66
Nussbaum, M. C., 65, 68

O

O'Brien, E. J., 231, 244, 246, 260, 261
O'Guinn, T. C., 176, 177, 180, 282, 285, 316, 341
Oatley, K., 8, 15, 39, 40, 41, 42, 43, 46, 48, 49, 50, 51, 53, 54, 59, 60, 61, 67, 68, 344, 345, 347, 350, 351, 352, 353
Oberschall, A., 207, 227
Ohtsuka, K., 231, 234, 238, 257, 259, 261

Olde, B., 11, 12, 229, 236, 237, 259, 350, 351
Olien, C. N., 168, 180
Olson, J. M., 78, 94
Omi, M., 224, 227
Ortony, A., 293, 312
Ostrom, T. M., xiii, xv, 334, 341
Ottati, V., 229, 239, 260
Ottaviani, B., 281, 286
Ovid, 42
Owens, J., 236, 261

P

Palsson, H., 34, 36
Parker, D. E., 113, 129
Patwardhan, M. V., 52, 67
Pausch, R., 113, 129
Pennington, N., 12, 15, 239, 255, 256, 261, 350, 354
Perez-Diaz, V., 210, 227
Perse, E. M., 104, 129, 168, 171, 180
Petersen, W., 281, 285
Petty, R. E., xiv, xv, 2, 15, 90, 93, 173, 174, 175, 179, 320, 328, 331, 332, 333, 334, 335, 336, 337, 339, 341, 352, 353, 354
Philips, R., 98, 121, 126
Phillips, A., 197, 198, 199, 204
Piaget, J., 48, 68
Picard, R., 122, 129
Pichert, J. W., 236, 258
Piotrow, P. T., 160, 161, 179
Pipher, M., 184, 200, 204
Polanyi, L., 213, 227
Polichak, J. W., 9, 71, 330, 345, 346, 347, 351, 352
Poliner, C., 140
Pollack, A., 268, 285
Polletta, F., 208, 210, 227
Pomeroy, V., 236, 237, 259
Pontalis, J. B., 203, 204
Postman, L. J., 294, 312
Potok, C., 3, 4, 15
Potter, W. J., 175, 179
Potts, G. R., 283, 285
Powell, M. C., 170, 178
Powell, R. A., 171, 180
Pratt, V., 121, 129
Prentice, D. A., 81, 89, 90, 94, 163, 174, 179, 257, 261, 328, 329, 330, 331, 340, 341, 350, 354
Press, A., 223, 227
Prevost, S., 98, 121, 126
Priester, J. R., 346, 353
Pritchert, J. W., 281, 285
Prochaska, J. O., 167, 179
Proffitt, D., 113, 129

Propp, V., 19, 20, 21, 36
Prothero, J. D., 113, 129
Proust, M., 65, 68
Prussog, A., 104, 128
Prybyla, D. J., 120, 126
Puskas, G., xv
Pyles, L. D., 240, 259
Pynchon, T., 264, 266
Pyszynski, T., 8, 14, 30, 31, 32, 34, 35, 36

Q

Quayle, D., 316

R

Rachlin, A., 32, 33, 36
Radvansky, G. A., 231, 244, 245, 252, 262
Radway, J., 7, 10, 11, 15, 183, 185, 186, 187, 188, 189, 204, 326, 328, 341, 345, 348, 349, 352, 353, 354
Ramesh, R., 102, 129
Raney, G. E., 231, 244, 246, 261
Ranger, T., 210, 226
Rapaport, W. J., 268, 275, 280, 285
Ratcliff, R., 72, 91, 94, 231, 235, 236, 260, 261, 293, 313
Ratterman, J. J., 293, 312
Raymond, P., 76, 93
Rayner, K., 231, 244, 246, 261
Reagan, R., 320
Reason, J. T., 117, 129
Redd, G. M., 344, 354
Redd, W. H., 321, 336, 340
Redd, S. J., 247, 261
Redeker, G., 266, 281, 285
Reeves, B., 113, 121, 122, 104, 129, 346, 354
Reeves-Kazelskis, C., 152
Reich, R., 113, 128
Rheingold, H., 104, 113, 129
Richards, I. A., 59, 68
Ricoeur, P., 206, 220, 227
Riesbeck, C. K., 288, 293, 312
Rimon, J. G., 160, 161, 179
Rinehart, W., 160, 161, 179
Rips, L., 239, 258
Roberts, D. F., 173, 180
Robertson, P., 147
Rockwell, T. H., 165, 178
Rodriguez, R., 90, 93
Roehl, B., 98, 129
Roese, N. J., 78, 94
Rogers, E. M., 10, 15, 158, 159, 161, 162, 166, 167, 180
Rokeach, M., 161, 164, 178, 180

Rolland, J., 118, 125
Romer, D., 316, 320, 340
Rorty, R., 221, 227
Ronsenbaum, P. S., 133, 155
Rosenberg, J., 200, 201, 204
Rosenberg, M., 105, 129
Rosenberg, S., 105, 129
Rosenblatt, L. M., 59, 68
Ross, B. H., 293, 299, 312
Ross, L., 86, 94, 322, 340
Ross, L. D., 293, 312
Rouner, D., 168, 172, 174, 175, 180
Rowling, J. K., 139
Rubin, A. M., 168, 171, 180, 325, 341
Rubin, D. C., 229, 239, 261, 319, 341
Rugeley, C., 154, 155
Rumelhart, D. E., 229, 253, 261
Ruvolo, A., 105, 128
Ryan, 268, 280, 285

S

Sabido, M., 158, 159
Sacks, H., 73, 94
Sakata, H., 113, 127
Sandak, R., 239, 262
Sanders, J., 266, 281, 285
Sarfati, J., 154, 155
Sartre, J. P., 104, 129
Schank, R. C., 12, 13, 15, 229, 235, 239, 246, 250, 254, 261, 278, 282, 285, 287, 288, 289, 290, 291, 292, 293, 294, 295, 297, 299, 300, 301, 303, 308, 309, 312, 313, 316, 341, 346, 351, 352, 353, 354
Scheff, T. J., 59, 60, 61, 64, 68
Schiffrin, D., 241, 261
Schlegoff, E. A., 73, 94
Schmidt, S., 264, 285
Schober, M. F., 74, 95, 238, 261
Scott, W., 270, 280, 285
Sears, D., 215, 227
Seifert, C. M., 235, 236, 261, 293, 313
Seilman, U., 60, 67, 278, 285
Sen, R. J., 129
Sendak, M., 142
Seneca, 30, 36
Sewell, W. H., Jr., 212, 213, 227
Shakespeare, W., 39, 43, 46, 48, 49, 50, 56, 57, 58, 61, 64, 65, 68, 192, 193
Shapiro, M., 114, 129
Shapiro, S. C., 268, 275, 285
Sharkey, T. J., 114, 128
Sharpton, A., 147
Shavitt, S., 2, 15
Shaw, A. M., 133, 155

AUTHOR INDEX 363

Shaw, D. L., 168, 180
Sheehan, P. W., 327, 333, 341
Sheffield, F. D., 2, 14
Shefner-Rogers, C. L., 10, 15, 161, 166, 180
Sheridan, T., 102, 103, 104, 106, 113, 117, 125, 129
Sherwood, S., 212, 222, 227
Shils, E., 210, 227
Shneiderman, B., 107, 129
Short, J., 102, 104, 129
Shrum, L. J., 176, 177, 180, 282, 285, 316, 341
Sidney, P., 48, 68
Signorielli, N., 2, 14, 167, 177, 178, 316, 340
Sikora, S., 50, 57, 68
Silver, I., 269, 285
Simon, L., 30, 31, 32, 35, 36
Simon, S., 150, 155
Sims, K., 98, 129
Singer, M. J., 102, 113, 127, 130
Singer, M., 11, 14, 59, 67, 72, 94, 231, 241, 242, 246, 248, 250, 258, 260, 261
Singhal, A., 158, 159, 161, 162, 180
Singhal, S., 120, 129
Slater, M. D., 10, 15, 157, 163, 167, 168, 169, 172, 174, 175, 176, 180, 283, 285, 316, 331, 347, 348, 352
Slater, M., 102, 103, 117, 125, 127
Slavin, R. E., 152
Slovic, P., 94, 286
Smith, A., 210, 211, 219, 227
Smith, E. E., 86, 94
Smith, E. R., 281, 282, 285
Smith, M., 154, 155
Smith, P., 206, 217, 219, 220, 221, 224, 227
Smith, R. H., 247, 260
Smith, W., 21
Snyder, C. R., 344, 354
Snygg, D., 105, 129
Soja, E. W., 224, 227
Solomon, S., 8, 14, 30, 31, 32, 35, 36
Somers, M., 205, 207, 209, 212, 213, 223, 227
Sonenshein, R., 216, 227
Spencer, S., 20, 21, 36
Srinivasan, M. A., 127
St. John, M. F., 283, 285
Stangor, C., 253, 254, 261
Stark, L., 113, 130
Steel, D., 283
Steele, D., 21
Steinbeck, J., 332

Steinmetz, G., 206, 208, 209, 227
Steuer, J., 103, 104, 107, 113, 129
Stevens, A. L., 292, 311, 312
Stone, B., 117, 129
Stone, O., 283
Storey, D., 163, 180
Stowe, H. B., 3, 15, 263, 265, 267, 276, 279, 286, 318, 341, 350
Strange, J. J., xiv, xv, 1, 12, 13, 15, 168, 180, 263, 269, 270, 273, 275, 276, 281, 282, 286, 302, 304, 313, 329, 341, 343, 346, 347, 350, 351, 354
Styron, W., 267
Suetonius, 30, 36
Sullivan, J., 98, 121, 126
Surmelian, L., 339, 341
Sutherland, I., 102, 114, 130
Swaggart, J., 308, 309
Sympson, S. C., 344, 354

T

Tan, E. S. H., 63, 68
Tarrow, S., 207, 228
Tatar, M. M., 30, 37
Taylor, C., 205, 212, 228
Taylor, P. B., 20, 37
Taylor, S. E., 322, 341, 344, 354
Tellegen, A., 326, 327, 333, 341
Tertullian, 30, 37
Tester, K., 30, 37
Tetsutani, N., 113, 125
Thackeray, 270
Thagard, P., 273, 286
Thompson, S. C., 322, 341
Thompson, S., 19, 37
Thornton, C. L., 125
Tichenor, P. J., 168, 180
Tierney, W., 152
Tiger, L., 31, 37
Tilly, C., 207, 210, 228
Tolstoy, L., 25, 37, 266, 286
Tompkins, J., 203, 204
Tolbert, M. J., 133, 155
Tooby, J., 24, 33, 35
Toombs, W., 152
Touraine, A., 223, 228
Trabasso, T., 11, 14, 59, 67, 72, 94, 231, 234, 241, 242, 246, 247, 248, 250, 258, 260, 261, 262
Tromp, J., 113, 130
Trope, Y., 13, 14, 352, 353
Tubbs, J., 152
Turkle, S., 119, 123, 130
Turner, T. J., 171, 178, 238, 250, 254, 258

Tversky, A., 87, 94, 176, 180, 273, 286, 299, 311, 313
Tweet, J., 119, 126
Tzeng, Y., 231, 244, 247, 262

V

Vakoch, D. A., 76, 77, 95
Van den Berghe, P., 210, 228
van den Broek, P., 229, 231, 234, 244, 247, 259, 262
van Dijk, T. A., 338, 341
van Doren, D., 264, 284
Van Hoy, B. W., 127
van Oostendorp, H., 338, 341
van Peer, W., 236, 262
Vaughan, P., 161, 162, 166, 180
Vaught, C., 165, 178
Velicer, W. F., 167, 179
Vilscek, E., 152
Vidmar, N., 161, 164, 180
Vilhjalmsson, H., 121, 126
Vorderer, P., 47, 69, 262
Voss, J. F., 239, 262

W

Walton, K. L., 80, 95, 325, 341
Walker-Dalhousie, D., 152
Wander, P., 164, 180
Warner, C. D., 263, 266, 286
Warner, G. C., 192, 204
Warren, D. H., 116, 130
Wason, P. C., 273, 286
Wegener, D. T., 2, 15
Weinstock, M., 239, 256, 260
Weintraub, B., 283, 286
Weisenberger, J. H., 113, 127
Weiss, H. J., 133, 155
Welch, R. B., 113, 116, 117, 118, 130
Wells, M. J., 113, 129
Wheeler, S. C., xiv, 90, 93, 95, 174, 181, 257, 262, 283, 286, 331, 332, 341, 346, 350, 354
White, E., 201
White, H., 213, 220, 228
Wicker, T., 33
Wicklund, R., 325, 340
Wiehagen, W. J., 165, 178
Wiemer-Hastings, K., 230, 231, 260
Wierwille, W. W., 114, 117, 126
Wilde, O., 267, 280, 286

Wiley, J., 239, 262
Willhoite, M., 146, 155
Williams, C. J., 170, 178
Williams, E., 102, 104, 129
Williams, G., 113, 129
Williams, J. P., 236, 262
Williams, S., 119, 126
Wilson, E. O., 25, 34, 37
Wilson, T. D., 279, 284
Wimsatt, W. K., 58, 69
Winant, H., 224, 227
Winfrey, O., 309
Winnicott, D. W., 64, 69
Witmer, B. G., 113, 130
Wittgenstein, L., 50, 69
Wolfe, T., 40, 69
Wolt, I., 215, 225
Wood, M., 318, 338, 341
Wright, C., 142
Wulff, H. J., 69, 239, 262
Wurm, L. H., 76, 77, 95
Wyer, R., 254, 262, 316, 341
Wynne, S. K., 140, 155

Y

Yan, H., 121, 126
Yaser, Y., 160, 179
Ybasco, F. C., 344, 354
Yoder, P. S., 163, 181
Young, M., 231, 244, 247, 262
Yun, S. H., 160, 179

Z

Zajonc, R. B., 76, 94, 95, 167, 181
Zald, M., 207, 226
Zeltzer, D., 106, 160
Zeltzer, B., 102, 103, 117, 125, 130
Zillmann, D., 2, 14, 83, 95, 115, 120, 130, 171, 172, 181, 276, 278, 282, 284, 286
Zimbardo, P. G., 30, 36
Zola, E., 276
Zubin, D., 280, 286
Zuckerman, M., 25, 34, 37
Zwaan, R. A., 231, 244, 245, 250, 252, 262, 338, 341
Zyda, M., 120, 129

Subject Index

A

A Feeling for Books, 188–190
Absorption, 18, 24, 191, 326
  see also entrancement, transportation, engagement, involvement, presence
  and entrancement, xiv
  factors influencing, 174
Abstract principles, 293–294, 309–310
Acompaname (*Come along with me*), 159
Affect, 76–77
  affective primacy, 76
  and priming, 76–77
  and remindings, 278
Affective fallacy, 59
Agency, 51, 283
Agenda setting, 276, 277
Agents, agent perspective, 236–239
  characters, 236–237
  fusion facilitation hypothesis, 237
  imaginary camera operator, 238
  narrator, 236–237
  point of view, 236–237
  pragmatic agents, 236
  reader, 238
  and source memory, 237
Alice in Wonderland, 274
All in the Family, 161, 164
"American way of life"
  Dick & Jane, 143–144
American Civil Liberties Union (ACLU), 148–149
Appraisal, 63
Aristotle, 45
Arousal, 114–116
Artistry, 327–328
Assimilation and accommodation, 48, 55, 61
Association Structure (see Suggestion Structure)

Attention, 100, 123
  zoom theories, 100
Attitude accessibility theory, ix, 170
Attitude strength, xiv
Attribution theory, 247
Authority attitudes
  in *Harry Potter*, 139
Avatar, 109
  and judgments of others, 120

B

Ban books (banning), 133, 140
  school-based, 347
  of schoolbooks, xiv
Banks, Russell, 53
Bardon Bus, 60
Binary code/discourse, 212, 216
Body, 184, 185
  schema, 116
  user's, 108–110, 113–118
Body Project, The, 184
Book of the Month Club, 185, 188–189, 196
Books
  book problem, 102
  interface, 120
Boxcar Children, 191–193

C

Case-based reasoning, 288
  analogies between cases, 293
  stories as "cases," 288–301
Casino Royale (James Bond), 83–85
Causal responsibility judgments, 276–277, 281
Causal generalization, 277
Causal consequence, 248–249
  see also expectation

365

SUBJECT INDEX

Causal antecedent, 248
Censors
   school, 347
Censorship, x, xi, 7, 9–10, 315
Center for Communications Programs
   (Johns Hopkins), 159
Character(s), 214, 216–218
   as role models, 163
   transitional, 161
Child support, 308
Chinese boxes, 18, 33
Christopher Columbus, 4–5, 6
Chronological order, 234, 319
Chunks (of discourse), 245–246
Cinderella, 274
Civil society, 206, 216–217, 218
Civil Rights Movement, 215
Civil participation, 349
Class, 207, 208–209
Coherence assumption, 245–246
   local coherence, 245
   global coherence, 245–246
   in story model, 256
Comic books, 163
Communication
   and persuasion, xiii
Completeness, 255
Comprehension, 229–231
   stability across individuals, 230
Computer-based simulations, 307
Computers, 97–99, 311
Confessions of Nat Turner, The, 267
Congo, 266
Consistency, 256
Constitutional rights, 132–133, 138
Constraint satisfaction, 252
Construction-integration model, 233, 244, 256
Constructionist theory, 11, 231, 241–257, 350
Context of fictional stories, 350
Context failure, modes of
   context activation failure, 270
   context comprehension failure, 269
   context discrimination failure (*see also* Reality monitoring), 269–270, 283
   context engulfment, 270
   context encoding failure, 269
   context specification failure, 269, 283
   context specification forgetting, 269
   context rejection, 269
Context specifications, 268
Conversational interaction, 73
   roles, 74
   turn-taking, 73
Counterarguing, 86, 173–175, 334–335
Courts, 132

Creationism, 148–150
Critical thinking, 133, 144
Cuando Estemos Juntos (When we are Together), 160
Culturally common stories, 219
   proverbs and fables, 301
Culture (cultural), 190, 205–206
   contested environment, 195
   selves intertwined with, 190
   zine, 199
Curriculum (curricular)
   controversies, 138–139
   decisions, 132

D

Daddy's Roommate, 146
Das Boot, 281
Daydreaming, 19, 27
Death, 28, 29
   denial of, 18
   tranquil, 344
Decay of Lying, The, 267
Decontextualized stories, 241
Defamiliarization, 55–56
Dhvani, 52
Digital world, 107
Disbelief, 18
   suspension of, 173, 257
Discourse Structure, 44, 46–47, 58
Discourse, 229–230
   components and assumptions, 241–243
   theory, 229–230
Dreaming, 18, 26, 197–198
   imperative reality of, 19
   language of, 33
Dreams, 49, 106, 274, 280–281
Dual process theories, 352

E

Edu-tainment (Education entertainment), xiii, 347–348
Elaboration Likelihood Model, 330–334
Embodiment, 108–118
   dimension, 110
   mediated, 108–110
   for narrative experience, 113
   progressive, 113–114
Emotion, ix, x, 8, 9, 188, 238, 325
   anger, 42, 54, 63
   engine of narrative impact, 344
   in fiction vs. life, 63
   mechanism, 344
   memories of, 26
   and reasoning, 54
   recollection of, 191

SUBJECT INDEX   367

sadness, 54, 63
unconscious, 26
Emotional distance, 60–61
Empathy 50, 66, 120, 172
   and remindings, 278
Engagement (see also transportation,absorption, involvement, presence), 277–278
   as moderator of causal generalization, 278
Entertainment Education 10, 157, 163, 347–348
   and AIDS, 161, 170, 177
   and alcohol use, 164, 172, 174, 175
   ethics of, 177
   evaluations of, 159, 163
   in Egypt, 159
   and family planning, 159–162
   in India, 160
   in Mexico, 160
   and occupational safety, 165
   in Pakistan, 159
   in Peru, 158
   in Tanzania, 161, 162
   in Turkey, 159
   in the United States, 163–164
   and use of epilogues, 162–163
Entrancement xiv, 18, 24, 278, 344
   see also transportation,absorption, engagement, involvement, presence
Episodic recruitment, 278
   see also remindings
Equal access
   of individuals, 195
Ersatz interaction, 346
Eternal cycle, 20–21
   with rebirth, 21
Eurocentric approach, 144
Evaluatory responses, 345
Event Structure, 44–46, 52, 58
Event indexing model, 245
Evolution, 18, 19, 133, 148–150
   perspective, 24
   psychological mechanisms, 33
   scale, 31
   teaching of, 148–150
   universals, 25
Expectation failures, 292, 293, 299, 302, 303
Expectations, 298–299, 303
Experience
   direct, 101–102
   mediated, 101–102
Experiential systems, 27
Experiential mode, 326–327
Explanation assumption, 245, 247
   why-questions, 247

Explanation-based reasoning, 247
Explanations, 299–300, 302
Explicit text, 230
   see also surface code

F

Fact, 302
   versus fiction, 317, 329, 352
False notes, 334–335
Familiarity, 240
Federal Express, 231
Feminism, feminist, 185
Fiction (narratives), 12, 41, 89, 302, 315, 316, 318–319, 328–329
   and agenda setting, 276–277
   and beliefs, 171, 319, 329
   and causal generalization, 277
   formulaic, 18, 21, 186
   and forms of impact, 282–283
   as "mere pretense", 264
   potboiler, 21, 345
Fidelity
   as image resolution, 113
Firsthand stories, 290
Fitness (purpose), 18, 24–25
   see also evolution
Flow, 325–326
Folktale, 19–21, 24, 28, 33
Frame of reference, 305–306, 308
Fred Smith, 231
Free speech, 132
Free exercise of religion, 132, 137
Functional fixedness, 84–85
Fundamentalist
   Christian, 133, 136

G

Games, 51
   video, 115
Gender
   expectations, 191
   order, 186
Generic knowledge structure
   see also script, 244, 254–255
Genre(s), 214, 218–222, 239–240
   comedy, 219, 221
   fotonovela, 163
   irony, 219, 221
   narrative simulation, 165
   as organizational structure, 219
   parable, 158
   romance, 186–187, 219–220, 221, 349
   soap opera, 157, 158
   and social movements, 218–222
   thriller, 41

368   SUBJECT INDEX

tragedy, 219–220, 221
Girls at risk, 183–185
Gleaning
    narrative, 202–203
    playful, 196–198
Goals, 73, 92, 291, 297, 307–308
Gravity's Rainbow, 264
Grrls, 10, 200–202
Gun safety, 308–309

H

Hamlet, 44, 45–46, 49, 55–58, 61–62, 65, 344–345
Harry Potter stories, 139–142
    witchcraft, 139–141
    satanic elements, 139
    magic elements, 139, 141–142
Heather Has Two Mommies, 146
Hero(es), 308, 349
    of all narratives, 18
    immortality, 18, 20
    invulnerability, 19
    single with thousand faces, 19
Herzl, Theodor, 3, 4
Heterosexuality
    and romance, 186
Holodeck, 101, 114
Hope, 21, 28, 344
    creation of, 23–24
    form of immortality, 21
    magic of, 23
    mechanisms of reading, 23
    message, 33
    and mortality in news, 29–30
    as news, 29
    Pandora's box, 344
    source of, 23
How to Read a Book, 264
How We Die, 318
Hunger
    for news, 23
    for stories, 23
Hum Log, 160, 161, 162, 170
Hypnotic susceptibility, 326
Hypothetical explanations, 272–273

I

Identification 46, 61–62, 66, 172
    with character, 251–252
Identity (identities), x, 11, 60
see also self, identification
    authorized models, 195
    collective, 205–223
    creation, 191
    group, national, 349
    individual, 205, 212
    multiple/Hybrid, 205, 209, 211
    narrative creation of, 205–206, 210, 222
    social, 349
    and social movements, 206–210
Imagery 13, 318, 319, 321–323, 348, 352
    investment in, 329–330
    and load, 336
    skill or ability, 327, 333–334
Imagination, 133, 134
Immersive technologies, 114
Immortality, 28, 33
    affirmation of, 20
    delusion of, 18, 22, 25–26
    domestication of, 344
    of gods, 20
    sense of, 18
    of world, 20
Inconsiderate texts, 232
Indexing, 288, 292
    and anomalous features, 293
    storage and retrieval, 292, 302–303
    surface features, 292, 293
    thematic features, 292
Image, 241
    intensity, 335–336
    as prompt for entire message, 337–338
Inferences, 75–76, 79, 230–231
    coherence-based, 249
    encoding score, 251
    explanation-based, 250
    knowledge-based, 241, 244
    novel situational, 251–252
    passive activation, 253–255
    reader goal-driven, 253
    script actions encoded as, 254, 255
    spatial, 252
    syllogistic or statistical, 244
    word-triggered, 251–252
Influence
    of public narratives, xiv
Insight, 64
Institute for Learning Sciences (Northwestern), 307
Institute for Communication Research, 159
Interactant (interactor), 98, 346
    Dungeons and Dragons, 119
    motor inputs of, 121
    sense of own body, 116–118
    with artificial characters, 122–123
Interactive environment, 97–124
    media, 99, 101, 346
    technologies, 99, 107, 165
Interest/interestingness, 235, 240, 304–305, 310

SUBJECT INDEX 369

Interface
　computer, 106–107
　facilitates ubiquity of access, 123
　information transformation point, 107
　intelligence, 120–123
　point of interaction, 106
　proscenium, 106
　"windows", 107
Intersubjectivity, 217
Invented stories, 290
Involvement (see also absorption, entrancement, transportation, engagement, narrative involvement, presence), 171–173
　forms of, 174
Invulnerability, 22, 25, 33
　delusion of, 18
Ivanhoe, 270, 280

J

Jane Eyre, 58
Jewish culture, 295–297
JFK, 283
Journalists, 29
Jury decision-making, x, 239, 255–256, 350
　see also story model

K

Kansas State School Board, 150
Keats, John, 55–56
Key to Uncle Tom's Cabin, The, 279
Kid Dynamite, 71–72, 75, 77–79, 85–86, 89, 92–93
Knowledge
　as constructed of stories, 287, 294, 351
　as narrative, 12

L

Laws of the mind, 100
Lawsuits, 132–133
Learning, 301–304
Leveling and sharpening, 294
Levels of discourse, 232, 240
Lexical decision task, 251
Lies, damned lies, and narrative, 279
Literary quality, 132, 328
Little Women, 192
Los Angeles Sentinel, 215–216
Los Angeles Times, 213, 215–216
Lost in a Book, 18, 21, 23–24

M

Marx, Karl, 208
Meaning representation, 230
Media advocacy, 164–165
　Harvard Alcohol project, 164
　by Office of National Drug Control Policy, 164
Media effects
　incidental vs. intentional, 157
Media consumption, 185
Media Interface and Network Design (MIND), 100
Medium
　coupled to mind, 100
Memory, 85, 233, 237, 240, 325
　autobiographical, 52, 59–61
　and emotions, 59, 60, 61
　priming, 59
　structures, 287, 290, 292, 294, 300, 301–302, 303, 309–310
Menarche, 184
Mental model, 58, 85–86
　see also situation model
Middlebrow, 188–189, 193, 348
　literature, xiv
　personalism, 188
　readers, 348
Mimesis, 48–49, 351
Mimicry, 192, 193, 195
Minds
　as repositories of cases, 351
Misogyny, 201
Missing, 281
Monsters (monsterization), 30
Mood
　management, 114–115
　states, 114
Mortality salience xiv, 31–33, 343, 344
Motor
　behavior of user, 110, 121
　immersion, 113
Mozert v. Hawkins Public Schools (1987), 133–138
MUDS, 100
Multicultural/Multiculturalism, 132, 133, 136, 349
　inclusiveness, 144
Multimedia environment, 98
Munro, Alice, 62
Murphy Brown, 176
Myth, 21–22, 28, 33
　speech of, 33
Mythic structure, 19–20, 344

N

Nappy Hair, 142–143

370 SUBJECT INDEX

Narrative influence
  in courtroom, 350
  factors and constraints, 343, 347
  mobilizing, 349
  versus nonnarrative, 347
Narrative(s)
  classic function of, 120
  collective, 206, 208–210, 211–213
  Cold War, 215
  coordination of public and personal, 208
  experience, 113, 119, 120, 122–124
  legal, 209
  mobilization, 206, 215
  multicultural, 132
  and nationalism, 210–211
  power, 18, 315
  pragmatic function of, 239
  quality, 335
  recollection of, 345
  structure, 211–213, 319, 320
  that convey attitudes, 131
  that convey ideals, 131
Narrative impact, 40
  and detail, 309–310
  determinants of, 304–310
  resistance to, 308–309
Nationalism, 210–211, 222
Need for cognition, 90, 333–334
Negative preferences, 87–88
Non-factive predicates, 268
Norm theory, 87
Norms, social, ix, 166, 170
Novela Health Education, 163

O

Official stories, 289
Old New Land, 3, 4, 345
Order of presentation, 332–333
Overhearer, 74–75

P

Pacing, 330
Participation (side-participation), 9, 345, 347, 351
  responses 345
Participatory responses, 7, 330, 345
  as-if response, 78, 81, 330
  and attentional resources, 86
  commitment to, 82
  content of, 91–92
  evaluatory, 79
  impact on (real-world) beliefs, 79, 89–91
  impact on emotional experiences, 80–82

and memory for narratives, 85, 89
problem-solving, 78–79, 82–85
replotting, 78, 87
Passive vs. active readers, 73, 75
Passive activations, 249–250, 253–255
Patriarchal (defined), 184
Perception
  mediated, 116–117
Persistence of attitude change, 336–338
Personal importance, 90
Personal experience, 304
  see also personal relevance
Personal relevance, 331–332
Perspective, types of, 281
Persuasion 2, 316, 321, 322, 323, 325, 329, 330–338
Phenomenology, 8
Phobias, 26
Photoplay, 99–100
Pinocchio circling, 334–335
Plans, 297–298
Plausibility, 257, 350
  criterion, 350
Plot, 206–213, 214–216
  structure, 234
Poetics, 48
Political Process Theory, 207
Population Communications Services
  (*see* Center for Communications Programs)
Population Communications International, 159
Positive preferences, 87–88
Practical Criticism, 59
Pragmatic context, 241
Presence, 346, 347
  and arousal, 114–116
  "being there," 101–106
  dimensions of, 104–105
  epiphenomenon, 106
  experience of, 99
  level of, 106, 116
  sense of moving into narrative, 119
  social, 106
  telepresence, 101–103, 113
President (William Jefferson) Clinton, 308–309
Pretense (nature of), 264–265
Processes within individuals, 343–346
Processes within social contexts, 346–349
Propositions, 233
Protesters
  justifications, 132
  progressive textbook, 144–145
Public Burning, The, 264
Public sphere, 212, 282

SUBJECT INDEX

Public narratives
   gleanings therefrom, 348
   impact of, ix-xi, 2-8, 343
   to refashion selves, 348
   role of imagery, 352
   underlying mechanisms, 343-353

R

Rainbow Curriculum, 145-148
Rasas, 52, 59
Rational systems, 27
Reader-Response Theory, 59
Reading the Romance, 186
Reading
   as connected to writing, 196
   effects of, 188-190
   exploratory, 187
   genuinely prospective, 188
   investments, 187
   variable practices, 185-188
Reading times, 233, 240, 244
Reality monitoring/testing (*see also* Context discrimination failure), x, xi, 113, 114
Realization, 47, 58
Recognition probe, 91
Referential Contexts, 268, 274
Reminding(s), 278-279, 281, 292, 299, 302-303, 309, 345, 351, 352
   see also episodic recruitment, suggestion structure
Representation(al)
   bodily, 109
   codes, 98, 107
   techniques, 98
Resource mobilization paradigm, 207
Reviving Ophelia, 184
Rhetoric, rhetorical persuasion, 2, 320-321
Rights of parents, 132
Rime of the Ancient Mariner, 57
Risk-taking
   human, 18, 24-25
   by young males, 24-25
Rock 'n Roll, 191-192
Rodney King, 217-218
Role models, 160-161, 168, 170
Roles and role-playing 42, 51, 54, 165
Romance (readers), 186-187, 345, 348
   mass market for, 186
   reading, 186-187
Roots, 164
Russian formalists, 55

S

Sabido, Miguel, 158-159

Safety 8, 17-18, 344
   cognitively driven, 19
   of myth, 19
Sarah Cole, 53-54
Scenes, 292-293
Schema, ix, 42, 48, 55
School boards
   power of, 132, 137-138
Schoolbooks, 131-139, 143-148
Science, 268-269
Scripts, 292-293
Scrutiny of arguments, 90, 331
Secondhand stories, 290
Secular humanism, 133-135
Self/selves, 51, 55, 65
   see also identity
   awareness, public, 325
   as collage, 194-196
   construction, 194-195, 199
   culturally constructed, 194
   dramatization, 195
   fashioning, 190-194, 198, 202, 348
   hood, 190
   lesbian, 196
   as projected, 193, 195
   reconfiguration, 348
   sense of, 183-184
Self-concept, 10
Self-defining story, 300
Self-reliance, 133, 134-135
Sensation seeking, 25
Sensory experience, 98
   channels, 108
   devices, 107
   immersion, 108-110
   motor disturbances, 118
Sesame Street, 274
Sexual orientation, 146-148
Shakespeare, 192-193
   see also Hamlet
Shogun, 176
Side-participants, 72-75, 91-92
   see also participation
Simplemente Maria, 158, 172, 348
Simpson, O.J. 217-218
Simulation, 41, 46, 48-50, 100, 268
   narratives as form of, 102
   of physics and dynamics of objects, 112
   sickness symptoms, 117
Situation model, 230, 234-235, 240, 241, 247-249, 281
Snow Falling on Cedars, 280, 281
Sociability, 109, 118-120
   higher levels via evolution of interactive technologies, 120
   as key defining feature of interactive narrative, 119

numbers of users, 118
synchronicity, 118
Social Learning theory (social cognitive theory), ix, 159, 165–166
and vicarious experience, 159, 165–166
Social Movements, 207–210
Social Psychology, xiv
Sociology, xiii, 206
"Sonny Liston was a Friend of Mine," 71
Source, The, 269
Spatial location, 249, 252
Speech acts, 58
Stages of change, 166–170
Star Wars, 175
Stereotypes, 282
Stories, 197, 199, 287–311
  and communication, 293
  construction of, 294
  definition of, 288–289
  external, 302
  internal, 302
  listening, 292, 303
  point of, 289
  and problem-solving, 292
  telling, 294
  timing, 306–307
  types of, 289–291
  and understanding, 292–294
Story world, 344, 350
Story-model of jury decision-making, 12, 255–257, 350
Story-world, 17
Storyteller, storytelling, 18, 27, 98
Structural-affect theory, 238
Structure-building framework, 233, 244
Structure(s)
  discourse, 44, 45, 46–47, 58, 344
  emotion facilitating, 347
  event, 344
  of narrative, 328, 344, 352
Subjective realism, 175
Subjective (deictic) recentering, 280, 281, 351
Subplan, 248
Suggestion structure, 45, 51, 58
Superordinate goal, 248, 251
Surface code, 232, 233
Suspense, 82–85, 238–239, 325, 328
  initiating event, 82
  magnitude of, 84
  and text structure, 82
Symbolic pollution, 217
Symbolic representation, 268
Sympathy, 62, 63, 65, 172

T

Teaching, 149–150, 151, 347
Technology, 106–124, 310
Telecommunication channels, 107
Telenovelas, 158
Televisa, 158, 159
Television, 158–161, 164, 176, 310
Terror management
  heightened mortality, 31
  own world-view, 31–33
  paradigm, 30
  self-esteem, 31
Text hegemony, 347, 349, 353
Textbase, 233–234
Textbooks, see schoolbooks
"The Pugilist at Rest," 81
Thematic point, 235–236, 246
  ability to construct, 235–236
  and conversations, 235
  on-line/off-line processing, 235–236
Theme, 300–301, 305
Theoretical perspectives, 349–352
Theory of planned behavior, 166
Theory of reasoned action, 166, 168
They Died with their Boots On, 266
Think-aloud protocols, 250, 256
Trance, 19, 116
Transformation of self, 41, 48, 54
Transportation, x, 13, 21, 24, 43, 48, 101, 171, 278, 316–339, 344
  see also absorption, engagement, entrancement, involvement, presence
Transportation-Imagery Model, 316–338, 352
Tropes
  hendiasis, 57
  metaphor, 54–55, 57
  metonymy, 54–57
  simile, 54
  synecdoche, 55
Truth
  kinds of, 41, 49, 50
  verification strategies, 274
Twende na Wakati (Let's Go with the Times), 161, 170
Typicality/representativeness of exemplars, 279–280

U

Uncle Tom's Cabin, 3, 263–264, 265–266, 279–280, 315, 318, 338–339, 345

SUBJECT INDEX 373

Unconscious processes, 250

V

Vection, 114
Ven Conmigo (Come with Me), 159
Virtual reality, 9, 98, 99, 113, 116–118, 119
 games, 115
 and head motion, 116, 121
 immersive, 98
 wearable system, 124
Virtual environment, 98, 101, 113, 119
 immersive, 121
 training and counseling, 119–120
Vividness, 322

W

War and Peace, 266
War of the Ghosts, 47–48, 52
War politics, 32
War of the Worlds, 269
Watts Uprising, 213, 215–216
Word-naming task, 251
Working memory, 241
 span, 91

Z

Zines
 creativity of girls', 199–200
 Riot Grrls and their, 200–202